AI in MENA Education Systems:

Local Innovations and Global Implications

Tendai Charles
https://orcid.org/0000-0002-0253-5960
The British University in Dubai, UAE

Christopher Hill
Canadian University in Dubai, UAE

IGI Global
Scientific Publishing
Publishing Tomorrow's Research Today

Vice President of Editorial	Melissa Wagner
Director of Acquisitions	Mikaela Felty
Director of Book Development	Jocelynn Hessler
Production Manager	Mike Brehm
Cover Design	Jose Rosado

Published in the United States of America by
IGI Global Scientific Publishing
701 East Chocolate Avenue
Hershey, PA, 17033, USA
Tel: 717-533-8845 | Fax: 717-533-7115
Website: https://www.igi-global.com E-mail: cust@igi-global.com

Library of Congress Cataloging-in-Publication Data

Names: Charles, Tendai, 1982- editor | Hill, Christopher, 1978- editor
Title: AI in MENA education systems : local innovations and global implications / Edited by Tendai Charles, Christopher Hill.
Other titles: Artificial intelligence in Middle East North Africa education systems
Description: Hershey, PA : IGI Global Scientific Publishing, [2026] | Includes bibliographical references and index. | Summary: "This book examines how artificial intelligence is transforming education across the MENA region, highlighting innovations, challenges, and ethical concerns in multilingual, diverse, and unevenly resourced contexts. It documents local practices while distilling globally relevant insights for policy, pedagogy, governance, and sustainable AI integration in K-12, higher, and vocational education"-- Provided by publisher.
Identifiers: LCCN 2025044970 (print) | LCCN 2025044971 (ebook) | ISBN 9798337367767 hardcover | ISBN 9798337367774 paperback | ISBN 9798337367781 ebook
Subjects: LCSH: Artificial intelligence--Educational applications--Middle East | Artificial intelligence--Educational applications--Africa, North | Education--Effect of technological innovations on--Middle East | Education--Effect of technological innovations on--Africa, North | Education and globalization--Middle East | Education and globalization--Africa, North | Education and state--Middle East | Education and state--Africa, North
Classification: LCC LB1028.44 .A44 2026 (print) | LCC LB1028.44 (ebook)
LC record available at https://lccn.loc.gov/2025044970
LC ebook record available at https://lccn.loc.gov/2025044971

British Cataloguing in Publication Data
A Cataloguing in Publication record for this book is available from the British Library.

Table of Contents

Detailed Table of Contents

This chapter presents a PRISMA-guided systematic review of AI-enabled assessment in MENA higher education (Jan 2023–Aug 2025). Searches of ERIC, Scopus, ProQuest and APA PsycINFO yielded studies synthesised narratively across three themes: Policy & Ethics, Assessment Tools & Analytics, and Learning & Feedback. Evidence indicates policy uncertainty and integrity risks alongside promising formative applications; early-warning analytics show utility, whereas automated scoring and AI detectors exhibit reliability concerns. We propose tiered, context-sensitive policies, professional development, authentic assessment designs, and feedback-literacy scaffolds. The chapter identifies methodological gaps and urges rigorous, mixed-method evaluations attuned to regional languages and cultures.

This study investigates how undergraduate students at a multicultural UAE university use Generative AI as an academic assistant and how they perceive its value, risks, and role in learning. Using a qualitative design grounded in constructivist and phenomenological approaches, the study draws on a focus group to examine emotional, cognitive, and behavioural dimensions of AI engagement. Findings show that students view Generative AI as an embedded study companion supporting idea generation, drafting, summarising, and problem solving, with accessibility and efficiency driving regular use. Participants also expressed concern about uneven institutional guidance, dependency risks, and uncertainty around acceptable and ethical use. Clear patterns emerged around developing prompt literacy, navigating inconsistent advice from instructors, and demand for transparent policies and practical instruction. Student readiness was shaped not only by technical familiarity but also by institutional clarity, pedagogical support, and confidence in responsible use within academic tasks and assessment use.

This chapter examines how artificial intelligence (AI) is conceived, used, and controlled in schools across the Middle East and North Africa (MENA). This chapter discusses the influence of national AI visions, teacher competencies, linguistic diversity, and ethical governance on the success or constraints of AI adoption, utilising policy analysis and regional case studies. There is much focus on problems with Arabic natural language processing, differences in infrastructure, and gaps in teacher training. This chapter combines ideas from responsible AI, culturally responsive design, and educational innovation to show how AI can help with fair learning, multilingual accessibility, and long-term growth. In general, the analysis shows that the MENA region is becoming an essential part of global AI-in-education research by using context-aware, ethically sound, and language-inclusive methods.

Artificial Intelligence (AI) is reshaping higher education, enabling personalization, efficiency, and innovation. Yet its impact on the psychological, social, and ethical wellbeing of students and educators remains underexamined, especially in rapidly evolving regions like the Middle East and North Africa (MENA). This chapter introduces the AI-CARE Framework, a multidimensional model for ethically and wellbeing-centered AI integration in education. Its six dimensions (Agency & Autonomy, Inclusive Design, Compassionate Integration, Adaptive Wellbeing Support, Resilience Building, and Ethical Governance) draw on education, psychology, and technology ethics to explain how AI affects human flourishing. The framework identifies causal pathways, contextual factors, and practical tools such as the AI-CARE Scorecard to support implementation and research. By centering wellbeing in AI design and governance, the AI-CARE Framework offers a roadmap for healthier, fairer, and more sustainable learning ecosystems globally and in MENA.

This quantitative study of 146 UAE K-12 teachers examines how gamification shapes collaborative learning and the prospective contribution of AI. An online survey captured perceptions of benefits, effectiveness (lessons/websites), and implementation barriers. Analyses (descriptives, Cronbach's alpha, regression, one-sample t-tests) show gamification significantly predicts collaborative outcomes, explaining 52.5% of variance. Kahoot and ClassDojo were viewed as highly effective for engagement, cohesion, and behaviour. Reported obstacles included time-intensive design, limited methodological expertise, and curriculum constraints. Although AI data were not collected, we outline how AI-enabled gamification could personalise learning, automate feedback, and optimise group dynamics. We recommend curricular and professional development integration

The integration of artificial intelligence (AI) into special education presents unprecedented opportunities to transform learning experiences for students with special educational needs (SEN). This chapter examines how AI-driven technologies are reshaping inclusive educational practices, and explores how AI supports personalised learning, enhances accessibility, fosters engagement, and promotes greater learner independence. The theoretical framing integrates Universal Design for Learning (UDL), Differentiated Instruction, and Assistive Technology theories, demonstrating how AI can address systemic challenges in special education. In addition, it offers evidence-based recommendations for educators, policymakers, and developers to ensure that AI technologies are deployed ethically, inclusively, and sustainably. By situating the discussion within the unique educational, cultural, and policy contexts of the MENA region, this chapter highlights AI's transformative potential to empower diverse learners and foster equitable participation in increasingly digital learning environments.

The aim of the study is to examine how Finland implemented programming skills in its national curriculum to offer lessons for the implementation of the new National AI Curriculum introduced in the United Arab Emirates using Bernstein's curriculum model. This chapter adopts a conceptual and comparative approach, drawing on secondary literature and policy documents, and uses Bernstein's Curriculum Model as an analytical framework to interpret Finland's case and extract lessons for the UAE. The findings highlight strategies to ease the transition and make the implementation process smoother for different stakeholders. By synthesizing international best practices with the UAE's digital transformation goals, the chapter provides actionable recommendations for policymakers, curriculum designers, and educators seeking to bridge the gap between technological innovation and classroom practice. This chapter contributes to the global discourse on AI literacy in education by presenting the UAE as a case study of policy-driven innovation in a rapidly transforming educational landscape.

This chapter examines how MENA education systems can regulate AI not as an afterthought but as a core dimension of academic quality and institutional legitimacy. It first traces the emerging uses of AI in schools and universities and shows how opaque algorithms unsettle traditional ideas of responsibility, authorship, and assessment. The chapter then explores how existing accreditation and quality assurance regimes—often designed for analogue institutions—can be reimagined to address issues such as data governance, algorithmic bias, learning analytics, and AI-assisted assessment. Drawing on regional policy documents and illustrative institutional practices, it proposes principles, indicators, and review processes that embed accountability into the design, procurement, and deployment of AI tools. Rather than importing ready-made global templates, the chapter argues for context-sensitive regulatory frameworks that align with MENA socio-political realities while safeguarding learners' rights and public trust.

Foreword

The widespread release of Generative AI (GenAI) platforms in 2022 has had a resounding impact on society, an impact that is still being felt across all sectors and perhaps none more so than education. At an institutional level, GenAI has caused at worst moral panic and at best serious concern as administrators have sought to control and contain what they see are serious threats to academic integrity. At the sharp end of classroom teaching, reactions have ranged from wholehearted enthusiasm to quiet – or not so quiet – despair as educators have sought to make sense of the challenges and affordances of these new tools. Among students, considerable uncertainty persists in the face of mixed messages, outdated assessment practices and incoherent policies. There is a clear distinction between ideas of control, policing and surveillance, and belief in adaptation, adoption and redefinition, a distinction that is at the same time clear yet opaque depending on context, viewpoint and personal experience.

More recently, however, research and practice are converging and new, clearer directions are emerging. This is particularly true in the MENA region. Institutions and classrooms have often been at the forefront of technology enhanced learning, and it is this collective experience and wisdom that this volume draws on. The contributors already function in technology-rich environments, and are thus able to approach GenAI with perspective and skill, and in doing so provide the reader with a state-of-the-art portrait of the current situation in the MENA context. The editors, Dr. Tendai Charles and Prof. Christopher Hill, are both highly experienced educators in the region, and this has helped them to compile a wide-ranging selection of work that crosses and connects the key elements of policy, ethics, readiness, assessment, pedagogy and inclusion around GenAI as it simultaneously disrupts and reshapes education from governance to classroom teaching.

This compilation is an important and timely contribution to the growing literature and takes an expert, balanced and informed approach to GenAI. The reader is encouraged to move beyond narratives of discontinuity and disruption and urged to consider instead how human agency, responsibility and redefined education need to be negotiated in the age of GenAI. Instead of merely adopting the new technology, this volume positions the MENA region as a key contributor shaping GenAI governance and pedagogy, and provides a valuable resource across governance, policy, pedagogy and practice. I hope you will enjoy it.

Rob Miles
Higher Colleges of Technology, UAE

Preface

Artificial intelligence has moved from the margins of educational innovation to the very center of teaching, learning, assessment, and governance. Nowhere is this transformation more visible and more contested than in the Middle East and North Africa (MENA), a region characterized by rapid digital ambition, linguistic diversity, youthful populations, and highly centralized education systems. This edited volume, *AI in MENA Education Systems: Local Innovations and Global Implications*, brings together scholars and practitioners to examine how AI is being interpreted, adopted, regulated, and resisted across educational contexts in the region.

Rather than treating AI as a purely technical intervention, the chapters in this book approach it as a socio-educational phenomenon shaped by culture, language, policy, ethics, and power. Collectively, the contributions move beyond deterministic narratives of disruption or efficiency to ask deeper questions: How does AI reshape professional identity, student agency, and academic integrity? What risks emerge when global AI tools meet local pedagogies and multilingual realities? And how can education systems in MENA design AI futures that are ethical, inclusive, and pedagogically sound?

The volume spans higher education and K–12 contexts, empirical studies and conceptual frameworks, and perspectives from the Gulf, the wider Arab world, and comparative global cases. While grounded in MENA realities, the insights offered resonate far beyond the region, contributing to international debates on responsible AI, assessment reform, teacher readiness, and hybrid human–AI intelligence. Below is a chapter-by-chapter summary of this material to supplement your reading.

CHAPTER OVERVIEW

Chapter 1 presents a PRISMA-guided systematic review of AI-enabled assessment in higher education across the MENA region between January 2023 and August 2025. Drawing from major academic databases, the chapter synthesizes findings across three themes: policy and ethics, assessment tools and analytics, and learning and feedback. The review identifies significant policy uncertainty and academic integrity concerns, alongside promising applications of AI for formative assessment and early-warning learning analytics. While predictive analytics show utility in identifying at-risk students, automated scoring systems and AI-detection tools raise reliability and fairness issues. The chapter concludes by recommending tiered, context-sensitive policy frameworks, professional development for educators, authentic assessment redesign, and more rigorous mixed-method research attentive to regional languages and cultures.

Chapter 2 explores how undergraduate students at a multicultural UAE university use generative AI as an academic assistant. Using a qualitative, constructivist, and phenomenological approach based on focus group data, the study reveals that students perceive AI as an embedded study companion that supports brainstorming, drafting, summarizing, and problem-solving. Accessibility and efficiency drive regular use, but students also express concern about dependency, unclear ethical boundaries, and inconsistent institutional guidance. The findings emphasize the importance of prompt literacy, transparent policies, and practical instruction. Student readiness is shown to depend not only on technical familiarity but also on institutional clarity, pedagogical support, and confidence in responsible academic use.

Chapter 3 examines how artificial intelligence is conceptualized, implemented, and governed across MENA school systems. Through policy analysis and regional case studies, the chapter highlights the influence of national AI strategies, teacher competencies, infrastructural disparities, and linguistic diversity on AI adoption. Particular attention is given to challenges in Arabic natural language processing and uneven access to technological resources. The chapter integrates perspectives from responsible AI, culturally responsive design, and educational innovation to argue that effective AI integration must be context-aware, ethically grounded, and linguistically inclusive. It positions MENA as an increasingly important contributor to global AI-in-education discourse through its locally responsive approaches.

Chapter 4 introduces the AI-CARE Framework, a multidimensional model designed to embed wellbeing and ethics into educational AI integration. The framework outlines six interconnected dimensions, Agency and Autonomy, Inclusive Design, Compassionate Integration, Adaptive Wellbeing Support, Resilience Building, and Ethical Governance, and explains how AI systems affect psychological, social, and institutional wellbeing. By mapping causal pathways and contextual factors, the chapter reframes AI adoption as a human-centered process that prioritizes flourishing over efficiency alone. It also offers practical tools, such as the AI-CARE Scorecard, to guide implementation and future research, particularly within MENA's rapidly evolving higher education landscape.

Chapter 5 presents a quantitative study of 146 UAE K–12 teachers examining the impact of gamification on collaborative learning and the potential contribution of AI. Survey data reveal that gamification significantly predicts collaborative outcomes, explaining over half of the variance observed. Teachers report that platforms such as Kahoot and ClassDojo enhance engagement, classroom cohesion, and student behavior. However, barriers include time-intensive lesson design, limited methodological expertise, and curriculum constraints. Although AI-specific data were not collected, the chapter outlines how AI-enabled gamification could personalize instruction, automate feedback, and optimize group dynamics, and it recommends integrating such approaches into professional development and curriculum planning.

Chapter 6 focuses on the transformative potential of AI in special education across the MENA region. Grounded in Universal Design for Learning, Differentiated Instruction, and Assistive Technology frameworks, the chapter demonstrates how AI can personalize learning pathways, enhance accessibility, foster engagement, and promote learner independence for students with special educational needs. It also addresses systemic and ethical considerations, providing recommendations for policymakers, educators, and developers to ensure inclusive and sustainable AI implementation. By situating its analysis within MENA's cultural and policy contexts, the chapter underscores AI's role in advancing equitable participation in digital learning environments.

Chapter 7 adopts a comparative and theoretical approach to examine Finland's implementation of programming skills in its national curriculum and extract lessons for the UAE's new National AI Curriculum. Using Bernstein's Curriculum Model as an analytical framework, the chapter analyses policy documents and secondary literature to identify strategies that facilitate smoother implementation across stakeholders. It highlights the importance of structured teacher preparation, phased integration, and alignment between technological ambition and classroom practice. The chapter offers actionable recommendations for policymakers and curriculum designers, positioning the UAE as a case study in policy-driven educational innovation.

Chapter 8 addresses the regulation of AI in education through the lenses of accountability, accreditation, and quality assurance in the MENA region. It argues that AI should be treated not as a peripheral innovation but as a core dimension of institutional legitimacy and academic quality. The chapter examines how opaque algorithms disrupt traditional notions of authorship, assessment, and responsibility, and it explores how existing accreditation systems can be adapted to address data governance, algorithmic bias, and AI-assisted evaluation. Rather than importing external regulatory models, the chapter advocates for context-sensitive frameworks that reflect MENA's socio-political realities while safeguarding learners' rights and public trust.

Chapter 9 investigates teachers' readiness for generative AI in K–12 education in Sharjah through an exploratory qualitative study. Drawing on interviews and written responses, the chapter finds widespread awareness of generative AI but fragmented pedagogical understanding and uneven confidence in supervising student use. Teachers express uncertainty regarding assessment practices and institutional expectations, reflecting broader governance ambiguities. The study conceptualizes readiness as institutionally mediated, shaped by professional confidence, ethical judgment, and policy clarity. It concludes that coordinated institutional support and structured professional development are essential for sustainable integration of generative AI in schools.

Chapter 1
A Systematic Literature Review of AI in Higher Education Assessment Across the MENA Region

Siham Abukhalaf
http://orcid.org/0009-0000-9894-6264
Deakin University, Australia

ABSTRACT

This chapter presents a PRISMA-guided systematic review of AI-enabled assessment in MENA higher education (Jan 2023–Aug 2025). Searches of ERIC, Scopus, ProQuest and APA PsycINFO yielded studies synthesised narratively across three themes: Policy & Ethics, Assessment Tools & Analytics, and Learning & Feedback. Evidence indicates policy uncertainty and integrity risks alongside promising formative applications; early-warning analytics show utility, whereas automated scoring and AI detectors exhibit reliability concerns. We propose tiered, context-sensitive policies, professional development, authentic assessment designs, and feedback-literacy scaffolds. The chapter identifies methodological gaps and urges rigorous, mixed-method evaluations attuned to regional languages and cultures.

INTRODUCTION

Definitions and Importance

Artificial intelligence (AI) can be defined as the science and engineering of building machines capable of performing tasks normally requiring human intelligence

DOI: 10.4018/979-8-3373-6776-7.ch001

(Luo et al., 2025b). Early definitions framed AI as creating "intelligent machines" (McCarthy et al., 2006), while later scholars emphasised rational agents that act adaptively in their environments (Berente et al., 2021). Modern AI encompasses a spectrum of technologies, including machine learning, deep learning and natural language processing (NLP), that enable systems to solve problems, make decisions and learn from data (Azzam & Charles, 2025). Recent breakthroughs in large language models (LLMs) such as generative pre-trained transformers (GPT) extend AI's capabilities to generate new content in the form of text, images, code and audio. Generative AI (GenAI), unlike earlier analytic forms of AI, produces novel outputs by learning from vast datasets (Azzam & Charles, 2024). Its emergence has catalysed a new era of efficiency and precision in education while simultaneously raising ethical concerns around bias, transparency and misuse.

AI's influence on higher education is multidimensional. Researchers report that AI technologies enhance and sometimes surpass human capabilities in complex instructional tasks, supporting personalised learning, adaptive feedback and efficient resource allocation (Charles & Charles, 2024). The AI market in higher education was valued at approximately USD 2 billion in 2022, with projections of a 36% compound annual growth rate through 2030 (Luo et al., 2025b). Such growth signals the sector's confidence that AI can deliver personalised instructional content, real-time feedback and improved student engagement (Charles, 2025). Within assessment, GenAI enables automated essay scoring, adaptive testing and predictive analytics, potentially reducing teachers' workload and providing timely feedback. However, the opacity of many AI systems, the so-called "black box" problem, makes it difficult for educators to understand how decisions are made, which can impede trust and raise fairness concerns (Charles & Hill, 2025). Studies also caution that overreliance on AI tools may erode students' motivation and critical thinking (Charles, 2022). Thus, while AI holds promise for enhancing assessment, its deployment must be balanced against issues of transparency, bias and academic integrity.

Purpose of the Study

The Middle East and North Africa (MENA) region has set ambitious digital transformation agendas, exemplified by the United Arab Emirates' (UAE) National AI Strategy 2031, that prioritise AI adoption in higher education and workforce development. These national strategies align with the United Nations' (UN) Sustainable Development Goals, particularly Goal 4 (quality education) and Goal 9 (industry, innovation and infrastructure). Yet existing reviews of AI-enabled assessment are dominated by studies from North America, Europe and East Asia. A recent scoping review of generative AI in assessment noted that most empirical research to date was conducted in 2023 and that evidence remains "limited" and "preliminary" (Xia et al., 2024). The same review highlighted the need for institutions to redesign policies and curricula to adapt to AI's implications. Weng et al. (2024) further reported that traditional assessment methods in higher education "do not operate effectively" in the GenAI era and identified three emergent assessment approaches — traditional, innovative/refocused, and GenAI-incorporated — alongside new learning outcomes such as career-driven competencies and lifelong learning skills. Importantly, most studies employ qualitative methodological designs, indicating a paucity of rigorous quantitative evidence.

Against this backdrop, the present chapter undertakes a systematic literature review of AI-driven assessment in higher education across the MENA region for the period January 2023 (post-ChatGPT release) to August 2025. By synthesising conceptual and empirical studies from countries within MENA, the review aims to map current AI-enabled assessment practices, evaluate reported benefits and challenges, and compare regional innovations with global trends. This inquiry addresses critical gaps identified in prior reviews, namely, the lack of geographic diversity in existing evidence (Xia et al., 2024), the need for more quantitative and mixed-method research (Weng et al., 2024), and the imperative to align AI adoption with national development goals. Additionally, the study situates AI-enhanced assessment within broader discourses on educational equity and academic integrity; such as concerns about plagiarism and cheating having intensified with the advent of GenAI tools, underscoring the importance of ethical guidelines and policy frameworks (Charles & Papadaki, 2025).

Research Questions

To guide this investigation, the chapter poses three research questions: (1) What AI-driven assessment practices are currently implemented in MENA universities? (2) What benefits and challenges have been reported in relation to learning outcomes, academic integrity and institutional policies? And (3) How do local innovations in MENA align with or diverge from global trends in AI-enabled assessment?

In addressing these questions, the review aims to inform regional stakeholders (i.e. educators, administrators and policymakers) about evidence-based strategies for integrating AI into assessment. The findings will also contribute to the global discourse on ethical and effective AI adoption in higher education, ensuring that innovations support student learning while safeguarding integrity, transparency and equity.

LITERATURE REVIEW

Theoretical Framework

To conceptualise acceptable AI use in assessment, recent scholarship has drawn on boundary work and social boundary theory. Corbin et al. (2025) argue that educators and students often employ metaphors of "drawing lines" when describing appropriate GenAI use in assessment. Social boundary theory views boundaries as symbolic constructs that protect professional legitimacy during periods of technological disruption. This perspective illuminates how participants distinguish legitimate from illegitimate practices and emphasises that boundary-making has real consequences for pedagogical and emotional well-being. Corbin et al. (2025) therefore call for frameworks that move beyond simple prohibitions or permissions to address enforcement feasibility, the preservation of authentic learning, and the emotional burden on educators and students. In short, boundary theory helps explain why "grey areas" persist and why institutional guidance must engage with lived experiences rather than imposing rigid rules.

A second relevant theoretical lens is the 'wicked problems' framework. Drawing on Rittel and Webber's (1973) typology, Corbin and colleagues (2025) argue that the GenAI-assessment challenge exhibits all ten characteristics of 'wicked problems'. Teachers interviewed for their study offered contradictory definitions of the problem: some framed GenAI as essential for workforce readiness, while others viewed it as educational fraud. Wicked problems resist definitive formulation, lack a stopping rule, and offer only "good" or "bad" solutions. Participants' experiences illustrated these features, as educators vacillated between integration and policing, struggled to decide when an assessment design was "done", and recognised that any solution involved trade-offs between authenticity, creativity and workload. Understanding AI in assessment as a 'wicked problem' suggests that universities should grant teachers the permission to iterate, compromise and diverge rather than seeking a definitive fix.

A complementary perspective comes from feedback literacy and self-regulation. Zhan et al. (2025) note that while feedback is theoretically powerful, student engagement is often low due to contextual constraints such as large classes and limited curriculum space. They propose a cyclical feedback framework in which students engage in *feedback forethought*, *feedback control* and *feedback retrospect* when interacting with GenAI tools. Crucially, GenAI's affordances such as interactivity, anxiety-reduction, communicative authenticity, student-centredness, repetitive practice and ubiquity, can enhance feedback but also introduce challenges like biased or misleading information, plagiarism and over-dependence. The extent to which students benefit from GenAI depends on their feedback literacy and capacity for metacognitive regulation.

Finally, grading practices must be understood through the lens of value judgments and epistemological development. Luo and Dawson's (2025) study of 33 university teachers demonstrates that grading GenAI-assisted work involves four interrelated value clusters — *person-oriented* (honesty, diligence), *capability-oriented* (independence vs. AI competence), *relation-oriented* (trust), and *justice-oriented* (fairness and beneficence). Ethics intersects these clusters, because teachers expressed concern about penalising honest students and rewarding hidden AI use. Teachers' judgments also reflected differing epistemological stages: absolutists tended to privilege independent, human-produced work, whereas multiplist and evaluativist teachers adopted more flexible approaches. Understanding these value positions is essential for interpreting teacher responses to AI-assisted assignments.

Context of the study

The MENA region is undergoing rapid digital transformation. Countries such as the UAE have articulated national strategies that emphasise AI-driven economic diversification and educational innovation. Yet, the global literature on AI-enabled assessment remains geographically imbalanced, with a predominance of studies from the West and East Asia. A recent scoping review of 969 publications identified only thirty-two empirical studies on generative AI in higher-education assessment, most published in 2023 (Xia et al., 2024). The review called for research that explores institutional and cultural variations and emphasised that assessment transformation must cultivate self-regulated learning, responsible AI use and integrity (ibid). Thus, there is an urgent need for systematic evidence from the MENA region to inform regional policy and practice. This chapter responds to that need by examining AI-enabled assessment across MENA universities, a context that has received little attention in existing literature.

Review of Literature

Opportunities and Affordances of AI-Driven Assessment

Across the literature, AI is portrayed as a double-edged sword. On the positive side, GenAI tools can produce personalised feedback, adapt assessment tasks to individual needs and enhance student engagement. Zhan et al. (2025) highlight six affordances —interactivity, anxiety reduction, communicative authenticity, student-centredness, repetitive practice and ubiquity — that allow GenAI to deliver rapid, context-sensitive feedback in human-like dialogues. These affordances may reduce teacher workload and enable ongoing formative assessment. The scoping review by Xia et al. (2024) similarly notes that GenAI offers innovative approaches to evaluating student performance and tailoring learning experiences, potentially reshaping time-intensive manual assessment practices. However, the same review emphasises that AI-driven assessment should cultivate students' self-regulation and responsible learning. For AI tools to act as enablers, students must develop feedback literacy and metacognitive strategies to engage productively with machine-generated comments.

Challenges and Ethical Concerns

Despite these affordances, scholars repeatedly underscore the ethical and pedagogical challenges posed by GenAI. Zhan et al. warn that GenAI can produce biased or misleading feedback and may encourage plagiarism or over-dependence. Xia et al. (2024) observe that GenAI has heightened concerns about cheating and academic integrity. Corbin et al. (2025) note that educators struggle to preserve assessment validity while preventing false accusations of AI misuse. The problem is further complicated by the fact that generative AI blurs the line between acceptable assistance and inappropriate delegation; outputs may not genuinely reflect a student's competencies, making it difficult for teachers to judge authenticity. Mistrust of AI detectors is also evident in empirical studies (Charles & Charles, 2024), where detectors produced false positives on handwritten exams, particularly for higher-scoring students. These issues highlight the need for transparency and ethical guidelines in AI-driven assessment.

Boundary and Policy Frameworks

Researchers emphasise that universities must move beyond binary prohibitions or blanket endorsements of AI use. Corbin et al. (2025) interviewed nineteen students and twelve educators and found widespread uncertainty about where "the line" lies. Participants described blurred boundaries, grey areas and the need for clear institutional guidance. The study uses social boundary theory to show that boundary-making is part of maintaining educational legitimacy and that policy must consider feasibility of enforcement, the preservation of authentic learning, and emotional wellbeing of teachers and students. Analogies to Grammarly and other proofreading tools suggest that some forms of AI assistance (e.g., grammar checking) are already accepted, while others remain contentious. In light of this ambiguity, the authors argue for institutional conversations that articulate permissible AI use and support educators in communicating policies consistently.

Grading Practices and Value Judgements

Luo and Dawson's (2025) interview study demonstrates that teacher judgments on AI-assisted work extend far beyond the quality of the assignment. Teachers drew on person-oriented values such as honesty and diligence; perceptions of students' honesty influenced whether AI use was seen as cheating. Capability-oriented values were also prominent: independence was often privileged, with some teachers instinctively ranking students higher if they worked without AI. However, other teachers argued that critical use of AI demonstrates discipline-specific competence, especially in fields like engineering or digital arts where tool use is integral. Relation-oriented values concerned trust; teachers emphasised maintaining trusting relationships and avoiding penalising students who openly declared AI use. Finally, justice-oriented values related to fairness and beneficence; educators were worried that equal grades for AI-assisted and unassisted work could create resentment among students. The study concludes that grading with AI assistance is shaped by educators' epistemological development: absolutist teachers tend to penalise AI use, whereas evaluativist teachers adopt more balanced approaches. These findings highlight the need for transparent grading criteria and professional development to surface and critically examine value judgements.

AI and Assessment as a Wicked Problem

Viewing AI in assessment as a 'wicked problem' provides a meta-framework for understanding these tensions. Corbin et al. (2025) found that teachers' experiences align with all ten characteristics of 'wicked problems'. Participants framed AI adoption in contradictory ways, either as an essential workplace skill or as educational fraud. They had no clear "stopping rule" for knowing when an assessment redesign was complete. Solutions were not right or wrong but involved trade-offs between competing values. For example, some teachers created dual submission streams (with and without AI) to preserve agency, but this doubled their workload. Recognising AI-enabled assessment as a 'wicked problem' implies that institutional responses should prioritise ongoing, adaptive strategies rather than definitive fixes and should provide educators with the authority and resources to iterate.

Global Trends and MENA Research Gaps

Comprehensive reviews reveal a rapidly expanding literature but also significant gaps. Xia et al. (2024) report that out of 969 publications on GenAI and assessment, only 32 empirical studies met their inclusion criteria. Most were qualitative and there was almost no representation from the MENA region. The review urges educational institutions to transform assessments to support self-regulated learning, responsible AI use and integrity, while emphasising teacher professional development and policy reform (ibid). Weng et al. (2024) similarly classify emerging assessment practices into traditional, innovative/refocused and GenAI-incorporated categories, noting a shift towards higher-order tasks and career-relevant learning outcomes. However, they caution that existing evidence is preliminary and call for more rigorous mixed-method research. Collectively, these reviews underscore the paucity of MENA-specific data. While some studies in the region explore AI adoption in teaching and early warning analytics, research directly examining AI-enhanced assessment remains scarce. For example, Waked et al. (2024) demonstrate that AI detectors mislabel authentic student work as AI-generated in Saudi Arabian English exams, raising fairness concerns; and Boubker (2024) shows widespread ChatGPT use among Moroccan students for exam preparation and writing, yet these findings have not been integrated into broader assessment frameworks. The present systematic review addresses this gap by synthesising the emerging yet fragmented evidence on AI-driven assessment across MENA institutions.

METHODOLOGY

This study employed a systematic literature review of AI-enabled assessment within higher education across the MENA region, in accordance with the Preferred Reporting Items for Systematic Reviews and Meta-Analyses (PRISMA 2020) guidelines (Page et al., 2021). PRISMA emphasises that, to be valuable to users, systematic reviews must transparently report why the review was conducted, how studies were identified and selected, and what the authors found (Liberati et al., 2009). The 2020 update to PRISMA provides a 27-item checklist and flow diagrams to reflect advances in search, appraisal and synthesis methods (Moher et al., 2015). A growing body of educational research has adopted these guidelines; for example, Choi-Lundberg et al. (2023) note that their review of digital innovations in higher-education learning designs followed PRISMA to ensure rigour and replicability. Following this precedent, the present review articulated a protocol specifying information sources, eligibility criteria, and procedures for screening, data extraction and synthesis. I developed this protocol prior to the search and it was used to guide all subsequent decisions. The review did not involve human subjects and thus did not require ethical approval; however, I still abided by the research ethics guidelines and requirements of the Centre for Research in Assessment and Digital Learning (CRADLE) at Deakin University, Australia.

Although the review did not include human participants, it systematically selected studies that met predefined eligibility criteria. Eligible studies were peer-reviewed journal articles (empirical or conceptual) published between 1 January 2023 and 31 August 2025 in English. To ensure contextual relevance, included studies had to:

1. *Population/Setting*: focus on higher-education institutions located in the MENA region, including Algeria, Bahrain, Egypt, Iran, Iraq, Jordan, Kuwait, Lebanon, Libya, Morocco, Oman, Palestine, Qatar, Saudi Arabia, Syria, Tunisia, UAE and Yemen. Studies examining multi-region samples were included only if MENA-specific findings were reported.
2. *Phenomenon of Interest*: examine the use of AI, including machine learning, deep learning, LLMs such as ChatGPT or other generative AI, in assessment or assessment-adjacent practices (e.g., automated scoring, feedback generation, plagiarism detection, adaptive testing, proctoring, early warning analytics). Studies focusing solely on teaching, tutoring, administration or recruitment were excluded.
3. *Context and Language*: be situated within a higher-education context (undergraduate, postgraduate or continuing education) and published in English to ensure accurate analysis. Conference proceedings, book chapters, theses and grey literature were excluded, as were studies published outside the specified date range.

Information Sources and Search Strategy

The review searched four bibliographic databases selected for their breadth and disciplinary coverage: ERIC, Scopus, ProQuest and APA PsycINFO. Search strings were tailored to each database using controlled vocabulary (e.g. ERIC descriptors) and keywords to capture variations in AI terminology, assessment concepts and regional identifiers. The generic search template was: ("artificial intelligence" OR "AI" OR "machine learning" OR "generative AI" OR "large language model") AND ("assessment" OR "grading" OR "evaluation" OR "feedback") AND

("higher education" OR "university" OR "college") AND

("Algeria" OR "Bahrain" OR "Egypt" OR "Iraq" OR "Jordan" OR "Kuwait" OR "Lebanon" OR "Libya" OR "Morocco" OR "Oman" OR "Palestine" OR "Qatar" OR "Saudi Arabia" OR "Syria" OR "Tunisia" OR "United Arab Emirates" OR "Yemen").

Field tags (e.g., TITLE-ABS-KEY in Scopus) were applied to restrict searches to titles, abstracts and keywords. Date limits (1 Jan 2023 – 31 Aug 2025) and language limits (English) were applied where possible at the database level; when only year-level filters were available (e.g., ERIC), month-level restrictions were enforced during screening. The search was executed on 1st September 2025 (Melbourne time).

To ensure completeness, reference lists of key articles were screened, and citation searching was conducted in Scopus.

A structured extraction form, developed in Google Sheets, captured bibliographic details (authors, year, journal, country), methodological characteristics (study design, sample size, discipline), AI modality (LLM, machine learning classifier, NLP analytics, predictive analytics), assessment focus (formative feedback, summative grading, proctoring, integrity analytics, early warning), outcomes (validity, reliability, accuracy, fairness, perceptions, learning impacts) and key findings.

Data Collection Procedure

Search results from each database were imported into Google Sheets. Deduplication was performed using a combination of title, author, publication year and DOI fields. Initial screening of titles and abstracts was conducted independently by two reviewers (myself and a colleague) using the eligibility criteria. Studies were coded as "include", "exclude" or "uncertain". Discrepancies were resolved through discussion, and articles labelled "uncertain" proceeded to full-text review.

Full texts of potentially eligible articles were retrieved and assessed for inclusion independently by the same reviewers. Reasons for exclusion at this stage were documented (e.g., not MENA, not assessment, not higher education, non-English, outside date range, inaccessible full text). The PRISMA flow diagram (*see* Figure 1) summarises the selection process: 346 records were identified, three duplicates were removed, leaving 343 for title/abstract screening; 274 were excluded, resulting in 69 articles for full-text retrieval; of these, 22 were excluded. Ultimately, 47 studies met the inclusion criteria and were included in the review.

Figure 1. PRISMA flow diagram, informed by Page et al. (2021).

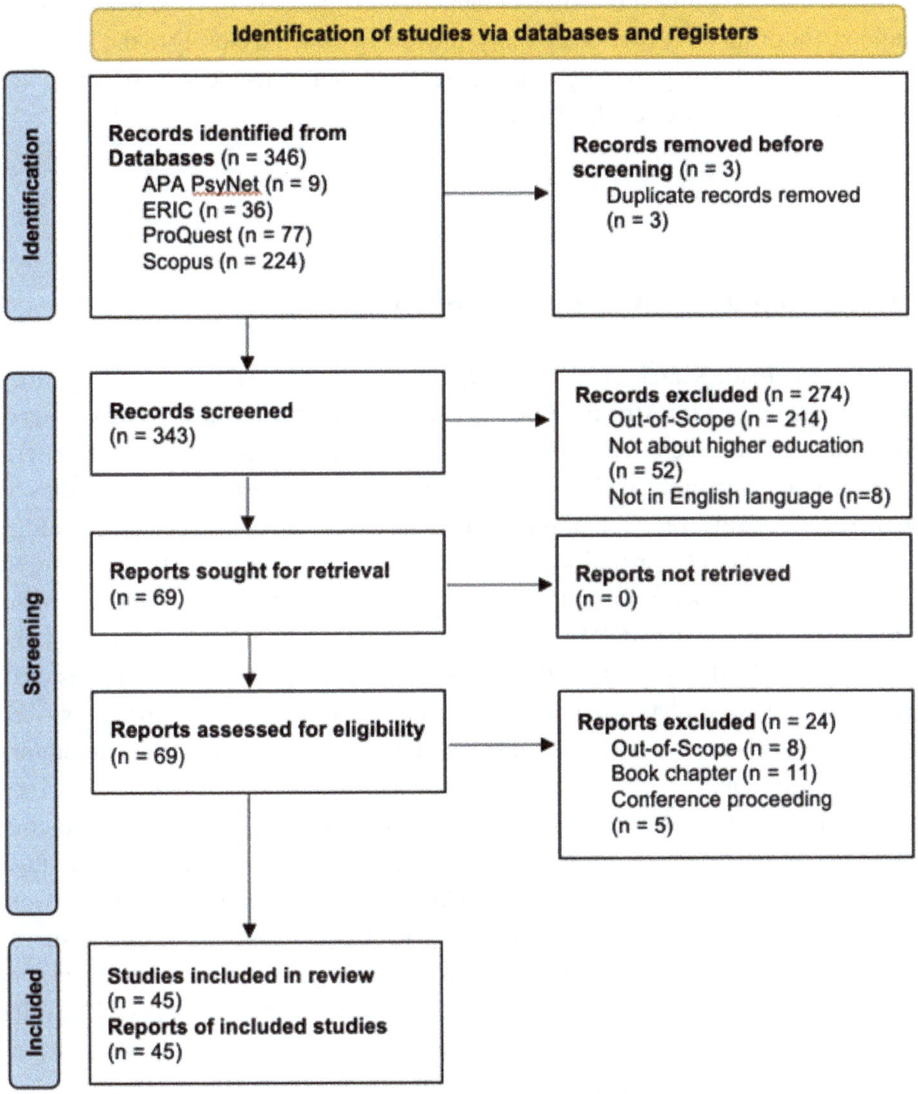

Data Analysis

Given the heterogeneity of interventions, contexts and outcome measures, meta-analysis was not feasible. Instead, a narrative synthesis approach was adopted, wherein studies were then grouped into thematic categories based on their primary assessment function. Within each category, findings were synthesised qualitatively to identify patterns in reported benefits, challenges, and outcomes. Particular attention was paid to the alignment of MENA practices with global trends and to any unique regional innovations or barriers. Finally, the review adhered closely to the PRISMA reporting guidelines, providing a transparent account of the search, selection and synthesis process (Page et al., 2021).

RESULTS

Study Selection and Characteristics

The systematic search of ERIC, Proquest, Scopus and APA PsycINFO yielded 346 records. After removing three duplicates, 343 titles and abstracts were screened. Sixty-nine records were retrieved in full, and 45 studies met the inclusion criteria and were included in the review. Table 1 summarises the distribution of studies by theme, AI modality, research design and country. The majority of included studies came from the Gulf Cooperation Council (GCC) states—particularly Saudi Arabia (KSA), the United Arab Emirates (UAE), Qatar and Bahrain—as well as Jordan, Egypt and Morocco. ChatGPT (or other large language models such as GPT-4 and Gemini) was the dominant modality across themes, although several studies evaluated general AI-analytics platforms or customised machine-learning classifiers. Cross-sectional surveys were the most common design, reflecting the exploratory nature of the field.

The 45 included studies spanned a variety of disciplines—education, medicine, engineering and business—and levels (undergraduate, postgraduate and faculty). Most (70%) were published in 2024–2025, reflecting a surge of empirical work following the public release of ChatGPT in late 2022. The predominance of survey designs underscores a nascent evidence base, with only a handful of experiments or quasi-experimental evaluations. Thematic analysis of the extracted data yielded three primary themes — Policy & Ethics, Assessment Tools & Analytics, and Learning & Feedback — alongside smaller clusters on adoption and other emerging topics.

Table 1. Distribution of studies across themes and methodological characteristics

Theme	No. of studies	Common AI modality	Dominant designs	Representative countries	Example studies
Policy & Ethics	22	ChatGPT; AI-detection programs	Cross-sectional surveys, qualitative interviews, and conceptual frameworks	Saudi Arabia, Jordan, UAE	Evangelista (2025); Aldossary (2024); Waked (2024)
Assessment Tools & Analytics	11	ChatGPT and related generative models; machine-learning classifiers	Quantitative experiments and surveys	Egypt, Jordan, Morocco	Al-Azzam (2025); Boubker (2024); Shabara (2024)
Learning & Feedback	5	ChatGPT; general AI	Cross-sectional surveys; mixed-methods	Bahrain, Oman, regional Middle East	Alrayes (2024); Salem (2025)
Adoption & Perceptions	4	General AI tools and GenAI	Q-methodology study; technology acceptance surveys	Qatar, Oman	Chaaban (2024); Alshamy (2025)
Other	3	General AI applications	Descriptive surveys; mixed methods	Jordan, Morocco	Alkaramneh (2025); Moukhliss (2024)

Thematic Analysis

Policy & Ethics

Nearly half of the included studies (22/45) focused on policy issues, academic integrity and ethical considerations related to AI-enabled assessment. Researchers consistently reported uncertainty among educators and students regarding permissible AI use and called for institutional guidelines that move beyond simple prohibitions. Interviews with Australian university staff and students revealed that participants frequently invoked metaphors of "blurred lines" or "grey areas" when describing acceptable GenAI use. This resonates with boundary-work theory, which posits that symbolic boundaries protect professional legitimacy and must evolve during periods of technological change. Corbin et al. (2025) argue that policy should consider enforcement feasibility and the emotional burden on educators and students, rather than simply drawing a line between allowed and forbidden practices.

Academic integrity was a recurrent concern across MENA studies. Several surveys in KSA, Jordan and Bahrain reported high awareness of ChatGPT's potential for cheating, with respondents expressing the need for proctoring tools, plagiarism detectors and honour codes. Waked et al. (2024) experimentally evaluated four AI-text detectors on handwritten English exams and found high false-positive rates, particularly for higher-scoring scripts. This finding highlights the risk of unfairly penalising students and underscores calls to evaluate the reliability of AI-detection technologies before implementation. Similarly, Luo and Dawson (2025) observed that teachers' grading decisions on AI-assisted assignments reflected person-, capability-, relation- and justice-oriented values. Some educators felt morally obliged to reward independent work, while others considered critical AI use a desirable skill; this tension illustrates the ethical complexity of assessment in the GenAI era.

Policy-oriented studies also emphasised the wicked nature of the AI-assessment problem. Drawing on Rittel and Webber's framework, Corbin et al. (2025) argued that AI in assessment exhibits all ten characteristics of wicked problems: there is no definitive formulation, solutions are not right or wrong, and every intervention leads to further consequences. Interviews revealed that some educators viewed AI as essential for preparing students for AI-rich workplaces, while others saw it as educational fraud. Recognising this wickedness implies that institutions should permit teachers to iterate and adapt assessment practices rather than seeking a definitive fix. Studies in the GCC echoed the need for flexible policies, suggesting that universities develop tiered guidelines (e.g., allowable AI use for drafting but not final submissions), invest in professional development, and engage students in co-creating ethical codes. Overall, the Policy & Ethics theme underscores the urgency of establishing clear, context-sensitive policies that balance innovation with integrity.

Assessment Tools & Analytics

The second major theme (11/48 studies) centred on AI-enabled assessment tools and predictive analytics. These studies examined the accuracy, reliability and educational impact of AI systems deployed to score assignments, generate formative feedback or classify at-risk students. Early warning systems were prominent: Al-Azzam and Al-Oudat (2025) developed a framework using GPT-4-assisted labelling and machine-learning classifiers to categorise students' academic and psychological challenges. Among various algorithms tested, support vector machines achieved the highest accuracy (88.2%), highlighting AI's potential for identifying students in need of support. Boubker (2024) reported widespread use of ChatGPT among Moroccan university students for exam preparation, assignments and idea generation, with structural-equation modelling indicating a positive relationship between AI use and perceived learning outcomes.

Experimental evaluations of automated scoring systems produced mixed results. Shabara et al. (2024) compared ChatGPT's scoring of 100 English essays with that of 11 human teachers; ChatGPT's scores showed weak–moderate agreement with teachers' assessments, and its intra-rater reliability was only moderate. The authors caution against using ChatGPT as a standalone grader without human oversight.

A proof-of-concept study at Qatar University compared ChatGPT and Gemini on multiple-choice questions (MCQs) in emergency medicine. Results indicated that generative AI performed better on text-only questions than on image-based items and that human students still outperformed both models. Such findings reinforce calls to treat AI as an assistive tool rather than a substitute for expert judgment. Studies evaluating plagiarism detectors and proctoring systems also highlighted technical limitations and raised concerns about biased outcomes.

Learning & Feedback

A smaller cluster of studies (5/48) focused on AI's role in enhancing student learning and feedback. These investigations often viewed AI as a tutor or study aid rather than as an assessor. Alrayes et al. (2024) surveyed Bahraini academics and found that only 7.6% of those who used ChatGPT employed it for assessment, whereas 46.8% used it for teaching and 33.4% for research. Respondents reported that performance expectancy, effort expectancy and hedonic motivation significantly predicted their intention to use ChatGPT. Salem (2025) surveyed over 250 medical educators across Saudi Arabia, Egypt and Jordan and found high levels of AI readiness, particularly in awareness and efficacy, although resource and training challenges remained.

The evidence points to GenAI's potential to enhance feedback engagement but also to the need for careful scaffolding. Zhan et al. (2025) propose a cyclical feedback framework comprising feedback forethought, feedback control and feedback retrospect. They argue that GenAI tools can reduce anxiety, increase interactivity and provide authentic dialogue, yet they also risk bias, plagiarism and over-dependence if students lack feedback literacy. This duality mirrors findings from MENA surveys: students in nursing and medical programmes appreciated AI's immediacy and flexibility but expressed concern about its accuracy and fairness. Mixed-methods studies emphasised the importance of developing students' metacognitive skills to engage productively with machine feedback. Overall, the Learning & Feedback theme suggests that AI can enrich formative assessment and study practices when integrated into a pedagogically sound framework that promotes self-regulated learning.

Adoption & Perceptions

Four studies examined adoption patterns and perceptions of AI more broadly, often using technology-acceptance frameworks. A Q-methodology study with 43 graduate students and faculty at Qatar University identified five distinct viewpoints ranging from enthusiastic adoption to cautious scepticism. The largest group prioritised ethical and policy considerations, reflecting the overlap with the Policy &

Ethics theme. Surveys in Oman and Jordan found moderate levels of AI adoption, with variability across disciplines and demographic factors. These studies provide contextual insight into faculty and student readiness but offer limited detail on assessment specifically; thus they complement rather than drive the main themes.

Other

The remaining few studies investigated general AI applications in higher education without explicit focus on assessment. For example, Alkaramneh et al. (2025) surveyed Jordanian faculty about AI use in teaching and research, while Moukhliss et al. (2024) explored AI adoption in Moroccan universities using a mixed-methods approach. Again, although these studies mention assessment as one of several AI applications, their findings contribute little to the core questions of this review and were therefore categorised separately.

Synthesis of Findings

Taken together, the thematic analysis reveals that research on AI in MENA higher-education assessment is still emergent and fragmented. Policy and ethical concerns dominate the discourse, reflecting widespread anxiety about integrity, fairness and the legitimacy of AI-assisted work. Empirical evidence for the effectiveness of AI-enabled assessment tools is mixed: early warning systems show promise, but automated scoring and detection tools exhibit reliability issues. Studies focusing on learning and feedback underscore AI's potential to personalise feedback and enhance engagement, but also highlight the need for metacognitive scaffolding and professional development. There is a notable absence of rigorous quantitative evaluations and a scarcity of longitudinal or experimental designs. Moreover, cross-regional comparisons suggest that MENA institutions are grappling with similar challenges to those documented globally—yet local cultural and policy contexts demand tailored solutions.

DISCUSSION

Interpretation of Findings

This review provides the first systematic synthesis of research on artificial-intelligence–enabled assessment in higher education across the MENA region. By examining 45 studies published between January 2023 and August 2025, I identified three dominant themes (policy & ethics, assessment tools & analytics, and learning & feedback) alongside smaller clusters on adoption and other applications. The prominence of policy and ethical concerns reflects a global discourse that has rapidly emerged in the wake of generative AI. Qualitative studies in Australia and the UK found that educators and students struggle to define acceptable AI use and call for guidance that goes beyond simple bans. My synthesis shows that MENA scholars echo these anxieties: surveys in Bahrain, Jordan and Saudi Arabia report heightened awareness of academic integrity issues, mistrust of AI detectors and confusion about permissible assistance. This aligns with international analyses of policy responses, which emphasise the need for accountability, human oversight, transparency and inclusiveness in generative AI use (Dabis, & Csáki, 2024). The AI Assessment Scale proposed by Perkins et al. (2024) similarly advocates a flexible framework that empowers educators to select appropriate AI involvement based on learning outcomes.

My second theme centres on assessment tools and analytics. Studies on early warning systems demonstrate promising accuracy in predicting at-risk students, suggesting that machine-learning classifiers can support timely intervention. However, evidence for automated scoring is mixed: experiments comparing ChatGPT with human raters found only moderate agreement and highlighted the risk of false positives when AI detectors label authentic work as machine-generated. Such findings caution against overreliance on AI for high-stakes grading and call for human oversight and calibration. The fact that most tool-oriented studies were cross-sectional rather than experimental underscores the nascent state of this research area.

The learning & feedback theme reveals that educators and students are beginning to leverage AI for formative purposes. Surveys report moderate adoption of ChatGPT for exam preparation and feedback, and educators perceive AI as a tool for enhancing engagement and reducing anxiety. Zhan et al. (2025) propose a cyclical feedback framework in which students engage in forethought, control and retrospection when interacting with AI tools. Yet participants in our included studies emphasised the need for training in metacognitive and feedback literacy to mitigate risks such as bias, plagiarism and over-dependence. Overall, the findings suggest that AI can enrich formative assessment when embedded within scaffolded pedagogical designs.

Comparisons with Global Evidence

The MENA findings broadly mirror global trends in AI-enabled assessment. International studies emphasise that generative AI has ushered in ethical challenges that universities are only beginning to address (Dabis, & Csáki, 2024). Content analyses of policy documents from top universities around the world highlight a central ethical imperative: student assignments must reflect individual learning, and human actors retain moral and legal responsibility for AI misuse (ibid). Moreover, global policy responses often combine preventive measures (e.g., modifying assessment tasks) with dialogue-based sanctions and encourage explicit communication of AI use in course syllabi. These patterns resonate with MENA institutions' emphasis on developing honor codes, proctoring tools and institutional guidelines.

At the same time, the MENA context introduces unique dynamics. National AI strategies, such as Saudi Arabia's Vision 2030, create strong incentives for rapid adoption of AI technologies in education. Many studies in my sample were produced by institutions within the GCC and were motivated by government directives to foster digital transformation. Yet other parts of the region (e.g., Yemen, Libya, Algeria) are underrepresented, reflecting disparities in research capacity and infrastructure. Cultural factors may also influence perceptions of AI: for example, surveys indicate that students and faculty express moral concerns about authenticity and fairness, often grounded in Islamic ethical frameworks. Future work should explore how Arabic language, local culture and religious values shape AI policy and practice in MENA higher education.

Implications for Practice and Policy

The synthesis suggests several actionable recommendations. First, institutions should develop multi-tiered policies that articulate permissible AI use across different assessment stages—drafting, editing, feedback and final submission. The AI Assessment Scale provides a template for such differentiation, enabling educators to align AI use with specific learning outcomes. Policies must be accompanied by clear communication strategies; the nature article on global policy responses notes that transparency about AI use in course syllabi is already considered good practice (Dabis, & Csáki, 2024). Second, universities should invest in professional development to enhance faculty's digital literacy and ethical decision-making. Interviews reveal that educators feel burdened by the responsibility to police AI use and need support to integrate AI meaningfully. Workshops and communities of practice can help teachers design assessments that leverage AI for higher-order skills while preserving academic integrity.

Third, assessment design should prioritise authentic, higher-order tasks that are less amenable to automation. Scholars argue that generative AI challenges traditional forms of assessment and necessitates innovative approaches such as project-based, oral and peer assessment that emphasise process over product. Our review supports this view: several included studies report shifting towards open-ended tasks and reflective assignments to mitigate the risk of AI misuse. Finally, institutions should adopt a cautious stance towards AI detectors and automated scoring systems. Evidence of high false-positive rates and moderate agreement with human scorers suggests that these tools should be used only as aids, not as sole arbiters, and that their performance must be rigorously evaluated in diverse linguistic and disciplinary contexts.

Limitations of the Evidence and of This Review

Three notable limitations characterise the body of evidence. First, the vast majority of studies employ cross-sectional surveys or qualitative interviews; robust experimental designs and longitudinal evaluations are scarce. This limits our ability to draw causal inferences about the effectiveness of AI-enabled assessment tools. Second, representation across the MENA region is uneven. Research is concentrated in the GCC and a few North African countries, leaving gaps in understanding of contexts such as Algeria, Libya, Sudan and Yemen. Third, most studies rely on self-reported perceptions rather than objective measures of learning outcomes or assessment quality. Only a handful of studies evaluate AI tools directly, and those that do often use small samples or single institutions.

This review itself has limitations. Although the search was comprehensive within ERIC, Proquest, Scopus and APA PsycINFO, I restricted the language to English and the publication period to January 2023–August 2025. Relevant studies published in Arabic or French, or works outside indexed journals, may have been missed. I also excluded conference papers and book chapters, which might contain emerging insights. The heterogeneity of included studies precluded meta-analysis; instead, I synthesised findings narratively and thematically. Despite these limitations, the review offers a timely and rigorous overview of AI-enabled assessment in MENA higher education.

Directions for Future Research

Future research should move beyond perceptions and policy analyses to evaluate AI integration in real classroom settings. Rigorous experimental and quasi-experimental designs are needed to measure the impact of AI tools on learning outcomes, equity and academic integrity. Comparative studies across disciplines and cultural contexts can illuminate how AI adoption is shaped by subject matter and institutional culture. Researchers should also investigate how AI can support formative assessment and feedback, perhaps drawing on the cyclical feedback model. Additionally, work is needed to develop and test fair, transparent AI detection and scoring systems, particularly in languages other than English. Finally, cross-national collaborations within MENA could help build research capacity and share best practices, ensuring that regional AI policies and innovations are informed by robust evidence.

CONCLUSION

This systematic review provides a comprehensive synthesis of how generative artificial intelligence is reshaping assessment practices in higher education across the MENA region. By analysing 45 studies published between January 2023 and August 2025, we identified three dominant themes (policy & ethics, assessment tools & analytics, and learning & feedback) that collectively illuminate both the promise and the peril of AI-enabled assessment. Research in the region mirrors global concerns that generative AI tools offer transformative pedagogical opportunities while simultaneously posing ethical and academic challenges. The prevalence of policy-oriented studies highlights the urgency of establishing clear guidelines: institutions are wrestling with accountability, human oversight, transparency and fairness. At the same time, experiments with AI-driven scoring and early-warning systems reveal technical limitations and underscore the need for robust human oversight.

Several overarching conclusions can be drawn. First, the integration of generative AI into assessment demands a unique policy response. Top-down mandates that emphasise individual responsibility and academic integrity must be balanced with flexible, context-sensitive frameworks that empower educators to select appropriate AI use based on learning outcomes. Second, the effectiveness of AI-enabled tools remains uncertain: while machine-learning classifiers can accurately flag at-risk students, automated grading systems and AI detectors often exhibit reliability issues and risk unfairly penalising students. Human oversight and iterative calibration are therefore essential.

Third, harnessing AI for formative assessment and feedback holds considerable promise but requires significant investment in feedback literacy and metacognitive training. As Zhan et al. (2025) argue, students must develop the skills to critically engage with AI-generated feedback; otherwise, the benefits of interactivity and personalisation may be outweighed by risks of bias, plagiarism and over-dependence. Fourth, the research landscape is uneven: most studies rely on cross-sectional surveys and are concentrated in a handful of countries, leaving substantial gaps in our understanding of AI-enabled assessment in other parts of the MENA region. Addressing these gaps will require longitudinal and experimental studies, inclusive sampling, and multilingual publication strategies.

Looking ahead, universities across the MENA region are uniquely positioned to lead in the ethical adoption of AI given their national AI strategies and rapid digital transformation. By developing multi-tiered policies, investing in professional development, designing assessments that emphasise higher-order thinking, and engaging students in co-creating ethical guidelines, institutions can harness AI to enhance learning while safeguarding integrity. As global policy analyses show, clear communication of AI use in course syllabi and a blend of preventive and dialogue-based approaches are emerging as good practice. Future research must build on these insights to develop culturally attuned frameworks that ensure AI serves as a catalyst for educational equity, innovation and lifelong learning in the region.

REFERENCES

Al-Azzam, S. H., & Al-Oudat, M. (2025). Artificial Intelligence-Based Classification and Prediction of Academic and Psychological Challenges in Higher Education. *Educational Process: International Journal, 15*, e2025150. DOI: 10.22521/edupij.2025.15.150

Aldossary, A. S., Aljindi, A. A., & Alamri, J. M. (2024). The role of generative AI in education: Perceptions of Saudi students. *Contemporary Educational Technology, 16*(4), ep536. DOI: 10.30935/cedtech/15496

Alkaramneh, M. S., Al-Taj, H., Ghanem, B. O., Sheirah, K. A., Ghedhaifi, H., & Shatat, N. (2025). The Degree to Which Faculty Members at Jordanian Universities Employ Artificial Intelligence Applications in Education and Scientific Research. *The Journal of Educators Online, 22*(3), n3.

Alrayes, A., Henari, T. F., & Ahmed, D. A. (2024). ChatGPT in education–Understanding the Bahraini academics perspective. *Electronic Journal of e-Learning, 22*(2), 112–134. DOI: 10.34190/ejel.22.2.3250

Alshamy, A., Al-Harthi, A. S. A., & Abdullah, S. (2025). Perceptions of Generative AI Tools in Higher Education: Insights from Students and Academics at Sultan Qaboos University. *Education Sciences, 15*(4), 501. DOI: 10.3390/educsci15040501

Azzam, A., & Charles, T. (2024). A Review of Artificial Intelligence in K-12 Education. *Open Journal of Applied Sciences, 14*, 2088–2100. DOI: 10.4236/ojapps.2024.148137

Azzam, A., & Charles, T. (2025). K-12 STEM Teachers' Experiences with Artificial Intelligence. *TEM Journal, 14*(1), 463-468. https://doi.org/DOI: 10.18421/TEM141-41

Berente, N., Gu, B., Recker, J., & Santhanam, R. (2021). Managing artificial intelligence. *Management Information Systems Quarterly, 45*(3), 1433–1450. DOI: 10.25300/MISQ/2021/16274

Boubker, O. (2024). From chatting to self-educating: Can AI tools boost student learning outcomes? *Expert Systems with Applications, 238*, 121820. DOI: 10.1016/j.eswa.2023.121820

Chaaban, Y., Qadhi, S., Chen, J., & Du, X. (2024). Understanding researchers' AI readiness in a higher education context: Q methodology research. *Education Sciences, 14*(7), 709. DOI: 10.3390/educsci14070709

Charles, R., & Charles, T. (2024). High school students' perceptions of using AI for learning. *Voice of the Publisher, 10*, 284–297. DOI: 10.4236/vp.2024.103024

Charles, T. (2022). The past, present, and future of assessments in the higher education sector. In Hill, C., Lamie, J., & Gore, T. (Eds.), *The evolution of transnational education* (pp. 126–136). Routledge., DOI: 10.4324/9781003225386

Charles, T. (2025). AI in Professional Development for English Language Teachers. In Ali, M., Anwar, M., Fazal, S., & Ayyaz, S. (Eds.), *AI Applications for English Language Learning* (pp. 73–92). IGI Global Scientific Publishing., DOI: 10.4018/979-8-3693-9077-1.ch004

Charles, T., & Hill, C. (2025). Micro-credentials and AI in higher education: Transforming professional development. In ElSayary, A. (Ed.), *Prompt engineering and generative AI applications for teaching and learning* (pp. 1–14). IGI Global Scientific Publishing., DOI: 10.4018/979-8-3693-7332-3.ch001

Charles, T., & Papadaki, M. (2025). Ethical Leadership in Technology Integration and Digital Education. In Soles, B., & Meyerott, T. (Eds.), *Diverse Leadership Perspectives in Education: From K-12 to Higher Education* (pp. 437–454). IGI Global Scientific Publishing., DOI: 10.4018/979-8-3693-6115-3.ch016

Choi-Lundberg, D. L., Butler-Henderson, K., Harman, K., & Crawford, J. (2023). A systematic review of digital innovations in technology-enhanced learning designs in higher education. *Australasian Journal of Educational Technology, 39*(3), 133–162. DOI: 10.14742/ajet.7615

Corbin, T., Bearman, M., Boud, D., & Dawson, P. (2025). The wicked problem of AI and assessment. *Assessment & Evaluation in Higher Education*, •••, 1–17. DOI: 10.1080/02602938.2025.2553340

Corbin, T., Dawson, P., Nicola-Richmond, K., & Partridge, H. (2025). 'Where's the line? It's an absurd line': Towards a framework for acceptable uses of AI in assessment. *Assessment & Evaluation in Higher Education*, •••, 1–13. DOI: 10.1080/02602938.2025.2456207

Dabis, A., & Csáki, C. (2024). AI and ethics: Investigating the first policy responses of higher education institutions to the challenge of generative AI. *Humanities & Social Sciences Communications, 11*(1), 1–13. DOI: 10.1057/s41599-024-03526-z

Evangelista, E. D. L. (2025). Ensuring academic integrity in the age of ChatGPT: Rethinking exam design, assessment strategies, and ethical AI policies in higher education. *Contemporary Educational Technology, 17*(1), ep559. DOI: 10.30935/cedtech/15775

Hossain, Z., Alwreikat, A., Khan, G. A., Alotaibi, F. A., Biswas, M. S., & Sbeity, F. (2025). AI Literacy and Perception Among Library and Information Science Students in South Asia and the Middle East. *Science & Technology Libraries*, •••, 1–21. DOI: 10.1080/0194262X.2025.2484280

Liberati, A., Altman, D. G., Tetzlaff, J., Mulrow, C., Gøtzsche, P. C., Ioannidis, J. P., Clarke, M., Devereaux, P. J., Kleijnen, J., & Moher, D. (2009). The PRISMA statement for reporting systematic reviews and meta-analyses of studies that evaluate healthcare interventions: Explanation and elaboration. *BMJ (Clinical Research Ed.), 339*. Advance online publication. DOI: 10.1136/bmj.b2700 PMID: 19622552

Luo, J., & Dawson, P. (2025). Exploring value judgements in grading: Will teachers mark down student work assisted by GenAI, and should they? *Studies in Higher Education*, •••, 1–15. DOI: 10.1080/03075079.2025.2552825

Luo, J., Zheng, C., Yin, J., & Teo, H. H. (2025b). Design and assessment of AI-based learning tools in higher education: A systematic review. *International Journal of Educational Technology in Higher Education*, *22*(1), 42. DOI: 10.1186/s41239-025-00540-2

McCarthy, J., Minsky, M. L., Rochester, N., & Shannon, C. E. (2006). A proposal for the dartmouth summer research project on artificial intelligence, august 31, 1955. *AI Magazine*, *27*(4), 12–12. DOI: 10.1609/aimag.v27i4.1904

Moher, D., Shamseer, L., Clarke, M., Ghersi, D., Liberati, A., Petticrew, M., Shekelle, P., & Stewart, L. A.Prisma-P Group. (2015). Preferred reporting items for systematic review and meta-analysis protocols (PRISMA-P) 2015 statement. *Systematic Reviews*, *4*(1), 1. DOI: 10.1186/2046-4053-4-1 PMID: 25554246

Moukhliss, G., Lahyani, K., & Diab, G. (2024). The Impact of Artificial Intelligence on Research and Higher Education in Morocco. [EduLearn]. *Journal of Education and Learning*, *18*(4), 1292–1300. DOI: 10.11591/edulearn.v18i4.21511

Page, M. J., McKenzie, J. E., Bossuyt, P. M., Boutron, I., Hoffmann, T. C., Mulrow, C. D., ... & Moher, D. (2021). The PRISMA 2020 statement: an updated guideline for reporting systematic reviews. *bmj, 372*. https://doi.org/DOI: 10.1136/bmj.n71

Perkins, M., Furze, L., Roe, J., & MacVaugh, J. (2024). The Artificial Intelligence Assessment Scale (AIAS): A framework for ethical integration of generative AI in educational assessment. *Journal of University Teaching & Learning Practice*, *21*(6), 49–66. DOI: 10.53761/q3azde36

Rittel, H. W., & Webber, M. M. (1973). Dilemmas in a general theory of planning. *Policy Sciences*, *4*(2), 155–169. DOI: 10.1007/BF01405730

Salem, M. A., Zakaria, O. M., Aldoughan, E. A., Khalil, Z. A., & Zakaria, H. M. (2025). Bridging the AI Gap in Medical Education: A Study of Competency, Readiness, and Ethical Perspectives in Developing Nations. *Computers*, *14*(6), 238. DOI: 10.3390/computers14060238

Shabara, R., ElEbyary, K., & Boraie, D. (2024). Teachers or ChatGPT: The issue of accuracy and consistency in l2 assessment. *Teaching English with Technology*, *24*(2), 71–92. DOI: 10.56297/vaca6841/LRDX3699/XSEZ5215

Waked, A. N., Abdelsalam, H., Ashraf, M. W., Pilotti, M., & El Alaoui, K. (2024). The impact of falsely detecting AI-generated text on academic assessment. In Shelley, M., & Ozturk, O. T. (Eds.), *Proceedings of ICRES 2024 International Conference on Research in Education and Science* (pp. 573-586), Antalya, Turkiye. ISTES.

Weng, X., XIA, Q., Gu, M., Rajaram, K., & Chiu, T. K. (2024). Assessment and learning outcomes for generative AI in higher education: A scoping review on current research status and trends. *Australasian Journal of Educational Technology*, *40*(6), 37–55. DOI: 10.14742/ajet.9540

Xia, Q., Weng, X., Ouyang, F., Lin, T. J., & Chiu, T. K. (2024). A scoping review on how generative artificial intelligence transforms assessment in higher education. *International Journal of Educational Technology in Higher Education*, *21*(1), 40. DOI: 10.1186/s41239-024-00468-z

Zhan, Y., Boud, D., Dawson, P., & Yan, Z. (2025). Generative artificial intelligence as an enabler of student feedback engagement: A framework. *Higher Education Research & Development*, *44*(5), 1289–1304. DOI: 10.1080/07294360.2025.2476513

Chapter 2
Adopting the New Academic Assistant:
Student Use and Perceptions of Generative AI in a Multicultural UAE University

Asim Bashir
http://orcid.org/0009-0000-2747-2874
University of Birmingham in Dubai, UAE

Pamela Johnson
https://orcid.org/0009-0006-6010-7936
University of Birmingham in Dubai, UAE

ABSTRACT

This study investigates how undergraduate students at a multicultural UAE university use Generative AI as an academic assistant and how they perceive its value, risks, and role in learning. Using a qualitative design grounded in constructivist and phenomenological approaches, the study draws on a focus group to examine emotional, cognitive, and behavioural dimensions of AI engagement. Findings show that students view Generative AI as an embedded study companion supporting idea generation, drafting, summarising, and problem solving, with accessibility and efficiency driving regular use. Participants also expressed concern about uneven institutional guidance, dependency risks, and uncertainty around acceptable and ethical use. Clear patterns emerged around developing prompt literacy, navigating inconsistent advice from instructors, and demand for transparent policies and practical instruction. Student readiness was shaped not only by technical familiarity but also by institutional clarity, pedagogical support, and confidence in responsible use within academic tasks and assessment use.

DOI: 10.4018/979-8-3373-6776-7.ch002

INTRODUCTION

Since its public release in late 2022, ChatGPT has catalysed a rapid and profound transformation in English for Academic Purposes (EAP) within higher education (HE). Generative artificial intelligence (GenAI) tools, powered by large language models (LLMs), can produce original content, such as text, images, and other media, by learning patterns from vast datasets (Sengar et al., 2024).

Student use of these capabilities ranges from productive use for learning to misuse, or substitution for one's original work. For EAP learners, the power and efficiency of LLMs to answer many traditional essay questions and writing tasks grammatically accurately and according to other specifications, such as word count or citations, has led some students to substitute their own work with GenAI content. Free, widespread access to tools such as ChatGPT, Copilot, Claude, Gemini, Scispace, Perplexity, and others has made them available to students of all income levels around the world. While many of these tools are only free to an extent, the free versions are often adequate for a wide range of academic tasks.

One MENA university code of practice prohibits submission of GenAI content in assessed student work unless its use is explicitly authorised. However, it is to date impossible to definitively prove a learner has submitted GenAI content as their own. Tools and applications that claim to detect GenAI content vary in accuracy, and even a one percent false positive rate could result in numerous incorrect misconduct accusations. Institutional guidelines indicate that when GenAI use is permitted, it must be acknowledged, and assessment specifications should outline the required form of acknowledgement. Citations, declarations, reflective statements, and the disclosure of prompts or chats are some acceptable forms of GenAI disclosure.

The inability of educators and institutions to definitively prove GenAI content in student work has meant that traditional means of enforcing academic integrity policies are no longer relevant, and this has resulted in misuse of GenAI, often without censure. While some students substitute AI generated content for their own work, others use these tools to provide critical feedback on or edit their original work, uses in which GenAI enhances their learning and improves the quality of their work (Escalante et al., 2023). Although AI research tools sometimes provide incorrect references and citations (Walters & Wilder, 2023), others expedite the research process and help students find the evidence they need in a fraction of the time.

While research exists on teacher experience and perspective of GenAI (Mohebi, 2025; Nazim & Alzubi, 2025), and there is research on student perspectives (Abdaljaleel et al., 2024), less work has been published to date on HE student perspectives in the Middle East and North Africa (MENA).

Purpose of the Study

The candid reflections of the five students who participated in this project have implications for policy, resourcing, and instruction. In terms of policy, clear understanding of when and why students seek GenAI support can inform institution policy as well as curriculum and assessment design. When educators ask their current students about GenAI use, students might not share candidly out of concern that they might be doing something that is prohibited or could lead to negative consequences. For this reason, this study selected learners who had already completed their EAP programme and moved into undergraduate studies. They were also reassured that their contributions to the discussions would be anonymised. This enabled the students to speak openly about their AI use.

Accurate views of student AI use can help MENA universities make realistic policy, as opposed to futile prohibitions, and help educators understand what students already know and what they need to learn to use GenAI effectively. One student in this project noted that they viewed discussion of academic integrity as so irrelevant that their attention was immediately lost once when the topic was raised in class or workshops.

Like some of its MENA neighbours, the UAE has federal HE institutions that offer free study to local high-school graduates. These institutions generally serve Emirati students, who predominantly speak Arabic as their native language. The UAE also hosts transnational universities, or universities that have a main campus in one country and at least one additional campus abroad. Students at these institutions come from diverse linguistic and cultural backgrounds. While the student demographics at each of these types of institutions varies significantly, academic integrity challenges are widespread.

Realistic views of student GenAI use can also inform course developers as they design assessments that reveal both what students know independently, and what they can do with all available resources. One student noted that rapid developments in GenAI necessitate continuously updated tasks and course content. It is one thing for researchers and educators to say curriculum and assessment need to adapt to new conditions, but quite another for students to say it. Even the most innovative, well-resourced EAP programmes will need to regularly revisit their learning experiences and materials as technology and contexts evolve. This will take skill and planning, and it may mean resource allocation changes.

Mitigating the aforementioned challenges while leveraging GenAI for learning advantage requires time. Instructors need GenAI skills, and time to develop these skills. Furthermore, as developments in GenAI emerge and students' competencies change, educators also need time to develop new learning resources. These are points to consider when deciding who to hire and how many people are needed.

Creating a team that can drive progress in a time of rapid change requires more than hardworking teachers. Skilful curriculum and assessment developers and course content creators, or teachers with these skills, can ensure programme agility and ability to manage change.

Students who are skilful, responsible GenAI users will also drive the UAE closer to its goal of being a world leader in artificial intelligence. The UAE National Strategy for Artificial Intelligence 2031 outlines the country's plans to train government employees, upskill working professionals, and train the country's STEM graduates (UAE Government, 2024) in AI skills. Furthermore, United Nations Sustainable Development Goal Four also calls for HE that provides students with relevant skills for employment (United Nations, 2015). This chapter explores perspectives of university students in the UAE and offers recommendations for sound institutional policy and leveraging GenAI for academic success.

What This Chapter Adds

In their own words, students share how they have been using a variety of GenAI tools. They had the opportunity to take long conversational turns and express themselves frankly and fully, as well as respond to their peers' perspectives. While there were relatively few participants, the depth of their contributions complements other studies in this volume and provides insight on essential aspects of GenAI in MENA HE.

Research Questions

This study is guided by the following research questions:

1. How do undergraduate students in a multicultural UAE university integrate generative AI tools into their everyday academic practices?
2. In what ways do students' digital and linguistic competencies shape their perceptions of generative AI's usefulness, ease of use, and accuracy?
3. What are students' perceptions of academic integrity and how should institutions respond?

LITERATURE REVIEW

Introduction

The rapid integration of GenAI tools into HE has reshaped how students plan, draft, revise, and evaluate academic work. Research consistently demonstrates widespread student use of such tools for summarising readings, generating ideas, clarifying concepts, and supporting linguistic accuracy, particularly under time pressure and heavy assessment demands. While this growing body of literature establishes the prevalence of GenAI adoption, it offers more limited insight into how students negotiate, regulate, and evaluate AI use during authentic academic tasks.

These limitations are especially salient in multilingual and multicultural HE environments, such as in the UAE and wider MENA region. In such contexts, linguistic diversity, disciplinary variation, and evolving institutional policies intersect to shape students' experiences of AI-mediated learning. This literature review adopts the Technology Acceptance Model (TAM) as its foundational framework (Davis, 1989), using perceived usefulness (PU) and perceived ease of use (PEOU) to explain student adoption of GenAI tools. However, because GenAI systems are interactive, probabilistic, and language-mediated, TAM alone is insufficient to capture the complexity of student experience.

Accordingly, this review synthesises research on AI literacy, accuracy and verification, linguistic equity, human–AI complementarity, and ethical confidence. These constructs are treated as context-sensitive refinements of TAM rather than parallel frameworks, enabling a more nuanced understanding of GenAI use in multilingual HE settings. The review situates the present study within international scholarship while foregrounding the specific conditions of UAE and MENA HE.

Theoretical Framework

The TAM explains technology uptake through PU and PEOU (Davis, 1989). It has been widely applied in educational technology research due to its conceptual clarity and empirical robustness, offering an expansive explanation of why users adopt new tools. In the context of GenAI, students often report high initial usefulness because AI tools provide rapid, flexible academic support, alongside high PEOU due to conversational interfaces requiring minimal technical training.

However, GenAI challenges several assumptions embedded in traditional TAM applications. Unlike earlier educational technologies, GenAI systems require users to actively co-construct meaning through language. Interaction quality depends not only on interface usability but also on students' ability to articulate intent, contextualise academic tasks, and interpret outputs critically. As a result, both PU and PEOU are shaped by communicative competence, metacognitive judgement, and contextual awareness rather than by system design alone.

Recent scholarship therefore argues for expanded interpretations of TAM that account for literacy demands, trust calibration, and ethical ambiguity in AI-supported learning (Bashir et al., 2025). Rather than replacing TAM, these refinements extend its explanatory power by recognising that GenAI use is embedded within linguistic, pedagogical, and institutional contexts that mediate how usefulness and ease of use are experienced in practice.

Context of the Study

GenAI has become embedded in everyday HE practices, with students routinely using AI tools to support writing, research, and comprehension (Liang et al., 2023). These tools align with contemporary patterns of self-directed learning by offering immediacy and personalised assistance. At the same time, concerns persist regarding authorship, cognitive engagement, and the reliability of AI-generated content. Student adoption has advanced more rapidly than institutional policy development, creating misalignment between practice and governance (Yeo, 2023; Dawson et al., 2024).

The UAE and wider MENA region provide a particularly relevant context for examining these dynamics. National strategies position artificial intelligence as a driver of educational and economic transformation (UAE Government, 2024), and universities increasingly promote AI-enhanced learning environments. Studies indicate that students particularly in UAE institutions expect advanced digital tools to be integrated into their academic experience (Khadragy et al., 2024; Shwedeh et al., 2024). However, institutional interpretations of AI policy vary across programmes and instructors, resulting in inconsistent guidance for students (Alsharefeen & Sayari, 2025).

HE across the MENA region is also characterised by exceptional linguistic and cultural diversity. Many students use English as an additional language, shaping academic communication and help-seeking practices (Jaleel & Saber, 2025). Thus, linguistic diversity has direct implications for GenAI use, as language proficiency influences prompt formulation, output interpretation, and verification effort (Liu et al., 2024). Compared with Western contexts that often assume greater linguistic homogeneity and more stable policy environments, UAE and MENA universities highlight how language, institutional clarity, and cultural expectations mediate technology acceptance.

GenAI Use and AI Literacy

Research consistently shows that students engage with GenAI as a routine academic assistant rather than an occasional or peripheral tool. Large-scale studies indicate that students commonly use GenAI for drafting text, summarising readings, clarifying concepts, planning assignments, and improving linguistic accuracy (Rudolph et al., 2023; Liang et al., 2023). PU is therefore a strong driver of adoption, particularly in assessment-intensive environments where students value efficiency and flexibility (Li et al., 2025).

Within the UAE, similar patterns are evident. Students frequently consult GenAI tools before approaching instructors due to their constant availability and rapid feedback (Swidan et al., 2025). While these practices highlight the practical value of GenAI, scholars caution that efficiency gains may come at the expense of deeper cognitive engagement if AI is used unreflectively for content generation (Yusuf et al., 2024). Despite growing evidence of everyday use, fewer studies examine how students strategically engage with GenAI across specific academic tasks or how these practices develop in multilingual settings.

Effective engagement with GenAI depends not only on access but also on AI literacy. Prompt formulation, often referred to as prompt engineering, is best understood as a communicative and metacognitive practice rather than a technical skill. Lee and Palmer (2025) conceptualise prompting as a rhetorical activity requiring disciplinary awareness and task understanding, while Mollick and Mollick (2024) emphasise that prompting involves clarifying intent and reflecting on desired outcomes. Students must anticipate how the system will interpret their input and refine requests iteratively to obtain meaningful responses.

Empirical studies suggest that most students develop these competencies informally through trial and error rather than structured instruction (Ji et al., 2025). Although targeted interventions can support greater learner autonomy and more deliberate engagement with academic tasks (Mzwri & Turcsányi-Szabo, 2025), explicit teaching of AI literacy remains uncommon. In multilingual learning environments, these demands are intensified, as linguistic variability affects how prompts are interpreted and how much effort is required to achieve satisfactory output, shaping PEOU.

Accuracy, Trust, and Linguistic Equity

Despite their fluency and apparent authority, GenAI systems frequently generate inaccurate or misleading information. Documented limitations include factual errors, flawed reasoning, and fabricated citations, commonly referred to as hallucinations (Borji, 2023). These issues complicate students' judgements of reliability and directly shape PU. Trust in GenAI is therefore not a stable attitude but an evaluative process that unfolds as students interact with outputs across tasks and contexts.

Verification literacy plays a central role in this process. Research shows that students who routinely cross-check AI-generated information against authoritative sources develop more calibrated trust and use GenAI more responsibly (Wang et al., 2025). In contrast, users often accept AI output uncritically in the absence of explicit guidance, particularly when responses are linguistically polished and confidently presented (Nimmo et al., 2024; Chiang & Lee, 2023). Verification thus becomes a key mechanism through which students manage risk, accuracy, and academic credibility.

Linguistic equity significantly shapes these dynamics. Large language models are trained predominantly on English-dominant datasets, resulting in uneven performance across users (Blodgett et al., 2020). Research demonstrates that prompts deviating from standard academic English, including non-native phrasing or code-switching, produce less consistent outputs (Suárez et al., 2020). For multilingual students, this variability increases the effort required to interpret and verify AI responses.

In multilingual HE contexts such as those found in the UAE and wider MENA region, linguistic equity therefore intersects directly with trust and verification practices. Students may need to reformulate prompts, simplify language, or rely on translation tools, increasing cognitive load and influencing confidence in AI-generated content (Liu et al., 2024). Therefore, linguistic background mediates both PEOU and PU, shaping how students evaluate AI output and decide when it can be integrated into academic work.

Human–AI Feedback Complementarity

As GenAI becomes embedded in everyday academic practice, research increasingly examines how students integrate AI-generated feedback with human guidance. Students commonly value GenAI for its immediacy and availability, particularly for surface-level concerns such as grammar, clarity, and structural coherence (Kotamjani et al., 2024). This form of feedback is often perceived as low-risk and supportive during early stages of drafting.

However, AI feedback remains limited in its capacity to support higher-order academic development. Studies consistently show that students continue to rely on instructors for disciplinary judgement, evaluative feedback, and guidance on academic standards (Vashishth et al., 2024). Godwin-Jones et al. (2024) observe that learners frequently sequence AI and human feedback strategically, using GenAI to address preliminary issues before engaging with instructor feedback for conceptual refinement. When integrated thoughtfully, AI-supported formative feedback can enhance learning efficiency without displacing the pedagogical role of instructors (Zhao, 2025).

At the same time, reliance on AI-mediated feedback raises concerns about authorship, voice, and academic identity. Since GenAI can generate polished language and coherent argumentation, students may struggle to distinguish between their own developing academic voice and AI-assisted output. Without clear pedagogical framing, AI feedback risks shifting responsibility for meaning-making away from learners, highlighting the importance of understanding how students negotiate these boundaries.

Ethics, Integrity, and Policy

The widespread adoption of GenAI has intensified debates surrounding academic integrity and ethical responsibility in HE. Early institutional responses often relied on restrictive or ambiguous policies, which research suggests can increase student uncertainty rather than promote responsible engagement (Yeo, 2023). Conventional integrity frameworks struggle to accommodate AI-mediated academic work, particularly given the difficulty of distinguishing between student-authored and AI-generated content (Dawson et al., 2024; Bashir et al., 2025).

Recent scholarship increasingly advocates for pedagogically grounded approaches that emphasise ethical confidence rather than compliance. Ethical confidence refers to students' capacity to make informed and transparent decisions about AI use in relation to learning outcomes, disciplinary norms, and institutional expectations. Studies indicate that clear guidance and constructive integration reduce anxiety and encourage responsible use more effectively than prohibition or surveillance-oriented policies (Porayska-Pomsta et al., 2023; Selwyn et al., 2025).

In HE contexts, ethical ambiguity is further amplified. Students may rely on GenAI for linguistic support while remaining uncertain about where acceptable assistance ends and academic misconduct begins. Within the UAE, institutional interpretations of AI policy vary across programmes and instructors, leaving students to negotiate ethical boundaries through personal judgement and peer norms (Alsharefeen & Sayari, 2025). Examining how students interpret and respond to these conditions is therefore essential for understanding the ethical dimensions of GenAI use.

Summary of Gaps

Existing research confirms widespread student adoption of GenAI but offers limited insight into how learners make evaluative decisions during authentic academic tasks. In particular, verification practices, post-output evaluation, and linguistic equity remain underexplored, despite their centrality to judgements of PU and PEOU. Studies of AI literacy have largely foregrounded prompting skills without examining how these competencies develop informally through use or how they shape trust, confidence, and academic judgement. Existing ethical and integrity scholarship similarly prioritises institutional policy perspectives, leaving student interpretations of policy ambiguity insufficiently understood.

These gaps are especially pronounced in multilingual HE contexts such as the UAE, where linguistic diversity and evolving governance structures intensify the interpretive demands placed on students. Addressing these limitations requires qualitative, student-centred research that examines how learners negotiate usefulness, ease of use, trust, and ethical boundaries in situ. The present study responds by applying an extended TAM to multilingual students' lived experiences of GenAI use.

METHODOLOGY

Study Design

This study adopted a qualitative exploratory design to investigate how undergraduate students at a multicultural university in the UAE engage with and interpret GenAI tools in their academic work. A qualitative approach allows close examination of lived experiences and meaning making, which is well suited to emerging and complex educational technologies (Patton, 2025). The study was situated within an interpretivist orientation, recognising that perceptions of GenAI are socially constructed and shaped through interaction. A focus group was selected as the sole data collection method because it encourages participants to respond to one another and co-construct shared understandings, a strength highlighted in the work of Kitzinger (1995) and Vaughn et al. (1996). This design enabled the study to capture how students discuss usefulness, ease of use, trust, and ethical considerations relating to GenAI within a naturalistic group environment.

Participants

Five undergraduate students took part in the focus group, recruited through purposive sampling to ensure variation in discipline, cultural background, and experience with GenAI tools. Participants previously completed a Foundation Year at the institution and were studying programmes in business, engineering, and the humanities, reflecting the diversity recommended for focus group composition (Krueger & Casey, 2014). Their ages ranged from eighteen to twenty-two, and they represented a mixture of nationalities and first languages typical of the UAE HE landscape. Levels of digital literacy and prior GenAI use also varied, which facilitated discussion of differing levels of familiarity and confidence in applying AI tools. All participants were enrolled full time during the period of data collection.

Ethical approval was obtained from the university's research ethics committee, and participants provided informed consent prior to taking part. Table 1 below summarises the key demographic and academic characteristics of the study participants.

Table 1. Participant Demographics

Participant	Gender	Major	Year of Study	L1
Participant 1	Male	Economics	First Year	Russian
Participant 2	Male	AI and Computer Science	Second Year	Arabic
Participant 3	Female	AI and Computer Science	First Year	Arabic/English
Participant 4	Female	Computer Science and Software Engineering	First Year	Arabic/English
Participant 5	Male	AI and Computer Science	First Year	English

Instruments

Data were collected using a semi structured focus group discussion guide informed by the TAM (Davis, 1989). The guide included prompts related to PU, PEOU, behavioural intention, prompt engineering, accuracy, trust, and ethical concerns, reflecting recent scholarship on student engagement with GenAI (Aldreabi et al., 2025; Li et al., 2025; Swidan et al., 2025). A digital audio/video recorder was used to capture the discussion for accurate verbatim transcription. Reflexive field notes were taken during and immediately after the session to document non-verbal cues, interactional dynamics, and initial analytic reflections. Participants were given an information sheet and signed a consent form, which clarified confidentiality procedures, voluntary participation, and the handling of research data.

Procedure

Data Collection

Potential participants were contacted through email invitations and those who agreed to take part signed the consent form on the day of the focus group. The session was held in a quiet, neutral room arranged to support open discussion. The researchers introduced the purpose of the study, reminded participants of their right to withdraw, and explained the recording process. The discussion lasted approximately one hour and followed the semi structured guide, with flexibility for participants to raise issues they considered important. Reflexive notes were taken throughout the session. At the end of the discussion, the recording was transferred to a password protected digital drive accessible only to the researchers. The recording was then transcribed verbatim, and all identifying information was removed to ensure anonymity. These steps reflect recommended standards for qualitative data management and credibility (Guest et al., 2017; Morgan, 1997; Tausch & Menold, 2016).

Data Analysis

The dataset consisted of qualitative material, specifically the verbatim transcript and the researcher's field notes. Analysis followed Braun and Clarke's (2006) six phase thematic analysis framework. The researchers first familiarised themselves with the data, then coded the transcript using NVivo® qualitative data analysis software, applying a combination of deductive codes based on TAM constructs and inductive codes that emerged from participants' contributions. Deductive codes reflected PU, PEOU, and behavioural intention, whereas inductive coding captured new areas such as prompt engineering strategies, linguistic challenges, accuracy concerns, and ethical reflections (Braun & Clarke, 2023). Codes were then grouped into broader themes and reviewed for coherence across the dataset. The themes were explicitly aligned with the research questions, ensuring that issues relating to usefulness, ease of use, and ethical trustworthiness mapped onto the corresponding analytical focus. Reflexive memoing was used throughout the analysis, and peer debriefing helped validate interpretations, consistent with guidance from Patton's (2025) work on reflexive thematic analysis. Final themes were reviewed and refined using the criteria outlined by Lochmiller (2021) to ensure clarity, coherence, and representational accuracy.

RESULTS

Introduction

This section presents the findings from the focus-group investigation exploring how undergraduate students in a multicultural UAE university use and experience GenAI tools within their academic lives. The analysis identifies a range of student-reported practices, experiences, and perspectives relating to GenAI use across academic tasks. Students described using tools such as ChatGPT and Perplexity to support writing, research, coding, and planning, illustrating the extent to which these technologies have become integrated into their learning practices.

Alongside this integration, students also demonstrated the emergence of new forms of digital literacy centred on how they communicate with AI systems. They spoke at length about the need for carefully structured prompts, strategic wording, and contextual framing, highlighting the considerable skill involved in eliciting useful responses. Their comments also underscored persistent concerns about accuracy, trustworthiness, and fairness, particularly for students whose first language is not English. These concerns shaped how students verified AI outputs and navigated limitations that could disadvantage them in comparison to more linguistically confident peers.

In addition to discussing their use of GenAI for task completion, students reflected on how its role intersects with more traditional sources of academic support. Their accounts also described how they use GenAI alongside other sources of academic support, drawing on each for different purposes and levels of depth. Finally, students offered strong views about the ethical and curricular implications of AI use, questioning the relevance of current academic integrity policies and expressing a desire for clearer, more up-to-date institutional guidance that aligns with real-world expectations.

GenAI as a Deeply Integrated Academic Assistant

Students described GenAI tools as an essential and routine part of their academic workflow. They explained that AI is used across a wide range of tasks, often forming the starting point for assignments, explanations, or problem-solving. Several students referred to GenAI as a dependable study companion that they return to frequently throughout the week to support their academic writing, including generating initial paragraph ideas, rephrasing sentences, and helping to structure essays. One student explained, "When I don't know how to begin my paragraph, I ask it to give me a starting point and then I build from there." Others highlighted the usefulness of AI for research-related tasks, particularly summarising long texts, extracting key ideas, or helping to interpret dense academic sources. As one participant noted, "If I have a long article, I paste it and ask it to summarise the main arguments, so I know where to focus."

Beyond writing and research, students also reported using AI for technical and discipline-specific tasks. Engineering and computing students described using AI to debug code, rewrite functions, or clarify errors. One student shared, "It helps me understand what my code is doing wrong and how to fix it." Others mentioned that AI assists with tasks such as formatting citations, checking grammar, or creating study plans.

A consistent feature of student accounts was the convenience and immediacy of AI access. Several participants described relying on AI when facing tight deadlines or managing multiple responsibilities. One student stated, "Sometimes I know I can do the task, but I don't have time with everything going on, so I get AI to help me finish it faster." The availability of support at any time, without waiting for tutor hours or peer availability, was frequently emphasised. As another student put it, "It's always there. You can ask it anytime, even late at night when no one else can help."

Students also described emotional reassurance in using AI for clarification or quick checks. One participant commented, "If I'm unsure whether my answer makes sense, I ask it to check. It gives me confidence before I submit." Others highlighted how AI helped them overcome moments of academic uncertainty, especially when they felt stuck or unsure how to proceed.

Prompt Engineering and the Emergence of New AI Literacies

Students reported that effective use of GenAI requires careful attention to how questions and instructions are phrased. They explained that the quality of AI output depends heavily on the specificity, clarity, and structure of the prompts they provide. Several participants noted that simply asking a general question often produces vague or unhelpful responses, prompting them to develop more detailed and strategic approaches to interacting with AI tools. One student described the need for precision, stating, "You can't just type something basic. You have to tell it exactly what you want, otherwise it gives you something too general." Others elaborated that successful prompting involves supplying sufficient context and constraints to guide the AI toward the expected output. As another participant explained, "You need to give it the full scenario, like all the details. If you don't, it will make assumptions and go in a different direction."

Several students discussed prompting as a skill they have learned through experimentation. One noted, "At first I didn't know how to get good answers, but the more I used it, the more I understood how to phrase things better." Another student described this learning process as iterative: "I try something, see what it gives me, and then adjust the prompt. Eventually I get the response I need." They also reported that AI sometimes produces outputs that do not fully align with assignment requirements, even when the prompt appears clear. To manage this, they described using "layered prompting" or sequential instructions to gradually refine the AI's output. One participant described this approach by saying, "You have to keep correcting it or adding more instructions, so it understands exactly what the teacher wants." A few students mentioned deliberately placing the AI into a specific "role" or scenario to improve the relevance of its responses. For example, one student shared, "I tell it, 'You are a university student doing this assignment,' and then it gives a more accurate answer."

Students also discussed instances where the AI seemed to "look for the easiest way out," producing answers that circumvented the intended task or misinterpreted the assignment brief. One participant commented, "Sometimes it tries to find a shortcut or gives something that doesn't follow the rubric, so you have to be very clear to stop that."

Overall, students described prompt engineering as an emerging literacy that develops over time. They recognised that effective AI use is not automatic but depends on their ability to craft prompts that are detailed, context-specific, and aligned with academic expectations.

Accuracy Failures, Verification Practices, and Linguistic Inequity

Students described clear post-output evaluation practices, with AI responses rarely accepted at face value. Instead, they reported cross-checking information against course materials and external sources, re-running prompts to test consistency, and selectively adapting outputs rather than reproducing them verbatim. These practices functioned as verification habits that shaped trust and confidence in AI use. Situations where GenAI produced results that were incorrect, misleading, or inconsistent were also described. They noted that the reliability of AI responses varied depending on the type of task, with some areas proving more problematic than others. Mathematics, quantitative subjects, and technical problem-solving were identified as areas where AI often performed poorly. One student explained, "When it comes to math, it gets things very, very wrong. Sometimes it gives a whole different answer even when two people write the exact same question." Another described similar inconsistency: "I asked it the same question twice and it gave me two different solutions. You can't trust it for calculations."

Several students also mentioned experiences with fabricated or inaccurate information, especially when requesting academic sources or detailed evidence. One participant commented, "Sometimes it makes up articles or citations. You think it's real until you check and realise it doesn't exist." Others described how earlier versions of AI tools were particularly unreliable, producing outputs that required extensive correction: "Before, it used to confuse me more than help me. I had to rewrite everything by myself because it gave nonsense." Due to these accuracy concerns, students developed their own verification practices to check the validity of AI-generated answers. They discussed cross-checking information using Google, textbooks, course materials, and tutor feedback. As one student stated, "I never trust it fully. I look at what it gives and then compare it with other sources to see if it makes sense." Another said, "It's good for getting the idea, but I always double-check before I use it."

Linguistic differences were also highlighted as a factor influencing AI accuracy. Several participants noted that the effectiveness of AI responses depended on the user's ability to express prompts clearly in English. One student shared, "For someone whose first language isn't English, it's harder to get the answer you want because you don't know how to be specific enough." Another explained that students with certain linguistic backgrounds faced greater difficulty: "If you write in Russian or try to get it to understand something in Russian, the output is horrible. English speakers get better results." This linguistic imbalance shaped students' overall experience of using AI. Some felt at a disadvantage compared to peers with stronger English proficiency because they struggled to formulate prompts with the required precision. The same participant observed, "Sometimes I know the answer in my language, but I can't phrase the question properly in English, so the AI doesn't understand me." Others found that the AI misinterpreted their prompts due to grammar or vocabulary issues, leading to inaccurate or irrelevant outputs.

Across the focus group, students approached AI-generated information with caution, relying on verification strategies and acknowledging that language differences influenced both the quality of the output and their confidence in using the tool.

The Complementary Roles of AI and Human Feedback

Clear differences were described between the type of feedback students receive from GenAI tools and the feedback offered by their tutors. Across the discussion, they emphasised that both sources serve important but distinct purposes, and many reported using them together as part of their learning process.

Students consistently characterised AI feedback as immediate, accessible, and useful for identifying surface-level issues. One participant noted, "When I finish a paragraph, I paste it in and ask it what sounds wrong. It tells me straight away." Another student highlighted the convenience of this rapid response, explaining, "If I need quick guidance, AI is faster. I don't have to wait for office hours." Several participants said they relied on AI for grammar checking, restructuring sentences, or clarifying basic misunderstandings before seeking further help. However, students also pointed out that AI feedback often lacked depth and specificity. One remarked, "It tells you the general things but doesn't go into detail. It's too nice sometimes." Another commented on the generic tone: "It tells you you're doing well even when you're not. It doesn't challenge you." Some students mentioned that AI occasionally misinterpreted assignment requirements or over-simplified suggestions.

In contrast, tutor feedback was described as more detailed, accurate, and tailored to the individual assignment. One student explained, "My tutor tells me exactly where my argument doesn't work. They tell you what to fix and why." Another said, "The tutor sees the whole picture. They know what the assignment is really asking for." Students also described tutor feedback as more reliable and aligned with assessment expectations. As one participant stated, "The tutor tells you what the rubric needs. AI doesn't always follow that." Others noted that tutors could explain disciplinary conventions or reasoning in ways AI could not replicate. Despite these differences, students frequently highlighted the value of combining both forms of feedback. One described this process by saying, "I use AI first to get the basic things out of the way, then I take my real questions to the tutor." Another explained, "AI helps you clean the draft, but the tutor helps you improve it."

Overall, students viewed AI and tutors as complementary rather than interchangeable. They used AI for quick checks and basic support, while relying on tutors for critical insight, contextual understanding, and guidance on more complex aspects of academic work.

Reimagining Academic Integrity, Ethics, and Curriculum Reform

During the focus group, students expressed strong views about the relevance and fairness of existing academic integrity policies in relation to GenAI use. Many felt that current rules do not adequately reflect how AI is used in real academic and professional contexts. Several participants described a sense of disconnect between university expectations and the realities of modern study practices.

One student commented, "The policies feel old. They don't match how people actually work now. In real jobs, AI is allowed." Another participant echoed this sentiment, saying, "Using AI isn't cheating. It's a tool, just like anything else. Outside university, no one gets fired for using it." Students repeatedly emphasised that institutional rules had not kept pace with technological change, leading to confusion about what constitutes acceptable use. Participants also reflected on how unclear or inconsistent guidance contributes to student uncertainty. One student explained, "Some teachers say it's okay in some parts, others say don't use it at all. There's no clear rule." Another added, "We need proper instructions, not warnings. If they want us to use it correctly, they should teach us how."

A number of students discussed the need for curriculum updates that integrate AI literacy and responsible use rather than relying on penalties or prohibitive messaging. One stated, "Instead of telling us not to use it, they should show us how to use it in the right way." Others suggested that AI training should be embedded into coursework, with one student saying, "Workshops aren't enough. It should be part of the class. Everyone should learn the same skills." Some participants also expressed that strict integrity rules often lead students to ignore them rather than comply. As one student put it, "Most students don't follow the rules anyway because the rules don't make sense anymore." Another added, "If you ban it, people will still use it. It's better to teach how to use it properly."

Across the discussion, students consistently framed AI as an unavoidable part of academic and professional life. They argued that universities should focus on teaching responsible use, redesigning assessments to reflect AI's presence, and updating policies to align with contemporary expectations.

Summary of Findings

The findings show that students use GenAI tools as a regular part of their academic work, relying on them for drafting, summarising, coding, proofreading, and quick clarification. They described developing prompt-engineering strategies through trial and refinement and highlighted the need for clear, specific instructions to obtain useful responses. Students also reported issues with accuracy, especially in quantitative tasks, and described verifying AI outputs through alternative sources. Non-native English speakers noted additional challenges due to linguistic limitations. Students distinguished the immediacy of AI feedback from the depth of tutor feedback, often using both together. They also questioned current academic integrity policies, expressing a desire for clearer guidance and curriculum-based training on responsible AI use.

Table 2 below summarises how the results are analytically aligned with the study's three research questions, providing a structural overview of how the findings are interpreted in the discussion section.

Table 2. Summary of Results

Themes	Linked RQ	TAM (PU / PEOU)	Extensions
GenAI as a Deeply Integrated Academic Assistant	RQ1	PU	Routine integration, efficiency
Prompt Engineering and Emerging AI Literacies	RQ1	PEOU	AI literacy, communicative effort
Accuracy Failures, Verification Practices, and Linguistic Inequity	RQ2	PU, PEOU	Trust calibration, verification, linguistic equity
Complementary Roles of AI and Human Feedback	RQ2	PU	Human–AI complementarity
Reimagining Academic Integrity, Ethics, and Curriculum Reform	RQ3	PU	Ethical confidence, institutional clarity

DISCUSSION

Introduction

The purpose of this section is to interpret the results of the study in relation to the research questions, the TAM, and the wider body of literature reviewed earlier. While the previous section presented the findings descriptively and foregrounded students' voices, this section explores the 'why' and 'how' behind these patterns, situating them within existing theoretical and empirical discussions. The analysis draws on the conceptual framework introduced earlier in the chapter, including PU, PEOU, digital and AI literacy, linguistic equity, and ethical adaptation, to develop a fuller understanding of student engagement with GenAI in a multicultural UAE university. Rather than claiming generalisability, the discussion presents the findings as insight into how students negotiate usefulness, trust, and ethics in AI-mediated learning that may resonate across comparable HE settings.

The findings revealed a complex picture of student interaction with GenAI, where the technology is not merely an optional aid but an integrated academic companion. Students' experiences reflected emerging digital literacies, variable trust in AI accuracy, and tensions between institutional policy and everyday study practices. At the same time, the results highlighted important challenges, particularly related to accuracy failures, linguistic disadvantage, and uncertainty surrounding academic integrity expectations.

This section is organised around the three research questions guiding the study. Each section examines how the findings support or contradict expectations derived from TAM and from recent literature, including regional studies in the UAE and broader debates in higher-education research. By connecting student experiences to these frameworks, the discussion identifies how this study confirms, extends, or challenges existing understandings of GenAI adoption. The section concludes by outlining the theoretical contribution of the study, its practical implications for curriculum design and institutional policy.

Table 3 below summarises how each research question is addressed through TAM-aligned analytical themes in the Discussion.

Table 3. Summary of Discussion

Research Question	Primary Focus	TAM-Aligned Themes
RQ1	Everyday adoption and routinisation of GenAI	Perceived usefulness (PU), habitual use, task efficiency, emergent behavioural intention
RQ2	Competence-mediated evaluations of GenAI	Perceived ease of use (PEOU), accuracy and trust calibration, verification literacy, linguistically mediated access
RQ3	Ethical judgement and institutional alignment	Ethical confidence, normative beliefs, perceived legitimacy of use, human–AI role differentiation

Research Question 1: How do undergraduate students in a multicultural UAE university integrate generative AI tools into their everyday academic practices?

The findings show that students in this study used GenAI pervasively, embedding it into a wide range of academic activities and returning to it repeatedly throughout their learning routines. This confirms the central role of PU, a core construct in the TAM (Davis, 1989) and aligns with research demonstrating that students adopt AI primarily to enhance efficiency, manage workload, and increase productivity (Li et al., 2025; Maxwell et al., 2025). Students described using GenAI across a wide range of academic tasks, reflecting its routine integration into everyday study practices. Their references to AI as "always there" show that they no longer view it as a supplementary tool used only when needed. Instead, they turn to it automatically as part of their normal study routines. This pattern reflects a shift in PU, where AI becomes woven into the flow of learning tasks and decision making. The technology moves beyond convenience and becomes a dependable academic partner that students rely on instinctively for idea generation, clarification, and verification.

This finding supports existing studies showing high-frequency AI use across disciplines (Sousa & Cardoso, 2025; Swidan et al., 2025), but it also extends the literature by demonstrating a level of normalisation not commonly addressed in current research. Much of the global literature still treats GenAI as a relatively new or supplementary technology (Yusuf et al., 2024), whereas the students in this study described it as indispensable. This suggests that earlier assumptions about voluntary, occasional AI use may no longer reflect actual student behaviour, particularly in digitally mature contexts like the UAE. At the same time, the findings also highlight risks associated with over-reliance on GenAI. Students described instances where AI output appeared authoritative despite being inaccurate, creating the potential for misplaced confidence in incorrect answers. Heavy dependence on AI for drafting and problem-solving also risks shallow engagement with content when outputs are adopted uncritically, while reliance on polished AI-generated language raises concerns about the dilution of students' academic voice.

A notable aspect of the findings was the emergence of prompt engineering as a central skill underpinning successful AI use. Students repeatedly emphasised the need for specificity, structured prompts, and contextual framing, revealing that prompt design operates as a form of academic literacy in its own right. This supports recent arguments that prompt engineering is an essential competency for effective AI interaction (Federiakin et al., 2024; Lee & Palmer, 2025), but the present study goes further by providing qualitative evidence of how students develop these skills, primarily through experimentation, refinement, and iterative learning. While literature typically proposes formal training frameworks, the students here demonstrated self-directed AI literacy development, indicating that students are already building capabilities that institutions have yet to formally recognise.

These patterns also indicate a nuanced expansion of TAM's construct of PEOU. Although students found AI interfaces technically easy to operate, they made clear that effective use requires communicative precision and strategic thinking. This aligns with recent critiques suggesting that PEOU must account for cognitive and linguistic demands, not just interface simplicity (Sergeeva et al., 2025). In this sense, ease of use is not evenly distributed; it depends on the user's linguistic proficiency, academic experience, and ability to express detailed prompts.

Overall, the results for Research Question 1 show that GenAI has become a deeply integrated academic assistant. Students use it extensively, frequently, and strategically. Their practices largely support existing technology-acceptance assumptions around usefulness but challenge the framing of GenAI as an optional tool. This instead suggests that it has become a normalised and expected component of student learning in the UAE's multicultural HE environment.

Research Question 2: In what ways do students' digital and linguistic competencies shape their perceptions of generative AI's usefulness, ease of use, and accuracy?

The findings revealed several recurring challenges that shaped how students interacted with GenAI tools. These limitations related primarily to accuracy failures, inconsistent output quality, and linguistic inequities, all of which influenced students' level of trust in AI. These results align with global concerns regarding hallucination and unreliability in AI systems (Wang et al., 2025) and help explain why students approached AI-generated content with caution, despite using it frequently. Students' perceptions of GenAI usefulness and ease of use were mediated by post-output verification habits, with evaluation and cross-checking functioning as central mechanisms for managing trust and accuracy.

A key limitation described by students was inaccuracy in quantitative and technical tasks. Their accounts of receiving multiple, conflicting answers to the same mathematics question reflect the broader literature on instability in AI problem-solving, particularly for numerically complex outputs. Contractor and Reyes (2025) similarly found that students struggled with inconsistent answers in STEM contexts, prompting them to verify outputs manually. This behaviour contradicts assumptions that students passively accept AI results; instead, the students in this study actively cross-checked and validated information through alternative sources. This form of engagement demonstrates that students are critical consumers of AI-generated output.

Another important challenge described in the findings is citation fabrication and factual errors, an issue widely documented in the literature and introduction. Students' observations that AI sometimes "makes up articles" align with earlier warnings that LLMs can generate plausible but incorrect references. This reflects Yusuf et al.'s (2024) argument that AI may reduce cognitive effort while simultaneously increasing verification workload.

The second major limitation was linguistic inequity, especially among non-native English speakers. Students explained that the quality of AI output was directly correlated with their ability to craft precise, detailed prompts in English. This pattern is rarely documented in TAM-based studies, which typically treat PEOU as a universal construct. The findings here show how and why PEOU is uneven: it is mediated by linguistic proficiency and the user's ability to articulate a detailed request. Swidan et al. (2025) similarly highlight multilingual challenges in the UAE context, but the present study adds depth by demonstrating how these challenges materially affect accuracy, trust, and overall user experience.

This linguistic dimension expands traditional understandings of ease of use. While TAM conceptualises PEOU as interface simplicity (Davis, 1989), students in this study viewed AI as only "easy" if they possessed strong enough linguistic and academic literacy to communicate effectively with it. The need for careful wording, contextual framing, and iterative prompting highlights the cognitive load involved in achieving accurate outputs. Students who lacked advanced English proficiency described receiving results that were less relevant or sometimes entirely misaligned with their original question, suggesting that AI may reinforce or exacerbate existing linguistic inequalities.

Collectively, the results for Research Question 2 support the literature on accuracy concerns and hallucinations in AI, but challenge assumptions that students trust AI uncritically. This highlights a more complex dynamic in which frequent AI use coexists with deliberate trust calibration and verification. Furthermore, the findings extend the literature by foregrounding linguistic equity as a significant barrier, suggesting that AI tools built on English-dominant datasets may not serve all learners equally, particularly in multicultural contexts like the UAE.

Research Question 3: What are students' perceptions of academic integrity and how should institutions respond?

The findings show that students viewed current academic integrity policies as outdated, unclear, and inconsistent with real-world professional practices. They repeatedly expressed frustration that institutional guidelines had not kept pace with the rapid integration of GenAI into academic work. This perception directly supports earlier arguments that traditional integrity frameworks no longer reflect the realities of contemporary learning or workplace expectations. More importantly, these results highlight why students increasingly disregard restrictive rules: they see a mismatch between institutional expectations and the everyday demands of digital literacy, employment contexts, and academic workload.

Students' concerns closely mirror recent research showing that ambiguity around AI rules is experienced not only by learners but also by faculty. Alsharefeen and Sayari (2025) found that educators themselves lack consensus on what constitutes acceptable AI use, while Zhai (2024) noted that institutional responses often default to prohibition driven by fear of academic misconduct rather than pedagogical reasoning. This pattern is reinforced by recent UAE-based research with EAP faculty, which shows that instructors increasingly struggle to determine where legitimate student work ends and AI-generated content begins, leading to significant uncertainty in how academic integrity should be interpreted in practice (Bashir et al., 2025). In the present study, students described the consequences of this institutional ambiguity, explaining that different instructors offered conflicting guidance and that the messaging they received was often punitive rather than developmental. Such inconsistency undermined student confidence and contributed to confusion about legitimate AI use, further illustrating why integrity policies grounded in pre-AI paradigms are no longer workable.

At the same time, the findings challenge assumptions that students are indifferent or irresponsible regarding academic integrity. Instead, participants expressed a strong desire for transparent, practical, and ethically grounded instruction on how to use AI responsibly. Rather than rejecting integrity values, students argued that universities should teach AI literacy, including prompt engineering, critical evaluation, and responsible use, directly within academic modules. This aligns closely with calls in the literature for ethical empowerment rather than punitive regulation (Shwedeh et al., 2024; von Winckelmann et al., 2024; Yusuf et al., 2024). Students' emphasis on mandatory, curriculum-based instruction further supports studies showing that optional workshops or ad-hoc training are insufficient for preparing students to navigate AI effectively (Li et al., 2025).

The findings also show how students currently balance integrity with practical needs: they combine AI support with tutor guidance, using AI for initial drafting or idea generation and relying on tutors for deeper analytical feedback. This supports research indicating that students value human feedback for its contextual depth (Vashishth et al., 2024) and that AI cannot replace the relational or disciplinary knowledge that tutors provide. The hybrid approach described by students suggests that they already engage in responsible academic practice, even when institutional guidance is lacking.

Finally, students' arguments that AI is widely accepted in professional settings reflect broader discussions that integrity policies must adapt to the expectations of labour markets and UAE Vision 2031 priorities. Students require AI skills to participate meaningfully in AI-driven economies, and the present findings reinforce this point as students view AI competence as a fundamental part of being 'future-ready.' Their call for updated policies, clearer guidelines, and curriculum redesign reflects not a desire to bypass academic standards but a wish to align institutional expectations with the evolving demands of education and employment. Overall, the results for Research Question 3 support literature highlighting policy gaps and ethical ambiguity, challenge assumptions that students are complacent about integrity, and extend the conversation by foregrounding students' active advocacy for pedagogical and institutional reform.

Theoretical Contribution

This study makes several contributions to theoretical understandings of GenAI adoption in higher education, particularly through its application and extension of the TAM. The findings show that while TAM constructs such as PU and PEOU remain relevant, they do not fully capture the complexity of student engagement with AI in a multicultural and linguistically diverse university environment. Students' descriptions of GenAI as deeply embedded in their everyday academic routines indicate that usefulness has evolved beyond task efficiency into a form of habitual integration, where AI becomes part of the cognitive infrastructure of learning. While grounded in a specific institutional and regional context, this reconceptualisation offers analytically transferable insight into student–AI interaction that can inform research and practice beyond the immediate study site.

The findings also extend TAM by highlighting the central role of AI literacy, particularly prompt engineering, as a prerequisite for effective use. Students' need to craft detailed, context-rich prompts demonstrates that ease of use is not merely determined by interface design but is significantly shaped by linguistic and communicative competence. This introduces a sociolinguistic dimension to the TAM, suggesting that adoption cannot be understood without considering language proficiency, academic literacy, and the cognitive demands of interacting with AI systems.

Furthermore, the study contributes theoretical insight into linguistic equity, showing that students' ability to benefit from AI varies according to their command of English and their capacity to articulate complex prompts. This extension of the TAM acknowledges that PEOU is unevenly distributed and mediated by cultural and linguistic factors, a finding rarely addressed in current technology adoption research.

Finally, the results demonstrate that AI adoption is not driven solely by individual attitudes or perceived benefits, but is intertwined with broader questions of ethics, institutional policy, and learner identity. Students' calls for updated integrity frameworks and curriculum integration highlight a shift from compliance-based models of academic conduct towards a more participatory and pedagogically grounded understanding of responsible AI use. This positions students as active agents shaping the ethical landscape of AI in higher education. Collectively, these contributions suggest that future applications of the TAM should incorporate dimensions of digital literacy, linguistic accessibility, ethical reasoning, and institutional alignment, providing a more holistic framework for understanding AI adoption in diverse educational contexts.

Implications for Policy, Curriculum, and Practice

The findings of this study highlight several implications for institutional policy, curriculum design, and teaching practice. At the policy level, students' perceptions of outdated and inconsistent academic integrity guidelines indicate a need for institutions to move beyond prohibition-oriented approaches. Existing frameworks assume that AI use is exceptional or undesirable, yet the results show that students already rely on AI as a normalised academic companion. This misalignment suggests that institutions must update policy to clearly differentiate between acceptable and unacceptable uses of AI, articulating expectations that are transparent, feasible, and aligned with professional realities. Policy revision should include student representation to ensure that guidelines reflect lived academic experience rather than top-down assumptions about learner behaviour.

From a curriculum perspective, the findings point to a pressing need to incorporate AI literacy into formal teaching. Students demonstrated emergent skills in prompt engineering, iterative refinement, and verification, but these were self-developed and unevenly distributed, particularly disadvantaging non-native English speakers. Embedding AI literacy, including prompt design, critical evaluation of outputs, citation verification, and ethical use, within modules would help ensure equity and consistency across cohorts. This aligns with the emphasis on future-ready competencies noted in broader UAE policy documents and echoed earlier in this chapter. Curriculum redesign should also consider assessment adaptations, shifting away from tasks that can be easily automated and towards those requiring reasoning, reflection, data interpretation, and human judgement.

Ways of mitigating AI misuse in an EAP context include:

1. Paper-based writing tasks completed without devices, ensuring that students rely on their own understanding;
2. Using secure exam browsers and online proctoring tools to restrict access to unauthorised resources during online assessments;
3. Creating assignment prompts and rubrics that require engagement with highly specific, course-delivered content, making it more difficult for AI tools to generate accurate responses;
4. Assigning in-class critical responses to previously unseen texts, which encourages real-time comprehension and original written output;
5. Incorporating viva-style interviews that require students to speak spontaneously to demonstrate understanding of course concepts;
6. Embedding in-class note-taking tasks from lectures or videos, which assess listening skills and the ability to synthesise information independently (AI Assessment Scale Project, 2026).

For teaching practice, the results underscore the continued significance of human feedback, which students valued for its depth, contextual relevance, and alignment with disciplinary expectations. Rather than viewing AI as a threat to pedagogical relationships, teachers can incorporate AI strategically into formative processes. For example, students might use AI for early-stage drafting, with tutor time directed toward higher-order critique and conceptual understanding. Such blended approaches can support efficiency while preserving academic integrity and critical thinking.

These implications collectively suggest that institutions should adopt a proactive and pedagogically informed strategy toward AI integration. Shifting from reactive restriction to guided empowerment can help ensure that students develop the skills, judgement, and ethical awareness needed to engage with AI responsibly and effectively in both academic and professional settings.

Summary

This section discussed how undergraduate students in a multicultural UAE university use GenAI in their academic work, the challenges they encounter, and how they interpret academic integrity in relation to AI. Students described using GenAI routinely for writing and study support, including drafting, summarising, language checking, coding support, and planning. They also reported developing practical strategies for effective use, particularly prompt refinement and post-output verification.

Students highlighted limitations linked to accuracy and reliability, including inconsistent answers, citation fabrication, and the need to cross-check outputs against other sources. They also described linguistic challenges, noting that prompt precision and the quality of AI responses were shaped by English proficiency. Finally, students reported mixed experiences of institutional guidance, describing uncertainty about acceptable use and a desire for clearer expectations.

CONCLUSION

Education leaders sometimes believe they must make decisions on behalf of students because they, the professionals, are the ones with the expertise and knowledge, perhaps believing that students are not capable of understanding the rationale for leadership choices. However, in this study, students themselves recognised the need for continuous update of curriculum and evolution of assessment tasks. It was the students who observed the limitations of GenAI feedback and understood the depth of tutor feedback, and it was the students who called for a new approach to academic integrity. Taken together, these perspectives suggest that effective AI governance requires not only policy revision but also curriculum and assessment redesign that students can recognise as legitimate and workable.

The focus group participants highlighted the need for a realistic, practical academic integrity and AI policy that students can understand and respect. A shift from prohibitions, which are difficult to enforce, to transparency can be one aspect of a more clear-eyed AI policy. Incorporating instruction on how to declare or cite GenAI use into coursework could provide students with positive guidance on how to use AI effectively and ethically, as opposed to focusing on rules and violations. Furthermore, communicating that policy cannot be left to chance. A single mention of it on a university webpage, an optional orientation workshop, and a brief reference at the beginning of a course, even if they are all combined, are insufficient to fully communicate a university's AI policy and the standards of ethics and good practice it aims to establish. For a durable integration of the policy, these measures must be present alongside classroom instruction on the role of AI in each assignment. As assessments are announced, instructors should clarify permissible uses of GenAI along with ways to appropriately declare its use. This information should also be embedded within assignment instructions to ensure consistency and reinforce expectations.

That said, not all faculty members themselves are confident to instruct students on institution policy or appropriate methods of declaring GenAI use. Without adequate professional development for faculty on institutional policy and appropriate methods of acknowledging AI use, student ambiguity around what is permissible could persist. However, requiring faculty development on AI is challenging due to differences in individuals' knowledge of it (Huma et al., 2025), politics, and resource constraints (Kurtz et al., 2024). Nonetheless, these challenges make professional learning no less necessary, and institutions and students would benefit from an institution-wide baseline of faculty AI skills. Consistent application of university policy is essential for credibility and adoption across the academic community, and inconsistent enforcement or frequent exceptions undermine the policy's integrity and weaken its core message about ethical AI use and the importance of transparent disclosure.

Educator AI skills impact student outcomes (Alwakid et al., 2025). A student who did not have teacher instruction on effective prompting for writing feedback said he found AI feedback unhelpful, but the student who had such instruction found that the AI writing feedback was useful. While many students are capable of using various AI tools productively and independently, teacher input on the specific steps to using them to greatest academic advantage can be beneficial. These learners' perspectives on academic integrity highlight the need for a new approach. Their disengagement with policies they view as irrelevant underscores a need to rethink what is taught, and how it is assessed.

Integrating tasks that require original thought, and ensuring original thought is rewarded in assessment criteria, can also reduce student temptation to submit unedited GenAI content as their own. GenAI content often gives similar answers to similar problems and prompts. The work of students who rely too heavily on GenAI may ultimately resemble the work of others who do the same. One way of cultivating critical thought would be classroom instruction that empowers the student to evaluate the suitability of GenAI output for instructional tasks. As one student in the group mentioned, the tasks themselves must also be updated regularly, frequently even. A shift from standard essays and presentations to case studies, product proposals, courtroom simulations, problem- and project-based tasks not only make the learning experience more GenAI resistant, but also more challenging and engaging.

Limitations

This study, based on a single focus group of five students from a selective British university in the United Arab Emirates, provides only a limited perspective on AI use among relatively high-achieving students and does not reflect the broader Middle Eastern context. The small sample size limits the generalisability of findings, and the nature of the university can result in some sampling bias in terms of socioeconomic status and previous academic achievement. Additionally, the participants' contributions may have been shaped by social dynamics, such as a desire to align with peers or make a favourable impression.

Recommendations

1. Broader research is needed. Multiple focus groups across a range of universities, including public and private, selective, and non-selective, would capture a wider spectrum of student experiences and attitudes toward AI. Including participants from diverse backgrounds across the Middle East would enhance representation and allow for comparative analysis.
2. Complementing qualitative data with large-scale anonymous surveys would strengthen the reliability of findings. Surveys could explore patterns of GenAI use, perceived benefits and risks, and ethical considerations, while focus groups would provide depth to these trends. Additionally, longitudinal studies tracking changes in attitudes and practices over time could offer insights into how policies and GenAI developments shape student behaviour.
3. Future research should examine the effectiveness of different policy strategies and instructional integrations, assessing whether transparency-based approaches and instructional guidance on declaring GenAI use lead to more ethical use compared to traditional, prohibitive policies.

The insights examined in this article indicate the need for deep reconsideration of the pillars of course design and institutional AI policy. They may also turn attention to achievement of graduate attributes and a broader question of who students actually become as a result of their academic journey (Grove, 2025). Curricula that challenge students to view the world critically, envision possibilities, and realise their ambitions can ensure that AI remains a tool for academic and professional growth, rather than a substitute for true achievement.

REFERENCES

Abdaljaleel, M., Barakat, M., Alsanafi, M., Salim, N. A., Abazid, H., Malaeb, D., Mohammed, A. H., Hassan, B. R., Wayyes, A. M., Farhan, S. S., Khatib, S. E., Rahal, M., Sahban, A., Abdelaziz, D. H., Mansour, N. O., AlZayer, R., Khalil, R., Fekih-Romdhane, F., Hallit, R., & Sallam, M. (2024). A multinational study on the factors influencing university students' attitudes and usage of ChatGPT. *Scientific Reports*, *14*(1), 1983. DOI: 10.1038/s41598-024-52549-8 PMID: 38263214

AI Assessment Scale Project. (2026). Custom AIAS GPT [Generative AI tool; response generated using prompt about examples of AI-resistant assessments]. AI Assessment Scale. https://aiassessmentscale.com/

Aldreabi, H., Dahdoul, N. K. S., Alhur, M., Alzboun, N., & Alsalhi, N. R. (2025). Determinants of student adoption of Generative AI in Higher Education. *Electronic Journal of e-Learning*, *23*(1), 15–33. DOI: 10.34190/ejel.23.1.3599

Alsharefeen, R., & Sayari, N. A. (2025). Examining academic integrity policy and practice in the era of AI: A case study of faculty perspectives. *Frontiers in Education*, *10*. Advance online publication. DOI: 10.3389/feduc.2025.1621743

Alwakid, W. N., Dahri, N. A., Humayun, M., & Alwakid, G. N. (2025). Exploring the role of AI and teacher competencies on instructional planning and student performance in an Outcome-Based Education System. *Systems*, *13*(7), 517. DOI: 10.3390/systems13070517

Bashir, A., Nomaan, S., & Hysaj, A. (2025). Generative AI in education: Exploring EAP faculty perspectives at a multicultural UAE university. In Coman, A., & Vasilache, S. (Eds.), Lecture Notes in Computer Science: Vol. 15786. *HCII 2025* (pp. 125–140). Springer., DOI: 10.1007/978-3-031-93539-8_9

Blodgett, S. L., Barocas, S., Daumé, H., & Wallach, H. (2020). Language (Technology) is Power: A Critical Survey of "Bias" in NLP. *arXiv*. DOI: 10.48550/arXiv.2005.14050

Borji, A. (2023). A categorical archive of ChatGPT failures. *arXiv*. DOI: 10.48550/arxiv.2302.03494

Braun, V., & Clarke, V. (2006). Using thematic analysis in psychology. *Qualitative Research in Psychology*, *3*(2), 77–101. DOI: 10.1191/1478088706qp063oa

Braun, V., & Clarke, V. (2023). Toward good practice in thematic analysis: Avoiding common problems and be(com)ing a knowing researcher. *International Journal of Transgender Health, 24*(1), 1–6. DOI: 10.1080/26895269.2022.2129597 PMID: 36713144

Chiang, C., & Lee, H. (2023). Can large language models be an alternative to human evaluations? *arXiv*. DOI: 10.48550/arxiv.2305.01937

Contractor, R., & Reyes, D. (2025). Generative AI in higher education: Evidence from an elite college. *arXiv*. https://arxiv.org/abs/2508.00717

Davis, F. D. (1989). Perceived usefulness, perceived ease of use, and user acceptance of information technology. *Management Information Systems Quarterly, 13*(3), 319–340. DOI: 10.2307/249008

Dawson, P., Bearman, M., Dollinger, M., & Boud, D. (2024). Validity matters more than cheating. *Assessment & Evaluation in Higher Education, 49*(7), 1005–1016. DOI: 10.1080/02602938.2024.2386662

Escalante, J., Pack, A., & Barrett, A. (2023). AI-generated feedback on writing: Insights into efficacy and ENL student preference. *International Journal of Educational Technology in Higher Education, 20*(1). Advance online publication. DOI: 10.1186/s41239-023-00425-2

Federiakin, D., Molerov, D., Zlatkin-Troitschanskaia, O., & Maur, A. (2024). Prompt engineering as a new 21st century skill. *Frontiers in Education, 9*. Advance online publication. DOI: 10.3389/feduc.2024.1366434

Godwin-Jones, R., O'Neill, E., & Ranalli, J. (2024). Integrating AI tools into instructed second language acquisition. In Chapelle, C. A., Beckett, G. H., & Ranalli, J. (Eds.), *Exploring artificial intelligence in applied linguistics* (pp. 9–23). Iowa State University Digital Press., DOI: 10.31274/isudp.2024.154.02

Government, U. A. E. (2024) '*UAE National Strategy for Artificial Intelligence 2031*'. Retrieved November 08, 2025, from https://ai.gov.ae/strategy

Grove, M. (2025). *It's time we moved the generative AI conversation on - HEPI*. HEPI. Retrieved November 29, 2025, from https://www.hepi.ac.uk/2025/07/16/its-time-we-moved-the-generative-ai-conversation-on/

Guest, G., Namey, E., Taylor, J., Eley, N., & McKenna, K. (2017). Comparing focus groups and individual interviews: Findings from a randomized study. *International Journal of Social Research Methodology, 20*(6), 693–708. DOI: 10.1080/13645579.2017.1281601

Huma, T., Ahmed, S., Mahmood, W., Khan, A., Afridi, A. K., Huma, T., Ahmed, S., Mahmood, W., Khan, A., & Afridi, A. K. (2025). AI adoption in Higher Education: A Comparative study of Institutional readiness and challenges. *Social Science Review Archives.*, *3*(4), 304–312. DOI: 10.70670/sra.v3i4.1117

Jaleel, B., & Saber, H. (2025). The United Arab Emirates as an International Education Hub: Assessing Progress Toward a Knowledge-Based Economy. *Journal of Studies in International Education*. Advance online publication. DOI: 10.1177/10283153251364511

Ji, Y., Zhong, M., Lyu, S., Li, T., Niu, S., & Zhan, Z. (2025). How does AI literacy affect individual innovative behavior: The mediating role of psychological need satisfaction, creative self-efficacy, and self-regulated learning. *Education and Information Technologies*, *30*(11), 16133–16162. DOI: 10.1007/s10639-025-13437-4

Khadragy, S., Selim, N., Hassan, D., Hegazy, A., & Ali, S. (2024). Exploring the effects of using AI technologies in higher education institutions in UAE. *Journal of Curriculum and Teaching*, *13*(5), 10. DOI: 10.5430/jct.v13n5p10

Kitzinger, J. (1995). Qualitative Research: Introducing focus groups. *BMJ (Clinical Research Ed.)*, *311*(7000), 299–302. DOI: 10.1136/bmj.311.7000.299 PMID: 7633241

Kotamjani, S. S., Shirinova, S., Muratova, K., & Sharma, M. (2024). Exploring Students' Perspectives on Generative AI for Academic Purposes in Uzbekistan's Higher Education. *Association for Computing Machinery*, 986–994. https://doi.org/ DOI: 10.1145/3726122.3726266

Krueger, R. A., & Casey, M. A. (2014). *Focus groups: A Practical Guide for Applied Research*. SAGE Publications.

Kurtz, G., Amzalag, M., Shaked, N., Zaguri, Y., Kohen-Vacs, D., Gal, E., Zailer, G., & Barak-Medina, E. (2024). Strategies for Integrating Generative AI into Higher Education: Navigating Challenges and Leveraging Opportunities. *Education Sciences*, *14*(5), 503. DOI: 10.3390/educsci14050503

Lee, D., & Palmer, E. (2025). Prompt engineering in higher education: A systematic review to help inform curricula. *International Journal of Educational Technology in Higher Education*, *22*(1). Advance online publication. DOI: 10.1186/s41239-025-00503-7

Li, K. C., Chong, G. H. L., Wong, B. T. M., & Wu, M. M. F. (2025). A TAM-Based analysis of Hong Kong undergraduate students' attitudes toward generative AI in higher education and employment. *Education Sciences*, *15*(7), 798. DOI: 10.3390/educsci15070798

Liang, W., Yuksekgonul, M., Mao, Y., Wu, E., & Zou, J. (2023). GPT detectors are biased against non-native English writers. *Patterns (New York, N.Y.)*, *4*(7), 100779. DOI: 10.1016/j.patter.2023.100779 PMID: 37521038

Liu, G. L., Darvin, R., & Ma, C. (2024). Exploring AI-mediated informal digital learning of English (AI-IDLE): A mixed-method investigation of Chinese EFL learners' AI adoption and experiences. *Computer Assisted Language Learning*, *38*(7), 1632–1660. DOI: 10.1080/09588221.2024.2310288

Lochmiller, C. (2021). Conducting Thematic Analysis with Qualitative Data. *The Qualitative Report*. Advance online publication. DOI: 10.46743/2160-3715/2021.5008

Maxwell, D., Oyarzun, B., Kim, S., & Bong, J. Y. (2025). Generative AI in Higher Education: Demographic differences in student perceived readiness, benefits, and challenges. *TechTrends*. Advance online publication. DOI: 10.1007/s11528-025-01109-6

Mohebi, L. (2025). A qualitative study on the integration of AI in Education: Perceptions, challenges, and opportunities among selective In-Service and Pre-service teachers in the UAE. In *Lecture notes in educational technology* (pp. 113–126). Springer., DOI: 10.1007/978-981-96-4952-5_8

Mollick, E., & Mollick, L. (2024). Instructors as Innovators: A future-focused approach to new AI learning opportunities, with prompts. *arXiv*. DOI: 10.48550/arxiv.2407.05181

Morgan, D. L. (1997). *Focus groups as qualitative research*. SAGE Publications.

Mzwri, K., & Turcsányi-Szabo, M. (2025). The impact of prompt engineering and a generative AI-Driven tool on autonomous learning: A case study. *Education Sciences*, *15*(2), 199. DOI: 10.3390/educsci15020199

Nazim, M., & Alzubi, A. A. F. (2025). Empowering EFL teachers' perceptions of generative AI-mediated self-professionalism. *PLoS One*, *20*(6), e0326735. DOI: 10.1371/journal.pone.0326735 PMID: 40549814

Nimmo, R., Constantinides, M., Zhou, K., Quercia, D., & Stumpf, S. (2024). User Characteristics in Explainable AI: The Rabbit Hole of Personalization? *Association for Computing Machinery*, 1–13. https://doi.org/DOI: 10.1145/3613904.3642352

Patton, M. Q. (2025). *Qualitative research & evaluation methods* (4th ed.). Sage Publications.

Porayska-Pomsta, K., Holmes, W., & Nemorin, S. (2023). The ethics of AI in education. In Du Boulay, B., Mitrovic, A., & Yacef, K. (Eds.), *Handbook of Artificial Intelligence in Education* (pp. 571–604). Edward Elgar Publishing., DOI: 10.4337/9781800375413.00038

Rudolph, J., Tan, S., & Tan, S. (2023). ChatGPT: Bullshit spewer or the end of traditional assessments in higher education? *Journal of Applied Learning & Teaching*, *6*(1), 342–363. https://search.informit.org/doi/10.3316/informit.T2025102700003092061569891

Selwyn, N., Ljungqvist, M., & Sonesson, A. (2025). When the prompting stops: Exploring teachers' work around the educational frailties of generative AI tools. *Learning, Media and Technology*, *50*(3), 310–323. DOI: 10.1080/17439884.2025.2537959

Sengar, S. S., Hasan, A. B., Kumar, S., & Carroll, F. (2024). Generative artificial intelligence: A systematic review and applications. *Multimedia Tools and Applications*, *84*(21), 23661–23700. DOI: 10.1007/s11042-024-20016-1

Sergeeva, O. V., Zheltukhina, M. R., Shoustikova, T., Tukhvatullina, L. R., Dobrokhotov, D. A., & Kondrashev, S. V. (2025). Understanding higher education students' adoption of generative AI technologies: An empirical investigation using UTAUT2. *Contemporary Educational Technology*, *17*(2), ep571. DOI: 10.30935/cedtech/16039

Shwedeh, F., Salloum, S. A., Aburayya, A., Fatin, B., Elbadawi, M. A., Ghurabli, Z. A., & Dabbagh, T. A. (2024). AI adoption and educational sustainability in higher education in the UAE. In Al-Marzouqi, A., Salloum, S. A., Al-Saidat, M., Aburayya, A., & Gupta, B. (Eds.), *Artificial Intelligence in Education: The Power and Dangers of ChatGPT in the Classroom* (pp. 201–229). Springer., DOI: 10.1007/978-3-031-52280-2_14

Sousa, A. E., & Cardoso, P. (2025). Use of generative AI by higher education students. *Electronics (Basel)*, *14*(7), 1258. DOI: 10.3390/electronics14071258

Suárez, P. J. O., Romary, L., & Sagot, B. (2020). A Monolingual Approach to Contextualized Word Embeddings for Mid-Resource Languages. *arXiv,* 1703–1714. https://aclanthology.org/2020.acl-main.156/

Swidan, A., Lee, S. Y., & Romdhane, S. B. (2025). College students' use and perceptions of AI tools in the UAE: Motivations, ethical concerns and institutional guidelines. *Education Sciences*, *15*(4), 461. DOI: 10.3390/educsci15040461

Tausch, A. P., & Menold, N. (2016). Methodological aspects of focus groups in health research. *Global Qualitative Nursing Research, 3*. Advance online publication. DOI: 10.1177/2333393616630466 PMID: 28462326

United Nations. (2015) *'Sustainable Development Goal 4: Ensure inclusive and equitable quality education and promote lifelong learning opportunities for all'*. Retrieved November 08, 2025, from https://sdgs.un.org/goals/goal4

Vashishth, T. K., Sharma, V., Sharma, K. K., Kumar, B., Panwar, R., & Chaudhary, S. (2024). AI-Driven Learning Analytics for Personalized Feedback and Assessment in Higher Education. In Nguyen, T., & Vo, N. (Eds.), *Using Traditional Design Methods to Enhance AI-Driven Decision Making* (pp. 206–230). IGI Global Scientific Publishing., DOI: 10.4018/979-8-3693-0639-0.ch009

Vaughn, S., Schumm, J., & Sinagub, J. (1996). *Focus group interviews in education and psychology*. SAGE Publications., DOI: 10.4135/9781452243641

Von Winckelmann, S., Henry, M., & Mackenzie, A. (2024). Empowering Educators: A Case Study on Establishing AI Competency and Confidence. In Crompton, H., & Burke, D. (Eds.), *Artificial Intelligence Applications in K-12 - Theories, Ethics, and Case Studies for Schools*. Routledge., DOI: 10.4324/9781003440192

Walters, W. H., & Wilder, E. I. (2023). Fabrication and errors in the bibliographic citations generated by ChatGPT. *Scientific Reports, 13*(1), 14045. DOI: 10.1038/s41598-023-41032-5 PMID: 37679503

Wang, F., Li, N., Cheung, A. C. K., & Wong, G. K. W. (2025). In GenAI we trust: An investigation of university students' reliance on and resistance to generative AI in language learning. *International Journal of Educational Technology in Higher Education, 22*(1). Advance online publication. DOI: 10.1186/s41239-025-00547-9

Yeo, M. A. (2023). Academic integrity in the age of Artificial Intelligence (AI) authoring apps. *TESOL Journal, 14*(3). Advance online publication. DOI: 10.1002/tesj.716

Yusuf, A., Pervin, N., & Román-González, M. (2024). Generative AI and the future of higher education: A threat to academic integrity or reformation? Evidence from multicultural perspectives. *International Journal of Educational Technology in Higher Education, 21*(1). Advance online publication. DOI: 10.1186/s41239-024-00453-6

Zhai, X. (2024). Transforming teachers' roles and agencies in the era of generative AI: Perceptions, acceptance, knowledge, and practices. *Journal of Science Education and Technology*. Advance online publication. DOI: 10.1007/s10956-024-10174-0

Zhao, C. (2025). AI-assisted assessment in higher education: A systematic review. *Journal of Educational Technology and Innovation*, *6*(4). Advance online publication. DOI: 10.61414/jeti.v6i4.209

Chapter 3
Artificial Intelligence in MENA Education:
AI, Governance, and Multilingual Innovation in MENA

Ghofran Yazbeck
http://orcid.org/0009-0002-9731-5203
The British University in Dubai, UAE

ABSTRACT

This chapter examines how artificial intelligence (AI) is conceived, used, and controlled in schools across the Middle East and North Africa (MENA). This chapter discusses the influence of national AI visions, teacher competencies, linguistic diversity, and ethical governance on the success or constraints of AI adoption, utilising policy analysis and regional case studies. There is much focus on problems with Arabic natural language processing, differences in infrastructure, and gaps in teacher training. This chapter combines ideas from responsible AI, culturally responsive design, and educational innovation to show how AI can help with fair learning, multilingual accessibility, and long-term growth. In general, the analysis shows that the MENA region is becoming an essential part of global AI-in-education research by using context-aware, ethically sound, and language-inclusive methods.

INTRODUCTION

1.1. The Rise of Artificial Intelligence in Education

Artificial intelligence (AI) is nowadays one of the most disruptive forces in education. AI is bringing new meanings to design, delivery, and evaluation of learning

DOI: 10.4018/979-8-3373-6776-7.ch003

through adaptive learning systems and intelligent tutoring, predictive analytics, and automated assessment (Chen, Chen, and Lin, 2020; Holmes, 2020). Teachers are increasingly using data-driven insights to promote personalised learning, improve efficiency, and expand accessibility. Nonetheless, local preparedness for AI — both technological and non-technological, including institutional and cultural factors — as Hwang et al. (2020) and Chen et al. (2022) describe, is a condition for the educational value of AI.

1.2. The Middle East North Africa Context: Hope and Reality

The Middle East and North Africa (MENA) are of the most challenging regions for AI applications. They have some of the most technologically ambitious states in the world, and, at the same time, the nations are under conflict or resource deficit. The Gulf Cooperation Council (GCC) member states (United Arab Emirates and Saudi Arabia) have developed comprehensive national AI strategies that enable AI to enter the field of education policy and practice (Alotaibi & Alshehri, 2023; Demaidi, 2025). In contrast, low-cost, mobile-first systems in some areas of North Africa and the Levant will ensure continuity of learning (Salah, Alves, and Guerreiro, 2014).

This two-sided fact establishes that MENA is neither a passive actor nor a unitary actor in the development of AI. It is diverse enough to enable context-based innovation and sustainable change in academic institutions, but it also poses challenges in governance, equity, and teacher readiness (Fadlelmula & Qadhi, 2024).

1.3. Global Narratives and Regional Marginality

Western or East Asian discourse on AI in education dominates global discussions, overlooking the issues faced by Arabic-speaking and multilingual regions (Knox, 2020). It has led to MENA being represented as an importer of technologies rather than an educational provider of AI (Adly, 2020). However, this is not the case today, as recent studies indicate that the region is also producing domestic AI models tailored to local linguistic and cultural needs. One such case in the military education sector in the UAE is the implementation of AI-powered e-learning platforms, which enhance the reliability of testing (Alnaqabi & Yassin, 2021). The situation at universities in Oman is different, as they consider careful yet potentially integrative strategies (Ayed, 2022). This is a pointer to an increasing regional involvement in global educational change.

1.4. Aligning AI with Sustainable Development Goals

It is not a secret that AI will help achieve Sustainable Development Goal 4 by providing inclusive and equitable quality education (Pedro et al., 2019; Kamalov, Santandreu Calonge, and Gurrib, 2023). Theoretically, AI can personalise the learning process, identify learning needs, and support underprivileged students. Nevertheless, comparable technologies may also increase inequalities in the event of weak infrastructure and poor governance, or when the teacher is incompetent (Ateeq et al., 2024). The digital capacity and policy coherence differences across MENA imply that achieving AI requires greater interactions among governments, institutions, and educators to foster an ethical, and culturally responsive innovation (Trigui et al., 2024).

1.5. Knowledge Co-Creation and Language-Aware Innovation

However, in contemporary pedagogy, a new phenomenon called knowledge co-creation, in which students, teachers, and AI systems contribute to knowledge creation, has become part of this process (Ouyang & Jiao, 2021). This is challenging to achieve in the multilingual (MENA) classrooms due to the linguistic diversity. The current languages are Arabic, English, and French, and the currently available AI tools can perform better in English. The weaknesses of Arabic natural-language processing (NLP) and dialect recognition render the AI inadequate (Hamed & Ismael, 2024). There is, therefore, a need to create language-sensitive AI systems that take into account cultural peculiarities and linguistic diversity to enable quality accessibility and educational sovereignty..

1.6. Teacher Competencies in the Age of AI

Teacher preparation is one of the most decisive factors in adopting AI. Teachers must acquire data, algorithmic, and ethical literacy skills to successfully operate the human-AI collaboration (Hwang et al., 2020; Khosrow et al., 2022). In the MENA region, in particular, teacher-training courses do not always include formal AI or professional development components (Ayed, 2022; Ateeq et al., 2024). Even well-resourced schools with no background preparation will likely implement it shallowly or unfairly. Continuous professional learning and institutional support are among the important aspects of sustainability that build capacity.

1.7. Governance, Ethics and Cultural Legitimacy

The AI integration leads to trust or mistrust, depending on the ethical and governance structures. The issues of privacy, responsibility, and data ownership are universal, but they are susceptible in the legal and cultural context of the MENA (Mes et al., 2022; Gutierrez Jr., 2024). There are also special AI ethics councils established by other parties that have not yet developed their policies (Trigui et al., 2024). In good governance, international, local, and custodial values of justice and stewardship should be part of it.

1.8. Increasing AI Admission: Towards Sustainable and Equal

Regardless of the disparities in development, it is impossible to ignore the movement of the regions. The AI application in tertiary education, vocational education, and the health sciences is reported to have increased investment (El-Kassas et al., 2025). The resilient and flexible innovations that use limited resources may be implemented in situations of necessity, such as artificial intelligence-aided mobile learning during emergencies (Salah et al., 2014). According to these trends, AI in MENA education is not a dream but an engine that changes and breathes.

1.9. Significance and Purpose of the Research

Based on the lenses of teacher skills, linguistic adaptation, and scalability, the paper will explain how AI is conceptualised, implemented, and regulated in the education systems of MENA countries. The policy analysis and the case studies of the regions are comparative, thus providing insight into the mechanisms that would promote or discourage the implementation of meaningful development. Last but not least, the study reinstates MENA as an innovator and part of the global AI-in-Education research community, focusing on moral regulation, multilingual awareness, and pedagogies that avoid vaccination.

2. BACKGROUND AND PROBLEM STATEMENT

2.1. Global Expansion of AI in Education

Among the brightest examples of change in education over the last 10 years is the emergence of artificial intelligence (AI). AI is applied in schools and universities worldwide to facilitate personalised learning, automate grading, monitor student performance, and support administrative decision-making (Chen, Chen, and Lin,

2020; Gocen & Aydemir, 2020). Intelligent feedback systems, predictive analytics, and adaptive tutoring are AI applications that are more efficient and that offer a personalised learning experience. According to Ouyang and Jiao (2021), educational AI currently operates under three paradigms — automation, augmentation, and co-creation —that are disrupting the roles of both teachers and students.

Globally, policymakers are introducing AI as a tool to realise United Nations Sustainable Development Goal 4 (SDG 4), which aims to provide inclusive and equitable quality education (Pedro et al., 2019). This vision, however, is not easily realised. Chen et al. (2022) argue that AI theory has never been aligned with classroom practice, and the gap in this area has become the most significant in under-invested systems, where access to digital infrastructure, teacher skills, and ethical considerations is limited. These are highly volatile international issues in the MENA region.

2.2. MENA Region: Variety and Digital Intention

The population of the North Africa and Middle East region exceeds 450 million, making it the world's most youthful region. It has highly centralised educational systems that are well-endowed in the Gulf Cooperation Council (GCC) and decentralised, underfunded systems in North Africa and the Levant. Such diversity opens the door to opportunities and asymmetries in the implementation of AI-based education.

The governments of GCC countries have made AI one of the pillars of their economic diversification and digital-transformation strategies (Nurunnabi et al., 2023). An example is the United Arab Emirates, one of the first countries in the world to appoint a Minister of State for Artificial Intelligence and to incorporate AI into school and higher education reforms (Alnaqbi & Yassin, 2021). According to Saudi Arabia's Vision 2030, AI is also a key to knowledge-based economic development and the modernisation of universities (Alotaibi & Alshehri, 2023). Oman has been strategic but cautious in its approach to priority areas, focusing more on teaching and capacity building and less on policy development (Ayed, 2022).

The North African and Levantine systems, on the other hand, are typically marred by resource inadequacy, ageing infrastructure, and political turmoil. Cost, mobile-based, and offline-enabled AI are all viable solutions in such situations to ensure the continuity of learning (Salah, Alves, and Guerreiro, 2014). This opposition amplifies the paradox of the central region. Although AI pilots enjoy the good life of the wealthiest states, some parts of the MENA population remain in the digital divide, preventing them from accessing equal opportunities.

2.2. Thematic Literature Review

The available research on artificial intelligence (AI) in education in the Middle East and North Africa (MENA) can be classified into four interconnected thematic strands: governance and ethics, teacher competencies, language-aware AI and equity and inclusion. Through these strands, the literature is shown to reflect increased scholarly interest in it as well as major gaps in its evidence within the region.

Governance and Ethics

International studies define the ethical practice of AI in the educational sector by introducing transparency, accountability, and equity (Holmes et al., 2022; Gutierrez Jr., 2024). Trigui et al. (2024) and Demaidi (2025) demonstrate in the MENA context the existence of an uncoordinated, poorly implemented educational governance mechanisms despite the national AI strategies of many countries. Although the states of the GCC including UAE and Saudi Arabia have constructed standardised ethics and AI regulatory structures (Alnaqbi and Yassin, 2021; Alotaibi and Alshehri, 2023), North African and Levantine models are mostly based on generic ICT or donor ethics frameworks (Adly, 2020). The question whose evidence is yet to be substantiated is how these governance structures can be translated into being systematic in classification of accountability and protection of their data in the classroom level.

Teacher Competencies

According to international studies, data literacy, AI literacy, and ethical literacy are the qualities that teachers need in order to use AI effectively (Hwang et al., 2020; Khosravi et al., 2022). Specific studies developed within the MENA reveal that interest of teachers is strong but there is a lack of structured professional development (Ayed, 2022; Ateeq et al., 2024). Fadlelmula and Qadhi (2024) single out the problem of constant capacity gap between technological adoption and pedagogical preparedness in the GCC universities. The question that remains to be resolved is the impacts of these competency gaps on long-term learning and equity in different MENA classrooms.

Language-Aware and Multilingual AI

The literature reports Arabic language processing as one of the greatest limitations to AI-powered education on a regular basis (Hamed and Ismael, 2024; El-Kassas et al., 2025). Auto assessment, speech recognition and tutoring systems are made tricky by Arabic diglossia, dialect variation as well as code-switching. In spite of the fact that new Arabic NLP datasets are also being generated in the GCC, Kamalov, Santandreu Calonge, and Gurrib (2023) claim that linguistic localisation should be supported by culturally responsive pedagogy. The body of evidence is still scanty on the multilingual AI systems effectiveness in the actual MENA classrooms.

Equity, Inclusion, and Fragile Contexts

AI has been generally advocated as the means of SDG-4 through access improvement to marginalised learners (Pedro et al., 2019). North Africa and Levant studies indicate that AI systems based on mobile and low bandwidth have the potential of facilitating continuity of learning in case of crises (Salah, Alves, and Guerreiro, 2014). Adly (2020) and Ateeq et al. (2024) caution, however, that the aspect of inequality due to the disparity in the infrastructure, gender bias, and institutional exclusion can repeat the existing inequalities. There is limited longitudinal evidence about the effects of equity.

Combined, the literature shows that among the concepts there is a high level of conceptual agreement regarding the significance of governance, teacher capacity, linguistic inclusion, and equity, but empirical synthesis is deficient in terms of MENA-specific. This is one of the reasons why this gap gives a ground to the current comparative and policy- and case-based analysis.

2.3. Opportunities: Sustainable Development and Innovation

Artificial intelligence can be a significant asset to quality and academic inclusiveness when developed responsibly. Pedro et al. (2019) are convinced that AI can be used to customise learning, reduce student drop-out rates, and provide real-time information to the administration. Another potential proponent of AI in education, as put forth by Kamalov, Santandreu Calonge, and Gurrib (2023), is that it can be the first to spark a sustainable, multi-tiered revolution in the sector, including green technology, ethical governance, and social responsibility.

Regarding multilingualism, gender equality, and accessibility for students with disabilities, these opportunities may be found in MENA. According to Hamed and Ismael (2024), opportunities exist for AI-based opportunistic learning systems to tailor the teaching process to the speed, style, and language preferences of Arab learners. Having equal proportions of such systems offer the chance to bridge the learning gap between rural and urban regions, as well as between boys and girls.

2.4. Hardships: Leadership, Conscience, Preparation

Despite the mentioned positive shifts, the sustainable deployment of AI in MENA education is threatened by several systemic problems.

Governance and Ethics

There are other significant issues related to data privacy and protection, bias, and algorithmic responsibility raised by AI. The concept of responsible AI, as postulated by Holmes et al. (2022), implies open-handed governance and ethics at the societal level.. According to Trigui et al. (2024), the critical governance gaps in the MENA region include inconsistent regulatory frameworks and insufficient coordination among ministries. In most instances, the educational institutions do not have specific policies that regulate data use or algorithmic fairness.

Teacher Preparedness

The teachers are left at the heart of implementing AI, but their willingness is not balanced. Saudi Arabian, Omani, and Qatari studies demonstrate that, although teachers are optimistic about the opportunities of AI, a significant number of them did not receive formal education on the ethical or pedagogical applications of the technology (Ateeq et al., 2024; Ayed, 2022). Without the specific professional development models, educators will likely turn into mere technology-delivery machines rather than become creators of AI-boosted education.

Infrastructure and Availability

Unequal internet penetration and access to hardware remain widespread across most regions, even in countries with national strategies in place, as noted by Adly (2020) and El-Kassas et al. (2025). Differences between elite and popular institutions constrain scalability. The linguistic and cultural differences exacerbate these disparities, as most artificial intelligence tools are developed in either English or Chinese, leaving Arabic and its dialects underrepresented in natural language processing (NLP) research.

2.5. Linguistic and Cultural Dimensions

Among the least-researched fields of AI use in education is language. Arabic is a diglossic language with numerous dialects and transliteration systems, which create an obstacle to the standard practices of NLP models (Hamed & Ismael, 2024).

Consequently, automated evaluation, speech recognition, and text analysis software tend to produce incorrect results in Arabic settings.

In addition to language, AI systems must navigate cultural conventions on privacy, gender interactions, and pedagogy. According to Gutierrez Jr (2024), ethical considerations in the MENA region regarding AI should be guided by the local values, including Islamic justice, trust, and human dignity. Ethical frameworks established globally cannot be easily imported; they must be tailored to the local context to be seen as legitimate and trusted by users.

2.6. Policy Gaps and Fragmentation

Many in MENA have introduced national AI education policies that are often disjointed. Demaidi (2025) demonstrates that generic national AI visions in the region's developing countries lack specific concepts for how teachers will be trained, the curriculum redesigned, or evaluated. Therefore, projects are often pilot-based and short-term.

Fadlelmula and Qadhi (2024) note that much of the current literature on AI in higher education in the GCC states focuses on describing it rather than evaluating its impact or sustainability. Little longitudinal research exists that examines the actual effects of AI on learning outcomes or on narrowing inequality. The absence of robust surveillance systems complicates the task of determining what works, in which circumstances, and to whom.

2.7. The Problem of Evidence and Evaluation

In MENA, AI interest tends to outpace its factual assessment. Ateeq et al. (2024) note that the implementation of ICTs and AI tools in universities has been rapid, without accompanying evaluation. Equally, Alotaibi and Alshehri (2023) note that Saudi organisations are willing to adopt AI but are also hesitant due to the lack of understanding of the ethical and pedagogical implications. Without accurate figures and studies conducted by other institutions, policymakers risk investing in technologies that are not beneficial to students or teachers.

2.8. Framing the Central Problem

The combination of these observations indicates a definite issue in the region. Artificial intelligence (AI) is gaining popularity in MENA education, even though the use is uneven; its evaluation and management are disproportionate. The standardisation of technology is not readily achievable because the number of languages varies, and national motivations are the opposite of local capabilities. Competency in the sustainable use of teachers and in the building of ethical frameworks is lacking.

The following research question is therefore the most crucial one that will be used in this study:

What would it be like to localise, control and sustain the introduction of AI through the MENA education systems in such a way that it will facilitate the fair delivery of learning and teacher proficiencies as well as linguistic and cultural variety?

The given issue points out three gaps, which are interrelated:

1. Gaps in knowledge An adequate amount of research has not been conducted to connect AI initiatives and tangible educational results.
2. Capacity gap between actual and desired limits of ethical use of AI: teacher training and institutional support.
3. A contextual gap- the lack of adaptation of the global AI schemes to linguistic and cultural conditions of MENA.

2.9. Toward a Research Agenda for Sustainable AI in MENA Education

This identified gap must then be filled through a holistic research agenda that comprises of policy, pedagogy, and technology. Future progress depends on:

- Developing evidence-based frameworks for evaluating AI effectiveness and equity.
- Building teacher-competency models that integrate data literacy, ethical reasoning, and Culturally responsive practice.
- Advancing Arabic NLP and multilingual AI resources to support inclusive learning.
- Designing governance mechanisms aligned with both global standards and regional moral codes.

These specifications align with the suggestions made by Holmes et al. (2022) and Kamalov et al. (2023) according to whom, innovation, accountability, transparency, and inclusivity are the main attributes of sustainable AI in education.

2.10. Summary

Overall, the history of AI in MENA education could be characterized by a high rate of development, uneven distribution, and high chances of local innovation. The field currently lies at the intersection of experimenting with imported solutions and attempting to develop models that can deploy AI globally in ways that are ethical, multilingual, and sustainable. It is this tension that is the urge behind the current research and basis of the subsequent sections defining the research purpose, questions, and conceptual frameworks.

3. RESEARCH OBJECTIVES AND QUESTIONS

3.1. Framing the Study Purpose

New technologies: The use of artificial intelligence (AI) in education in the Middle East and North Africa (MENA) has been met with both excitement and trepidation. Although the national plans of the United Arab Emirates, Saudi Arabia, and Oman are oriented to AI in support of the economic development and innovation (Alotaibi & Alshehri, 2023; Ayed, 2022), the imbalance in the preparation of teachers, their acquisition of the language and management of it remains characteristic of the region. These arguments constitute the rationale for the conceptualised systematic study of AI, its application, and its continued maintenance across different educational systems.

The proposed research will thus not merely provide descriptive reasons for why AI is adopted. However, it will provide an evidence-based, theory-grounded explanation of how AI will help develop or destabilise the education system. The general aim is to discover systems that link the use of technology to fair learning outcomes and the pursuit of institutional change on a long-term scale.

3.2. General Aim

The primary objective of the research is to discuss the bright future of AI in education in the MENA region (K12, universities and colleges, and vocational education) and to explore how regional systems can strike a balance among innovation, ethics, and inclusion. It discusses how AI can enhance knowledge co-creation, empower teachers, and enable governance in multilingual and culturally diverse environments.

3.3. Specific Objectives

The research has three explicit aims that are interrelated and jointly determine the direction of analysis of the research:

This should be done to identify and map AI-driven innovations within the education systems of MENA and includes reviewing policies, institutional initiatives, and classroom activities based on AI, teaching, learning, and evaluation (Alnaqbi & Yassin, 2021; Fadlelmula & Qadhi, 2024).

The evaluation of mechanisms and situational requirements that constitute AI implementation involves an analysis of governance models, educator credentials, systems, and cultural-linguistic factors that predispose to AI implementation or failure (Trigui et al., 2024; Gutierrez Jr., 2024).

The study to be carried out will employ international standards, such as those of UNESCO and the OECD, to explain how the region can build on global theory and practice in ethical and sustainable AI in education (Holmes et al., 2022; Pedro et al., 2019).

3.4. Guiding Research Question

To operationalize these objectives, four key research questions will be used to shape the research:

1. What is both the conceptualisation and design of AI-in-education strategies in the realms of national and institutional structures by MENA countries?
2. What are context-relevant factors, such as governance, infrastructure, teacher preparedness, and linguistic environment that lead to the success or failure of AI implementation?
3. Which are the ethical, cultural, and pedagogical issues of incorporating AI in education that teachers, students, and policymakers encounter?
4. What can global strategies of multilingual, equitable, and ethically controlled AI in education learn from what has been done in MENA?

3.5. Significance of the Inquiry

The study addresses these questions and, hence, it contributes to the three major academic and practical spheres:

Policy and Governance: Giving evidence in the hands of decision-makers who are supposed to discover the means of how to approach AI initiatives in a manner that adheres to ethical and legal authorisations.

Teacher Development: Determining competency to work well with AI and be a professionally resilient human.

Linguistic and Cultural Relevance: The implementation of AI tools must advance the diversity of the Arabic language and local pedagogy. Finally, the study will seek to rebrand the MENA region as the source of knowledge, not the recipient of technology, proving that AI in education can be inclusive, locally relevant, and globally educative.

4. CONCEPTUAL AND THEORETICAL FRAMEWORKS

4.1. Introduction

The discussion on how artificial intelligence (AI) is transforming education in the Middle East and North Africa (MENA) requires theoretical foundations to help bridge the concepts of technology, pedagogy, and governance. AI in education can not be perceived as a technological innovation; it is a socio-technical system that relies on human capabilities, values, and institutional arrangements (Ouyang & Jiao, 2021; Holmes, 2020).

This section is an integration of four frameworks that are interrelated and collectively guide the study:

- Theories of Change in AI-Enhanced Education: How the inputs of technology and policy result in learning outcomes.
- Governance and Ethics Frameworks, describing responsible, culturally-based ways of regulating AI;
- The Culturally Responsive and Language-Aware AI Design deals with the issue of linguistic diversity and accessibility.
- Tackling the phenomenon of AI moving to sustainable use, Educational Innovation Ecosystems.

These paradigms are beneficial in shedding light on the interactive aspects of policy, pedagogy, and culture in the MENA environment.

4.2. Theories of Change in AI-Enhanced Education

Change of Theories (ToC) are systematic explanations of how educational reforms can generate desired results. When applied to AI in education, a ToC approach establishes links among the inputs (e.g., infrastructure, teacher training, data policies), processes (e.g., incorporating AI into teaching), and outcomes (e.g., better learning, inclusion, governance).

According to Hwang and Chen (2020) and Chen et al. (2022), effective AI implementation is a multi-stage process that involves technological readiness, pedagogical change, and, finally, institutionalisation. The operation is based on the congruence of the policy aspirations and classroom realities. Isolated pilots with a low level of alignment will be called AI projects, but these are not the reform of the system (Fadlelmula & Qadhi, 2024).

The MENA environment is viewed through a ToC lens, and some of the most important assumptions are highlighted. First, the national AI strategies presuppose that technology will automatically enhance educational outcomes (Demaidi, 2025). Nevertheless, research findings indicate that this success lies in educators' skills, cultural acclimatisation, and moral governance (Ayed, 2022; Alotaibi & Alshehri, 2023). Second, the ToC highlights the value of feedback loops, i.e., how information generated by AI systems can inform policy, curriculum, and teacher development modifications.

An important point to highlight is that Pedro et al. (2019) argue that AI applications should be implemented to fulfil Sustainable Development Goal 4, using evidence-based, context-specific methods to accelerate its achievement. Similarly, Kamalov, Santandreu Calonge, and Gurrib (2023) state that the sustainability of AI education is not a result of automation but rather the symbiosis of professional judgment skills and educator assistance.

Accordingly, AI in MENA education change theory is not a linear approval process, but rather an accentuative and adaptive process, in which alignment among technology, pedagogy, and policy is a continuous endeavour.

4.3. Governance and Ethics Frameworks

The Need for Responsible AI Governance

The artificial intelligence in education has specific ethical issues, which are not the same as technical efficiency. The responsible use of it primarily concerns bias, transparency, privacy, and accountability (Holmes et al., 2022; Gutierrez Jr., 2024). Frameworks such as the UNESCO Recommendation on the Ethics of Artificial Intelligence and the OECD AI Principles serve as global reference points. Nevertheless, these global standards should be appropriate to both the cultural, legal, and religious realities of MENA (Trigui et al., 2024).

One of the ethical frameworks suggested by Holmes et al. (2022) is grounded in transparency, fairness, and accountability in AI-based education at the community level. The application of this model in MENA must be adjusted to the region's diverse governance regimes, i.e., centralised policy frameworks in the Gulf and decentralised ones in North Africa. For example, the AI governance model in the UAE incorporates a national code of ethics and institutional codes of conduct, and it is a multi-level governance model (Alnaqbi & Yassin, 2021).

Cultural and Religious Dimensions of Ethics

In MENA, AI should also abide by Islamic moral values, which emphasise justice (adl), trust (amana), and the benefit to society (maslaha). Gutierrez Jr (2024) states that the principles can deepen global AI ethics by providing a holistic perspective of technology as a moral and social agent. For example, the Islamic value of adl can be understood as fairness in the use of algorithms in decision-making to encourage fair access to education and to avoid discrimination.

In addition, Western culture's emphasis on privacy and data ownership does not align with Eastern culture. Family consent, shared responsibility, and respect for authority shape perceptions of acceptable AI behaviour (Trigui et al., 2024). International ethics and local cultures should therefore also have governance structures to encourage compliance and integrity.

Ethics and duties of the teacher in institutions. Teachers mediate the ethics of AI in educational institutions. They ought to understand the mechanisms of recommendation generation, the biases they might carry, and how to handle AI-informed recommendations when they do not align with pedagogical decisions (Khosravi et al., 2022). It requires new ethical literacy, which is a convergence of technical literacy and moral cognition.

The use of AI ethics during teacher training would enhance transparency and accountability, helping prevent the overuse of opaque systems. According to Holmes (2020), teachers not only consume technology but also serve as ethical guardians, ensuring that it serves rather than vice versa.

4.4. Language-Aware and Culturally Responsive AI Design

The Linguistic Challenge

Language is one such big obstacle to the use of AI in the MENA education setting. Arabic is not the simplest language to deal with, as it is a diglossic language with many variants of A.L.B.. As such, it is not readily handled under natural language processing (NLP) and machine learning (Hamed & Ismael, 2024). The majority of AI systems installed in the world are trained in English and Mandarin, and hence are not effective in working with Arabic texts and speech, along with the writing (El-Kassas et al., 2025).

It is a linguistic ambiguity that influences the quality of AI-based assessments, translation tools, and chatbots. As an example, suppose that the automatic essay-scoring algorithms being trained on the English corpora are affected by the Arabic syntax or morphology, which results in biased outcomes. Simultaneously, voice recognition applications will not detect regional dialects.

Language-Aware Innovation

One way for language-conscious AI to minimise these gaps is to incorporate the system's linguistic variance into its design and to account for its cultural context.

Hamed and Ismael (2024) even acknowledge that opportunistic learning systems based on AI can be dialectical to the learners. This growth of fairness and inclusivity can be ensured by designing region-specific NLP datasets and free Arabic corpora.

AI tools should also be developed to improve the process of code-switching between Arabic, English, and French, which is prevalent in teaching and testing in multilingual MENA classrooms. Active and interactive interfaces, as Lampou (2023) and Gocen and Aydemir (2020) observe, attract more student attention and foster greater comprehension. Thus, AI localization can be characterised as less technical than pedagogical localization.

Cultural responsiveness and Accessibility

In addition to language, AI must also conform to broader cultural identities. The AI can discover a culturally responsive approach; in other words, all its visual, textual, and behavioural features are tailored to learners' values and experiences. The authors suggest involving students with disabilities in the inclusive, gender-balanced, and accessible AI systems (Kamalov et al., 2023). To illustrate this point, assistive devices that learning institutions in rural areas can implement for people with visual disabilities include integrating and synthesising Arabic speech using AI.

The desire for such initiatives is supported by UNESCO's human-centred AI concept, which views technology as an empowerment tool for educators rather than a substitute. As the language and culture converge, not only will MENA education be digitised, but it will also be education-sovereign, meaning it can alter AI systems through local philosophies of education.

The AD theory offers insight into how AI adoption is progressing —from small pilot use to system-wide use. According to Chen et al. (2020), the adventurers adopt new technologies early, but large-scale change is mainly driven by institutional support, reinforcement, and example-setting.

There are pilot initiatives; they are feasible in the MENA, particularly in the GCC; however, most lack sustainability provisions (Fadlelmula & Qadhi, 2024). Pilots will stagnate without specifically outlined and committed funding models, interoperability models, and the building of teacher capacity. A sound innovation system should therefore be internally harmonised in terms of policies, invest in infrastructure, and develop human capital (Adly, 2020; Nurunnabi et al., 2023).

The Public-Private Partnership Role

To achieve sustainable scale in AI, the private sector's input is required. Partnerships between universities, EdTech, and the Ministry would accelerate the development of Arabic NLP tools and AI school programmes, as well as information management

(Alotaibi & Alshehri, 2023). Nevertheless, Ateeq et al. (2024) also underline that excessive reliance on proprietary technologies might also lead to dependence and reduce transparency. The interoperable models are open source, ensuring long-term survivability and knowledge sharing.

The Balance in the Innovation- Ethics

Ethics should be introduced along with innovation. The dilemma of innovation rates and ethical regulations will persist because, as Trigui et al. (2024) note, AI governance in the MENA remains somewhat fragmented. Sustainable ecosystems should be built on two fronts: one focused on promoting experimentation and equality, and the other on privacy and information safety. Kamalov et al. (2023) state that such a balance is needed in advancing the so-called sustainable AI revolution, which can benefit learners and societies.

4.5. Incorporating Frameworks of Educational Transformation of MENA

These visions are unified in this paper into a multidimensional ecosystem representation of AI in MENA education (Figure not shown). The change theories demonstrate the causal relationships among technology, pedagogy, and outcomes. Under governance and ethics, guidelines and the principles involved in the use of AI are provided. The language-conscious design would ensure the inclusion of cultures and languages, and the innovation-ecosystem theory would be used to explain how this would be achievable on a large scale.

This unified approach can enable MENA not only to be a simple consumer of global technologies but also to be a co-author of knowledge in education. It recognises the need for top-down governance (policies and funding) and bottom-up agency (teacher adaptation and learner participation) to achieve sustainable innovation. With ethics, language, and inclusion as the key tenets of the theoretical background, the framework would help guide policymakers, educators, and researchers in creating a more equitable, rooted-in-context AI vision for the future of education in the field.

5. METHODOLOGY AND APPROACH

5.1. Research Design

The study will use a comparative mixed-methods design to generate generalisable evidence across different educational settings in the MENA. The comparative factor allows examining differences between high-resource systems, such as those based in the Gulf Cooperation Council (GCC), and systems with greater resource constraints in North Africa and the Levant. The mixed-methods element entails policy review, document analysis, and the synthesis of case studies to develop a holistic view of the conceptualisation, implementation, and sustenance of artificial intelligence (AI) in education.

The structure will be appropriate given the multi-layered character of AI in education, which operates at the technical, pedagogical, and ethical levels (Holmes, 2020; Chen et al., 2022). It enables analysis of macro-level policy systems and micro-level teacher and learner work. The idea that quantitative data (e.g., adoption rates, pilot assessments) is broader suggests that mixed methods are helpful in AI studies (Roll & Wylie, 2016). Conversely, qualitative data (e.g., teacher perceptions, institutional stories) is in-depth.

The design is based on a theory-informed investigation under the influence of the conceptual frames mentioned above, the theories of change, governance, and ethics, and language-conscious innovation. Those frameworks guide the selection of cases, the coding of themes, and the interpretation of findings.

5.2. Methodological Orientation

This study is predominantly oriented toward interpretivism because educational technologies are viewed as gaining meaning under conditions of cultural and institutional practices (Ouyang & Jiao, 2021). The AI in MENA education cannot be conceptualised solely in terms of counting tools or policies; it must be viewed as a social phenomenon conditioned by beliefs, modes of governance, and linguistic facts.

Simultaneously, the constructivist lens will inform the investigation of shared knowledge construction among researchers, educators, and policymakers. The role of AI in education is not only technical, as Hwang et al. (2020) highlight, but pedagogical and relational. Hence, contextual interpretation and human experience are important to this study as key to comprehending technological adoption.

5.3. Data Sources and Evidence Base

The study draws upon three main categories of data sources:

Table 1. Evidence Identification and Selection Protocol

Criterion	Description
Databases and sources	Scopus, Web of Science, Google Scholar, UNESCO, OECD, and national AI strategy documents
Keywords	"AI in education", "MENA education", "Arabic NLP", "teacher AI competencies", "AI governance", "educational equity"
Time frame	2019–2025
Inclusion criteria	Peer-reviewed studies, national AI strategies, and institutional reports focused on MENA education
Exclusion criteria	Commercial blogs, non-educational AI sources, and non-MENA-focused studies
Quality check	Preference for peer-reviewed journals and official policy documents (e.g., Holmes et al., 2022; Pedro et al., 2019; Fadlelmula & Qadhi, 2024)

Documentation Policies and Strategy:

The policies of national AI, policies of the education sector, and plans of digital transformation of the selected MENA countries (e.g., UAE, Saudi Arabia, Oman, Egypt, and Tunisia) are analysed to determine the goals, priorities, and implementation frameworks (Alotaibi & Alshehri, 2023; Demaidi, 2025).

The academic and institutional research:

Empirical evidence on teacher preparation, government policies, and ethical issues is presented by peer-reviewed literature along with institutional reports (Fadlelmula & Qadhi, 2024; Ayed, 2022; Trigui et al., 2024). These comprise qualitative interviews, surveys, and systematic reviews on AI adoption in the region.

Case and Comparison Reports:

It has been reported through case evidence based on the local contexts of military education in the UAE (Alnaqbi & Yassin, 2021), Omani higher-education programs (Ayed, 2022), and reforms in Saudi universities (Alotaibi & Alshehri, 2023). Complementary evidence from the UNESCO and OECD reports provides the comparative benchmarks (Pedro et al., 2019).

According to Whitehead et al. (2019), such a combination of data outcomes yields a multi-level evidence base that links national strategies, institutional practices, and scholarly outcomes.

5.4. Case choice and Scope Comparison

To maintain representativeness, five countries were purposely chosen to provide diversity in economic capacity, government schemes, and education-related priorities:

1. United Arab Emirates (UAE) – 1.An AI governance and educational technology innovation leader (Alnaqbi & Yassin, 2021).

2. Saudi Arabia - A fast-changing system of higher education with its focus on the concept of Vision 2030 and AI-assisted learning outcomes (Alotaibi & Alshehri, 2023).
3. Oman - Oman is an example of integration implemented with attention to teacher capacity through policy, i.e., it is measured (Ayed, 2022).
4. Egypt - This is a densely populated system with digital programs and poorly developed infrastructure.
5. Tunisia - Displays grassroots, low-end innovation in the context of popular educational environments (Salah, Alves, and Guerreiro, 2014).

5.5. Data Collection and Analysis

Document and Policy Analysis

- Qualitative content analysis was conducted to analyze the documents, with the recurring themes that were examined being teacher competencies, data governance, inclusivity, and language adaptation. The coding was done using both inductive (as it occurs in [data]) and deductive (based on frameworks) coding methods.
- The following were some of the important analytical questions: How do national AI strategies define education-related objectives?
- What governance mechanisms ensure ethical and inclusive implementation?
- How is teacher capacity addressed in policy and practice?

This approach aligns with Kamalov, Santandreu Calonge, and Gurrib (2023), who argue for evaluating AI strategies on the basis of sustainability and inclusiveness rather than technological novelty.

Comparative Case Synthesis

Using cross-case comparison, synthesized case studies have revealed standard drivers and barriers. All the cases were summarized according to five dimensions:

- Policy leadership and vision;
- Infrastructure and assets;
- Instructional improvement of teachers;
- Governance mechanisms and Ethical mechanisms;
- Language and cultural accommodation.

This discussion relies on such solutions used in earlier comparative education investigation (Pedro et al., 2019; Fadlelmula and Qadhi, 2024), which provides the general picture of the region.

Thematic Coding

NVivo analysis was conducted to code themes into a systematic categorisation. The teacher competencies category included terms such as data literacy, AI training, and human-AI collaboration, while terms such as privacy, bias, and accountability were placed in the governance and ethics category (Holmes et al., 2022; Khosravi et al., 2022).

Valid findings were applied in thematic triangulation by comparing policy narratives to empirical research findings and institutional experiences.

5.6. Ensuring Reliability and Validity

Data triangulation across sources and levels (national, institutional, and scholarly) enhanced the validity of the findings. Member checking was designed so that regional specialists would review previous research to ensure that the research studies were culturally and linguistically accurate (Hamed & Ismael, 2024).

The coding instructions were documented to maintain consistency, and the interpretation of the independent datasets was compared. The analysis concerns transparency and replicability, not numerical generalization, as Chen et al. (2020) claim.

5.7. Ethical Considerations

Ethics is given center stage as a methodology grounded in the study of governance and cultural settings. The research is ethical and adheres to the principles of beneficence, justice, and respect for autonomy. Although no primary data collection was conducted, all secondary data were selected as credible, peer-reviewed, or policy-verified.

Besides, it analytically appeals to regional ethics, particularly Islam, which is concerned with social responsibility and justice (adl). These align with the consideration of Holmes et al. (2022), who propose moral regulation of AI in education at the community level.

Another area of ethical application regarding cultural bias is in the interpretation of policy and local agency in the decision to design technology.

5.8. Methodological Limitations

Although this study appears very comprehensive, it has several limitations.

- o Availability: National AI strategies are not published in all countries, as some are only available in Arabic, hindering cross-verification (El-Kassas et al., 2025).
- o Comparability: There are significant disparities in the governance and funding of educational systems across the MENA, hindering direct comparisons.
- o Rapid Change: AI policy and execution change rapidly, suggesting that data collected between 2020 and 2025 may become outdated in the near term (Trigui et al., 2024).

Nonetheless, the study has minimized these shortcomings through the use of multiple forms of data, a focus on processes as opposed to a set of outcomes, and an analytical relevance.

6. POLICY AND GOVERNANCE OF AI IN MENA EDUCATION

6.1. Introduction

Artificial Intelligence (AI) governance in the educational sector is among the most notable in the Middle East and North Africa (MENA), both in terms of the rate and quality of implementation. Even though AI policies worldwide focus on innovation, efficiency, and access, which should be mentioned, the development of AI policies at the national level needs to be synchronised with institutional frameworks and to consider ethical aspects as well (Holmes et al., 2022; Trigui et al., 2024). Such processes are particularly evident in MENA: the Gulf Cooperation Council (GCC) states are advancing rapidly under top-down national policies, whereas systems in the North African and Levantine regions are characterised by disjointed, reactive policy adjustments (Adly, 2020; Demaidi, 2025).

This section analyses four interlinked dimensions of policy and governance: **national strategies, institutional frameworks, ethical and regulatory structures**, and **equity and inclusivity considerations**.

6.2. National Strategies and Policy Frameworks

Regional Overview

Policies on AI in education in the MENA region are often incorporated into broader national digital transformation policies. Governments consider AI a force that promotes economic diversification, labor-market modernization, and sustainable development (Nurunnabi et al., 2023; Pedro et al., 2019). Nevertheless, although almost all MENA countries have adopted AI or ICT policies, few state specifications mention educational uses or teacher education.

A full-fledged AI strategy was established in the United Arab Emirates (UAE) in 2017, when the country was the first in the world to have a Minister of State of Artificial Intelligence. In education, the UAE's policy system encourages AI-based learning analytics, predictive assessment, and lifelong learning systems (Alnaqbi & Yassin, 2021). The government's vision for Centennial 2071 is to adapt AI to support national sustainability and tie education reform to future economic competitiveness.

The National Strategy on Data and Artificial Intelligence (NSDAI) is one of the pillars of Vision 2030 in Saudi Arabia, which is making AI a significant tool for quality assurance and higher education reform. AI-led analytics are also urged to be implemented in universities to monitor student performance and adjust curricula in line with labor-market predictions (Alotaibi & Alshehri, 2023). However, this has not been implemented evenly across institutions, with elite universities being the first and public institutions following behind, as they do not have the resources to comply with these programs.

Oman has a more balanced policy that integrates capacity-building and policy ambition. Ayed (2022) further noted that higher education institutions in Oman established specialised AI committees and pilot projects on staff preparedness and ethical consciousness, rather than deploying the systems on a large scale. It is also an element of adaptive governance, since this incremental strategy allows evaluation before expansion.

Egypt, Tunisia, and Jordan are currently moving in the same direction with AI implementation, primarily through digital education reforms encouraged by UNESCO and the World Bank. Demaidi (2025) notes that, despite all this, the majority of the effort is based on externally financed projects rather than nationally laid-down structures.

Policy Coherence and Fragmentation

Prominent among them in MENA is the spread and disintegration of policies. Most ministries (education, technology, higher education, and labour) usually have their respective AI initiatives and minimal coordination (Trigui et al., 2024). This is due to the absence of cross-sectoral governance systems, which lead to the duplication of mandates and inconsistent data-sharing provisions.

According to Adly (2020), this kind of fragmentation is a legacy of centralised bureaucratic cultures, and top-level strategies are announced quickly without specific execution plans. In the example of Saudi Arabia, as NSDAI establishes general educational goals, there are not many quantifiable indicators to determine the influence on the quality of teaching or participation (Alotaibi & Alshehri, 2023). Likewise, the Digital School 2030 initiative in Egypt encourages AI but lacks a coherent data-governance system connecting schools, universities, and ministries.

Proper AI governance thus requires integrating policies, i.e., connections between the objectives of digital education and teacher competency, assessment methodologies, and ethical standards (Holmes et al., 2022).

6.3. Institutional Governance and Implementation Mechanisms

Universities as Policy Laboratories

Colleges are instrumental in the realisation of AI national visions. Universities across the Gulf are policy laboratories, experimenting with AI tools in teaching and administration. As a case in point, student services, plagiarism detection, and predictive learning analytics are all AI-based chatbots used in UAE universities (Alnaqbi & Yassin, 2021). In Saudi Arabia, higher education institutions are implementing AI in e-assessment systems to align learning outcomes with national accreditation criteria (Alotaibi & Alshehri, 2023).

The professional development programs and the inclusion of AI ethics modules in teacher education programs are also among the institutional strategies in Oman (Ayed, 2022). These programs demonstrate how universities can put the policy aspiration into practice. However, according to Fadlelmula and Qadhi (2024), these innovations are not systemically integrated at all, which means they are structurally oriented projects. The change must be sustained through long-term investment, assessment structures, and cooperation between universities.

Institutional Level of Governance

Institutional governance defines how AI aligns with academic integrity, data privacy, and accreditation requirements. According to Trigui et al. (2024), formal AI governance charters defining roles in data protection, bias mitigation, and algorithmic transparency have been adopted by only a limited number of universities in the region. The majority of them are based on general ICT or e-learning policies that predate AI.

Ateeq et al. (2024) emphasise that in the absence of institutional governance frameworks, decision-making will be reactive, based on what vendors offer rather than strategic pedagogical objectives. Universities need AI guidance committees which comprise teachers, network system specialists, ethicists, and student leaders. These formations would guarantee participative decision-making and ongoing risk evaluation.

6.4. Ethics and Regulatory Governance

Emergence of Regional Ethical Frameworks

The most important, yet underdeveloped, element of AI policy in MENA education is ethical governance. Holmes et al. (2022) posit that responsible AI practices should be based on the general principles of fairness, transparency, and accountability that apply to the community. Trigui et al. (2024) note that, as MENA countries increasingly discuss ethical AI, most lack enforcement mechanisms or oversight bodies.

The source of the codified systems of ethics is in the UAE AI Ethics Guidelines and the Data and AI Authority (SDAIA) of Saudi Arabia. These programs are focused on data privacy and algorithmic fairness. Nevertheless, Gutierrez Jr. (2024) also adds that global moral principles, when applied to the MENA context, require sensitivity to cultural and religious principles, specifically the Islamic concepts of adl (justice) and maslaha (public good).

Adaptation of Ethics Scientifically: Culture, Religion

AI ethics in MENA cannot be imported wholesale or imitated along Western lines; it must reflect local social conventions. According to Gutierrez Jr. (2024), they could employ a so-called value-integrated model that assumes Islamic moral values are separate from global standards. For example, the fair design of algorithms is also adl, but information custodianship is similar to amana (trustworthiness).

It is a culturally based approach that enables the concept of legitimacy and confidence in using AI in learning. Kamalov et al. also share this view, explaining that AI should be developed sustainably, premised on moral ideals rather than on the foundation of community compliance (2023). This sort of adaptation will help receive ethics not as a dictate of an external government and pedagogy, but as an entity that is impossible to separate from.

Other legal and regulatory instruments

Law: MENA countries have data-protection laws in most cases (including the EU General Data Protection Regulation (GDPR))—however, a few address AI in learning. El-Kassas et al. (2025) assert that the health and finance industries are more regulated. On the other hand, education is a loosely regulated phenomenon, hence rendering institutions susceptible to privacy violations and accountability gaps.

This legal gap would be closed by developing specific rules governing the use of AI in education, including standards for data collection, consent mechanisms, and algorithmic auditing. It would also lead to international collaboration and academic accreditation.

6.5. Equity, Inclusion, and Linguistic Considerations in Governance

The Digital-Equity Imperative

Equity is one of the main issues of AI policy. Although digital access is unequal across cities and rural regions, as well as in government- and privately provided schools, the national ambitions are high (Adly, 2020; Ateeq et al., 2024). Pedro et al. (2019) caution that, unless implemented with inclusive strategies, AI will only exacerbate existing disparities rather than eliminate them.

Other countries, such as Oman and Tunisia, are adopting frugal innovation models, such as low-cost mobile-based AI apps that work in connectivity-constrained settings (Salah, Alves, and Guerreiro, 2014). Such initiatives demonstrate that fairness can be achieved through the innovations enabled by a responsive government and social interactions.

Gender and Accessibility

AI governance should also address gender equity and accessibility for learners with disabilities. Kamalov et al. (2023) stress that algorithms perpetuate gender bias, whereas the exclusion of users of assistive technologies hampers the establishment of inclusivity. In the nation's policies, bias audits must be mandatory, and AI tools should be available in Arabic and other modified dialects.

Language Policy and Data Sovereignty

The government of language comes directly in contact with the use of AI. Arabic natural-language processing (NLP) is not yet well developed, which limits the development of fair AI systems (Hamed & Ismael, 2024). The governments should then invest in open-source Arabic datasets and multilingual AI research hubs. Ethically and linguistically conscious AI governance depends on data sovereignty, i.e., the ability to store, process, and manage data locally, as described by Lampou (2023) and El-Kassas et al. (2025).

6.6. Cross-Sector Collaboration and Policy Learning

Public–Private Partnerships

Government-university and government-privacy-collaboration are vital in creating good governance. The collaboration with EdTech companies has increased the pace of AI implementation but has also raised dependency risks. Ateeq et al. (2024) warn that vendor-provided implementations can negatively affect pedagogical objectives and data ownership. These risks can be mitigated through transparent procurement policies, open-source solutions, and the development of local capacity.

Local Collaboration and Exchange of Knowledge

There is little collaboration between the regions, despite their shared linguistic and cultural background. The efforts of the Arab AI Network and the Arab States Arab AI in Education Forum of UNESCO are halfway toward integrated governance. To make benchmarking and monitoring across MENA countries more feasible, Nurunnabi et al. (2023) propose aligning AI monitoring in the region with the Sustainable Development Goals to ensure the monitoring process can be approached at similar levels.

Another role this servitude would play is harmonisation, especially in the areas of teacher competencies, ethics training, and the development of Arabic NLP.

6.7. The Results and the Accountability Systems

The governance should also have appropriate mechanisms for monitoring, evaluation, and accountability. According to Fadlelmula and Qadhi (2024), the available literature rarely quantifies the effect of AI on learning performance, so there is plenty of data in the policy environment, yet it lacks evidence. Policy feedback indicators would be developed based on aspects such as individual inclusion, teacher readiness, and ethical compliance.

In their reference to Kamalov et al. (2023), the authors should consider the use of so-called AI sustainability scorecards that measure performance against environmental, social, and governance (ESG) criteria. The use of AI in MENA can be linked to integrating AI educational campaigns into national sustainability reporting systems to achieve greater coherence and social confidence.

7. TEACHER COMPETENCIES AND HUMAN-AI COOPERATION

7.1. Introduction

The adoption of artificial intelligence (AI) in education requires instructor involvement. The effectiveness of AI lies in providing educators with an opportunity to read more than they do, reorganize pedagogy, and readjust ethical practices in classrooms. However, it is due to the policies of the countries and the technological equipment that determines such an accomplishment at this level. The need to build practical AI-related pedagogical competencies is a pedagogical and administrative priority in the Middle East and North Africa (MENA), where multilingualism, cultural diversity, and inequalities in access to digital services are the new norm (Ayed, 2022; Fadlelmula & Qadhi, 2024).

7.2. Rethinking Teacher Roles in the AI Era

With AI entering the picture, the role of a teacher shifts from a content presenter to a learning organiser and a moral negotiator. According to Hwang et al. (2020), AI helps teachers to transition to facilitation, mentorship, and individualised feedback. That said, the new dimensions of literacy are necessary: data literacy (the knowledge of analytics), AI literacy (the ability to interpret algorithmic results), and ethical literacy (the need to ensure fairness and privacy).

Cultural and linguistic awareness should also be included among the competencies in the MENA context, as most AI tools were developed in English and not fully translated into Arabic (Hamed & Ismael, 2024). The teachers then become mediators between imported technologies and classroom realities. According to Chen et al. (2022), to close this gap, it is necessary to find teachers who can critically evaluate AI recommendations rather than passively accept them.

7.3. Current Status of Teacher Preparedness in MENA

Research in the field indicates that there is an interest and scant preparation among teachers. Ayed (2022) found that teachers are eager to explore the potential of AI in their research on Oman, yet they lack organized training courses and institutional support. Similarly, as noted by Ateeq et al. (2024), although universities in the Gulf are investing in AI infrastructure, learners prefer traditional pedagogical approaches. In Saudi Arabia, few higher education institutions have introduced AI-aided assessment and grading, yet teachers are not taught much in data analysis or ethical behavior (Alotaibi & Alshehri, 2023).

These findings demonstrate that the unyielding capacity difference between the technological delivery and human preparedness exists. This, Fadlelmula and Qadhi (2024) say, is one of the missing links in the AI-in-education approaches of the region: the deficiency of professional development systems to support the digital reform. Without teachers' lifelong learning, AI projects will be either superficial or unfair.

7.4. Frameworks for Teacher Competencies

Teacher-competency models related to AI globally focus on four domains that are tied together:

1. Technical Proficiency - having an understanding of AI tools functionality and how to apply them (Chen, Chen and Lin, 2020);
2. Pedagogical Design - how AI knowledge applies in the lesson design and the assessment (Ouyang and Jiao, 2021);
3. Ethical and Data Governance Litany - awareness of the issues of bias, privacy, and transparency (Holmes et al., 2022);
4. Human-AI Collaboration Skills - integrating equal collaboration as regards to the human judgment and machine assistance (Khosravi et al., 2022).

In the case of MENA, one more linguistic-cultural dimension is necessary. The teachers should be able to determine the appropriateness of AI applications to Arabic linguistic subtleties and cultural norms. According to Gutierrez Jr. (2024), incorporating Islamic ethical considerations, such as adl (justice) and amana (trust), into teacher preparation could enhance moral responsibility in the application of AI.

7.5. Building Capacity through Professional Development

The main factor in the sustainable use of AI is professional development. The competency-building process introduced by Kamalov, Santandreu Calonge, and Gurrib (2023) must be long-term, with the process structure grounded in continuous training systems rather than workshops. More and more GCC-based initiatives (such as AI Campus in the UAE or the Future Skills Program) will include nationally based programs but involve little teacher input (Alnaqbi & Yassin, 2021).

The author proposes that the discussed degrees of training are basic digital literacy for all teachers, high-level AI, expertise-based pedagogy, and leadership in administration (Ayed, 2022). This kind of differentiation guarantees scale and context relevance. Cooperation with EdTech companies can be used to transfer skills, but, according to Ateeq et al. (2024), the interaction must not be based on academic freedom or on the openness of data use.

Other online professional learning communities and open-access MOOCs can be used in less-resourced settings. Lampou (2023) reminds us that modular training is also flexible, in that a teacher is not restricted in any way when he or she tries experimenting with AI, provided he or she considers its ethical implications.

7.6. Human–AI Collaboration and Pedagogical Balance

AI can only be successfully implemented through human-focused pedagogy. Holmes (2020) cautions against excessive automation, as it tends to reduce teachers' agency and students' creativity. Instead, teachers should rely on AI to facilitate, not exclude, human judgment. The explainable AI presented by Khosravi et al. (2022) is described as a pedagogical tool that provides greater transparency and enables the teacher to understand the reasons behind the system's recommendations.

Human-AI cooperation in multilingual classrooms in MENA extends to cultural translation. Instructors put AI results in context to align with learners' understanding, based on their linguistic contexts and socio-cultural conventions (Hamed & Ismael, 2024). This mediation will be educational and allow technological innovation.

7.7. Future Directions and Policy Implications

The development of teacher competencies should be coordinated among ministries, universities, and accreditation bodies. The AI literacy standards should be incorporated into teacher education and performance systems. According to Nurunnabi et al. (2023), aligning AI competencies with the Sustainable Development Goals will ensure that teacher development is relevant to the national innovation agenda.

Also, collaboration across regions may occur through networking, e.g., via the Arab AI in Education Alliance, where mutual training and study on culturally responsive teaching may be conducted. The evaluation systems should also monitor the outcomes of teacher-competency plans, reflected in improved student outcomes and ethical practice (Fadlelmula & Qadhi, 2024).

8. LANGUAGE, INCLUSION, AND ACCESSIBILITY IN AI EDUCATION

8.1. Introduction

The two essential aspects of artificial intelligence (AI) in education are language and inclusion, especially in the Middle East and North Africa (MENA). Learners experience Digital and AI-driven education in areas influenced by linguistic diversity, socio-economic disparities, and cultural heterogeneity. Although AI has the potential to advance access, personalisation, and equity, systems are not culturally and linguistically sensitive, and therefore the inequalities may multiply (Hamed & Ismael, 2024; Pedro et al., 2019).

In this part, the authors discuss the possibilities of language-conscious innovation and inclusive design, which can enable AI to contribute to equal learning in the MENA region. It deals with three broad areas of interest: Arabic language technologies and multilingualism; AI, inclusion, and accessibility; and governance strategies for linguistic equity and social justice.

8.2. The LingLSC of MENA Education.

The MENA region is linguistically diverse. The most prevalent is Arabic, with several varieties, including Classical Arabic, Modern Standard Arabic (MSA), and other dialects (Hamed & Ismael, 2024). In addition, English and French are often used as languages of instruction in science and higher education. This diglossic and multilingual situation poses unprecedented challenges for AI-based educational tools, which are typically trained on English-language data.

In the local context, the functionality of AI systems is constrained by the lack of effective Arabic natural language processing (NLP) systems, as Hamed and Ismael (2024) state. Arabic morphology and syntax are likely to be misinterpreted in text summarisation, speech recognition and automated essay assessment. Similarly, machine translation systems are not accurate at recognising dialect or cultural allusions. El-Kassas et al. (2025) note that, due to the lack of Arabic-language datasets, research and innovation in the field are disrupted, preventing the creation of local AI solutions in education and other areas.

Such language obstacles are transformed into an educational discrepancy. Anglophone programs or Francophone programs have easy access to AI-enhanced learning platforms, whereas Arabic-speaking students are economically disadvantaged. It is due to this imbalance that strongly promotes the growth of the digital divide both within and outside MENA countries, underscoring the necessity of language-sensitive AI innovation.

8.3. Language-Aware AI Innovation

Localising AI Systems for Arabic

A language-conscious AI is a concept that describes the creation of intelligent systems that take into account users' linguistic, cultural, and social realities (Hamed & Ismael, 2024). In learning, this can be achieved by training AI models on local-language data and incorporating local semantics and discourse patterns.

The development of Arabic NLP infrastructure has been increasing. Corpora development in Saudi Arabia, the UAE, and Qatar is being done on sentiment analysis, essay scoring, and automated tutoring (El-Kassas et al., 2025). Nevertheless, Kamalov, Santandreu Calonge, and Gurrib (2023) insist that translation should also be associated with innovation and culturally valuable pedagogy; i.e., AI tools should represent local histories, values, and learning patterns.

Language-conscious innovation is, therefore, a question of educational sovereignty —the ability of a nation to shape digital learning as a cultural identity or language. Lampou (2023) and Ouyang and Jiao (2021) emphasise that local adaptation positively affects learners' motivation and cognitive engagement, as learners relate AI-mediated learning to their daily language use.

Cross-Lingual and Multicultural Artificial Intelligence Learning Spaces

The MENA learners are exposed to mixed linguistic conditions in which Arabic, English, and French exist, and forms must facilitate multilingual interaction and code-switching. According to Chen, Chen, and Lin (2020), the concept of inclusivity in multilingual AI can be viewed as enabling, in which language hybridity is accepted in place of monolingualism.

In practice, this would involve creating chatbots in education and assessment software that can comprehend multiple languages or dialects in the same conversation. Examples of such systems might include enabling Arab students to answer some questions in English and others in their native dialect, with the AI interpreting the words based on their meanings. This flexibility encourages authenticity and participation, particularly in tertiary learning and in workplaces (Hamed & Ismael, 2024).

Generative AI and Large Language Models in MENA Education

Generative artificial intelligence and especially language models (LLM) have brought both new opportunities and threats to MENA education. Programmes that can create essays, feedback, translations, and tutorial can aid in decreasing the workload of the teacher and empower multilingual students, particularly when the Arabic NLP is integrated into their architecture (Hamed and Ismael, 2024; El-Kassas et al., 2025). Nonetheless, Holmes et al. (2022) warn that applied lack of governance of one can stem from either academic dishonesty or verifiability of assessments using generative AI. Inaccurate productions of Arabic or misunderstanding dialect can be a possible result in multilingual MENA classrooms, which results in biased scoring or misleading feedback. Thus, the fair usage of generative-AI should be regulated by the transparent assessment redesign, educator control, and culture-appropriate standards of ethics, where automation will enrich and not substitute pedagogical decisions (Khosravi et al., 2022; Gutierrez Jr., 2024).

8.4. AI for Inclusion and Accessibility

Promoting Educational Access

With an excellent opportunity to encourage inclusion, AI will help to eliminate the barriers to marginalised populations such as rural learners, refugees, students with disabilities, and girls in conservative environments. Pedro et al. (2019) see AI as a means of providing high-quality education to underserved populations through adaptive, mobile solutions.

North African and Levantine areas with limited resources have adopted AI-driven mobile learning and offline apps to maintain educational continuity even in the face of crises, such as conflicts or pandemics (Salah, Alves and Guerreiro, 2014). Such frugal innovations leverage low-cost, locally applicable technologies to make learning available even without a stable internet connection. The above examples show that inclusion can be achieved through design decisions that prioritise resilience and contextual flexibility.

AI and Gender Inclusion

The issue of gender equity is a significant educational problem in MENA. Nurunnabi et al. (2023) and Kamalov et al. (2023) emphasise the power and empowerment of women, as well as their marginalisation, depending on the design and deployment of AI. Inclusive AI systems can offer customised learning to women and girls who are culturally constrained in their physical movement, in virtual classrooms and adaptive tutoring.

Nevertheless, this will not be possible unless the data and controls are gender-sensitive, ensuring that women are not restricted in the virtual world. To achieve gender equity, it is necessary to gather representative data and integrate gender-awareness into AI governance systems (Trigui et al., 2024). This can be facilitated by the ministries of education and teacher-training institutes by incorporating gender literacy into AI competency models for educators to follow (Ayed, 2022).

Learner with Disabilities Accessibility

Students with disabilities have new opportunities because AI opens the door to assistive technologies. Learners with visual, auditory or cognitive disabilities can be assisted by speech recognition, predictive typing, or AI-based reading applications. Kamalov et al. (2023) and Holmes et al. (2022) state that inclusive design cannot be considered an extension; rather, it should be considered part of the design.

Assistive AI in Arabic is underdeveloped; nevertheless, improvements are evident. New projects in Saudi Arabia and the UAE are developing Arabic voice assistants and AI-powered captioning devices to help deaf students (El-Kassas et al., 2025). To expand these programs across the region, ministries, NGOs, and technology developers will have to work together to produce accessible content repositories and open-source datasets.

8.5. Governance and Policy for Linguistic and Inclusive Equity

Integrating Inclusion into AI Policy

A focus on innovation and efficiency, alongside lower levels of inclusion and accessibility, can characterise MENA AI policies. According to Fadlelmula and Qadhi (2024), few national AI strategies have quantifiable objectives for reaching underprivileged learners. Integrating inclusion into policy systems would mean that technology adoption supports a fair learning process rather than exacerbates inequality.

For example, the gradual nature of AI adoption in Oman involves providing teacher education on the principles of inclusive pedagogy and accessibility (Ayed, 2022). Equally, the AI strategy of the UAE includes the pillar of no learner left behind, which aims to improve accessibility for students with disabilities (Alnaqbi & Yassin, 2021). Such practices require policy alignment and budgetary commitment to scale across the region.

Creating Data and Language Sovereignty

The sovereignty of data, i.e. the control over data gathering, storage, and utilisation of national linguistic and educational data, is essential to fair AI development. El-Kassas et al. (2025) argue that the lack of regional data sovereignty means Arabic

NLP will remain reliant on external datasets, thereby restricting its representation and innovation.

The governments are thus advised to invest in national AI research centres that emphasise Arabic-language sources, open-source corpora, and culturally oriented teaching datasets. Nurunnabi et al. (2023) also support the establishment of a cross-border data-sharing infrastructure among Arab states to accelerate AI development in line with the Sustainable Development Goals.

Good Governance and Lingual Equity

Holmes et al. (2022) and Gutierrez Jr. (2024) emphasise that fairness across languages and social groups should be incorporated into ethical AI governance. Exclusion can be supported by linguistic bias or by algorithms that favour a specific dialect or sociolect. The integration of linguistic fairness measures into AI assessment systems is helpful because it allows policymakers to understand whether the systems are fair to all language users.

Fairness (adl) and trust (amana) are the most important values of Islamic ethics and are, at the same time, in line with global principles of AI ethics. Adopting these moral ideas into governance systems will enhance cultural legitimacy and foster inclusive innovation (Gutierrez Jr., 2024).

8.6. Future Directions and Collaboration

Future progress in inclusive and language-aware AI education depends on collaboration across multiple levels:

- **Governmental:** Ministries of Education and AI councils should fund national Arabic NLP initiatives and open-data repositories.
- **Institutional:** Universities should embed language-aware AI and accessibility design into teacher-education curricula (Ayed, 2022).
- **Regional:** Cross-national partnerships can accelerate Arabic NLP research and share inclusive AI standards (Trigui et al., 2024).
- **Private sector:** EdTech companies should co-design AI platforms with local educators to ensure cultural alignment and accessibility (Ateeq et al., 2024).

9. PATHWAYS FROM PILOT TO SCALE AND SUSTAINABLE IMPLEMENTATION

9.1. Introduction

The emerging rush of artificial intelligence (AI) projects in the Middle East and North Africa (MENA) education sector has led to the launch of pilot projects, smart classrooms, AI tutors, learning analytics dashboards, and national AI academies. Although these experiments show the potential of innovation, most are single or temporary, and there are few signs that system-wide implementation will be sustainable (Fadlelmula & Qadhi, 2024; Ateeq et al., 2024).

To scale AI initiatives, a systematic framework for the spread of innovation, the enablers of sustainability, and the interaction between governance and teacher capacity, accompanied by cultural adaptation, is required. In this section, the mechanisms, challenges, and strategies for transitioning AI from pilot implementation to long-term institutional and national integration are explained.

9.2. The Difficulty of Scaling AI in Education

Pilot programs are essential for determining feasibility, but scaling is highly coordinated and involves infrastructure, policy, and pedagogy. According to Chen, Chen, and Lin (2020) and Kamalov, Santandreu Calonge, and Gurrib (2023), scaling AI education implies not only the imitation of technologies but also the introduction of innovation into institutional practices and routines.

Some recurring difficulties in MENA include incomplete rating systems, an uneven range of policies, and a lack of teacher training and language support (Ayed, 2022; Trigui et al., 2024). The majority of them are taken due to short-term funding or global co-operation that is not directly connected to the national curriculum or accreditation programmes (Adly, 2020). It is the one that prevents innovative prototypes from meeting the sustainability threshold.

9.3. Facts of Successful Scaling

Coherence of Policy and Governance

The initial measure towards sustainable scaling is policy coherence. Rather than the visionary rhetoric, Fadlelmula and Qadhi (2024) are expected to set targets, assign responsibility for policies, and make them available. Examples of countries that use central coordination to accelerate the adoption of institutions include the United Arab Emirates (UAE) and Saudi Arabia. The national objectives of the UAE to introduce AI could be related to the plan to introduce the technologies, comprising the objective to design AI education within the framework of the nationwide Strategy 2031 to stabilise the policy framework (Alnaqbi & Yassin, 2021).

On the contrary, disintegrated systems are too complex to keep afloat. Demaidi (2025) claims that developing countries tend to implement high-level AI strategies without specific implementation frameworks, leading to policy drift. In response to this, Oman's incremental model, which integrates capacity building with pilot testing, demonstrates how smaller systems can grow through adaptive learning and continuous feedback (Ayed, 2022).

Resource Allocation and Infrastructure

Any scaling endeavour is supported by physical and digital infrastructure. AI expansion requires robust internet access, information centres, and compatible learning management systems (Pedro et al., 2019). However, the difference between MENA countries remains considerable: in GCC countries, cloud systems and AI laboratories are highly developed, whereas in North African and Levantine countries, basic ICT infrastructure is still in place (Salah, Alves and Guerreiro, 2014).

According to Kamalov et al. (2023), fair infrastructure development should be implemented alongside the introduction of AI; otherwise, expansion only widens inequality. The regional collaboration might also be involved in this case, such as collective digital libraries with Arabic-language didactic materials or international AI research (El-Kassas et al., 2025).

Educator Ability and School Culture

Teachers play the key role of scaling. Even highly funded AI systems fail to continue without their active participation. As Hwang et al. (2020) and Khosrowavi et al. (2022) note, growing AI demands educator trust in the use, adaptation, and criticism of AI systems. Nevertheless, the number of MENA teachers trained in AI-related skills, especially in ethical and data-literacy skills, remains low (Ateeq et al., 2024; Ayed, 2022).

Peer learning and knowledge transfer can be achieved through the development of communities of practice in universities and schools. According to Lampou (2023), digital collaborative platforms among teachers are more open and aim to facilitate greater adoption and pedagogical innovation. The institutional culture needs to change too: from technology-as-tool thinking to technology-as-partner thinking, and it should be based on experimentation and feedback rather than compliance.

9.4. Models of Sustainable Implementation

The GCC Model: Top-Down Acceleration

The GCC states, especially the UAE and Saudi Arabia, are ideal examples of the top-down acceleration models. Their national AI plans provide centralised funding, regulatory certainty, and performance standards (Alotaibi & Alshehri, 2023). Innovation has its flagship locations in universities, where AI has been tried in admissions, learning analytics, and assessment.

Although these models provide scale quickly, they risk overlooking bottom-up innovation and teacher agency. Fadlelmula and Qadhi (2024) warn that implementation should not occur at a high rate without adequate professional development, as it will foster dependency on vendors and curtail the imagination of pedagogical processes. These situations require sustainable scaling that involves institutionalising teacher education and moral supervision into the national policies.

BOTTOM-UP Adaptation Frugal Innovation Model

However, this differs from other countries such as Tunisia, Egypt, and Jordan, which use bottom-up adaptation models grounded in local ingenuity. Salah, Alves and Guerreiro (2014) report the use of remote labs and mobile AI apps by Tunisian universities to deliver low-cost science education. These low-cost developments are based on open-source software, domesticization of local code development, and scaling up through alliances.

Adly (2020) defends frugality as a means of promoting sustainability, as it fosters local ownership and resilience. Nevertheless, unless these grassroots campaigns are coordinated at the national level, they find it hard to change the mainstream policy. The centralisation versus decentralisation of vision and innovations is a significant problem in the MENA region educational systems.

Adaptive Scaling: The Hybrid Model

Oman's hybrid strategy has been adaptive scaling, in which pilot projects are developed, continuously assessed and evaluated, and then scaled up (Ayed, 2022). Teacher training, ethical concerns, and cultural fit drive the use of AI in higher education in Oman. This model is a slow, steady process that appreciates learning through doing rather than radical change.

The theories-of-change framework (Section 4), which consists of constant feedback and situational learning, is associated with these adaptive models. They can show that scaling may be sustainable not in terms of scale and velocity but in consistency among technology, government, and learning.

9.5. Coalitions and Ecosystem Creation

Public-Private Collaboration

PPP is actively engaged in scaling AI. Business organisations involved in the provision of technical services include EdTech firms, and governments fund such organisations by providing regulations (Ateeq et al., 2024). However, Fadlelmula and Qadhi (2024) and Trigui et al. (2024) claim that PPPs must strike a balance between innovation and ethics, and between education and integrity.

In practice, vendor-controlled AI systems place heavy emphasis on data acquisition for commercial use. In the absence of regulation, it may result in privacy violations or algorithmic bias. It is excellent to implement open partnerships through open-source, transparent procurement and institutional data-ethics committees to achieve accountability (Holmes et al., 2022).

Local Co-operation and Knowledge Sharing

AI requires international collaboration to become sustainable. Nurunnabi et al. (2023) would prefer a local paradigm that entails the sharing of information among Arab universities, ministries, and technology centres to exchange best practices and databases. The plan would help expedite the development of Arabic NLP, ethical oversight, and teacher training.

The authors propose creating a Regional AI Education Observatory—a general institution that will monitor implementation outcomes, define the impact of pilots, and invest (El-Kassas et al., 2025). This kind of co-operation would enable decision-making and prevent overlapping efforts across the MENA countries.

9.6. Sustainability of Financing and Cost

Another aspect of long-term financial planning concerns sustainability. Although most pioneer AI pilots are funded by donors or government seed funding, few include lifecycle cost analysis. Demaidi (2025) and Adly (2020) note that cost modelling must incorporate maintenance, data storage, professional development, and software upkeep.

They suggest financing a multi-channel model, which would imply the use of state budgetary funds, business community investment, and open-source development (Kamalov et al., 2023). This is a risk-free form of diversification that encourages innovation. The first part is that Saudi Arabia and the UAE already invest in AI-specific projects through national education budgets, which is a new best practice to emulate across the entire region (Alotaibi & Alshehri, 2023).

9.7. Loop of Monitoring, Evaluation and Feedback

This is the greatest weakness of most MENA AI programs, which are not systematically evaluated. According to Fadlelmula and Qadhi (2024), the number of studies evaluating learning outcomes or equity effects is few compared with the number of descriptive reports. To ensure accountability, it is necessary to adopt evidence-based monitoring structures for AI projects.

Pedro et al. (2019) and Holmes et al. (2022) introduce the evaluation models, which relate the AI introduction to the Sustainable Development Goals (SDG 4) and are focused on access, quality, and inclusion. The assessment is an appurtenance to national plans, which would contribute to improving and training on what is learnt each time.

Data analytics tools can only support evaluation, as they can provide real-time data on teachers' and students' performance and on the general efficacy of the governance/pedagogical tool itself (Khosravi et al., 2022).

9.8. Projections in the future: Report to Sustainable Ecosystems

The AI solution to education in MENA focuses on resilient ecologies that combine top-down leadership with bottom-up agency. It will be based on four pillars of sustainability:

1. **Governance alignment** – coherent policies connecting visions of the national level with institutional performance;
2. **Human capacity** – continuous teacher development and ethical literacy;
3. **Cultural adaptation** – language-aware, context-sensitive AI systems; and
4. **Financial continuity** – diversified funding and open-source innovation.

10. DISCUSSION AND SYNTHESIS

Artificial intelligence (AI) is changing education in the Middle East and North Africa (MENA), but not as much in terms of technological advancement as in its fit within the context, teacher empowerment, and governance. The above paragraphs demonstrate that national policies are ambitious, especially within the Gulf

Cooperation Council (GCC), but the region's success in sustainable, inclusive, and culturally-based AI integration is not yet evident (Alotaibi & Alshehri, 2023; Demaidi, 2025).

Table 2. Policy, Practice, and Equity Patterns across MENA

Theme	GCC Example	North Africa / Levant Example	Key Problem	Policy / Learning Implication
Governance	UAE AI ethics codes and national AI authority (Alnaqbi & Yassin, 2021)	Fragmented AI regulation in Egypt and Tunisia (Demaidi, 2025; Adly, 2020)	Weak enforcement	Need for education-specific AI regulation
Teacher Capacity	AI pilots in Saudi universities (Alotaibi & Alshehri, 2023)	Limited teacher training in Tunisia and Egypt (Ayed, 2022)	Skills gap	Embed AI literacy in teacher education
Language & NLP	Arabic corpora in GCC (El-Kassas et al., 2025)	Weak dialect support in North Africa (Hamed & Ismael, 2024)	Biased assessment	Invest in Arabic NLP
Equity & Access	Special-needs AI in UAE (Alnaqbi & Yassin, 2021)	Mobile learning for refugees (Salah et al., 2014)	Digital divide	Prioritise inclusive AI design

Most countries in the MENA region perceive AI as an economic diversifier and a driver of global competitiveness at the policy level (Nurunnabi et al., 2023). Nevertheless, policy fragmentation and overlapping mandates across ministries persist, as do ineffective accountability mechanisms (Trigui et al., 2024). In the context of a well-established governance, such as the centralised model of the UAE, the implementation of AI proceeds rapidly. It is backed by a clear strategy and investment (Alnaqbi & Yassin, 2021). However, rapid top-down scaling may result in dependence on and neglect of employees' professional development needs (Fadlelmula & Qadhi, 2024). On the other hand, the slower yet more frequently demonstrated local ownership and flexibility in bottom-up initiatives are evident in North Africa and the Levant (Salah, Alves and Guerreiro, 2014). The problem facing MENA is balancing the pace of innovation with the need for contextual learning and moral values.

Teachers' competencies are a determinant of the sustainable integration of AI. In the region, teachers show interest but lack systematic support and ethical literacy (Ayed, 2022; Ateeq et al., 2024). Unless teachers invest in training, they risk becoming passive users of technology rather than active organisers of learning (Khosravi et al., 2022). An environmental sustainability-based AI ecosystem involves incorporating continuous professional growth, data literacy, and human-AI cooperation into national standards for teachers (Hwang et al., 2020).

Another way AI characterises MENA is through language and inclusion. In this context, diglossia negatively affects the natural language processing (NLP) performance of Arabic-medium learners (Hamed & Ismael, 2024). The AI tools are mostly English-based, and they replicate language inequities and cultural bias. Creating open-source Arabic NLP data and culturally responsive systems is thus a technological, as well as an ethical necessity (El-Kassas et al., 2025). In the same way, gender coverage and accessibility for students with disabilities are not yet well-developed aspects of AI governance (Kamalov, Santandreu Calonge and Gurrib, 2023). Global ethics can align with Islamic values through inclusive AI design grounded in fairness (adl) and trust (amana) (Gutierrez Jr, 2024).

The policy, heavy investment, and the institution's commitment are necessary for sustainability and the expansion of successful pilots. GCC models of the top-down type are very effective in the investment sphere, and the idea of frugal innovation in North Africa is a sign of strength and localisation (Adly, 2020). Regional cooperation can unite these strengths by sharing data, providing training opportunities, and developing assessment models. Hybrid models —national leadership and grassroots innovation — are the way forward to control the development of AI so that it is fair and culturally valid.

Lastly, AI in education in MENA will need to evolve beyond a collection of technology projects into an infrastructure of care that supports a human-centred system in which teachers, learners, and institutions co-create knowledge responsibly. The institutionalisation of ethics, language awareness, and inclusion at the policy-making and classroom levels will make the MENA region a participant rather than a follower in global, sustainable, and equitable AI for learning.

11. CONCLUSION AND RECOMMENDATIONS

11.1. Conclusion

Artificial intelligence (AI) is another historical opportunity for the Middle East and North Africa (MENA) to overhaul education with the support of innovation, inclusivity, and sustainability. Governments across the region are also striving to make AI more accessible and to develop high-quality national education strategies (Nurunnabi et al., 2023; Alotaibi & Alshehri, 2023). According to the current paper, however, the fundamental change that should be experienced in MENA education is not technological growth but moral principles, teacher competence, and language inclusivity.

The extent of such efforts that will be scaled and sustained is relative to the institutional commitment of the long-term and the cooperation of the region even though the states of the gulf cooperation council (GCC) like the United Arab Emirates (UAE) and Saudi Arabia have been pioneering their ambitious national policies and enormous investor despite the challenges of scaling them (Alnaqbi & Yassin, 2021; Demaidi, 2025). North African states and the Levant state argue that lean innovation can deliver significant results even in a context-driven, resource-constrained environment (Salah, Alves and Guerreiro, 2014). Combined, these experiences highlight the significance of the equilibrium between technological ambitions and social and cultural realities.

Implementing AI will make teacher preparation one of the success factors. The educators in the region are eager but not ready yet, as they lack a professional development framework grounded in data literacy, algorithmic thinking, and ethics (Ayed, 2022; Ateeq et al., 2024). AI can be used to support passive learning rather than stimulate critical thinking, without empowering the teacher as a co-creator of innovation. Simultaneously, linguistic inequalities and exclusion of learners with disabilities are maintained by the lack of Arabic natural-language processing (NLP) and inclusive design resources (Hamed & Ismael, 2024; El-Kassas et al., 2025). Hence, human-oriented AI, grounded in cultural and linguistic relevance, should be the guiding principle for regional change.

In the end, the MENA region is at a crossroads: it may remain an importer of foreign AI systems or become the knowledge-creating centre that provides models of ethical, multilingual, and sustainable AI in education relevant worldwide.

11.2. Recommendations

Incorporate AI Governance into the Education Policy:

The AI ethics, data privacy, and accountability should be incorporated into the education acts and accreditation standards by ministries (Holmes et al., 2022; Trigui et al., 2024). There will be a set of rules on transparency and bias to increase trust and legitimacy.

Build Teacher AI- Competency Frameworks:

They must teach AI literacy, data control, and ethical decision-making as fundamental elements of instructor education and make them institutional (Hwang et al., 2020; Khosravi et al., 2022). It is oriented towards lifelong professional growth, and the learning hubs currently available in the region can achieve this.

Manifest Destiny Enhanced Localization Cultural/ Arabic NLP:

I would also put more effort into opening both the Arabic open-source databases and language technologies, and be more even in the education derived from AI (Hamed & Ismael, 2024; El-Kassas et al., 2025). There is also the requirement that local AI researchers collaborate across MENA to accommodate both language and culture.

Design AI Gender responsive and Inclusive AI design:

The national AI councils are expected to ensure that people with disabilities can access different systems and that their responsiveness aligns with gender equality (Kamalov, Santandreu Calonge, and Gurrib, 2023). Any educational AI platform should provide capabilities such as Arabic voice recognition and adaptive tutoring.

Installs Regional Cooperation and Evaluation Systems:

It is possible to share information on it with the assistance of the Regional AI in Education Observatory, which enables one to assess it and disseminate best practices (Nurunnabi et al., 2023). They ought to possess uniform measures that offer equity, ethics and sustainability outcomes.

Accordingly, such a proposal would enable MENA education systems to afford the phase of experimentation of the process and move to a transformation that will produce the AI ecosystems, which will not become invasions of the local culture of the territory, but will be reconciled with the linguistic diversity of this group of people, as well as its humanist values. This is how the region shall be the model of responsible, inclusive, and responsible AI in learning and reconciliation, integrating innovation with morals and living identity for the rest of the world.

REFERENCES

Adly, A. A. (2020). On the quest for economic prosperity: A higher education strategic perspective for the MENA region. *arXiv preprint arXiv:2009.14408.*

Alnaqbi, A. M. A., & Yassin, A. M. (2021). Current status, challenges, and strategies of artificial intelligence and e-learning in the UAE military education system. *International journal of sustainable construction engineering and technology, 12*(3), 352-361.

Alotaibi, N. S., & Alshehri, A. H. (2023). Prospers and obstacles in using artificial intelligence in Saudi Arabia higher education institutions—The potential of AI-based learning outcomes. *Sustainability, 15*(13), 10723.

Ateeq, A., Alzoraiki, M., Milhem, M., Beshr, B. A. H., & Al Meer, S. (2024). Does Information Communication Technology Has Influence on Quality University Education on Gulf University: Literature Review. *The AI Revolution: Driving Business Innovation and Research, 1*, 565–574.

Ayed, I. A. H. (2022). *Oman higher education institutions dealing with artificial intelligence* (Doctoral dissertation, Universidade do Minho (Portugal)).

Chen, L., Chen, P., & Lin, Z. (2020). Artificial intelligence in education: A review. *IEEE Access : Practical Innovations, Open Solutions, 8*, 75264–75278.

Chen, X., Xie, H., Zou, D., & Hwang, G. J. (2020). Application and theory gaps during the rise of artificial intelligence in education. *Computers and Education: Artificial Intelligence, 1*, 100002.

Chen, X., Zou, D., Xie, H., Cheng, G., & Liu, C. (2022). Two decades of artificial intelligence in education. *Journal of Educational Technology & Society, 25*(1), 28–47.

Demaidi, M. N. (2025). Artificial intelligence national strategy in a developing country. *AI & Society, 40*(2), 423–435.

El-Kassas, M., Khalifa, R., Medhat, M. A., Yilmaz, Y., Tumi, A., Labidi, A., & AlNaamani, K. M. (2025). Mapping artificial intelligence adoption in hepatology practice and research: Challenges and opportunities in MENA region. *Frontiers in Medicine, 12*, 1630831. PMID: 41020250

Fadlelmula, F. K., & Qadhi, S. M. (2024). A systematic review of research on artificial intelligence in higher education: Practice, gaps, and future directions in the GCC. *Journal of University Teaching & Learning Practice, 21*(6), 146–173.

Gocen, A., & Aydemir, F. (2020). Artificial intelligence in education and schools. *Research on Education and Media*, *12*(1), 13–21.

Gutierrez Jr, R. (2024). Ethical Horizons in AI: Navigating Opportunities and Upholding Values in the MENA Landscape. *Volume (2). Mağalla al-Nūr li-l-dirāsāt al-insāniyya .. doi:. v2*, (4).DOI: <ALIGNMENT.qj></ALIGNMENT>10.69513/jnfh

Hamed, A. E., & Ismael, B. B. (2024). AI-Driven Opportunistic Learning: Enhancing Personalized Educational Experiences for Arab Learners in the MENA Region. *Journal of Scientific Development for Studies and Research (JSD), 5*(20), 206_225-206_225.

Holmes, W. (2020). Artificial intelligence in education. In *Encyclopedia of education and information technologies* (pp. 88–103). Springer International Publishing.

Holmes, W., Porayska-Pomsta, K., Holstein, K., Sutherland, E., Baker, T., Shum, S. B., & Koedinger, K. R. (2022). Ethics of AI in education: Towards a community-wide framework. *International Journal of Artificial Intelligence in Education*, *32*(3), 504–526.

Hwang, G. J., Xie, H., Wah, B. W., & Gašević, D. (2020). Vision, challenges, roles and research issues of Artificial Intelligence in Education. *Computers and Education: Artificial Intelligence*, *1*, 100001.

Kamalov, F., Santandreu Calonge, D., & Gurrib, I. (2023). New era of artificial intelligence in education: Towards a sustainable multifaceted revolution. *Sustainability*, *15*(16), 12451.

Khosravi, H., Shum, S. B., Chen, G., Conati, C., Tsai, Y. S., Kay, J., ... & Gašević, D. (2022). Explainable artificial intelligence in education. *Computers and education: artificial intelligence, 3*, 100074.

Knox, J. (2020). Artificial intelligence and education in China. *Learning, Media and Technology*, *45*(3), 298–311.

Lampou, R. (2023). The integration of artificial intelligence in education: Opportunities and challenges. *Review of Artificial Intelligence in Education*, *4*, e15–e15.

Nurunnabi, M., Mitchell, C., Koubaa, A., & Hoke, T. (2023). *Sustainable Development Goals and AI integration into Curricula in the MENA Region. Report*. Prince Sultan University.

Ouyang, F., & Jiao, P. (2021). Artificial intelligence in education: The three paradigms. *Computers and Education: Artificial Intelligence*, *2*, 100020.

Pedro, F., Subosa, M., Rivas, A., & Valverde, P. (2019). Artificial intelligence in education: Challenges and opportunities for sustainable development.

Roll, I., & Wylie, R. (2016). Evolution and revolution in artificial intelligence in education. *International Journal of Artificial Intelligence in Education*, *26*(2), 582–599.

Salah, R. M., Alves, G. R., & Guerreiro, P. (2014, February). Reshaping higher education systems in the MENA region: The contribution of remote and virtual labs. In *2014 11th International Conference on Remote Engineering and Virtual Instrumentation (REV)* (pp. 240-245). IEEE.

Trigui, H., Guerfali, F., Harigua-Souiai, E., Qasrawi, R., Atri, C., Sokhn, E. S., & Znaidi, S. (2024). Exploring AI governance in the Middle East and North Africa (MENA) region: Gaps, efforts, and initiatives. *Data & Policy*, *6*, e83.

Chapter 4
Embedding Wellbeing and Ethics in Educational AI:
The AI-CARE Framework for MENA Contexts

Emre Uygun
http://orcid.org/0000-0003-2027-4394
School of Foreign Languages, Bursa Uludağ University, Turkey

ABSTRACT

Artificial Intelligence (AI) is reshaping higher education, enabling personalization, efficiency, and innovation. Yet its impact on the psychological, social, and ethical wellbeing of students and educators remains underexamined, especially in rapidly evolving regions like the Middle East and North Africa (MENA). This chapter introduces the AI-CARE Framework, a multidimensional model for ethically and wellbeing-centered AI integration in education. Its six dimensions (Agency & Autonomy, Inclusive Design, Compassionate Integration, Adaptive Wellbeing Support, Resilience Building, and Ethical Governance) draw on education, psychology, and technology ethics to explain how AI affects human flourishing. The framework identifies causal pathways, contextual factors, and practical tools such as the AI-CARE Scorecard to support implementation and research. By centering wellbeing in AI design and governance, the AI-CARE Framework offers a roadmap for healthier, fairer, and more sustainable learning ecosystems globally and in MENA.

DOI: 10.4018/979-8-3373-6776-7.ch004

INTRODUCTION

Artificial intelligence (AI) is rapidly reshaping global education, changing how students learn, how educators teach, and how institutions operate. By 2024, over 80% of educational organizations had adopted some form of generative AI, representing the highest uptake across major sectors (World Economic Forum, 2025). These developments are often framed in terms of personalization, efficiency, and expanded access. Yet critical scholarship cautions that these promises are not neutral: AI can intensify surveillance, reproduce social inequities, and reorient educational priorities toward optimization and data extraction rather than care and human development (Benjamin, 2019; Crawford, 2021; Kwet, 2019). As UNESCO (2023) notes, AI's impact therefore extends beyond academic outcomes and into the ethical, social, and emotional dimensions of education.

Wellbeing in education concerns the emotional, social, and psychological flourishing of both learners and educators, not only cognitive achievement (Collie, 2023; Curren et al., 2024). Research consistently links positive mental health, engagement, and supportive relationships with academic success and long-term development. At the same time, learning environments dominated by efficiency, competition, and continuous monitoring can erode autonomy, trust, and relational quality (Deci & Ryan, 2000; Seligman, 2011). These tensions become sharper in AI-mediated systems, where algorithmic feedback and data-driven decision-making can support personalization while also generating stress, dependency, uncertainty, or loss of agency. Recent studies highlight this ambivalence in students' everyday experiences: AI-enabled convenience and responsiveness may co-occur with heightened anxiety, reduced trust, or feelings of being monitored when systems are opaque or evaluative in tone (Giannakos et al., 2024; Selwyn, 2022).

These dynamics are particularly pronounced in the Middle East and North Africa (MENA), where rapid digital expansion intersects with uneven infrastructure, diverse governance arrangements, and significant demographic pressures. Empirical studies indicate that, alongside growing adoption, both educators and students express concerns about privacy, fairness, surveillance, and professional autonomy (Alnsour et al., 2025; Liebherr et al., 2025). Across these contexts, two tensions are especially consequential: surveillance versus agency, and efficiency versus well-being. This chapter centers these tensions as the key problem space in which AI's educational value and harm are negotiated.

CONCEPTUAL GAP AND SIGNIFICANCE

This chapter proceeds from a simple diagnosis: the literatures most influential in AI adoption and the literatures most relevant to wellbeing often develop in parallel. Much AI-in-education research remains oriented toward efficiency, scalability, and performance optimization, with emphasis on learning analytics, automation, and productivity gains (Luckin et al., 2016; Mustafa et al., 2024; Williamson & Eynon, 2020). In parallel, AI ethics has tended to foreground high-level principles such as transparency, fairness, and accountability, but often without sustained engagement with day-to-day learning and teaching experiences (Floridi et al., 2018; Jobin et al., 2019; Uygun, 2026; Yan et al., 2025). By contrast, educational wellbeing research foregrounds psychological, relational, and occupational dimensions of learning and teaching, but has only recently begun to examine how AI systems reshape these experiences in practice (Collie, 2023; Curren et al., 2024; Seligman, 2011). As a result, many existing AI-in-education and AI ethics frameworks under-theorize educator wellbeing, implementation-level conditions, and the lived realities of AI-mediated education, especially in non-Western and resource-constrained contexts (Abdelnour-Nocera et al., 2021; Selwyn, 2022). The gap is visible in the limited attention to how students experience AI in daily learning, including trust, anxiety, motivation, and perceptions of surveillance.

The AI-CARE Framework addresses this gap by repositioning wellbeing as a central design and governance concern in AI adoption rather than a secondary outcome or ethical add-on. Unlike efficiency-oriented approaches that prioritize optimization, prediction, or personalization at scale, AI-CARE foregrounds human agency, inclusion, compassion, adaptability, resilience, and ethical governance as interdependent conditions shaping both student and educator wellbeing. These dimensions draw on established wellbeing and organizational theories (Bakker & Demerouti, 2017; Baxter & Sommerville, 2011; Deci & Ryan, 2000) while integrating critical scholarship that explains how surveillance, datafication, and professional devaluation can emerge from AI-enabled institutional logics (Benjamin, 2019; Crawford, 2021; Kwet, 2019). The framework is also designed for context sensitivity, particularly in MENA, where digital expansion can outpace governance capacity and professional support structures (Baytiyeh, 2022; Saqr et al., 2023).

For clarity, this chapter adopts a broad definition of AI encompassing generative systems (for example, conversational agents and content-generation tools) and non-generative educational applications (for example, predictive analytics, adaptive tutoring, and automated assessment). Where relevant, distinctions between these categories are noted, particularly in relation to autonomy, trust, academic integrity, and wellbeing (Giannakos et al., 2024; Klimova & Pikhart, 2025). AI-CARE is intended as a diagnostic and theory-building tool rather than a validated explanatory model. It supports hypothesis generation, informs procurement and governance decisions, and enables educators to reflect critically on classroom-level AI adoption. Rather than assuming that AI inherently promotes human flourishing, the framework specifies conditions under which AI may support or undermine wellbeing for learners and educators. The chapter is guided by three questions:

(1) Which AI design and governance features most effectively foster well-being in education?
(2) Through what mechanisms do these features exert influence?
(3) Under what conditions are positive outcomes most likely to occur?

CONCEPTUAL BACKGROUND

This section clarifies how wellbeing is understood in education, why AI changes the wellbeing problem, and why MENA contexts make implementation conditions especially consequential. Drawing on education, psychology, ethics, and policy, the AI-CARE Framework positions wellbeing as an organizing principle for AI integration in higher education, particularly in systems experiencing rapid transformation where innovation pressures can outpace governance, support, and capacity (UNESCO, 2021; World Economic Forum, 2025).

Wellbeing in Education

In educational research, wellbeing is increasingly conceptualized as multidimensional, encompassing emotional, psychological, and relational dimensions of lived experience rather than merely the absence of distress (Curren et al., 2024; Oades et al., 2011). For students, wellbeing is closely associated with motivation, engagement, persistence, and long-term life satisfaction, and is commonly theorized through PERMA and Self-Determination Theory (Deci & Ryan, 2000; Seligman, 2011). Empirical evidence links autonomy, competence, and relatedness to sustained engagement and academic success, including in higher education (Jeno et al., 2019; Li, 2025).

At the same time, wellbeing research highlights boundary conditions that matter for AI. Institutional environments that prioritize performance metrics, efficiency, and continuous monitoring may achieve short-term gains while undermining autonomy, trust, and relational quality, thereby eroding wellbeing over time (Larcombe et al., 2021). These dynamics become more consequential when digital systems amplify technocratic logics that privilege measurable outputs over educational experience and meaning-making.

Educator wellbeing is shaped by the balance between professional demands and available resources. It is increasingly treated as a determinant of instructional quality, retention, and classroom climate, not as an individual resilience issue (Collie, 2023; Sokal et al., 2020). Rapid digital transformation, when weakly supported by training, governance, and institutional dialogue, can intensify emotional labor and technostress, particularly in higher education settings (Dreer, 2023).

AI and Wellbeing

AI systems now permeate higher education through adaptive learning platforms, intelligent tutoring systems, predictive analytics, and automated assessment tools (Merino-Campos, 2025; Mustafa et al., 2024). While these technologies can support personalization and administrative efficiency, growing evidence highlights risks linked to surveillance, opacity, data bias, and diminished human agency (Williamson & Eynon, 2020; Yan et al., 2025). From a wellbeing perspective, these risks are structurally tied to design choices, governance arrangements, and how systems are embedded in institutional practices, not merely to technical performance.

Recent research foregrounds students' lived experiences of AI-mediated learning and repeatedly shows ambivalence. Students often report convenience, faster feedback, and perceived support, yet also describe anxiety, reduced trust, and feelings of being monitored when algorithmic processes are opaque or experienced as evaluative rather than assistive (Giannakos et al., 2024; Klimova & Pikhart, 2025; Selwyn, 2022). Uncertainty about how data are collected and used, and whether systems can be questioned or contested, can weaken motivation and psychological safety, particularly when AI is positioned as authoritative or punitive (Yan et al., 2025). These findings indicate that wellbeing outcomes depend as much on interpretation and perceived intent as on system functionality.

These tensions are pronounced in MENA, where higher education systems operate under heterogeneous conditions of infrastructure, regulatory maturity, and professional support. Some contexts have strong policy investment and technological capacity, while others face fragmented governance, limited faculty preparation, and uneven access to digital resources, increasing the likelihood of technostress and inequitable outcomes for students and educators (Abdelnour-Nocera et al., 2021; Baytiyeh, 2022; Saqr et al., 2023). Weak or uneven data protection regimes further heighten the psychological stakes of AI deployment at scale, especially where students have limited avenues to question or contest algorithmic decisions.

At the global level, frameworks such as Sustainable Development Goal 4 and UNESCO's Recommendation on the Ethics of Artificial Intelligence emphasize inclusive, equitable, and human-centered education, linking technological innovation to wellbeing, dignity, and agency (UNESCO, 2021, 2023). Complementary initiatives, including the OECD Learning Compass 2030, foreground learner agency, emotional health, and social connectedness as core educational outcomes (OECD, n.d.; Schleicher, 2020). AI-CARE builds on these commitments by translating them into an analytic lens for examining how AI systems shape student and educator wellbeing in practice, particularly in rapidly evolving contexts such as MENA..

THEORETICAL FOUNDATIONS

The AI-CARE Framework is grounded in interdisciplinary theories spanning psychology, education, occupational wellbeing, ethics, and sociotechnical systems thinking. Together, these perspectives share a central premise: AI is neither inherently supportive nor inherently detrimental to wellbeing; its effects depend on design, governance, and institutional embedding. Critical AI scholarship strengthens this premise by conceptualizing AI systems as sociotechnical arrangements shaped by power, surveillance, and extraction dynamics rather than neutral tools (Benjamin, 2019; Crawford, 2021; Kwet, 2019). This critical lens motivates AI-CARE's emphasis on ethical governance, agency, and institutional accountability, and it is especially salient in MENA, where uneven infrastructure and evolving regulatory frameworks can amplify both promise and risk.

Positive psychology provides a foundational wellbeing lens through Seligman's (2011) PERMA model, which conceptualizes flourishing in terms of Positive Emotion, Engagement, Relationships, Meaning, and Accomplishment. These domains inform AI-CARE's emphasis on compassionate integration and resilience building by clarifying what "supporting wellbeing" should mean beyond achievement. AI may contribute by supporting engagement through adaptive learning, strengthening accomplishment via formative feedback, and facilitating relationships through timely communication. However, research on optimization and surveillance cultures cautions that continuous monitoring, behavioral nudging, and performance analytics can undermine intrinsic motivation and relational depth, producing alienation rather than flourishing (Crawford, 2021; Kern et al., 2015). In MENA contexts characterized by large cohorts and assessment-driven pedagogies, PERMA therefore foregrounds a condition: wellbeing gains depend on whether AI designs preserve meaningful human interaction rather than replacing it with monitoring and compliance.

Self-Determination Theory further anchors AI-CARE's emphasis on agency and autonomy by identifying autonomy, competence, and relatedness as core psychological needs (Deci & Ryan, 2000). AI-mediated environments can support these needs through flexible pacing, formative feedback, and collaborative tools. Yet SDT also clarifies boundary conditions: AI that prescribes rigid pathways, obscures decision-making, or displaces human judgment can undermine autonomy and relatedness.

These risks are more likely under top-down or vendor-driven implementations that prioritize scalability over pedagogical agency (Benjamin, 2019; Kwet, 2019), and they can be intensified in MENA institutions with limited capacity for local adaptation (Jeno et al., 2019).

Educator wellbeing is further illuminated through the Job Demands–Resources (JD–R) model, which conceptualizes wellbeing as a balance between occupational demands and available supports (Bakker & Demerouti, 2017). This perspective underpins AI-CARE's attention to workload, emotional labor, professional identity, and long-term sustainability. AI can function as a resource when it reduces administrative workload or supports instructional decision-making, but it can become a demand when it intensifies surveillance, accelerates performance expectations, or requires continuous adaptation without adequate training. Beyond workload, AI-mediated teaching can reshape educators' sense of purpose and professional identity by repositioning teachers as interpreters of algorithmic outputs and managers of system-driven expectations. Critical political-economy analyses connect these shifts to wider datafication and accountability regimes that reconfigure educators' roles and relational work (Benjamin, 2019; Crawford, 2021). In several MENA higher education systems, rapid digitalization has outpaced governance and professional development, contributing to technostress and heightened emotional labor (Collie, 2023; Dreer, 2023).

Ethical foundations within AI-CARE draw on human-centered AI principles emphasizing transparency, accountability, fairness, and meaningful human oversight (Shneiderman, 2020; UNESCO, 2021; Uygun, 2026). From a wellbeing perspective, these principles are protective infrastructure: opaque algorithms, biased datasets, and fully automated high-stakes decisions can erode trust, heighten anxiety, and marginalize vulnerable groups, especially where data protection and enforcement are weak. Across much of MENA, ethical governance therefore functions as a boundary condition that determines whether AI adoption supports wellbeing or reproduces inequity (Kwet, 2019).

Finally, sociotechnical and ecological systems perspectives underscore that AI's effects emerge through interaction with institutional cultures, leadership practices, infrastructure, and policy environments rather than technical features alone (Baxter & Sommerville, 2011; Bronfenbrenner, 1979). This systems lens supports AI-CARE's integrative architecture and its focus on implementation context. It also clarifies why vendor dependence and global AI markets can constrain institutional autonomy, particularly in Global South contexts (Crawford, 2021). AI may reinforce coherent teaching and learning strategies in well-resourced universities, while producing fragmented implementation and unintended harms in under-resourced or conflict-affected settings.

Taken together, these theoretical perspectives position AI's relationship to wellbeing as contingent rather than deterministic. By integrating wellbeing-oriented theories with critical AI scholarship, the AI-CARE Framework provides a theoretically grounded and explicitly conditional account of how AI may contribute to, or detract from, human flourishing in higher education.

THE AI-CARE FRAMEWORK

Before detailing the six dimensions of the AI-CARE Framework, it is necessary to calibrate their evidentiary status and associated risks. Although each dimension is grounded in established theory and supported by selected empirical findings, the current evidence base remains uneven, context dependent, and in several areas contested (Giannakos et al., 2024; Klimova & Pikhart, 2025). Accordingly, AI-CARE should be read as a theory-building and diagnostic framework rather than a validated explanatory model.

This section does three things to strengthen the framework's analytic clarity. First, it distinguishes short-term from long-term wellbeing effects. Second, it links recurring implementation challenges to specific AI-CARE dimensions so that the framework can be used diagnostically. Third, it summarizes where evidence is stronger or weaker, and why those differences matter in practice.

Wellbeing effects should be considered across time horizons. In the short term, AI may influence stress, anxiety, perceived support, and engagement. Over longer periods, however, AI can shape learners' self-regulation and autonomy trajectories, including the risk of dependency on automated feedback or decision-support and the gradual displacement of self-monitoring, planning, and reflection by system prompts. From this perspective, AI-CARE treats autonomy not only as immediate perceived choice but also as sustained capacity to regulate learning over time, which is central to online learning success and can be measured through established self-regulation instruments (Broadbent et al., 2023). This distinction also clarifies why efficiency gains are an insufficient proxy for flourishing: reducing short-term friction can still undermine long-term agency if it externalizes core regulatory processes.

To make the framework's explanatory logic more explicit, recurring implementation challenges can be mapped onto the six dimensions. Opaque recommendations and automation overreach primarily implicate Agency & Autonomy and Ethical Governance (Shneiderman, 2020; UNESCO, 2021). Bias amplification and linguistic misrecognition implicate Inclusive Design and Ethical Governance (Mehrabi et al., 2022). Surveillance creep and labeling harm implicate Ethical Governance and can also weaken Compassionate Integration by eroding trust and psychological safety (Selwyn, 2022; Williamson & Hogan, 2020). Redistributed emotional labor and relational repair work implicate Compassionate Integration and Resilience Building, since educators are often expected to stabilize student emotions after AI-mediated decisions (Dreer, 2023; Jennings & Greenberg, 2009). These mappings are not exclusive. Their purpose is diagnostic: they clarify which dimensions should be foregrounded when a particular risk dominates, and which cross-dimensional safeguards must be activated.

Empirical support is strongest for agency-supportive and inclusive design principles. Research grounded in Self-Determination Theory and Universal Design for Learning consistently links autonomy support, accessibility, and perceived fairness to higher engagement, reduced anxiety, and improved wellbeing (Allen et al., 2018; Deci & Ryan, 2000; Korpershoek et al., 2019; Zheng et al., 2022). However, these effects are sensitive to implementation conditions: AI systems introduced through top-down mandates or opaque, vendor-driven deployments may undermine agency and trust despite personalization features (Saqr et al., 2023; Williamson & Eynon, 2020). A key long-term risk is autonomy drift: learners may initially feel supported by continuous guidance, yet gradually shift from self-regulated learning toward compliance with system cues, especially when feedback is instantaneous, authoritative, and difficult to contest.

Compassionate integration and resilience-building dimensions are supported by emerging but limited evidence. Studies suggest that empathetic communication, supportive feedback, and growth-oriented framing can reduce academic stress and foster persistence (Jennings & Greenberg, 2009; Killingback et al., 2024; Yeager & Dweck, 2012). Yet uncertainties remain regarding scalability, authenticity, and the redistribution of educators' emotional labor when these functions are mediated by AI (Acton & Glasgow, 2015; Dreer, 2023). A future-facing concern is that as automation expands, relational work can become increasingly invisible but still required: teachers may be tasked with legitimizing outputs, mediating disputes, and restoring trust after perceived misclassification or unfairness, even if they had no role in procurement or model configuration.

The most contested domain concerns adaptive wellbeing support and affect-sensitive AI. While affective computing demonstrates technical feasibility (D'Mello & Kory, 2015), substantial risks persist, including misclassification, surveillance creep, labeling harms, and privacy violations, particularly when emotional data are interpreted without sufficient contextual or cultural grounding (Selwyn, 2022; Tarafdar et al., 2019). These risks are amplified in settings with weak governance or limited support infrastructures, including parts of the MENA region (Baytiyeh, 2022; Saqr et al., 2023). Beyond immediate harms, affect-sensitive interventions may also influence long-term self-regulation by replacing learner-initiated coping strategies with system-triggered nudges, potentially weakening autonomy if learners become reliant on external prompts for emotion regulation.

Across all dimensions, ethical governance functions as cross-cutting infrastructure rather than a standalone solution. Evidence suggests that transparency, human oversight, and participatory governance can mitigate anxiety and enhance trust (Floridi et al., 2018; Jobin et al., 2019), yet their effectiveness is constrained by vendor power, data sovereignty challenges, and regulatory capacity. Where AI systems are shaped by global commercial priorities rather than local pedagogical and wellbeing goals, even well-designed features may fail to deliver intended benefits (Abdelnour-Nocera et al., 2021; Crawford, 2021; Kwet, 2019). Ethical governance should therefore be treated as longitudinal infrastructure: it requires monitoring for function creep, periodic auditing, and revision of institutional policies as systems evolve and automation pressures increase.

Overall, the AI-CARE dimensions represent plausible but conditional pathways. Analytically, they operate as interdependent layers: design conditions (Agency & Autonomy, Inclusive Design), relational-pedagogical conditions (Compassionate Integration, Resilience Building), high-risk support functions (Adaptive Wellbeing Support), and enabling safeguards (Ethical Governance). Their wellbeing effects depend on design choices, implementation contexts, governance arrangements, and the lived experiences of learners and educators, both in the short term and as patterns of dependence, self-regulation, and professional role reconfiguration accumulate over time. The sections that follow elaborate each dimension with these evidentiary limits, time horizons, and risks in view.

Agency & Autonomy

Agency and autonomy refer to the ability of learners and educators to exercise meaningful control over educational processes, including setting learning goals, selecting topics, adjusting pacing, and choosing instructional strategies. This dimension draws on Self-Determination Theory, which identifies autonomy as one of three basic psychological needs that contribute to intrinsic motivation, wellbeing, and engagement (Deci & Ryan, 2000; Howard et al., 2021). In the context of AI in higher education, autonomy-supportive technologies uphold human-centered principles by ensuring that final decision-making authority remains with human users rather than automated systems (Shneiderman, 2020; UNESCO, 2021).

In AI-mediated learning environments, perceived control can reduce helplessness and support alignment between study behaviors and personal goals. For example, adaptive platforms that offer students multiple pathways toward course objectives, rather than a single optimized route, can preserve choice, especially in multilingual classrooms where learners may need different pacing and representations (Baytiyeh, 2022; Saqr et al., 2023). However, autonomy is also a developmental capability: if AI provides constant micro-corrections and prescriptive next steps, learners may come to outsource planning, self-checking, and error diagnosis, increasing long-term dependency on automated feedback and weakening self-regulated learning habits (Broadbent et al., 2023). AI-CARE therefore treats autonomy as both choice now and capacity over time.

From a learner perspective, this tension is often experienced affectively. Some students interpret structured prompts and guided pathways as supportive, reducing anxiety and uncertainty. Others experience persistent nudging and progress tracking as pressure or covert surveillance. Over time, these experiences can shift motivation from self-directed goal setting toward compliance with algorithmic signals, complicating the development of durable learner autonomy.

For educators, maintaining agency means having the ability to accept, modify, or reject AI-generated recommendations, and to justify that discretion within institutional accountability regimes. A concrete example is an early-alert dashboard that flags at-risk students: agency-supportive use would allow instructors to review the basis of the flag, contextualize it with local knowledge, and decide whether and how to intervene, rather than being pressured to follow automated scripts. This balance is especially crucial in MENA systems where high workloads and limited professional development can make defaulting to the tool feel inevitable (Abdelnour-Nocera et al., 2021). When autonomy is protected, AI can remain an assistive resource rather than a directive authority.

To summarize, the following propositions guide how agency and autonomy contribute to wellbeing in AI-integrated educational systems:

- **P1.** AI that offers learners meaningful choice in task selection, sequencing, or pacing enhances intrinsic motivation, engagement, and wellbeing, and is more likely to support autonomy development over time than systems that rely on prescriptive pathways.
- **P2.** Instructor control over AI-generated outputs, including the ability to modify, reject, or contextualize recommendations, promotes professional satisfaction and mitigates burnout, particularly when automation pressures intensify.

Inclusive Design

Inclusive design refers to the intentional creation of AI-powered educational tools that are accessible, equitable, and responsive to the diverse needs, identities, and circumstances of learners and educators. Grounded in the Universal Design for Learning (UDL) framework, it emphasizes multiple modes of engagement, representation, and expression to reduce learning barriers and expand participation (CAST, 2018). In higher education, inclusive design contributes directly to psychological wellbeing by signaling recognition, fairness, and belonging, outcomes linked to persistence and social-emotional adjustment (Allen et al., 2018; Korpershoek et al., 2019).

AI technologies can support inclusive pedagogy when accessibility and fairness are embedded into system design rather than treated as afterthoughts. For instance, captioning and transcription tools can reduce language-related anxiety in multilingual cohorts, while adjustable feedback formats can support neurodiverse learners. Yet inclusion is also where long-term harms can accumulate: systematic misrecognition, such as persistent errors in Arabic varieties or dialectal inputs, can gradually erode trust and belonging, shifting students from struggling with a task to feeling excluded by the system, with downstream effects on engagement and retention (Baytiyeh, 2022; Saqr et al., 2023). In AI-CARE terms, these are not merely usability issues; they are wellbeing risks mediated through belonging and identity-relevant participation.

Inclusive design also requires explicit attention to gendered and linguistic inequities reproduced through AI systems. Critical AI scholarship shows that bias embedded in training data or interaction design can disadvantage marginalized groups and normalize inequitable academic norms (Benjamin, 2019; Mehrabi et al., 2022; Selwyn, 2022). When global vendors prioritize standardization, institutions may inherit defaults that misfit local pedagogies unless they actively audit, localize, and co-design with stakeholders (Crawford, 2021; Kwet, 2019; Williamson & Hogan, 2020). Under AI-CARE, the challenge-to-dimension link is direct: bias amplification and misrecognition primarily implicate Inclusive Design, but governance determines whether these issues are detectable, contestable, and correctable.

To guide future research and practice, the following propositions articulate how inclusive design in AI systems can support wellbeing in higher education:

- **P3.** AI systems incorporating UDL-aligned features, such as adaptive content delivery, multimodal feedback, and linguistic accessibility, help narrow participation gaps and increase students' sense of belonging.
- **P4.** Students' perceptions of AI systems as fair, inclusive, and accessible predict lower academic anxiety and higher overall satisfaction with their educational experience.

Compassionate Integration

Compassionate integration refers to the deliberate incorporation of empathy and emotional awareness into the design, implementation, and function of AI systems in education. Grounded in compassionate pedagogy, it emphasizes recognizing distress, responding with care, and cultivating holistic wellbeing (Killingback et al., 2024). This approach aligns with PERMA's relational emphasis (Seligman, 2011) and with the Job Demands–Resources model, which treats social support as protective against burnout (Bakker & Demerouti, 2017). When AI systems communicate with warmth and respect, they may reduce cognitive load and mitigate stress. Yet compassion must be evaluated as a sociotechnical claim, not a stylistic feature: empathetic phrasing may feel supportive in the short term while still operating inside monitoring and compliance infrastructures that undermine trust and dignity.

In higher education, practical applications include chatbots that respond to routine questions using supportive language, or systems that flag disengagement and trigger outreach. A concrete example is a chatbot reminding a student about missed deadlines: a compassionate design would acknowledge difficulty, provide options, and route the student to human support rather than escalating immediately to punitive workflows. Such tools can be valuable in resource-constrained settings where student services are limited. However, AI-CARE emphasizes a relational risk: compassion features can become a veneer if students perceive that care is primarily a mechanism for monitoring or performance control, which can intensify anxiety rather than reduce it (Selwyn, 2022; Williamson & Hogan, 2020).

While AI may reduce certain administrative demands, it does not eliminate emotional labor; it often redistributes it. Educators remain responsible for interpreting outputs, managing student reactions to automated feedback, and repairing trust when algorithmic decisions are perceived as unfair. Over time, this can reposition teachers as the human buffer for automation, especially when AI is scaled primarily for efficiency (Dreer, 2023; Jennings & Greenberg, 2009).

The following propositions outline how compassionate integration can enhance wellbeing in educational settings:

- **P5.** AI tutors that use explicitly empathetic responses can reduce academic anxiety and increase perceived support compared to neutral systems, but only when compassion is not paired with coercive monitoring or punitive escalation.
- **P6.** Offloading routine tasks to AI can increase instructor time available for mentoring and reduce emotional exhaustion, unless the implementation shifts additional relational repair work onto educators without recognition or support.

Adaptive Wellbeing Support

Adaptive wellbeing support refers to AI systems that sense learners' emotional or cognitive states and respond with timely, personalized interventions. This concept is rooted in affective computing, which recognizes that emotions shape attention, memory, motivation, and performance (D'Mello & Kory, 2015). When applied carefully, adaptive AI may sustain engagement and reduce overload. However, AI-CARE treats affect-sensitive support as high risk: misclassification and surveillance creep can produce psychological harm, and frequent nudging can externalize self-regulation if learners come to depend on system prompts to manage focus and stress (Selwyn, 2022; Tarafdar et al., 2019).

For some learners, such systems are experienced as supportive scaffolds, while others perceive the same interventions as intrusive monitoring that heightens anxiety rather than alleviating it. Examples include tutoring platforms that adjust difficulty after detecting frustration, or wellbeing assistants that suggest breaks during prolonged study sessions. A more contentious example is systems that infer distress from engagement traces and recommend mental health resources. Even when well-intended, such interventions can blur boundaries between learning analytics and psychological monitoring, particularly in contexts without strong governance and consent infrastructure (Williamson & Hogan, 2020). AI-CARE therefore links this dimension tightly to Ethical Governance: adaptivity without oversight risks converting wellbeing support into surveillance.

The following propositions articulate the potential benefits of adaptive wellbeing features in AI-enhanced education:

- **P7.** Students using affect-adaptive systems may report lower stress and achieve higher mastery compared to those using non-adaptive systems, conditional on robust consent, transparency, and culturally grounded interpretation.
- **P8.** Personalized wellbeing nudges can support anxiety regulation and completion, but designs should avoid creating long-term dependency on external prompts by gradually scaffolding learners toward self-initiated regulation (see Broadbent et al., 2023).

Resilience Building

Resilience building through AI involves leveraging technology to help students and educators persist through challenges, adapt to setbacks, and cultivate a growth-oriented mindset. This approach is informed by growth mindset theory, which emphasizes that framing mistakes as learning opportunities supports perseverance and self-efficacy (Dweck, 2006; Yeager & Dweck, 2012). The Job Demands–Resources model similarly notes that developing personal resources reduces burnout and promotes engagement (Xanthopoulou et al., 2007). In AI-CARE, resilience is treated as a long-term capability shaped by how learners interpret difficulty, sustain effort, and regulate strategies during extended learning trajectories.

In practice, resilience-promoting AI features might include scaffolded retries, reflective prompts after errors, and feedback that highlights progress rather than only deficits. A writing assistant, for example, can support resilience if it makes revision a visible process and prompts the learner to explain what changed and why, instead of merely providing a corrected answer. AI-CARE also flags a future risk: overly smooth automation can remove productive struggle, narrowing opportunities to develop perseverance and independent problem-solving. Resilience-building therefore requires calibrated assistance that supports effort without replacing it.

To guide implementation and research, the following propositions are proposed:

- **P9.** Safe-failure environments with scaffolded retries increase persistence and transfer compared to always-easy or unsupported-failure conditions.
- **P10.** Regular AI-prompted error reflection can increase academic self-efficacy and adaptive attributions over time, especially when prompts promote metacognitive explanation rather than answer provision.

Ethical Governance

Ethical governance ensures that the development, deployment, and monitoring of AI systems in education align with principles of transparency, accountability, equity, and meaningful human oversight. These values are central to human-centered AI approaches (Shneiderman, 2020) and articulated in UNESCO's Recommendation on the Ethics of Artificial Intelligence, which explicitly links AI to dignity and wellbeing (UNESCO, 2021). From a wellbeing perspective, ethical governance is protective infrastructure that reduces uncertainty, mitigates technostress, and sustains psychological safety (Floridi et al., 2018; Jobin et al., 2019; Selwyn, 2022).

Concrete strategies for ethical governance include transparent policies, stakeholder participation in procurement and evaluation, meaningful user control over data, and human review mechanisms for high-stakes decisions. For example, plagiarism detection systems that allow students to review flagged outputs, contest results, and engage in dialogic resolution are more likely to sustain trust and reduce anxiety than fully automated enforcement regimes (Selwyn, 2022; Williamson & Hogan, 2020). A second example is predictive analytics for retention: governance safeguards should prevent labeling harm by requiring explainability, appeal routes, and clear limits on how labels can be used in advising or disciplinary contexts (Selwyn, 2022).

Ethical governance also requires explicit attention to vendor dynamics and data sovereignty, particularly in regions where institutional bargaining power and regulatory enforcement are uneven. Critical analyses of datafication show that global vendors shape defaults and evaluative metrics in ways that privilege scalability and commercial efficiency over local pedagogical values (Crawford, 2021; Kwet, 2019). In the MENA region, where governance frameworks may be emergent, reliance on externally developed platforms can heighten risks related to cross-border data extraction and opaque decision-making (Abdelnour-Nocera et al., 2021; Saqr et al., 2023). Ethical governance should therefore be longitudinal (Uygun, 2026): it should include periodic audits, monitoring for function creep, and revision of policies as systems evolve and institutional reliance deepens.

To support these goals, the following propositions are advanced:

- **P11.** Institutions that implement transparent AI policies and involve stakeholders in oversight processes report higher levels of trust and lower AI-related anxiety among students and staff.
- **P12.** Human oversight of AI-supported decisions yields higher perceptions of fairness and lower stress than fully automated decision-making, particularly as automation pressures increase over time.

MODEL DYNAMICS

The AI-CARE Framework operates through interconnected pathways linking its six dimensions to student and educator wellbeing outcomes. These pathways are mediated by psychologically meaningful and context-sensitive mechanisms, most centrally engagement, belonging, workload, and technostress. Critically, AI-CARE treats these mechanisms as experiential and interpretive, not only functional. In other words, the same AI feature can produce different wellbeing effects depending on whether learners and educators experience it as supportive, intrusive, fair, or coercive (Selwyn, 2022; Williamson & Hogan, 2020).

Engagement functions as a key cognitive and affective mediator, reflecting sustained attention, interest, and effort in learning activities (Fredricks et al., 2004). Agency-supportive and inclusive systems can strengthen engagement when they increase perceived control and reduce uncertainty, while compassionate and resilience-oriented designs can sustain engagement by buffering stress and normalizing productive struggle (Deci & Ryan, 2000; Yeager & Dweck, 2012). However, AI-CARE emphasizes a temporal caution: engagement gains achieved through persistent prompting or prescriptive next-step guidance may be fragile if they externalize self-regulation and cultivate long-term reliance on system cues rather than learner-initiated planning and monitoring (Broadbent et al., 2023). In the MENA region, where learners may experience additional external stressors and institutional volatility, engagement-supportive AI can reduce dropout risk, but only when perceived as enabling rather than surveilling.

Belonging, defined as feeling accepted, valued, and connected within the learning environment, is consistently linked to academic persistence and psychological wellbeing (Walton & Cohen, 2011). Within AI-CARE, Inclusive Design and Compassionate Integration are the primary routes through which belonging is strengthened, because they determine whether AI systems communicate respect, fairness, and cultural-linguistic recognition. This is especially salient in multilingual and culturally diverse MENA higher education settings, where misrecognition, biased defaults, or English-centric assumptions can gradually shift student experiences from temporary difficulty to identity-relevant exclusion (Abdelnour-Nocera et al., 2021; Baytiyeh, 2022; Saqr et al., 2023). In AI-CARE terms, belonging is therefore not merely an affective outcome but a pathway through which equity and wellbeing become coupled over time.

Workload captures both perceived and actual demands on learners and educators. AI can reduce workload by automating routine processes, offering timely feedback, or supporting differentiation. Yet AI-CARE treats workload as a sociotechnical variable, shaped by implementation choices rather than the technology alone. Poorly implemented systems can increase workload through training burdens, usability friction, error handling, and the need to justify or repair trust after AI-mediated decisions (Dreer, 2023; Tondeur et al., 2021). For educators, this matters beyond time cost: as automation expands, relational labor can become more central and less visible, with instructors positioned as the human interface responsible for contextualizing algorithmic outputs and managing student reactions. This identity-relevant redistribution of labor helps explain why some efficiency-oriented deployments yield burnout rather than relief, particularly where professional autonomy is limited or accountability pressures are high (Benjamin, 2019; Crawford, 2021). In MENA systems with uneven infrastructure and limited professional development capacity, these risks can be amplified, as adoption is often faster than governance or support structures (Baytiyeh, 2022; Saqr et al., 2023).

Technostress refers to psychological strain associated with digital technologies, including fatigue, anxiety, frustration, and reduced performance (Tarafdar et al., 2019). AI-CARE conceptualizes technostress as partly driven by opacity and loss of control. Systems that are difficult to understand, contest, or opt out of are more likely to generate stress responses than tools experienced as transparent and user-governed (Selwyn, 2022). Ethical Governance mitigates technostress by instituting explainability, appeal routes, and clear boundaries on data use, while Agency & Autonomy reduces technostress by preserving meaningful discretion for students and instructors (Shneiderman, 2020; UNESCO, 2021). Adaptive Wellbeing Support can reduce strain when it scaffolds coping and self-regulation, but it can also intensify technostress when affect-sensitive monitoring is experienced as surveillance or when nudging creates pressure and dependency (Selwyn, 2022; Williamson & Hogan, 2020).

These pathways are shaped by moderators, or boundary conditions that influence the strength, direction, and equity of AI-CARE's effects. Key moderators include digital readiness, prior self-regulation capacity, cultural norms around monitoring and authority, socioeconomic status, infrastructure reliability, language ecology, and professional autonomy (Howard et al., 2021; OECD, 2021). For example, learners in digitally mature environments may benefit more quickly from adaptive systems, whereas students in under-resourced settings may experience the same tools as unstable, exclusionary, or punitive due to connectivity constraints and limited support. Similarly, instructors with high professional agency can integrate AI tools in pedagogically coherent ways, whereas those in rigid accountability environments may be pressured into compliance-oriented uses that undermine trust and wellbeing.

A defining feature of the model is a feedback loop between student and educator wellbeing. When student wellbeing improves, for example through increased belonging or reduced anxiety, instructors may experience fewer conflicts, fewer crisis interventions, and more instructional momentum, which can reduce emotional exhaustion and support professional satisfaction (Jennings & Greenberg, 2009). Conversely, when educator wellbeing is supported, including recognition of relational labor and protection of professional discretion, instructors are better positioned to create psychologically safe learning climates and to interpret AI outputs with contextual sensitivity, thereby strengthening student motivation and belonging. This loop clarifies why AI-CARE rejects trade-off framings that treat efficiency and wellbeing as independently optimizable. Instead, it treats wellbeing as system-level capacity sustained through trust, agency, and relational quality over time.

As illustrated in Figure 1, the six AI-CARE dimensions connect to these mediators as follows:

- Agency & Autonomy primarily strengthens engagement by increasing perceived control and reduces technostress by limiting coercive automation; it can also reduce workload when AI functions as assistive support rather than directive authority (Deci & Ryan, 2000; Zheng et al., 2022).
- Inclusive Design strengthens belonging by reducing exclusionary friction and bias, with longer-term effects on participation and retention; governance determines whether misrecognition and inequities are detectable and correctable (CAST, 2018; Walton & Cohen, 2011).
- Compassionate Integration supports belonging and engagement by making support feel relational rather than punitive; its wellbeing value collapses when "empathy" is layered onto monitoring infrastructures that undermine dignity and trust (Killingback et al., 2024; Selwyn, 2022).
- Adaptive Wellbeing Support can reduce technostress and sustain engagement when it scaffolds coping and self-regulation, but carries elevated risks of surveillance creep and long-term dependency if nudges replace learner-initiated regulation (Broadbent et al., 2023; Tarafdar et al., 2019).

- Resilience Building supports engagement over time by normalizing difficulty and promoting reflective adaptation; it is weakened when automation removes productive struggle and reduces opportunities for independent problem-solving (Yeager & Dweck, 2012).
- Ethical Governance reduces technostress by increasing transparency and contestability and constrains workload escalation by preventing function creep and clarifying responsibility boundaries; it also moderates all other dimensions by setting enforceable limits on data use, vendor power, and automated decision authority (Floridi et al., 2018; Jobin et al., 2019; Kwet, 2019).

Figure 1. AI-CARE Framework for Wellbeing-Centered Education

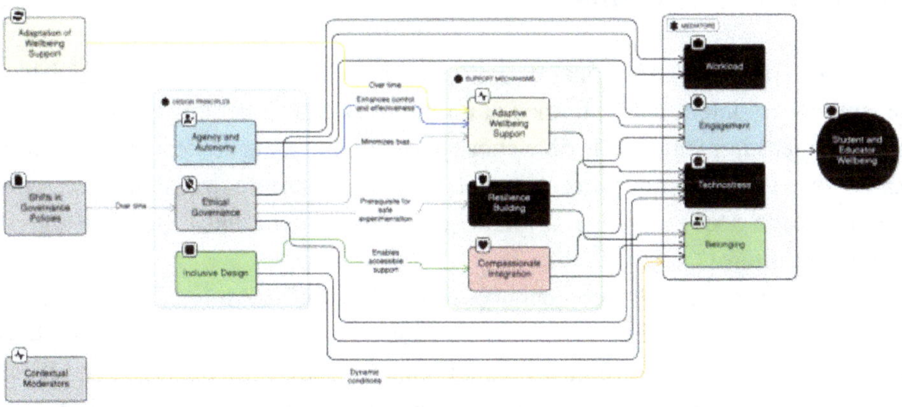

Together, these interactions reinforce a core claim: AI's wellbeing effects in higher education are contingent, cumulative, and mediated through lived experience. The AI-CARE Framework therefore functions as a context-sensitive model for evaluating how AI systems shape engagement, belonging, workload, and technostress across time, including longer-term risks such as autonomy drift, dependency on automated feedback, and the redistribution of educators' relational labor as automation intensifies (Broadbent et al., 2023; Dreer, 2023; Selwyn, 2022).

OPERATIONALIZATION AND MEASUREMENT

Translating the AI-CARE framework into empirical research and institutional evaluation requires careful operationalization that is theoretically coherent, methodologically defensible, and culturally responsive. Because AI-CARE is advanced as a theory-building framework rather than a validated explanatory model, the purpose of operationalization is not to prematurely fix constructs, but to provide plausible, testable indicators that allow researchers and institutions to examine how wellbeing-related mechanisms may function across contexts.

Operationalization within AI-CARE therefore follows three guiding principles. First, instruments are selected based on theoretical alignment with each dimension rather than superficial topical overlap. Second, measurement choices explicitly acknowledge cultural, linguistic, and institutional variation, particularly relevant for MENA contexts. Third, the framework incorporates methodological caution, recognizing that constructs such as autonomy, belonging, or compassion are not culturally invariant and require adaptation rather than direct transfer.

Operational Definitions

Table 1 presents operational definitions for each AI-CARE dimension. These definitions are intentionally framed at a mid-level of abstraction: specific enough to guide measurement, yet flexible enough to accommodate contextual adaptation. Rather than assuming uniform enactment, the definitions foreground *function* (what the dimension does for wellbeing) rather than *form* (how it must appear in a given system or culture).

This approach supports comparative research while avoiding the imposition of culturally narrow interpretations, such as equating autonomy exclusively with individual choice or compassion with emotionally expressive interaction. In MENA higher education settings, for example, autonomy may be enacted through negotiated instructor discretion rather than learner independence, and compassion may be expressed through responsiveness and fairness rather than affective language.

Table 1. Operational Definitions of AI-CARE Dimensions

Dimension	Operational Definition
Agency & Autonomy	The extent to which AI systems enable learners and educators to exercise control over decisions such as learning pathways, pacing, and instructional methods. Emphasizes user choice and decision-making aligned with Self-Determination Theory (Deci & Ryan, 2000; Zheng et al., 2022).
Inclusive Design	The degree to which AI tools integrate features that support accessibility, cultural and linguistic inclusivity, and equitable user engagement. Particularly relevant in multilingual and socioeconomically diverse regions such as MENA (Rose & Dalton, 2009).
Compassionate Integration	The incorporation of empathetic design principles and emotional intelligence in AI-mediated interactions, fostering relational trust and emotional safety in learning environments (Giannakos et al., 2024).

continued on following page

Table 1. Continued

Dimension	Operational Definition
Adaptive Wellbeing Support	The use of AI to detect, respond to, and personalize interventions related to learners' cognitive and emotional states, such as stress mitigation or motivational scaffolding (Klimova & Pikhart, 2025).
Resilience Building	The facilitation of psychological resilience through AI features that normalize failure, promote self-efficacy, and encourage adaptive coping strategies, especially important in high-pressure academic environments (Yeager & Dweck, 2012).
Ethical Governance	The implementation of transparent, fair, and participatory AI systems that safeguard user rights and data, with mechanisms for human oversight and algorithmic accountability (Jobin et al., 2019; Floridi et al., 2018).

Instrument Selection Rationale and Adaptation Logic

The instruments proposed in Table 2 were selected based on three criteria: (1) theoretical congruence with AI-CARE dimensions, (2) prior validation in digital or higher education contexts, and(3) demonstrated adaptability across cultural settings, including non-Western contexts where available.

Importantly, these instruments are not presented as a fixed battery. Rather, they illustrate *measurement families* that correspond to each dimension and can be adapted, shortened, or combined depending on research purpose, institutional constraints, and cultural context.

For example, the Self-Regulation for Learning Online Questionnaire (SRL-O) is recommended not because it measures AI use per se, but because its subscales align with AI-CARE's distinction between short-term support and long-term autonomy development. Similarly, the Teacher Agency Questionnaire is included because it captures ecological dimensions of professional agency, allowing researchers to examine how AI reshapes instructional discretion rather than simply workload.

Cultural and linguistic adaptation is not optional. Constructs such as *belonging*, *care*, or *intimacy* carry different social meanings across educational cultures. In MENA contexts, direct translations of items related to emotional closeness or intimacy may require conceptual reframing (e.g., approachability, fairness, responsiveness) to preserve construct validity while respecting cultural norms. Back-translation, cognitive interviewing, and pilot testing with local stakeholders are therefore essential steps prior to deployment.

Table 2. Suggested Metrics and Instruments for the AI-CARE Framework

Assessed	Suggested Instrument	Adaptability Notes
Student Agency & Self-Regulation	Self-Regulation for Learning Online Questionnaire (SRL-O) – A comprehensive 12-subscale instrument measuring students' motivational beliefs and self-regulated learning strategies in online/blended contexts (Broadent et al. 2023).	Content can be adapted to AI-driven tools (e.g. AI tutors), as it assesses general self-regulatory skills in digital environments.
Educator Autonomy & Agency	Teacher Agency Questionnaire (8-dimensions) – with eight dimensions of teacher professional agency (planning, pedagogy, ICT use, etc.) in ecological context (Leijen et al., 2024).	Can be adapted to measure educators' agency in adopting AI tools (e.g. decision-making in AI-enhanced teaching) due to its dedicated ICT-use domain.
Inclusive Environment	Inclusive Management in Tertiary Institutions Scale (IMTIS) – A 22-item scale (6-factor structure) assessing how well higher ed institutions foster inclusive culture, policies, and practices (Solis-Grant et al., 2022).	Designed for use by students, faculty, and administrators, making it globally adaptable. (Grounded in the Index for Inclusion, it has conceptual translations in 37 languages and has been adapted regionally, supporting use in MENA contexts.)
Caring Teacher–Student Relationships	Private-College Student–Teacher Relationship Scale (PCSTRS) – A 29-item scale capturing six dimensions of professor–student relationships: trust, interaction, intimacy, care, approval, and comfort (Bai et al., 2022).	While developed in a private-college context, its constructs (e.g. trust, care) are universal, allowing use in diverse cultural settings. It can be adapted linguistically for MENA; e.g. items on "intimacy" can be framed as approachability to respect cultural norms.
Well-Being & Resilience	Tripartite Occupational Well-Being Scale (TOWBS) – A 3-factor teacher well-being scale measuring "feeling good" (vitality) and "functioning well" (work engagement and professional growth) (Collie, 2023).	While designed for K–12, its focus on workplace well-being is transferable to higher education faculty. For students, complementary scales like the Brief Resilience Scale by Smith et al. (2008) remains a robust general measure widely validated internationally, including in Arabic contexts.
AI Literacy & Ethical Competence	AI Ethical Reflection Scale (AIERS) – A validated 12-item scale measuring individuals' ability to identify, use, and evaluate AI technologies under ethical standards, across four dimensions: awareness, usage, evaluation, and ethics (Wang et al., 2025).	Adaptable to higher education contexts, it measures ethical awareness, critical evaluation, and "AI for social good" – indicating growing cross-cultural tools to ensure responsible AI use in education.

Measurement Validity and Cross-Cultural Cautions

A central methodological risk in wellbeing-oriented AI research could be construct slippage: the assumption that psychometric equivalence implies experiential equivalence. AI-CARE explicitly cautions against interpreting scale scores as transparent indicators of lived wellbeing without contextual interpretation.

For instance, high scores on autonomy-related items may reflect compliance with system prompts rather than genuine self-regulation, particularly in highly automated environments. Similarly, perceptions of compassionate interaction may be shaped by cultural expectations of authority and care, complicating cross-context comparison.

Accordingly, AI-CARE recommends triangulation wherever possible. Quantitative measures should be complemented by qualitative methods such as interviews, reflective prompts, or participatory evaluation workshops. This is especially important when studying Adaptive Wellbeing Support or Ethical Governance, where trust, consent, and perceived legitimacy cannot be fully captured through survey instruments alone.

The AI-CARE Scorecard as a Developmental Tool

To facilitate practical implementation while preserving theoretical caution, the AI-CARE Scorecard provides a structured yet flexible rubric for assessing how well AI tools, institutional practices, or vendor proposals align with wellbeing-centered principles in education. The scorecard is explicitly designed to operationalize the AI-CARE framework without implying empirical validation. Consistent with sociotechnical evaluation traditions and human-centered AI scholarship, its purpose is diagnostic and developmental rather than summative or prescriptive, supporting reflective decision-making in both research and institutional contexts (Floridi et al., 2018; Sanders & Stappers, 2008; Selwyn, 2022).

Each of the six AI-CARE dimensions is rated on a 0–4 scale, where scores represent degrees of enactment rather than normative judgments of quality. Scoring is grounded in concrete evidence, including documented system features, observed institutional practices, and stakeholder perspectives, reflecting the view that wellbeing effects emerge from the interaction between technical design, governance arrangements, and lived educational experience (Baxter & Sommerville, 2011; Crawford, 2021). A score of 0 indicates no meaningful recognition of a dimension, while a score of 4 indicates sustained and embedded enactment across design, governance, and everyday practice. This approach avoids reducing evaluation to technical functionality alone and instead foregrounds the human, relational, and institutional conditions under which AI systems operate.

Table 3 presents the full rubric, offering calibrated descriptors for each score point. For interpretive clarity, cumulative scores may be used to indicate broad levels of wellbeing alignment:

- 0–8 = Minimal wellbeing alignment

- 9–14 = Developing wellbeing alignment
- 15–20 = Strong wellbeing alignment
- 21–24 = Exemplary wellbeing alignment

These categories are intended to support sense-making and strategic reflection rather than to function as certification thresholds, quality labels, or comparative rankings between institutions.

AI-CARE explicitly cautions against treating aggregate scores as definitive indicators of overall system quality. The scorecard is intentionally dimension-specific, enabling institutions to identify where strengths, vulnerabilities, and ethical tensions concentrate rather than encouraging maximal scoring across all domains. For example, an AI system may score highly on efficiency-oriented adaptivity while remaining underdeveloped in Ethical Governance or Agency & Autonomy. In such cases, the scorecard highlights where wellbeing risks are most likely to emerge, particularly risks associated with surveillance, autonomy erosion, or opaque decision-making, rather than labeling the system as globally deficient (Benjamin, 2019; Williamson & Hogan, 2020; Selwyn, 2022).

Importantly, the scorecard is conceived as a developmental instrument. Institutions can use it iteratively to surface underdeveloped dimensions, articulate targeted improvement priorities, and monitor change over time as AI systems evolve or scale. This longitudinal orientation is critical because many wellbeing risks identified in the AI-CARE framework, such as autonomy drift, technostress, or the redistribution of emotional and relational labor, tend to emerge gradually rather than at initial deployment (Tarafdar et al., 2019; Broadbent et al., 2023; Dreer, 2023). Repeated application therefore supports early detection of function creep and shifting risk profiles.

Crucially, AI-CARE recommends that the scorecard be applied through participatory processes involving educators, students, administrators, and, where appropriate, technical staff. Participatory scoring mitigates the risk of technocratic evaluation and aligns with the framework's emphasis on shared accountability, transparency, and contextual interpretation (Jobin et al., 2019; UNESCO, 2021). In regions such as the Middle East and North Africa, where governance structures, institutional authority, and infrastructural capacity vary widely, participatory use enhances legitimacy, supports cultural and linguistic adaptation, and enables bottom-up engagement alongside top-down oversight (Abdelnour-Nocera et al., 2021; Saqr et al., 2023).

In summary, the AI-CARE Scorecard translates abstract wellbeing and ethical principles into evaluative criteria while preserving the framework's conditional, theory-building orientation. It should be understood not as a compliance checklist or validation instrument, but as a structured analytic lens for surfacing trade-offs, tensions, and improvement pathways in AI-enabled education.

Table 3. AI-CARE Scorecard for Evaluating AI in Education

Dimension	0 – Not Addressed	1 – Minimal	2 – Emerging	3 – Established	4 – Fully Operationalized
Agency & Autonomy	No user control	1–2 basic options	≥25% self-pacing/ customization	≥50% goal-setting or overrides	≥75% adaptive control + override logs
Inclusive Design	No accessibility/ language	Basic visual options only	≥25% content accessible/adapted	≥50% multilingual or culturally adapted	≥90% WCAG* 2.1 AA*, 3+ languages, annual audits
Compassionate Integration	No empathy features	Polite tone in <25% of outputs	25–49% outputs show empathy	≥50% affective interaction + staff review	≥75% empathy-driven messages + escalation
Adaptive Wellbeing Support	No wellbeing inputs	1 generic prompt/ term	25–49% adaptive response	≥50% real-time personalization + referral	≥75% stress-aware nudges, multimodal tracking
Resilience Building	No retry/motivation	Basic retry, no feedback	≥25% retry with feedback	≥50% retry + reflection prompts	≥75% retry, tracking, improvement data logged
Ethical Governance	No safeguards	One-time privacy notice	<50% oversight + opt-out	>50% decisions audited + appeal route	100% transparency, recourse, bias audits 2x/yr

Note. *WCAG 2.1 AA refers to the Web Content Accessibility Guidelines. Level AA is ensuring digital tools are accessible, navigable, and readable for users with diverse needs, including screen readers and color contrast.

IMPLEMENTATION GUIDE

Effective implementation of AI-CARE requires treating wellbeing as a design constraint, not a downstream outcome. Because AI-CARE is a theory-building and diagnostic framework, implementation should be iterative and evaluative, with explicit acknowledgement that benefits are conditional on context, governance, and lived experience. In practice, this means making trade-offs visible early, constraining high-risk features until safeguards exist, and monitoring not only short-term affective outcomes but also longer-term trajectories such as autonomy development, dependency on AI feedback, and shifts in educator role and emotional labor.

Step 1. Make the trade-offs explicit before tool selection

AI adoption in higher education routinely frames "efficiency" as inherently beneficial, yet AI-CARE assumes that efficiency can either support wellbeing (by freeing time for mentoring) or erode it (by intensifying monitoring and compliance pressures). Implementation should therefore begin by explicitly negotiating three core trade-offs that recur across all six dimensions: efficiency versus relationality, personalization versus surveillance, and adaptive support versus privacy risk (Crawford, 2021; Selwyn, 2022; Williamson & Hogan, 2020). These are not abstract tensions; they shape day-to-day learner trust, anxiety, and motivation, as well as educators' sense of professional purpose and autonomy. A practical starting point is to define, in plain terms, what the institution will not automate (for example, high-stakes judgments without human review) and what data it will not collect (for example, inferred affect without robust consent and oversight).

Step 2. Conduct a feasibility triage for MENA contexts

AI-CARE's wellbeing claims are contingent on feasibility constraints that vary widely across MENA. Implementation should therefore include a readiness triage that prioritizes: (a) infrastructure (bandwidth, device access, LMS stability), (b) professional development capacity (time, facilitation expertise, critical AI literacy), (c) counseling and student support availability (referral pathways if risk is detected), and (d) procurement and vendor bargaining power (ability to demand audits, localization, data controls, and exit options) (Abdelnour-Nocera et al., 2021; Baytiyeh, 2022; Saqr et al., 2023). Where these capacities are limited, implementation should favor low-risk AI functions (for example, optional drafting support, accessibility features) and delay high-risk functions (for example, affect inference, automated risk labeling, coercive nudging).

Step 3. Implement AI-CARE by dimension with explicit operational checks

(1) Agency and Autonomy

Operationalization should protect "choice now" and "capacity over time." In the short term, autonomy-supportive design means learners can meaningfully choose pathways, pacing, and feedback modes, and instructors can override system recommendations (Deci & Ryan, 2000; Shneiderman, 2020; UNESCO, 2021). In the long term, AI-CARE treats autonomy as a developmental capability. If systems provide continuous micro-corrections and prescriptive next steps, learners may gradually outsource planning, self-checking, and error diagnosis, creating dependency and weakening self-regulated learning habits (Broadbent et al., 2023). Implementation should therefore include "autonomy scaffolding" rules, such as gradually reducing directive prompts and requiring learner reflection before revealing solutions in formative contexts.

(2) Inclusive Design

Inclusive design is not only accessibility compliance but also protection against cumulative belonging harms. Implementation should require multilingual usability and culturally responsive configurations, and it should explicitly address gendered and linguistic inequities that can be reproduced through biased data and standardized vendor defaults (Benjamin, 2019; Mehrabi et al., 2022; Selwyn, 2022). In MENA, Arabic diglossia and dialectal variation create predictable misrecognition risks. If the system repeatedly fails to recognize learners' linguistic inputs, the harm can shift from "difficulty with content" to "exclusion by the system," with downstream effects on trust, persistence, and identity-relevant participation (Baytiyeh, 2022; Saqr et al., 2023). Operationally, this implies periodic local bias checks, language-specific error audits, and stakeholder co-design rather than passive acceptance of vendor settings (Crawford, 2021; Kwet, 2019; Williamson & Hogan, 2020).

(3) Compassionate Integration

Compassion must be treated as relational practice, not interface tone. Supportive phrasing can reduce anxiety in the moment, but it can also function as a "care veneer" if it is embedded in surveillance or punitive escalation infrastructures that undermine trust (Selwyn, 2022; Williamson & Hogan, 2020). Implementation should therefore include clear human escalation routes and boundaries: AI can acknowledge difficulty and offer options, but accountability and high-stakes consequences should remain dialogic. Crucially, institutions should anticipate redistribution of emotional labor. As AI scales, educators often become the "human buffer" who explains system outputs, mediates disputes, and repairs trust, even when they did not choose the tool (Dreer, 2023; Jennings & Greenberg, 2009). Implementation plans should explicitly recognize, resource, and time this relational work, otherwise "efficiency gains" can translate into hidden workload and identity strain.

(4) Adaptive Wellbeing Support

Affective adaptivity is the highest-risk wellbeing pathway in AI-CARE. Even if technically feasible (D'Mello & Kory, 2015), affect-sensitive systems raise substantial risks of misclassification, function creep, labeling harms, and privacy violations, especially when interpreted outside cultural context (Selwyn, 2022; Tarafdar et al., 2019). Implementation should therefore treat adaptive wellbeing support as conditional: deploy only when consent is robust, governance is mature, and counseling pathways exist. In addition, AI-CARE foregrounds a long-term autonomy risk: frequent nudging can externalize self-regulation if learners come to rely on system prompts to manage focus and stress (Broadbent et al., 2023). A wellbeing feature is not automatically a wellbeing outcome; adaptivity should be designed to scaffold learners toward self-initiated regulation, not replace it.

(5) Resilience Building

Resilience is a long-horizon capability shaped by how learners interpret difficulty and persist over time (Dweck, 2006; Yeager & Dweck, 2012). Implementation should avoid "over-smoothing" learning through automation. If AI removes productive struggle, it can reduce opportunities to develop perseverance and independent problem-solving. Resilience-oriented AI should therefore be calibrated to support effort without replacing it: scaffold retries, prompt metacognitive explanation, and reward revision trajectories rather than only correctness. This aligns with occupational wellbeing logic too: resilience supports educators when feedback and evaluation systems emphasize growth and reflective practice rather than compliance (Bakker & Demerouti, 2017; Xanthopoulou et al., 2007).

(6) Ethical Governance

Ethical governance is longitudinal infrastructure, not a one-time checklist. It should include transparent policies, stakeholder participation in procurement, user control over data, human review in high-stakes decisions, and enforceable contestability routes (Floridi et al., 2018; Jobin et al., 2019; UNESCO, 2021). In MENA settings with uneven regulatory maturity, governance must also address vendor power and data sovereignty. Vendor defaults and metrics can privilege scalability and commercial efficiency over local pedagogical values, so procurement should require auditability, localization commitments, and exit options (Crawford, 2021; Kwet, 2019; Saqr et al., 2023). Governance also intersects with educator identity: when teachers are positioned as responsible for AI outcomes without authority over selection or configuration, role tension and emotional labor intensify. Implementation should therefore protect educator discretion through policy, not just interface controls (Dreer, 2023; Shneiderman, 2020).

Step 4. Use the AI-CARE Scorecard as a diagnostic gate, then evaluate longitudinally

The AI-CARE Scorecard should be used as a diagnostic tool during procurement and piloting, not as proof of wellbeing impact. A pragmatic approach is a two-stage gate: (a) score the tool against Table 3 to identify "missing safeguards," then (b) pilot with a predefined evaluation plan that includes both short-term outcomes (anxiety, trust, perceived support) and longer-term outcomes (self-regulation, autonomy development, dependency signals, educator agency, and emotional labor). The "cumulative score bands" can inform decision thresholds, but they should never substitute for contextual evaluation because the same score can produce different lived experiences under different governance regimes and institutional cultures (Selwyn, 2022; Williamson & Hogan, 2020).

WORKED EXAMPLE: APPYING AI-CARE IN A HYPOTHETICAL SCENARIO

To illustrate how the AI-CARE Implementation Guide can be operationalized in practice, this section presents a hypothetical but representative scenario involving a commonly adopted AI tool category in higher education. The example is not intended to report empirical findings or validate the framework. Rather, it demonstrates how AI-CARE can be used diagnostically and analytically to surface trade-offs, anticipate risks, and guide decision-making across design, governance, and evaluation stages.

Consistent with the framework's theoretical status, the example treats AI-CARE as a sense-making and decision-support tool rather than a prescriptive checklist. The aim is to show how institutions might move from abstract wellbeing and ethics principles to concrete implementation conditions, aligned measurement strategies, and defensible scale-or-stop decisions. The worked example proceeds through five steps, each corresponding to a critical phase in responsible AI adoption: contextual framing, structured evaluation, conditional implementation, aligned measurement, and longitudinal decision-making.

While the scenario is situated in a higher education context that reflects conditions common in MENA systems, the logic of the example is deliberately portable. The steps and reasoning are intended to be adaptable to diverse institutional, regulatory, and cultural contexts where AI adoption raises similar tensions between efficiency, autonomy, relationality, and wellbeing.

Step 1. Define the tool category, use context, and the primary trade-offs

As a worked example, consider an LMS-integrated system that combines (a) an AI tutor for practice and Q and A, (b) automated formative feedback (e.g., writing support), (c) an early-alert dashboard that flags "at-risk" students using trace data, and (d) optional wellbeing nudges (e.g., break reminders or motivational prompts). This tool class is common in higher education because it is framed as efficiency-enhancing, scalable, and supportive.

Under AI-CARE, it should be treated as a high-tension category because it activates several core trade-offs at once. Typical fault lines include personalization versus surveillance (early-alert analytics), efficiency versus relationality (automation displacing human contact), adaptive support versus privacy risk (wellbeing nudges and inference), and short-term support versus long-term autonomy development (constant micro-feedback shaping self-regulation habits).

In MENA settings, these tensions can be amplified by uneven infrastructure, variable counseling capacity, multilingual classrooms (including Arabic diglossia and dialectal variation), and heterogeneous governance capacity. These conditions increase the likelihood of technostress, misrecognition, and labeling harm if safeguards are weak.

Step 2. Score the tool with the AI-CARE Scorecard and interpret the total

Apply the AI-CARE Scorecard rubric (see Table 3) as a structured screening step, not as "validation." The goal is to surface where a tool is strong, where it is brittle, and which dimensions become gating constraints for safe adoption.

For this tool category, a plausible initial profile is mixed. Agency and Autonomy can reach "established" if learners genuinely control pacing and pathways and instructors can override or contextualize recommendations. Inclusive Design often lands at "emerging" when accessibility and multilingual performance are partial, and when Arabic variety support is weak.

Compassionate Integration commonly remains "emerging" when "supportive tone" exists without credible routes to human support, or when messaging is experienced as compliance-oriented rather than relational. Adaptive Wellbeing Support is typically "emerging" when nudges and adaptivity exist without robust consent, explainability, and limits on inference.

Resilience Building can be "established" if retry cycles and reflective prompts preserve productive struggle rather than remove it. Ethical Governance often becomes the bottleneck if early-alert logic is opaque, appeal routes are weak, or data boundaries invite function creep.

Once the six scores are assigned using Table 3 descriptors, interpret the cumulative range using the bands under Table 3 to decide whether the tool qualifies for a limited pilot, requires redesign before piloting, or should be rejected at procurement.

Step 3. Convert scores into non-negotiable implementation conditions

Implementation should specify conditions that actively manage the trade-offs identified in Step 1 and the weaknesses revealed in Step 2, rather than listing generic "best practices."

For early-alert analytics, Ethical Governance and Agency and Autonomy should be treated as gating dimensions. Flags must be explainable in terms meaningful to instructors and students, contestable via an explicit appeal route, and bounded in use (e.g., advising support only rather than disciplinary escalation). Without these constraints, the same system that claims to "support retention" can function as surveillance and labeling infrastructure that erodes trust and psychological safety.

For wellbeing nudges, Adaptive Wellbeing Support should be bounded to low-risk functions in early pilots (e.g., opt-in break reminders) with explicit prohibitions on affect inference or mental health "recommendations" unless governance and consent infrastructure are demonstrably strong. This is not a rhetorical ethical preference; it responds to the contested evidence base and high misclassification risk associated with affect-sensitive interventions.

For autonomy development, Agency and Autonomy and Resilience Building should be operationalized longitudinally. Feedback and prompts should gradually scaffold learners toward self-initiated planning and monitoring instead of sustaining dependence on system cues, because short-term convenience can still generate long-term "autonomy drift."

Finally, feasibility constraints should be written into implementation conditions, not left as background context. Infrastructure limits require low-bandwidth alternatives, professional development capacity constrains dashboard complexity, counseling availability constrains what "wellbeing support" can ethically mean, and procurement limitations constrain localization unless vendors contractually commit to audits, documentation, and data sovereignty protections.

Step 4. Evaluate the pilot with measures aligned to AI-CARE dimensions

Because AI-CARE is theory-building and diagnostic rather than validated, evaluation should be framed as hypothesis testing under constraints. The measurement strategy should include both short-term wellbeing states and longer-term capability trajectories, since AI may reduce short-term friction while weakening autonomy and self-regulation over time.

Use the suggested instruments in Table 2 to align measurement to dimensions and to detect long-term risks that "satisfaction" indicators often miss. Learner autonomy and self-regulation trajectories can be tracked via the Self-Regulation for Learning Online Questionnaire (SRL-O) (see Table 2), which helps test whether micro-feedback scaffolds regulation or externalizes it into dependency patterns.

Inclusive environment and belonging can be assessed via the Inclusive Management in Tertiary Institutions Scale (IMTIS) (see Table 2), which is useful for identifying cumulative exclusion arising from persistent misrecognition or unequal accessibility. Relational experience and perceived care can be tracked using the Private-College Student–Teacher Relationship Scale (PCSTRS) (see Table 2), since "compassionate phrasing" can still be experienced as surveillance if paired with monitoring workflows.

Educator agency and discretion can be measured with the Teacher Agency Questionnaire (see Table 2) to test whether instructors feel empowered to override and contextualize algorithmic suggestions rather than being pressured into compliance. Educator wellbeing and sustainability can be tracked via the Tripartite Occupational Well-Being Scale (TOWBS) (see Table 2) to detect whether efficiency gains are offset by hidden emotional labor and role tension.

Finally, ethical competence and reflective capacity can be assessed via the AI Ethical Reflection Scale (AIERS) (see Table 2). This helps check whether students and educators can critically interpret AI outputs rather than deferring to them, which is central to preventing automation bias and sustaining agency over time.

Step 5. Decide: scale, adapt, or stop, using AI-CARE as the decision logic

The decision rule should be explicit: scaling requires more than positive feedback or efficiency improvements. A tool that raises satisfaction while producing declining SRL-O scores at follow-up should be treated as an autonomy risk, because it suggests long-term externalization of regulation.

Similarly, a system that expands early-alert flags without transparent explanations, appeal routes, and bounded use should be treated as a governance failure because it shifts the environment toward surveillance and labeling harm.

A third failure pattern is lived-experience mismatch: if belonging or relationship measures deteriorate while performance metrics rise, AI-CARE requires privileging wellbeing-relevant experience signals over optimization claims. In that scenario, the appropriate response is not "more training" alone but redesign of interaction patterns, governance boundaries, and escalation routes.

A Summary of All

This worked example shows how AI-CARE can translate abstract principles into an implementable logic: identify the trade-offs first, score the tool to locate bottlenecks (Table 3), convert weak dimensions into non-negotiable conditions, and evaluate both short-term wellbeing and longer-term autonomy and identity trajectories using aligned measures (Table 2). The key point is that "efficiency" is not a stable proxy for flourishing: the same features that reduce friction today can accumulate into dependency, surveillance normalization, or role tension over time.

Finally, although MENA contexts sharpen the visibility of feasibility constraints and governance gaps, AI-CARE is not confined to MENA. It is a theoretical, diagnostic framework intended to be portable across higher education systems. Its value is in making trade-offs, boundary conditions, and time-horizon effects explicit, so the same implementation logic can be adapted to any region where AI adoption pressures intersect with wellbeing, equity, and accountability concerns.

RESEARCH AGENDA

As a theoretically grounded and diagnostic framework, AI-CARE does not require immediate validation in the narrow predictive sense. Rather, its value lies in guiding theory refinement, conditional testing, and critical examination of how AI reshapes wellbeing across time, contexts, and governance arrangements. A coherent research agenda should therefore prioritize designs that illuminate mechanisms, trade-offs, and unintended consequences, rather than seeking universal effect sizes. The following priorities outline how empirical research can progressively strengthen the framework's explanatory and practical utility.

Theory Refinement Through Longitudinal and Comparative Designs

Understanding AI's relationship to wellbeing requires attention to temporal dynamics, not only short-term outcomes. While experimental and quasi-experimental designs can examine proximal effects on stress, engagement, or perceived support, longer-term studies are essential for assessing how repeated AI interaction reshapes learner autonomy, self-regulation, and educator professional identity. Longitudinal panel designs, cohort studies, and delayed-intervention comparisons are particularly suited to capturing phenomena such as dependency on automated feedback, shifts in planning and monitoring behavior, or gradual normalization of surveillance practices.

Experimental approaches, including randomized or matched designs, can be valuable when used theoretically, for example to test whether autonomy-supportive configurations attenuate autonomy drift over time compared to prescriptive systems (Deci & Ryan, 2000; Zheng et al., 2022). However, such studies should be interpreted as boundary-testing exercises rather than definitive validation, given the sociotechnical complexity of AI-mediated education.

Micro-Longitudinal and Process-Oriented Approaches

Many wellbeing effects unfold at the level of everyday interaction. Micro-longitudinal designs, including Experience Sampling Method (ESM), learning analytics combined with self-report, or digital trace-informed reflection, can reveal how students experience AI moment-to-moment: when support feels enabling, when it becomes intrusive, and when self-regulation is externally displaced. These approaches are particularly relevant for examining Adaptive Wellbeing Support and Resilience Building, where the distinction between scaffolding and dependency is subtle and dynamic (Myin-Germeys et al., 2018; Tarafdar et al., 2019).

Process-oriented methods also allow researchers to study function creep, showing how systems initially introduced as supportive may gradually assume evaluative or disciplinary roles, with implications for trust and psychological safety.

Mixed-Methods Inquiry and Lived Experience

Because wellbeing is experienced subjectively and relationally, mixed-methods designs remain central to AI-CARE research. Quantitative indicators of stress, engagement, or self-efficacy gain interpretive depth when paired with interviews, diaries, or classroom ethnographies that capture how learners and educators make sense of AI systems in practice. Such designs are particularly important for understanding Compassionate Integration and Ethical Governance, where perceived intent, legitimacy, and fairness often matter more than technical performance.

Rather than treating qualitative findings as ancillary, AI-CARE invites their use as theory-generating evidence, surfacing mechanisms such as algorithmic fatigue, emotional buffering work by educators, or identity tension in AI-mediated teaching roles.

Cross-Contextual Testing and Fairness-Oriented Evaluation

Although AI-CARE has been developed with attention to MENA contexts, its constructs are intentionally portable. Cross-contextual research can examine how dimensions such as autonomy, inclusion, or ethical governance manifest differently across regulatory regimes, infrastructural capacities, and cultural norms. In this regard, MENA settings provide analytically rich cases for studying governance gaps, multilingual complexity, and rapid digitalization, but they do not delimit the framework's relevance.

Fairness audits should be embedded within such studies, not as standalone technical checks but as wellbeing-relevant analyses that examine differential impacts across gender, language background, disability status, or socioeconomic position (Mitchell et al., 2019). Persistent misrecognition or biased system behavior should be treated as longitudinal wellbeing risks rather than isolated technical errors.

Participatory and Governance-Focused Research Models

Participatory Action Research (PAR) aligns closely with AI-CARE's emphasis on agency, inclusion, and ethical governance. By engaging students, educators, and administrators as co-researchers, PAR can reveal how AI systems are negotiated, resisted, adapted, or normalized within institutions. Such approaches are especially valuable for examining how governance structures shape lived experience, and for testing whether participatory procurement or oversight mechanisms meaningfully reduce technostress and trust erosion.

Governance-focused research should also examine institutional decision-making over time, including procurement constraints, vendor lock-in, professional development capacity, and counseling availability, as these feasibility conditions strongly moderate wellbeing outcomes but are often absent from experimental designs.

Open and Reflexive Research Infrastructure

Finally, cumulative knowledge-building around AI-CARE depends on transparent and reflexive research practices. Pre-registered protocols, open measurement instruments, and shared analytic strategies can support comparison across studies without imposing artificial standardization. Importantly, openness should extend to documenting negative or ambiguous findings, including cases where AI-CARE-aligned designs fail under specific constraints.

As AI-mediated education continues to expand globally, such an infrastructure will enable researchers to identify not only where AI-CARE supports wellbeing, but where its assumptions break down, thereby strengthening the framework's theoretical integrity.

ETHICAL CONSIDERATIONS

Although the AI-CARE framework foregrounds wellbeing as a central concern in AI-supported education, its effectiveness ultimately depends on sustained and critical engagement with the ethical conditions under which AI systems are designed, procured, and governed. Ethical risks are not peripheral constraints on otherwise beneficial technologies; they actively shape psychological safety, trust, equity, and the relational dynamics of learning environments. Critical AI scholarship has repeatedly shown that educational AI systems are embedded within broader logics of surveillance, data extraction, and institutional control, which may conflict with pedagogical values of care, autonomy, and human development if left unexamined (Benjamin, 2019; Crawford, 2021; Kwet, 2019). From a wellbeing perspective, ethical governance therefore functions as enabling infrastructure rather than a supplementary safeguard.

Ethical Risks

One of the most pervasive risks is surveillance creep, the gradual expansion of monitoring practices beyond their initial pedagogical justification. AI systems introduced to support learning or early intervention may increasingly collect fine-grained behavioral or affective data, normalizing continuous observation and diminishing perceived autonomy over time (Williamson & Hogan, 2020; Crawford, 2021). Such dynamics are closely tied to technostress and self-censorship, particularly in institutional contexts where students and educators have limited avenues to contest data practices. In parts of the MENA region, where institutional trust and data protection regimes may be uneven, surveillance creep poses a direct threat to psychological safety and open participation.

A related concern involves labeling harm. Predictive analytics that classify learners as "at-risk," "low engagement," or "underperforming" can shape expectations, interactions, and self-perception in ways that extend far beyond their technical intent

(Selwyn, 2022). Labels may solidify deficit narratives, reduce self-efficacy, and narrow perceived academic futures, particularly when they are opaque or difficult to contest. These effects are not culturally neutral. In many MENA contexts, where educational identity is closely tied to social belonging and family reputation, algorithmic labels may carry amplified emotional and social consequences (Benjamin, 2019).

Bias amplification constitutes a further ethical challenge with direct wellbeing implications. AI systems trained on Western-centric, linguistically narrow, or historically unbalanced datasets may systematically misrecognize or disadvantage learners across gender, language background, disability status, or socioeconomic position (Mehrabi et al., 2022; Kwet, 2019). In linguistically diverse contexts, persistent misclassification, such as inaccurate handling of Arabic varieties, can erode trust incrementally, shifting learners' experiences from temporary frustration to sustained exclusion. Within AI-CARE, such risks implicate both Inclusive Design and Ethical Governance, underscoring that fairness failures are simultaneously technical and relational harms.

Finally, automation overreach, the displacement of human discretion in grading, advising, or support services, poses a structural risk to educational wellbeing. While automation is often justified in terms of efficiency and scalability, critical political-economy perspectives highlight how such shifts reconfigure educators' professional roles, redistributing emotional and relational labor rather than eliminating it (Crawford, 2021; Benjamin, 2019). When educators are positioned as the human interface responsible for explaining, justifying, or repairing algorithmic decisions they did not design or select, professional identity strain and emotional exhaustion may intensify. These risks are particularly acute during transitional educational moments, such as first-year study or academic probation, where relational judgment and care are central.

Ethical Safeguards

To mitigate these risks, human oversight must be treated as a foundational condition rather than a procedural afterthought. AI-CARE conceptualizes oversight not only as an accountability mechanism but as a wellbeing safeguard that preserves agency, trust, and psychological reassurance. High-stakes decisions affecting assessment, progression, or support should remain contestable and reversible, with AI systems operating in an assistive capacity rather than as authoritative arbiters (Floridi et al., 2018).

Complementing oversight, systematic red-teaming and adversarial testing can surface misclassifications, edge-case failures, and unintended harms prior to large-scale deployment (Raji et al., 2022). When integrated into procurement and evaluation processes alongside transparent documentation practices, such as model cards, red-teaming helps counter technocratic overconfidence and vendor-driven opacity, a concern repeatedly highlighted in critical analyses of educational AI markets (Kwet, 2019).

From a data ethics perspective, data minimization and privacy-preserving techniques, including differential privacy, can reduce risks of re-identification and secondary data use while preserving analytic utility (Dwork & Roth, 2014). These protections are especially salient in regions where legal enforcement mechanisms are still evolving, and where students may lack meaningful recourse against data misuse.

Equally important are participatory governance and co-design processes. Involving educators and students in decision-making around AI selection, configuration, and evaluation surfaces local values, cultural sensitivities, and wellbeing concerns that standardized solutions often overlook (Luckin et al., 2016). Such participation counters extractive or colonial dynamics in AI adoption and strengthens institutional legitimacy and trust, particularly in contexts marked by historical or geopolitical asymmetries (Benjamin, 2019; Kwet, 2019).

Taken together, Ethical Governance and Inclusive Design within AI-CARE should be understood as structural determinants shaping how all other dimensions operate over time. Ethical alignment must be embedded early, revisited iteratively, and monitored longitudinally as systems evolve, institutional reliance deepens, and automation pressures intensify. Without such sustained engagement, even well-intentioned AI systems risk undermining the wellbeing outcomes they are designed to promote.

LIMITATIONS AND SCOPE

The AI-CARE framework is advanced as a theory-building and integrative contribution that synthesizes insights from education, psychology, ethics, and critical AI studies. It is not intended as a systematic review and therefore reflects a purposive and conceptually driven selection of scholarly literature rather than an exhaustive mapping of all empirical or regional strands within the rapidly expanding AI and wellbeing field. While the framework draws on both foundational theories and recent research, particularly from the 2020s, it cannot capture the full diversity of methodological debates, sector-specific applications, or emerging perspectives that continue to evolve at pace.

A defining characteristic of AI-CARE is its normative orientation. The framework explicitly advances the position that student and educator wellbeing should function as a guiding principle in AI design, governance, and implementation. Although this stance aligns with global initiatives such as Sustainable Development Goal 4 and UNESCO's ethics recommendations, it should not be assumed that wellbeing is uniformly prioritized across institutional, market, or policy contexts. In systems dominated by performance metrics, high-stakes assessment, or competitive accountability regimes, wellbeing considerations may be subordinated to efficiency, ranking, or cost-reduction pressures. In such environments, AI-CARE may function more as a critical diagnostic lens than as an immediately actionable implementation model.

A further limitation concerns the empirical status of the framework. AI-CARE currently operates as a conceptual and heuristic model rather than a validated explanatory theory. Although its dimensions, mediators, and proposed pathways are grounded in established theoretical traditions, they have not yet been systematically tested as an integrated whole. Accordingly, claims regarding causal mechanisms and wellbeing outcomes should be interpreted as theoretically plausible rather than empirically conclusive. Rigorous validation through experimental, longitudinal, mixed-methods, and participatory research designs remains a necessary next step.

Implementation feasibility also varies substantially across contexts. In low-resource, crisis-affected, or governance-fragmented environments, constraints such as limited digital infrastructure, uneven professional development capacity, restricted counseling services, or weak regulatory oversight may limit the operationalization of certain dimensions, particularly Adaptive Wellbeing Support or Ethical Governance. These constraints are salient in parts of the Global South, including segments of the MENA region, where rapid digital expansion often outpaces institutional capacity. Without careful contextual adaptation, AI interventions intended to support wellbeing may inadvertently intensify inequities, technostress, or dependency.

Finally, the scope of AI-CARE is intentionally bounded to formal education, with a primary emphasis on higher education. While its six dimensions, agency, inclusion, compassion, adaptability, resilience, and ethical governance, are likely to resonate with K–12, vocational, or informal learning contexts, differences in developmental needs, pedagogical structures, and AI use cases require careful reinterpretation. Claims advanced in this chapter should therefore not be generalized beyond tertiary education without additional contextual and empirical support.

CONCLUSION

AI is no longer a peripheral innovation in education; it is increasingly embedded in the everyday practices, decision-making structures, and relational dynamics of higher education institutions worldwide. While dominant narratives have emphasized AI's capacity to enhance efficiency, personalization, and performance, growing evidence suggests that such gains are neither neutral nor cost-free. Without deliberate attention to human experience, AI adoption risks intensifying surveillance, eroding agency, and redistributing emotional and professional burdens in ways that undermine wellbeing.

The AI-CARE framework responds to this challenge by repositioning student and educator wellbeing as a central analytic and normative concern in AI integration. By articulating six interdependent dimensions, Agency & Autonomy, Inclusive Design, Compassionate Integration, Adaptive Wellbeing Support, Resilience Building, and Ethical Governance, the framework offers a structured account of how AI systems may support or undermine flourishing, depending on design choices, governance arrangements, and implementation contexts. Its attention to mediators, feedback loops, and contextual moderators reflects the complex, non-linear nature of AI's effects in educational environments.

The framework's contribution lies not only in conceptual synthesis but also in practical orientation. Instruments such as the AI-CARE Scorecard translate abstract ethical and wellbeing principles into evaluative criteria that can inform procurement, governance, and reflective practice. Used critically, these tools enable institutions to surface trade-offs, such as efficiency versus relationality or personalization versus surveillance, rather than assuming that technological optimization inherently produces positive outcomes.

The implications extend across multiple levels of the educational ecosystem. For educators, AI-CARE offers a lens to evaluate technologies in ways that preserve professional judgment and relational integrity. For institutional leaders, it informs policy, training, and procurement strategies that align innovation with ethical and wellbeing commitments. For policymakers, it provides a coherent structure to guide regulation and accountability without reducing wellbeing to a secondary concern. For developers and vendors, the framework clarifies design priorities that foreground trust, agency, and human dignity.

Ultimately, the promise of AI in education should not be measured solely by efficiency gains or predictive accuracy. Its more consequential impact lies in how it reshapes learning as a human experience: how it influences autonomy, belonging, emotional safety, and professional identity over time. Without explicit wellbeing-oriented governance, AI risks entrenching inequities and amplifying alienation. Guided by frameworks such as AI-CARE, however, AI can be oriented toward empowerment, equity, and sustainable educational futures.

Embedding wellbeing as a design and governance imperative is therefore not aspirational but foundational. As AI continues to evolve, responsible integration will require ongoing critical reflection, empirical scrutiny, and collaboration across disciplines and sectors, informed by the lived realities of those who teach and learn.

REFERENCES

Abdelnour-Nocera, J., Nobarany, S., & Parmiggiani, E. (2021). Contextual and cultural perspectives in human-centred computing. *Interacting with Computers, 33*(2), 117–123. DOI: 10.1093/iwc/iwab006

Acton, R., & Glasgow, P. (2015). Teacher wellbeing in Neoliberal contexts: A review of the literature. *The Australian Journal of Teacher Education, 40*(8). Advance online publication. DOI: 10.14221/ajte.2015v40n8.6

Allen, K., Kern, M. L., Vella-Brodrick, D., Hattie, J., & Waters, L. (2018). What schools need to know about fostering school belonging: A meta-analysis. *Educational Psychology Review, 30*(1), 1–34. DOI: 10.1007/s10648-016-9389-8

Bai, L. Y., Li, Z. Y., Wu, W. X., Liu, L. Y., Chen, S. P., Zhang, J., & Zhu, J. N. Y. (2022). Student-Teacher Relationship: Its Measurement and Effect on Students' Trait, Performance, and Wellbeing in Private College. *Frontiers in Psychology, 13*, 793483. DOI: 10.3389/fpsyg.2022.793483 PMID: 35360560

Bakker, A. B., & Demerouti, E. (2017). Job demands-resources theory: Taking stock and looking forward. *Journal of Occupational Health Psychology, 22*(3), 273–285. DOI: 10.1037/ocp0000056 PMID: 27732008

Baxter, G., & Sommerville, I. (2011). Socio-technical systems: From design methods to systems engineering. *Interacting with Computers, 23*(1), 4–17. DOI: 10.1016/j.intcom.2010.07.003

Baytiyeh, H. (2022). Artificial intelligence and the future of higher education in the Arab world. *International Journal of Educational Development, 89*, 102550. DOI: 10.1016/j.ijedudev.2021.102550

Benjamin, R. (2019). *Race after technology: Abolitionist tools for the new Jim Code*. Polity Press.

Broadbent, J., Panadero, E., Lodge, J. M., & Fuller-Tyszkiewicz, M. (2023). The self-regulation for learning online (SRL-O) questionnaire. *Metacognition and Learning, 18*(1), 135–163. DOI: 10.1007/s11409-022-09319-6 PMID: 36065225

Bronfenbrenner, U. (1979). *The ecology of human development: Experiments by nature and design*. Harvard University Press.

CAST. (2018). *Universal Design for Learning Guidelines version 2.2*. https://udlguidelines.cast.org/

Collie, R. J. (2023). The Tripartite Occupational Well-Being Scale: Evidence of Validity Among Teachers. *Journal of Psychoeducational Assessment*, *42*(1), 46–59. DOI: 10.1177/07342829231202313

Crawford, K. (2021). *Atlas of AI: Power, politics, and the planetary costs of artificial intelligence*. Yale University Press.

Curren, R., Boniwell, I., Ryan, R. M., Oades, L., Brighouse, H., Unterhalter, E., Kristjánsson, K., de Ruyter, D., Macleod, C., Morris, I., & White, M. (2024). Finding consensus on well-being in education. *Theory and Research in Education*, *22*(2), 117–157. DOI: 10.1177/14778785241259852

D'Mello, S., & Kory, J. (2015). A review and meta-analysis of multimodal affect detection systems. *ACM Computing Surveys*, *47*(3), 1–36. DOI: 10.1145/2682899

Deci, E. L., & Ryan, R. M. (2000). The "what" and "why" of goal pursuits: Human needs and the self-determination of behavior. *Psychological Inquiry*, *11*(4), 227–268.

Dreer, B. (2023). On the outcomes of teacher wellbeing: A systematic review of research. *Frontiers in Education*, *14*, 1205179. Advance online publication. DOI: 10.3389/fpsyg.2023.1205179 PMID: 37575417

Dweck, C. S. (2006). *Mindset: The new psychology of success*. Random House.

Dwork, C., & Roth, A. (2014). The algorithmic foundations of Differential Privacy. *Foundations and Trends in Theoretical Computer Science*, *9*(3–4), 211–407. DOI: 10.1561/0400000042

Floridi, L., Cowls, J., Beltrametti, M., Chatila, R., Chazerand, P., Dignum, V., Luetge, C., Madelin, R., Pagallo, U., Rossi, F., Schafer, B., Valcke, P., & Vayena, E. (2018). AI4People, an ethical framework for a good AI Society: Opportunities, Risks, principles, and recommendations. *Minds and Machines*, *28*(4), 689–707. DOI: 10.1007/s11023-018-9482-5 PMID: 30930541

Fredricks, J. A., Blumenfeld, P. C., & Paris, A. H. (2004). School Engagement: Potential of the Concept, State of the Evidence. *Review of Educational Research*, *74*(1), 59–109. DOI: 10.3102/00346543074001059

Giannakos, M., Azevedo, R., Brusilovsky, P., Cukurova, M., Dimitriadis, Y., Hernandez-Leo, D., & Rienties, B. (2024). The promise and challenges of generative AI in education. *Behaviour & Information Technology*, *44*(11), 2518–2544. DOI: 10.1080/0144929X.2024.2394886

Howard, J. L., Bureau, J., Guay, F., Chong, J. X., & Ryan, R. M. (2021). Student motivation and associated outcomes: A meta-analysis from self-determination theory. *Perspectives on Psychological Science, 16*(6), 1300–1323. DOI: 10.1177/1745691620966789 PMID: 33593153

Jennings, P. A., & Greenberg, M. T. (2009). The prosocial classroom: Teacher social and emotional competence in relation to student and classroom outcomes. *Review of Educational Research, 79*, 491–525. DOI: 10.3102/0034654308325693

Jeno, L. M., Vandvik, V., Eliassen, S., & Grytnes, J. A. (2019). Testing the novelty effect of an m-learning tool on internalization and achievement: A Self-Determination Theory approach. *Computers & Education, 128*, 398–413. DOI: 10.1016/j.compedu.2018.10.008

Jobin, A., Ienca, M., & Vayena, E. (2019). The global landscape of AI ethics guidelines. *Nature Machine Intelligence, 1*(9), 389–399. DOI: 10.1038/s42256-019-0088-2

Kern, M., Waters, L. E., Adler, A., & White, M. A. (2015). A multidimensional approach to measuring well-being in students: Application of the PERMA Framework. *The Journal of Positive Psychology, 10*, 262–271. DOI: 10.1080/17439760.2014.936962 PMID: 25745508

Killingback, C., Tomlinson, A., & Stern, J. (2024). Compassionate pedagogy in higher education: A scoping review. *Journal of University Teaching & Learning Practice, 21*(10). Advance online publication. DOI: 10.53761/7yvrw787

Klimova, B., & Pikhart, M. (2025). Exploring the effects of artificial intelligence on student and academic well-being in Higher Education: A mini-review. *Frontiers in Psychology, 16*. Advance online publication. DOI: 10.3389/fpsyg.2025.1498132 PMID: 39963679

Korpershoek, H., Canrinus, E. T., Fokkens-Bruinsma, M., & de Boer, H. (2019). The relationships between school belonging and students' motivational, social-emotional, behavioural, and academic outcomes in secondary education: A meta-analytic review. *Research Papers in Education, 35*(6), 641–680. DOI: 10.1080/02671522.2019.1615116

Kwet, M. (2019). Digital colonialism: US Empire and the new imperialism in the Global South. *Race & Class, 60*(4). Advance online publication. DOI: 10.1177/0306396818823172

Larcombe, W., Baik, C., & Finch, S. (2021). Exploring course experiences that predict psychological distress and mental wellbeing in Australian undergraduate and graduate coursework students. *Higher Education Research & Development*, •••, 1–16. DOI: 10.1080/07294360.2020.1865284

Leijen, Ä., Pedaste, M., & Baucal, A. (2024). A new psychometrically validated questionnaire for assessing teacher agency in eight dimensions across pre-service and in-service teachers. *Frontiers in Education*, *9*. Advance online publication. DOI: 10.3389/feduc.2024.1336401

Li, H. (2025). Students' wellbeing in positive higher education: Conceptual frameworks and influencing factors. *Frontiers in Education*, *10*. Advance online publication. DOI: 10.3389/feduc.2025.1607364

Luckin, R., Holmes, W., Griffiths, M., & Forcier, L. B. (2016). *Intelligence unleashed: An argument for AI in education*. Pearson.

Mehrabi, N., Morstatter, F., Saxena, N., Lerman, K., & Galstyan, A. (2022). A survey on bias and fairness in machine learning. *ACM Computing Surveys*, *54*(6), 1–35. DOI: 10.1145/3457607

Merino-Campos, C. (2025). The impact of artificial intelligence on personalized learning in higher education: A systematic review. *Trends in Higher Education*, *4*(2), 17. DOI: 10.3390/higheredu4020017

Mustafa, M. Y., Tlili, A., Lampropoulos, G., Huang, R., Jandrić, P., Zhao, J., Salha, S., Xu, L., & Panda, S., Kinshuk, López-Pernas, S., & Saqr, M. (2024). A systematic review of literature reviews on artificial intelligence in education (AIED): A roadmap to a future research agenda. *Smart Learning Environments*, *11*, 59. DOI: 10.1186/s40561-024-00350-5

Myin-Germeys, I., Kasanova, Z., Vaessen, T., Vachon, H., Kirtley, O., Viechtbauer, W., & Reininghaus, U. (2018). Experience sampling methodology in mental health research: New insights and technical developments. *World Psychiatry; Official Journal of the World Psychiatric Association (WPA)*, *17*(2), 123–132. DOI: 10.1002/wps.20513 PMID: 29856567

Oades, L. G., Robinson, P., Green, S., & Spence, G. B. (2011). Towards a positive university. *The Journal of Positive Psychology*, *6*(6), 432–439. DOI: 10.1080/17439760.2011.634828

OECD. (n.d.). *Teachers' occupational well-being framework*. OECD.

Raji, I. D., Kumar, I. E., Horowitz, A., & Selbst, A. (2022). The fallacy of AI functionality. *2022 ACM Conference on Fairness Accountability and Transparency,* 959–972. https://doi.org/DOI: 10.1145/3531146.3533158

Rose, D., & Dalton, B. (2009). Learning to read in the digital age. *Mind, Brain and Education : the Official Journal of the International Mind, Brain, and Education Society, 3*(2), 74–83. DOI: 10.1111/j.1751-228X.2009.01057.x

Saqr, M., Fors, U., & Tedre, M. (2023). Digital transformation in MENA higher education: A review and framework. *Education and Information Technologies, 28*(1), 43–64. DOI: 10.1007/s10639-022-11098-7

Seligman, M. E. P. (2011). *Flourish: A visionary new understanding of happiness and well-being*. Free Press.

Selwyn, N. (2022). The future of AI and education: Some cautionary notes. *European Journal of Education, 57*, 620–631. DOI: 10.1111/ejed.12532

Shneiderman, B. (2020). Human-Centered Artificial Intelligence: Reliable, Safe & Trustworthy. *International Journal of Human-Computer Interaction, 36*(6), 495–504. DOI: 10.1080/10447318.2020.1741118

Smith, B. W., Dalen, J., Wiggins, K., Tooley, E., Christopher, P., & Bernard, J. (2008). The brief resilience scale: Assessing the ability to bounce back. *International Journal of Behavioral Medicine, 15*(3), 194–200. DOI: 10.1080/10705500802222972 PMID: 18696313

Sokal, L., Trudel, L. E., & Babb, J. (2020). Canadian teachers' attitudes toward change, efficacy, and burnout during the COVID-19 Pandemic. *International Journal of Educational Research Open, 1*, 100016. Advance online publication. DOI: 10.1016/j.ijedro.2020.100016

Solis-Grant, M. J., Espinoza-Parçet, C., Sepúlveda-Carrasco, C., Pérez-Villalobos, C., Rodríguez-Núñez, I., Pincheira-Martínez, C., Gómez-Varela, J. P., & Aránguiz-Ibarra, D. (2022). Inclusion at universities: Psychometric properties of an inclusive management scale as perceived by students. *PLoS One, 17*(1), e0262011. DOI: 10.1371/journal.pone.0262011 PMID: 34995314

Tarafdar, M., Cooper, C. L., & Stich, J. (2019). The Technostress Trifecta - techno eustress, techno distress and design: Theoretical directions and an agenda for research. *Information Systems Journal, 29*(1), 6–42. DOI: 10.1111/isj.12169

Tondeur, J., Howard, S. K., & Yang, J. (2021). One-size does not fit all: Towards an adaptive model to develop preservice teachers' digital competencies. *Computers in Human Behavior, 116*, 106659. DOI: 10.1016/j.chb.2020.106659

UNESCO. (2021). *Recommendation on the ethics of artificial intelligence*. Paris: UNESCO. https://unesdoc.unesco.org/ark:/48223/pf0000381137

UNESCO. (2023). *Global Education Monitoring Report Summary 2023: Technology in education, A tool on whose terms?* Paris: UNESCO. https://www.unesco.org/gem-report/en/publication/technology-education

Uygun, E. (2026). Clashing AIs: Artificial intelligence literacy and academic integrity in an EFL context. *Journal of Academic Ethics*, *24*, 7. DOI: 10.1007/s10805-025-09676-2

Walton, G. M., & Cohen, G. L. (2011). A brief social-belonging intervention improves academic and health outcomes of minority students. *Science*, *331*(6023), 1447–1451. DOI: 10.1126/science.1198364 PMID: 21415354

Wang, Z., Chai, C.-S., Li, J., & Lee, V. W. (2025). Assessment of AI ethical reflection: The development and validation of the AI Ethical Reflection Scale (AIERS) for university students. *International Journal of Educational Technology in Higher Education*, *22*(1). Advance online publication. DOI: 10.1186/s41239-025-00519-z

Williamson, B., & Eynon, R. (2020). Historical threads, missing links, and future directions in AI in education. *Learning, Media and Technology*, *45*(3), 223–235. DOI: 10.1080/17439884.2020.1798995

Williamson, B., & Hogan, A. (2020). *Commercialisation and privatisation in/of education in the context of Covid-19*. Education International. https://eprints.qut.edu.au/216577/

World Economic Forum. (2025). *AI in Action: Beyond Experimentation to Transform Industry*. Retrieved from https://reports.weforum.org/docs/WEF_AI_in_Action_Beyond_Experimentation_to_Transform_Industry_2025.pdf

Xanthopoulou, D., Bakker, A. B., Demerouti, E., & Schaufeli, W. B. (2007). The role of personal resources in the job demands-resources model. *International Journal of Stress Management*, *14*(2), 121–141. DOI: 10.1037/1072-5245.14.2.121

Yan, Y., Liu, H., & Chau, T. (2025). A systematic review of AI ethics in education: Challenges, policy gaps, and future directions. *Journal of Global Information Management*, *33*(1), 1–50. DOI: 10.4018/JGIM.386381

Yeager, D. S., & Dweck, C. S. (2012). Mindsets that promote resilience: When students believe that personal characteristics can be developed. *Educational Psychologist*, *47*(4), 302–314. DOI: 10.1080/00461520.2012.722805

Zheng, L., Long, M., Zhong, L., & Gyasi, J. F. (2022). The effectiveness of technology-facilitated personalized learning on learning achievements and learning perceptions: A meta-analysis. *Education and Information Technologies*, *27*(8), 11807–11830. DOI: 10.1007/s10639-022-11092-7

Chapter 5
Enhancing Collaborative Learning Through Gamification in UAE Schools:
Evidence From Teachers' Perspectives

Khadeegha Alzouebi
http://orcid.org/0000-0001-7624-7040
Hamdan Bin Mohammed Smart University, UAE

Dua Alhammadi
http://orcid.org/0000-0002-0782-0111
Ministry of Education, UAE

ABSTRACT

This quantitative study of 146 UAE K-12 teachers examines how gamification shapes collaborative learning and the prospective contribution of AI. An online survey captured perceptions of benefits, effectiveness (lessons/websites), and implementation barriers. Analyses (descriptives, Cronbach's alpha, regression, one-sample t-tests) show gamification significantly predicts collaborative outcomes, explaining 52.5% of variance. Kahoot and ClassDojo were viewed as highly effective for engagement, cohesion, and behaviour. Reported obstacles included time-intensive design, limited methodological expertise, and curriculum constraints. Although AI data were not collected, we outline how AI-enabled gamification could personalise learning, automate feedback, and optimise group dynamics. We recommend curricular and professional development integration

DOI: 10.4018/979-8-3373-6776-7.ch005

INTRODUCTION

Definitions and Importance

Learning has evolved considerably in the digital age with the emergence of the internet, social media, e-learning tools, and intelligent educational technologies. One of the most challenging aspects of this transformation is facilitating effective online collaborative learning (Elsawah & Charles, 2023). Being an intrinsically social activity, e-learning cannot function properly without active interaction among participants. However, many learners find the process of engaging with peers overwhelming, and educators face increasing difficulties in sustaining meaningful collaboration in virtual and hybrid classrooms (Hill et al., 2023). As technology advances, researchers continue to explore innovative approaches to increase student motivation and enhance collaborative engagement (Abukhalaf et al., 2024). Among these, gamification has been highlighted as an effective pedagogical strategy to foster student participation and improve collaborative learning outcomes (Azmi et al., 2015).

Gamification, according to Kapp (2012), is the use of game-based mechanics, aesthetics, and game thinking to engage people, encourage action, promote learning, and solve problems. Educational gamification involves reimagining traditional academic activities through game-inspired elements such as points, badges, leaderboards, and challenges (Charles et al., 2025). Its primary objective is to enhance student learning by improving participation and sustaining engagement (Alshehhi et al., 2024). Gamification can also be viewed as the application of game design principles to educational contexts to increase learner motivation and enjoyment (Dichev & Dicheva, 2017).

Purpose of the Study

In recent years, artificial intelligence (AI) has begun to transform the potential of gamification in educational contexts by enabling adaptive, personalised, and data-driven learning experiences (Charles, 2025). AI-powered platforms can analyse real-time student interactions, provide automated feedback, and dynamically adjust task difficulty based on individual learner needs (Azzam & Charles, 2025). These innovations extend the value of gamification by enhancing its capacity to improve motivation, collaboration, and group cohesion—critical components of 21st-century classrooms (Charles & Hill, 2025). While the current study does not directly investigate AI, understanding its integration alongside gamification offers a broader perspective on how emerging technologies can enhance collaborative learning outcomes.

In education, the concept of collaborative learning refers to approaches where students and teachers work together intellectually to construct knowledge. Students collaborate in small groups to solve problems, generate ideas, or produce shared outputs. While lecture-based instruction still plays a role, collaborative classrooms are characterised by active participation, peer-to-peer learning, and student-centred dialogue (Smith & MacGregor, 1992). With the increasing availability of digital tools, students can now co-create documents, develop presentations remotely, and engage in synchronous and asynchronous group activities. However, despite this technological progress, sustaining motivation for collaborative group work remains a persistent challenge.

Research Questions

The purpose of this research is to examine the impact of gamification on collaborative learning and to evaluate its benefits and challenges within K-12 education in the UAE. While gamification has been shown to enhance student motivation and group engagement, the growing potential of AI-driven educational platforms offers promising opportunities for further amplifying these effects. This study investigates teachers' perceptions of gamification in the classroom, identifies barriers to effective implementation, and highlights future pathways for integrating emerging technologies such as AI to strengthen collaborative learning practices. Crucially, the research addresses the following questions:

- What are the key benefits of gamification on learning?
- What is the impact of gamification on student motivation to work collaboratively in group work activities?
- What are the key challenges of implementing gamification in schools?

LITERATURE REVIEW

Gamification and its Educational Significance

Collaborative learning has long been recognised as a key approach for fostering deeper understanding, enhancing communication, and improving student performance. According to Laal and Ghodsi (2012), collaborative learning generates numerous benefits—social, psychological, academic, and assessment-related—by promoting mutual support and collective knowledge-building rather than competition.

In parallel, the integration of gamification in educational contexts has emerged as a transformative strategy for enhancing engagement and motivation.

Gamification, as defined by Kapp (2012), involves incorporating game-based mechanics, aesthetics, and thinking into educational settings to encourage participation, promote learning, and solve instructional challenges. Typical features of gamification include points, badges, leaderboards, avatars, and interactive challenges, all of which are designed to make learning more interactive and enjoyable (Alshehhi et al., 2024). By turning academic concepts into game-like experiences, educators aim to increase learners' motivation, persistence, and engagement (Dichev & Dicheva, 2017).

Emerging research has shown that gamification not only boosts student motivation but also supports more dynamic learning environments. For example, Yaşar et al. (2020) found that primary school teachers frequently rely on elements such as badges and leaderboards to enhance motivation and student performance. Similarly, Lutfi, Suyono, and Hidayah (2021) demonstrated that integrating gamified tools, particularly computer-assisted learning platforms, significantly improves engagement and fosters a more student-centred learning environment.

The Emergence of AI-Driven Gamification

Recent advances in AI are reshaping the educational technology landscape, expanding the potential of gamification to deliver personalised and adaptive learning experiences (Charles & Charles, 2024). AI-powered gamification platforms can dynamically analyse learner behaviours, identify performance patterns, and provide real-time recommendations based on individual learning needs. This capacity enables educators to move beyond static game elements towards data-driven gamification, in which feedback, task complexity, and rewards are customised for each student's abilities and progress.

AI-driven tools such as Classcraft, Century Tech, and Smart Sparrow have demonstrated the ability to automatically track engagement, adapt challenges, and optimise group dynamics. By combining AI analytics with gamification mechanics, these systems enhance collaboration, motivation, and social presence—critical aspects of 21st-century learning environments. Importantly, while the current study does not examine AI empirically, positioning gamification within this broader technological context highlights its growing role in shaping the future of collaborative education.

Gamification and Collaborative Learning

Collaborative learning relies on students working together in small groups to solve problems, create shared outputs, and negotiate meaning, thus enhancing critical thinking and knowledge construction. Gamification has been shown to amplify these processes by increasing peer interaction, group cohesion, and shared goal orientation (Sailer & Homner, 2020). Their meta-analysis found that combining competition and collaboration in gamified learning environments produced significant improvements in behavioural and motivational learning outcomes.

Similarly, Bilgin and Gul (2020) investigated the effectiveness of gamification in collaborative learning environments and found that gamification elements improved group cohesion, strengthened academic performance, and promoted positive social interactions. These findings are echoed by Wiethof, Tavanapour, and Bittner (2021), who examined the integration of gamification into collaborative writing tasks. Their study revealed that carefully designed gamified environments enhance hedonic motivation, encourage creativity, and increase the intention to sustain participation over time.

AI further strengthens this dynamic by using predictive analytics to monitor group engagement and identify patterns of disengagement early. For example, AI-driven gamification platforms can detect when specific students contribute less during group tasks and automatically recommend targeted interventions, such as assigning new roles, adjusting challenge levels, or providing personalised feedback. This alignment between AI, gamification, and collaboration highlights a new frontier in educational technology where adaptive systems support both group and individual learning trajectories.

Benefits and Challenges of Gamification

Research highlights numerous benefits of gamification, including improved engagement, enhanced academic outcomes, and stronger learner motivation. Studies such as Bicen and Kocakoyun (2018) demonstrate that gamified environments enable students to track their progress, earn rewards, and remain committed to their tasks, while Barahona Mora (2020) showed that integrating gamified platforms like ClassDojo promotes positive behavioural development and reduces disruptive classroom behaviours.

However, implementing gamification is not without challenges. Yasar et al. (2020) reported that excessive competition can cause disengagement, while Bálint-Svella (2021) highlighted that many educators and pre-service teachers struggle to differentiate between game-based learning and gamification. Additionally, this study found that planning gamified lessons is time-intensive, teacher training remains limited, and curriculum constraints often hinder adoption.

AI-powered tools have the potential to address several of these obstacles. Intelligent gamification systems can automate lesson design, generate adaptive activities based on predefined learning objectives, and assist teachers in monitoring progress with minimal manual intervention. Moreover, AI-driven feedback mechanisms can help identify learning gaps early and offer tailored recommendations, thereby reducing the workload on educators while supporting differentiated learning pathways.

Summary of Literature

The reviewed literature demonstrates that gamification significantly enhances learner motivation, engagement, and collaboration across K-12 educational contexts. However, emerging AI technologies represent an evolutionary step in this process, enabling gamification to become more personalised, adaptive, and data-driven. While the current study focuses on teachers' perceptions of gamification in UAE schools, recognising the potential synergy between gamification and AI provides a broader framework for interpreting findings and informing future research directions.

METHODOLOGY

The research is meant to describe and provide explanations to answer questions and objectives. The data was gathered through an online survey filled out by teachers. This study will collect data using a quantitative research approach by use of questionnaires. Since an online (email) survey is the most time- and cost-effective method, that's how the research collected data for this study. The survey was sent to educators who have already used gamification their classes. The study's results can serve as a roadmap for addressing challenges that may occur in educational settings when gamification is implemented, and they can assist guide educators as they refine and perfect their own teaching methods to maximise the potential of gamification.

Teachers in the UAE serve as the study population, and an online survey was used to collect information about gamification impact benefits and challenges. Due to logistical reasons and covid 19 precautions, the responses were limited participation in this study to 146 teachers in the UAE using random sampling method. The primary method of data collecting for this study was an online survey. Participants will receive the online questionnaire through email and can take their time filling it out at their convenience. The research targeted UAE educators. Educators from all over the UAE participated in the study, and their replies was used to explore how well they employ gamification strategies in the classroom.

There were a series of questions examining the influence of gamification and the ways in which it might propel students toward greater levels of learning and collaborative learning. The survey contains five parts, each containing five questions, and it is anonymous. It takes the responder around 10–15 minutes to complete the survey. The questionnaire was disseminated and sent to teachers to be completed between September 1 and 7, 2022. It was aimed to gather information from at least 100 private and government teachers throughout the UAE. To reach a wide population, the researchers used Microsoft Forms to create and host the survey, which would then be disseminated to potential respondents via email and messaging apps like WhatsApp and Telegram. To boost the probability that participants will complete the whole survey, some items was marked as mandatory. Each educator can answer the survey just once from a single device to ensure an accurate total. The main variables in this study were:

- Benefits of Gamification
- Gamification & Collaborative Learning
- Gamified Lessons & Websites
- Gamification Challenges

RESULTS

The result of the analysis carried out in the course of this research are outlined and presented in this section. The data set used for analysis was derived from the survey conducted by the researchers which seeks to elicit or gather information on the impact of gamification on collaborative learning in UAE schools. The data set comprises of 146 responses, that is observations. The survey, as well as the data set, are in 5 sections, the demographic characteristics, items scale measuring and evaluating benefits of gamification, gamification and collaborative learning, gamified websites, and Gamification challenges. The questions measuring the factors in the data set are measured on a likert scale of five (Strongly disagree, disagree, Neutral, agree, and strongly agree).

The data set which was originally in excel format was exported from google form and subjected to computational analysis using special package for social sciences. Thus, the data set was converted to SPSS Sav format. Responses were recoded from string form into numeric forms, strongly disagree – 1, disagree – 2, neutral – 3, disagree- 4, and strongly disagree – 5. Questions and items measuring each of the 4 factors and measures were validated and examined for reliability using the reliability test (Cronbach's Alpha test). This study made use of three basic analytical procedures which were conducted to addresses the major objective of this study. Analysis carried out in the study includes Descriptive statistics, preliminary tests and inferential analysis. Descriptive statistics used for this data set involves the use of frequency and percentages to explain the distribution of the variables especially for categorical variables as well as the use of mean and standard deviation of variables that are numerical or ordinal in nature. The preliminary tests utilized to examine the reliability of the items is the Cronbach's Alpha test. Lastly, inferential statistics used involved the use of linear regression analysis to address the research questions and objectives of the study.

Demographic Characteristics

The frequency and percentage distribution of demographic characteristics of respondents is provided in Table 1. It can be observed that there are 118 females (80.8%) and 28 males (19.2%) in the survey. In terms of age distribution which have been categorized into 4 age groups, it can be observed that 12 of the respondents are between the ages of 20 to 30 years, 51 are between the ages of 31 to 40 years, 68 of the respondents are between the ages of 41 to 50 years and the remaining are between the ages of 51 to 60 years.

Findings have also revealed that 3 of the respondents reside in Abu Dhabi, 5 reside in Ajman, 10 reside in Dubai, 4 respondents reside in Ras Al Khaima, 1 respondent reside in Al Quwain, 88 respondents reside in Sharjah, and 35 reside in Fujairah. The distribution of years of experience of respondents shows that, 83 respondents have experience of between 10 to 20 years, 23 have below 10 years, and 40 individuals have experience of more than 20 years. In terms of educational background or degree findings have shown that 114 individuals have bachelor's degree, 6 have a diploma, 23 have attained a master's degree and the remaining 3 have a PhD. Lastly, 141 individuals attended a government school and 5 attended a private school.

Table 1. Participants' demographic information

Demographic Characteristics		n	%
Gender	Female	118	80.8%
	Male	28	19.2%
Age of Respondents	20-30	12	8.2%
	31-40	51	34.9%
	41-50	68	46.6%
	51-60	15	10.3%
City of Residence	Abu Dhabi	3	2.1%
	Ajman	5	3.4%
	Dubai	10	6.8%
	Ras Al Khaima	4	2.7%
	Um Al Quwain	1	0.7%

continued on following page

Table 1. Continued

Demographic Characteristics		*n*	%
	Sharjah	88	60.3%
	Fujairah	35	24.0%
Years of Experience	Between 10-20 Years	83	56.8%
	Below 10 Years	23	15.8%
	More than Twenty years	40	27.4%
Degree	Bachelor	114	78.1%
	Diploma	6	4.1%
	Master	23	15.8%
	PhD	3	2.1%
Type of School	Government School	141	96.6%
	Private school	5	3.4%

Descriptive statistics was used in evaluating and exploring the responses and views of respondents to questions on issues raised. Each of the items or questions have been answered on a likert scale of 5 (strongly disagree 1 to strongly agree 5). The mean and standard deviation for the five items measuring and evaluating the benefits of gamification have been provided in table 2. Since the responses are in likert scale with 4 and 5 signifying agree and strongly agree respectively. Mean responses that are 4 and above implies that most respondents agree with the particular questions being asked or item. However, responses lower than 3.0 would suggest that most respondents do not agree with the question or statement. While the standard deviation is a measure of how wide apart, dispersed or far apart the responses of the participants are from the mean or average response to each question being asked. A higher standard deviation suggests that the responses are far apart from the mean, while a lower standard deviation means participants' responses are not far apart or not dispersed from the mean. In Table 2, it can be observed that all the average responses to each statement measuring and evaluating the benefits of Gamification are above 4.0. This implies that respondents agree to all statements made in the survey concerning the benefit of gamification.

Table 2. Benefits of Gamification

	n	*M*	*SD*
Gamification makes learning fun and interactive	146	4.5274	.78076
Gamification in education has a strong positive impact on students' perceptions of its usefulness	146	4.3288	.80609
Gamification fosters loving, supportive, and long-term connections among students	146	4.2877	.84657
Gamification increase students' success and motivation in lessons	146	4.3767	.80636
Gamification improve learning outcomes by improving the engagement of students and creating an inspiring environment.	146	4.3904	.67847

In Table 3, it can be observed that all the average responses to each statement measuring and evaluating the collaborative learning using Gamification are above 4.0. This implies that respondents agree to all statements made in the survey concerning the Collaborative learning.

Table 3. Gamification & Collaborative Learning

	n	*M*	*SD*
The use of gamification and the combination of competition and collaboration is beneficial in gamification for developing behavioral learning outcomes	145	4.2828	.82246
The impacts of competition supplemented with collaboration is applicable for motivational learning outcomes	146	4.2603	.83917
Using gamification in a collaborative learning environment enhanced group cohesion and achievement	146	4.2808	.88468
Gamification enhances hedonic motivation and meaningful engagement	146	4.3630	.77797
Gamification Features operates as an enticing factor among group members, resulting in more commitment and improved learning	146	4.3288	.73447

In Table 4, findings from the descriptive statistics have shown that the average responses to each statement measuring and evaluating the use of gamified lessons and websites are above 4.0. This implies that respondents agree to all statements made in the survey concerning gamified lessons and websites.

Table 4. Gamified Lessons & Websites

	n	*M*	*SD*
Incorporating gamification techniques has a positive impact on student motivation	146	4.3973	.73793
Gamification allowed students to see their achievement status and improve in areas where they were weak	146	4.3082	.73873
Merging a gamification approach with a hybrid method of learning allowed students to understand the lesson better	146	4.3973	.66932

continued on following page

Table 4. Continued

	n	*M*	*SD*
Using gamified websites like class dojo helps in improving desired behaviors while reducing disruptive ones, using game design mechanics and principles in the environment of learning to trigger in	146	4.3082	.72934
Gamified websites improve students' behavioral growth, allow them to perform better	146	4.2671	.74548

In Table 5, findings from the descriptive statistics of items and questions of gamification challenges have shown that 4 out of the 5 items have their average responses above 4.0 as shown in the table below while the average response of the fourth items is 3.55 which is below 4.0. This implies that not all respondents agreed to these statements.

Table 5. Gamification Challenges

	n	*M*	*SD*
The most significant issue that teachers confront when implementing gamification features is the children's over-competitive actions	146	4.0479	.79942
Planning and preparing a gamified lesson is a major challenge of gamification as it takes a long time for the teacher to plan and prepare the gamified lesson	146	4.0959	.84142
The absence of methodological knowledge as well as curriculum constraints as obstacles to gamification	146	4.1096	.79761
The time allotted to implement the gamified lessons can be better used in the traditional	146	3.5479	1.07692
Incorporating gamification aspects while considering other actions rather than just success in lessons is the most successful method.	146	4.1781	.71134

Items in each of the four sections (factors) were summed up and averaged to form composite variables which are shown in Table 6. Descriptive statistics was carried out for the newly formed variables with their mean and standard deviation distribution. It can be observed that the average of these items after summing them up and averaging them are all above 4.0 except for gamification challenges.

Table 6. Composite variables

	n	*M*	*SD*
Benefits of Gamification	146	4.3822	.67422
Gamification & Collaborative Learning	146	4.3021	.71828
Gamified Lessons & Websites	146	4.3356	.69795
Gamification Challenges	146	3.9959	.80908

Preliminary test was carried out on the item variables of the data set. The reliability test in form of the Cronbach's alpha test was carried out to examine the reliability and consistency of the items (*see* Table 7). The Cronbach's alpha is a measure of internal consistency; how closely related a number of items are as a group. The coefficient ranges between 0 and 1. A high alpha value indicates that items measure an underlying factor. However, it is not a statistical test but a test of reliability/consistency. The result of the Cronbach's Alpha is provided in the table above with the Alpha values. It can be observed that the Cronbach's Alpha value for all the Four composite variables are greater than 0.70 which means that the observations, that is items, in the variables are reliable except for the data accountability variables.

Table 7. Reliability test

Variable / Measure	Cronbach's Alpha	Items
Benefits of Gamification	0.910	5
Gamification & Collaborative Learning	0.929	5
Gamified Lessons & Websites	0.980	5
Gamification Challenges	0.971	5

Impact of Gamification on Collaborative learning

The objectives and research question of the study are addressed and answered respectively in this section. The major objective is to examine the impact of gamification on collaborative learning. To address this objective an ordinary linear square regression was conducted. The Ordinary Least Squares (OLS) regression also known as simple linear regression helps examine the extent to which a variable is linearly related to another variable and also the extent to which a variable (independent) predicts another variable (outcome or predicted variable) (statistics.laerd.com). The independent variable is the benefit of gamification while the dependent variable is collaborative learning. Table 8 is the model summary table which shows the R square value, and the R square shows the variation and changes in the dependent variable accounted. It can be observed that R square is 0.525L This implies that the benefits of gamification account for a 52.5% change or variation in collaborative learning.

Table 8. OLS regression analysis [a]

Model	R	R Square	Adjusted R Square	Std. Error of the Estimate
1	.725[a]	.525	.522	.49670

a. Predictors: (Constant), Benefits of Gamification

The ANOVA result (*see* Table 9) shows the level of significance of the regression model in predicting the dependent variable, collaborative learning. It can be observed that the regression model significantly predicts collaborative learning, F (1, 144) = 159.231, $p < 0.05$.

Table 9. Results of ANOVA [a]

Model		Sum of Squares	df	Mean Square	F	Sig.
1	Regression	39.283	1	39.283	159.231	.000[b]
	Residual	35.526	144	.247		
	Total	74.809	145			

a. Dependent Variable: Gamification & Collaborative Learning
b. Predictors: (Constant), Benefits of Gamification

The coefficient of the independent variable is provided in the coefficient Table 10 below and it can be observed that gamification (benefits of Gamification) has a significant effect or influence on collaborative learning, $p < 0.01$. This implies that Gamification influence or affect collaborative learning. The value of the regression coefficient which is 0.779 suggests that the impact of Gamification on collaborative learning is positive.

Table 10. Coefficient of the independent variable [a]

Model		Unstandardized Coefficients		Standardized Coefficients	t	Sig.
		B	Std. Error	Beta		
1	(Constant)	.919	.271		3.388	.001
	Benefits of Gamification	.772	.061	.725	12.619	.000

a. Dependent Variable: Gamification & Collaborative Learning

To address the objectives on significant benefit and utilization of gamified lessons and websites, a one-sample T-test (*see* Table 11). The one-sample T-test is used to determine whether a sample comes from a population with a specific mean. Here the goal is to examine if respondents significantly agree with responses on the benefits of gamified lessons and websites. Therefore, the test value is 4.0 which is the Likert value for agreeing. It can be observed from the one-sample statistics that the average responses in on Gamified lessons and websites is 4.34 ± 0.70.

Table 11. Benefits of Gamified lessons and Websites

	n	*M*	*SD*	Std. Error Mean
Gamified Lessons & Websites	146	4.3356	.69795	.05776

The one-sample Test shows the actual result of the one-sample test, by observing the sig (2-tailed) value or p-value. It can be observed that the p-value is 0.000 which implies that respondents significantly agree that gamified lessons and websites are beneficial (*see* Table 12).

Table 12. One-Sample Test

	Test Value = 4					
	t	df	Sig. (2-tailed)	Mean Difference	95% Confidence Interval of the Difference	
					Lower	Upper
Gamified Lessons & Websites	5.810	145	.000	.33562	.2215	.4498

A one-way sample t-test was carried out to examine those challenges which respondents believe are affecting Gamification. It can be observed that respondents significantly agree that the absence of methodological knowledge as well as curriculum constraints as obstacles to gamification, time allotted to implement the gamified lessons, and the incorporation of gamification aspects while taking into account other actions rather than just success in lessons are major challenges of Gamification, $p < 0.05$ (*see* Table 13).

Table 13. Challenges of Gamification

	Test Value = 4					
	t	df	Sig. (2-tailed)	Mean Difference	95% Confidence Interval of the Difference	
					Lower	Upper
The most significant issue that teachers confront when implementing gamification features is the children's over-competitive actions	.725	145	.470	.04795	-.0828	.1787
Planning and preparing a gamified lesson is a major challenge of gamification as it takes a long time for the teacher to plan and prepare the gamified lesson	1.377	145	.171	.09589	-.0417	.2335
The absence of methodological knowledge as well as curriculum constraints as obstacles to gamification	1.660	145	.099	.10959	-.0209	.2401
The time allotted to implement the gamified lessons can be better used in the traditional	-5.072	145	.000	-.45205	-.6282	-.2759
Incorporating gamification aspects while taking into account other actions rather than just success in lessons is the most successful method.	3.025	145	.003	.17808	.0617	.2944

DISCUSSION

This study sought to examine the impact of gamification on collaborative learning within K-12 schools in the United Arab Emirates (UAE), focusing on teachers' perceptions of its benefits, challenges, and overall influence on student motivation and engagement. Using a quantitative approach, data from 146 teachers were analysed through descriptive statistics, reliability testing, linear regression, and one-sample t-tests. The findings demonstrate that gamification significantly enhances collaborative learning, accounting for 52.5% of the variance in group-based outcomes, confirming its effectiveness in fostering student participation, group cohesion, and knowledge-sharing.

Gamification's Impact on Collaborative Learning

The regression analysis indicated that gamification positively predicts collaborative learning outcomes ($R^2 = 0.525$), supporting previous findings that game-based instructional strategies encourage motivation, peer interaction, and a sense of belonging among learners (Sailer & Homner, 2020). Teachers reported that gamified lessons increased student engagement, promoted teamwork, and improved classroom participation. Platforms such as Kahoot and ClassDojo were identified as particularly effective for stimulating collaboration, providing opportunities for students to compete, share insights, and celebrate collective success.

These findings align with prior studies demonstrating that gamification enhances group learning by fostering both competition and cooperation (Bilgin & Gul, 2020; Wiethof et al., 2021). In the context of UAE classrooms, where diverse student populations often require differentiated strategies, gamification appears to create shared incentives that strengthen students' intrinsic and extrinsic motivation to work collaboratively.

Addressing Challenges Through AI-Enhanced Gamification

Despite its positive effects, the study also revealed several challenges reported by teachers, including time-intensive lesson planning, limited methodological knowledge, and curriculum constraints. These findings are consistent with previous research indicating that educators often face resource limitations and lack structured training when implementing gamification strategies (Yaşar et al., 2020; Bálint-Svella, 2021).

This is where AI presents an important opportunity to extend the benefits of gamification while mitigating its practical barriers. AI-powered platforms can automate significant aspects of gamification design, such as:

- Adaptive personalisation: AI algorithms can tailor difficulty levels, feedback, and rewards based on individual student performance, ensuring that gamified tasks remain engaging for both advanced and struggling learners.
- Automated lesson planning: Intelligent gamification tools can generate data-driven activity recommendations aligned with curricular goals, reducing teacher preparation time.
- Real-time engagement monitoring: AI analytics can track participation trends within collaborative groups, identify disengaged students, and prompt teachers with targeted intervention strategies.

By integrating AI, gamification can evolve from static, teacher-driven designs to dynamic, adaptive ecosystems that provide continuous, personalised support while strengthening group collaboration. Although the present study did not collect AI-specific data, these insights create a foundation for understanding how emerging technologies can amplify the collaborative outcomes observed in this research.

Implications for Educational Practice

The findings of this study have several implications for UAE schools and similar educational contexts. First, teacher professional development should focus not only on designing effective gamified experiences but also on leveraging AI-driven platforms to enhance efficiency and effectiveness. AI-powered tools such as Classcraft, Knewton Alta, and Century Tech provide ready-made gamification frameworks that enable educators to focus more on facilitating collaboration rather than designing every activity manually.

Second, AI can enhance equity in collaborative learning by identifying individual learning gaps and recommending differentiated gamified pathways that keep all students engaged. In classrooms where students possess varied language proficiencies, abilities, and motivations, AI's adaptive intelligence can ensure that collaborative learning opportunities remain accessible to everyone.

Finally, these findings highlight the need for policy-level strategies to integrate AI-supported gamification into UAE education. This includes curriculum design, procurement of intelligent gamified platforms, and structured training programmes to equip teachers with the technical and pedagogical skills necessary to maximise student engagement.

Future Research Directions

While this study focused on teachers' perceptions of gamification's impact, future research could empirically investigate AI-enhanced gamification to build on these findings. Potential research avenues include:

1. Evaluating AI-driven gamification tools and their effects on collaboration, motivation, and learning performance in K-12 contexts.
2. Comparative studies between traditional gamification platforms and AI-powered adaptive systems to measure differences in student engagement and group outcomes.
3. Longitudinal analyses examining how AI-assisted gamification influences sustained motivation and collaborative skill development over time.

By integrating AI-based frameworks into future investigations, researchers can explore the next generation of gamification—one that uses automation, predictive analytics, and personalisation to further enhance collaborative learning.

Summary of Findings

This study establishes that gamification is a powerful pedagogical strategy for promoting collaborative learning, motivation, and engagement in UAE classrooms. Teachers' perceptions highlight gamification's ability to make learning interactive and enjoyable, with statistical analyses confirming its significant positive impact. However, by incorporating AI-driven solutions, schools can overcome key challenges and unlock new opportunities for personalised, data-driven, and highly adaptive collaborative learning environments.

Ultimately, the integration of gamification and AI represents a promising trajectory for future education, positioning technology as a co-designer of learning experiences that empower both teachers and students.

CONCLUSION

This study investigated the impact of gamification on collaborative learning within K-12 schools in the United Arab Emirates, focusing on teachers' perceptions of its benefits, challenges, and overall influence on student motivation and engagement. Using a quantitative research design, data from 146 teachers revealed that gamification significantly improves collaborative learning, accounting for 52.5% of the variance in group-based outcomes. Teachers consistently highlighted that gamified platforms such as Kahoot and ClassDojo enhance student motivation, group cohesion, and overall engagement, reinforcing the value of gamification as a powerful pedagogical tool.

However, the findings also underscore persistent challenges, including time-intensive lesson planning, limited methodological knowledge, and curriculum constraints. While these barriers limit widespread adoption, emerging AI-driven gamification tools provide promising solutions. AI-powered platforms can personalise learning experiences, automate feedback, monitor real-time engagement, and recommend adaptive challenges, enabling teachers to create dynamic and inclusive collaborative environments with reduced workload.

The integration of AI-enhanced gamification represents the next phase of educational innovation. By leveraging intelligent systems alongside established gamified frameworks, schools can foster personalised, adaptive, and data-driven learning ecosystems that strengthen collaboration, equity, and engagement across diverse student populations.

Moving forward, future research should investigate the direct impact of AI-driven gamification tools on collaboration, motivation, and learning outcomes in K-12 classrooms. Comparative and longitudinal studies are needed to evaluate the effectiveness of AI-enhanced systems relative to traditional gamification approaches and to examine how adaptive technologies influence student participation over time.

In conclusion, this study establishes gamification as a transformative strategy for improving collaborative learning in UAE classrooms while positioning AI as a key driver of future advancements. Integrating these technologies into educational practice has the potential to redefine teaching and learning by creating intelligent, personalised, and highly engaging environments that empower both educators and students.

REFERENCES

Abukhalaf, S., Charles, T., & Hill, C. (2024). The Metaverse as a Virtual Learning Space: Perceptions from the UAE. *Journal of Ecohumanism*, *3*(5), 1037–1052. DOI: 10.62754/joe.v3i5.3954

Alshehhi, N., Alzouebi, K., & Charles, T. (2024). Perspectives On Game-Based Learning Within The Higher Education Sector. *Educational Administration: Theory and Practice*, *30*(5), 3229–3233. DOI: 10.53555/kuey.v30i5.2153

Azmi, S., Iahad, N. A., & Ahmad, N. (2015). Gamification in online collaborative learning for programming courses: A literature review. *Journal of Engineering and Applied Sciences (Asian Research Publishing Network)*, *10*(23), 1–3.

Azzam, A., & Charles, T. (2025). K-12 STEM Teachers' Experiences with Artificial Intelligence. *TEM Journal, 14*(1), 463. DOI: 10.18421/TEM141-41

Bálint-Svella, É. (2021). Prospective Preschool and Primary School Teachers' Knowledge and Opinion about Gamification. *Acta Didactica Napocensia*, *14*(1), 104–114.

Barahona Mora, A. (2020). Gamification for classroom management: An implementation using classdojo. *Sustainability*, *12*(22), 9371. DOI: 10.3390/su12229371

Bicen, H., & Kocakoyun, S. (2018). Perceptions of students for gamification approach: Kahoot as a case study. *International Journal of Emerging Technologies in Learning*, *13*(2).

Bilgin, C. U., & Gul, A. (2020). Investigating the effectiveness of gamification on group cohesion, attitude, and academic achievement in collaborative learning environments. *TechTrends*, *64*(1), 124–136.

Charles, R., & Charles, T. (2024). High School Students' Perceptions of Using AI for Learning. *Voice of the Publisher*, *10*(3), 284–297. DOI: 10.4236/vp.2024.103024

Charles, T. (2025). AI in Professional Development for English Language Teachers. In *AI Applications for English Language Learning* (pp. 73–92). IGI Global Scientific Publishing., DOI: 10.4018/979-8-3693-9077-1.ch004

Charles, T., & Hill, C. (2025). Micro-Credentials and AI in Higher Education: Transforming Professional Development. In *Prompt Engineering and Generative AI Applications for Teaching and Learning* (pp. 1-14). IGI Global Scientific Publishing. DOI: 10.4018/979-8-3693-7332-3.ch001

Charles, T., Zoelfakar, S., & Sebastian, S. (2025). Micro-Credentials in Vocational and Professional Training. In *Integrating Micro-Credentials With AI in Open Education* (pp. 217–250). IGI Global Scientific Publishing., DOI: 10.4018/979-8-3693-5488-9.ch010

Dichev, C., & Dicheva, D. (2017). Gamifying education: what is known, what is believed and what remains uncertain: a critical review. *International Journal of Educational Technology in Higher Education, 14*, 1–36. DOI: 10.1186/s41239-017-0042-5

Elsawah, W., & Charles, T. (2023). Investigating Emirati Students' Practices of Learning Block-Based Programming in an Online Learning Context: Evidence from a UAE National Program. In *BUiD Doctoral Research Conference 2022: Multidisciplinary Studies* (pp. 131-142). Cham: Springer Nature Switzerland. DOI: 10.1007/978-3-031-27462-6_12

Hill, C., Abu-Ayyash, E., & Charles, T. (2023). By nature, a social animal: An exploration of perceptions of online group work. *Cambridge Journal of Education, 53*(5), 665–681. DOI: 10.1080/0305764X.2023.2206795

Kapp, K. M. (2012). *The gamification of learning and instruction: Game-based methods and strategies for training and education*. Pfeiffer.

Laal, M., & Ghodsi, S. M. (2012). Benefits of collaborative learning. *Procedia: Social and Behavioral Sciences, 31*, 486–490. DOI: 10.1016/j.sbspro.2011.12.091

Lutfi, A., & Hidayah, R. (2021). Applying gamification to improve the quality of teaching and learning of Chemistry in high schools: A case study of Indonesia. *Asia-Pacific Forum on Science Learning & Teaching, 20*(2), 1–17.

Sailer, M., & Homner, L. (2020). The gamification of learning: A meta-analysis. *Educational Psychology Review, 32*(1), 77–112. DOI: 10.1007/s10648-019-09498-w

Smith, B. L., & MacGregor, J. T. (1992) "What is collaborative learning?" In Goodsell, A., Maher, M., Tinto, V., Smith, B.L., MacGregor J. T. (Eds.), *Collaborative Learning: A Sourcebook for Higher Education*. National Center on postsecondary teaching, learning, and assessment publishing, Pennsylvania State University, USA.

Wiethof, C., Tavanapour, N., & Bittner, E. (2021). Designing and evaluating a collaborative writing process with gamification elements: Toward a framework for gamifying collaboration processes. *AIS Transactions on Human-Computer Interaction, 13*(1), 38–61. DOI: 10.17705/1thci.00141

Yaşar, H., Kıyıcı, M., & Karatas, A. (2020). The views and adoption levels of primary school teachers on gamification, problems and possible solutions. *Participatory Educational Research*, *7*(3), 265–279. DOI: 10.17275/per.20.46.7.3

Chapter 6
Harnessing AI for Inclusive Special Education in the MENA Context

Rania Al-Tanna
http://orcid.org/0009-0002-1230-7045
The British University in Dubai, UAE

ABSTRACT

The integration of artificial intelligence (AI) into special education presents unprecedented opportunities to transform learning experiences for students with special educational needs (SEN). This chapter examines how AI-driven technologies are reshaping inclusive educational practices, and explores how AI supports personalised learning, enhances accessibility, fosters engagement, and promotes greater learner independence. The theoretical framing integrates Universal Design for Learning (UDL), Differentiated Instruction, and Assistive Technology theories, demonstrating how AI can address systemic challenges in special education. In addition, it offers evidence-based recommendations for educators, policymakers, and developers to ensure that AI technologies are deployed ethically, inclusively, and sustainably. By situating the discussion within the unique educational, cultural, and policy contexts of the MENA region, this chapter highlights AI's transformative potential to empower diverse learners and foster equitable participation in increasingly digital learning environments.

DOI: 10.4018/979-8-3373-6776-7.ch006

INTRODUCTION

Globally, the landscape of special education is evolving rapidly as educators, policymakers, and technology developers work to meet the diverse needs of students with special educational needs (SEN). Yet, despite these systemic efforts, these students often require highly individualized support, something that traditional educational models struggle to provide adequately. Although governments and schools have adopted comprehensive, inclusive education policies and initiatives, these systemic changes have not fully bridged the gap between the students' needs and classroom practices. Therefore, students with disabilities continue to face significant challenges in both academic success and social integration. These challenges are rooted in factors such as limited access to tailored learning resources, insufficient teacher training in special education methodologies, and the persistence of stigma and negative perceptions regarding disabilities. One of the most critical issues in special education is the lack of personalized instructional strategies that cater to the specific learning profiles of students with SEN. Traditional models of education frequently adopt a one-size-fits-all approach, which can be particularly detrimental for students requiring more individualized attention. This is especially evident among students with neurodevelopmental disorders such as autism, attention deficit hyperactivity disorder (ADHD), or dyslexia, who often need specialized learning environments and adaptive technologies that align with their cognitive and behavioral needs (Barua et al., 2022).

Artificial Intelligence (AI) presents transformative potential in meeting the diverse needs of students with special educational needs (SEN) by providing personalized learning experiences and improving overall inclusivity in educational settings. AI-assisted tools can enhance learning outcomes by adapting instructional materials, offering individualized feedback, and adjusting both the pace and content of learning according to the student's unique learning profiles. Such adaptability is crucial for promoting inclusive learning environments where educators can respond to the varying challenges faced by students with disabilities. Moreover, AI technologies can bridge learning and communication gaps by providing assistive solutions that promote accessibility, collaboration, and social participation. For instance, AI-driven technologies can create immersive and interactive learning experiences that cater to the diverse needs of students with SEN, fostering greater engagement and participation in the classroom (Zdravkova et al., 2022). Importantly, these technologies also empower students by promoting independence and self-directed learning, which are essential for their long-term academic success and personal development.

In addition to supporting students directly, AI technologies can also enhance teacher training and professional development. Many educators report feeling underprepared to address the needs of students with disabilities, which may contribute to frustration, inconsistent instructional quality, and reduced student engagement. AI-based tools can provide real-time feedback on teaching practices and suggest instructional adjustments, and offer professional resources aligned with specific classroom needs. These capabilities can help educators deliver more targeted support and promote inclusive Learning environments. For example, hybrid human-AI tutoring systems can offer additional support to students, augmenting the work of teachers and ensuring that students receive the specialized attention they need to succeed in inclusive educational settings (Thomas et al., 2024).

Despite its promising potential, the integration of AI in special education also presents ethical and practical challenges, including concerns about data privacy, the potential for algorithmic bias if AI systems are trained on non-representative datasets, potentially disadvantaging students with disabilities. Over-reliance on technology could further limit judgment and inadvertently widen existing inequalities, particularly in under-resourced schools where access to reliable infrastructure and training may be limited. As such, it is essential to ensure that AI systems are developed and implemented with inclusivity, transparency, and accountability at the forefront, prioritizing the well-being and rights of students with SEN. This chapter aims to explore these issues because by harnessing the potential of AI, educators can create more equitable and supportive learning environments that empower all students to thrive.

SYNTHESIS OF EXISTING RESEARCH

Current research on AI in special education suggests promising but uneven evidence across application areas. Studies examining AI-supported communication and literacy tools—such as text-to-speech, speech recognition, and predictive writing supports—show the most consistent benefits for improving access and learner participation. In contrast, AI-driven personalization platforms and adaptive learning systems remain an emerging area, with much of the evidence drawn from small-scale or short-term classroom implementations rather than longitudinal or cross-context studies. Experimental technologies such as robotics and augmented reality demonstrate innovative potential but are still largely exploratory in terms of validated educational impact. Across these strands, a recurring limitation is the context-specific nature of findings, which makes generalization difficult, particularly in low-resource or non-Western educational settings. Consequently, while AI technologies offer substantial opportunities for inclusive education, the current evidence base requires cautious interpretation, and further research is needed to clarify long-term outcomes, equity implications, and sustainable implementation models.

DEFINITIONS AND SCOPE OF THIS CHAPTER

In this chapter, the term *artificial intelligence (AI)* refers to adaptive digital systems capable of analysing data, recognizing patterns, and modifying outputs in response to learner interaction. This includes technologies such as intelligent tutoring systems, natural language processing (NLP) tools, predictive text applications, speech recognition, and AI-supported personalization platforms. While many of these tools overlap with assistive technology (AT), AI is distinguished here by its capacity for data-driven adaptation rather than solely providing static functional support. The discussion focuses primarily on inclusive K–12 educational settings, where students with special educational needs (SEN) learn alongside their peers. SEN profiles considered most centrally include learning disabilities, autism spectrum disorder (ASD), communication disorders, and physical or sensory impairments. However, many of the principles discussed may extend to broader disability categories. By clarifying these boundaries, the chapter aims to examine AI not as a general educational technology trend, but specifically as a set of tools with the potential to enhance inclusive practice.

While this chapter focuses specifically on AI-enabled systems, it is important to distinguish AI from broader categories of educational technology. General educational technologies include digital tools that deliver content but do not adapt based on learner data. Assistive technologies (AT) provide functional support that helps students overcome specific disability-related barriers, such as screen readers or alternative input devices. AI differs in its capacity to analyze learner interaction data and dynamically adjust outputs, recommendations, or content in response. In practice, many modern tools combine elements of AT and AI, but this chapter emphasizes AI's adaptive and data-driven features as its defining characteristic.

THEORETICAL FRAMEWORK

To understand how AI can transform special education, it is important to consider the theoretical frameworks that support inclusive educational practices. Three key frameworks provide the foundation for integrating AI technologies in special education: Universal Design for Learning (UDL), Differentiated Instruction, and Assistive Technology (AT) theories. These frameworks emphasize the importance of creating flexible, adaptable, and accessible learning environments that respond to the diverse needs of students with disabilities.

Universal Design for Learning (UDL) is a pedagogical framework that advocates for designing educational environments that are accessible and effective for all learners, regardless of their abilities. UDL is based on the principles of flexibility and inclusivity, encouraging educators to provide multiple means of engagement, representation, and action/expression (Quinde, 2024). These principles align well with the capabilities of AI technologies, which can analyze student data to identify learning preferences and challenges, enabling educators to tailor their instructional approaches accordingly. AI technologies are particularly effective in facilitating the development of adaptive learning environments that promote UDL principles (CAST, 2018). For example, AI can track a student's progress in real-time, identifying areas where they struggle and providing targeted interventions to address these challenges. This level of adaptability expands access to curriculum content and provides multiple modes of representation, such as converting text into speech for visually impaired students or providing visual aids for students with hearing impairments. Crucially, the integration of AI with UDL principles not only benefits students with disabilities but also enhances the learning experience for all students. By providing personalized and flexible learning options, AI technologies can help create a more inclusive and supportive classroom environment that accommodates diverse learning styles and abilities.

Differentiated Instruction is another critical framework that supports inclusive education by recognizing that students have varying levels of readiness, interests, and learning needs (Tomlinson, 2014). Differentiated Instruction requires educators to use a range of instructional strategies to meet the diverse needs of students and optimize their learning outcomes (Song, 2024). AI technologies play a significant role in differentiating instruction by providing continuous performance monitoring, adaptive task difficulty, and resource recommendations tailored to individual learners. Dynamic adjustments prevent both frustration and boredom, particularly for students with disabilities who may require intensive support. AI-driven platforms can assess student progress and modify instructional content and pacing accordingly, offering targeted intervention when necessary. They can also recommend appropriate engagement formats based on individual interests or motivation levels. In this way, AI-supported differentiated instruction promotes more responsive and inclusive learning environments by enabling educators to personalize support for students with SEN and ensure equitable access to academic success.

Assistive Technology (AT) refers to a wide range of tools and devices designed to support individuals with disabilities in their learning processes. AT theories emphasize the importance of providing technological solutions that address the specific needs of students with SEN, helping them overcome barriers to learning and participation (Uluyol & Aslan, 2022). AI technologies have the potential to enhance traditional assistive tools by providing more sophisticated and responsive solutions tailored to individual learning challenges. For instance, AI can improve the functionality of speech recognition software, making it more effective for students with communication difficulties. AI-powered tools can also enhance assistive technologies such as predictive text, text-to-speech (TTS) systems, and augmented communication devices, allowing students with disabilities to interact more effectively with the learning environment. These technologies can be particularly beneficial for students with severe disabilities, helping them communicate, complete assignments, and engage in classroom activities independently. By leveraging machine learning algorithms and natural language processing (NLP), AI can provide personalized solutions that adapt to the unique needs of each student, empowering them to achieve greater independence and academic success. Ultimately, the integration of AI into assistive technologies aligns with the overarching goal of fostering inclusivity in education, ensuring that all students have access to the resources and support they need to succeed

The integration of UDL, Differentiated Instruction, and AT theories with AI technologies presents numerous opportunities for enhancing inclusive education. AI facilitates the implementation of UDL by providing data-driven insights that inform instructional design, allowing educators to create flexible learning environments that accommodate diverse learning styles. AI also strengthens Differentiated Instruction through real-time monitoring, adaptive pacing, and targeted intervention, ensuring that students with disabilities receive instructional support matched to their progress and readiness. In parallel, AI enhances the functionality of assistive technologies by offering more sophisticated features such as predictive text, speech processing, and personalized learning pathways, which assist students with communication or cognitive challenges to engage more independently. Collectively, this integration of AI into assistive technologies ensures that all students have access to the resources and support they need to succeed, fostering greater inclusivity in education.

However, the successful implementation of these frameworks and AI technologies in inclusive education is not without challenges. Issues such as data privacy, accessibility, and the need for teacher training in AI applications must be addressed to maximize the benefits of these innovations. As discussed by Kamalov et al. (2023), the ethical implications of AI in education must be carefully considered to ensure that these technologies are used responsibly and effectively. Additionally, educators must be equipped with the necessary skills and knowledge to leverage AI tools in their teaching practices, which may require ongoing professional development and support. Arguably, the theoretical frameworks of Universal Design for Learning, Differentiated Instruction, and Assistive Technology provide a robust foundation for understanding the integration of AI in inclusive education. These frameworks emphasize the importance of creating accessible and responsive learning environments that cater to the diverse needs of all students, particularly those with disabilities. By harnessing the potential of AI technologies, educators can enhance their instructional practices and foster inclusivity in the classroom, ultimately promoting better learning outcomes for all learners.

Collectively, this integration of AI into assistive technologies ensures that all students have access to the resources and support they need to succeed, fostering greater inclusivity in education.

The relationships among these theoretical frameworks, AI-supported affordances, and inclusive learning outcomes are summarized in Table 1.

Table 1. Theoretical Frameworks and AI-Supported Inclusive Outcomes

Theoretical Framework	Key Principle	AI-Supported Affordances	Inclusive Learning Outcome
Universal Design for Learning (UDL)	Multiple means of representation, engagement, and expression	Multimodal AI tools, adaptive content delivery, text-to-speech, speech-to-text	Increased curriculum access and flexible participation
Differentiated Instruction	Instruction adjusted to readiness, interests, and learning profiles	AI-driven pacing, adaptive task difficulty, personalized feedback	Level-appropriate learning and improved engagement
Assistive Technology (AT)	Functional support to reduce disability-related barriers	AI-powered AAC tools, predictive text, speech recognition, accessibility interfaces	Greater independence, communication, and task completion

LINKING INCLUSIVE FRAMEWORKS TO AI AFFORDANCES

This alignment illustrates that AI technologies do not function independently of established inclusive pedagogy; rather, they operationalize long-standing principles of flexible design, individualized support, and barrier reduction. Framing AI within these theoretical traditions reinforces the view that technology should extend—not replace—effective instructional practice.

CURRENT AI TECHNOLOGIES IN SPECIAL EDUCATION

The integration of AI tools in education has significantly transformed the learning experience for students with SEN (Kuzdeuov et al., 2024). These tools are designed to address specific challenges faced by these learners, enhancing their ability to communicate, comprehend, and engage with educational content. The following discussion outlines various AI tools currently used to support students with disabilities, including speech recognition software, text-to-speech programs, predictive text tools, personalized learning platforms, and augmentative and alternative communication (AAC) devices.

Speech recognition software is a vital tool for students with SEN, particularly those with speech impairments or motor difficulties. This technology allows users to convert spoken language into text, enabling communication and academic engagement. For instance, smartphone-aided programs that utilize speech recognition technology have been shown to support individuals with severe neuro-motor disabilities, allowing them to engage in meaningful communication and learning activities (D'Amico et al., 2023). Also, the integration of automatic speech recognition (ASR) systems with AI platforms has further enhanced the accessibility of educational materials for students with disabilities. ASR technology enables students with speech or motor impairments to interact with digital devices using voice commands, eliminating the need for traditional keyboard and mouse inputs. This capability not only enhances communication but also fosters independence and self-reliance among students with disabilities, allowing them to participate more fully in classroom activities and academic tasks. Despite these benefits, speech recognition systems may misinterpret non-standard speech patterns, accents, or speech differences associated with certain disabilities. This can lead to frustration or inaccurate outputs that require human correction. Ongoing monitoring and teacher support are therefore necessary to ensure that the technology enhances rather than hinders communication.

Text-to-speech (TTS) programs are another essential AI tool that assists students with reading disabilities or visual impairments. TTS technology converts written text into spoken words, allowing students to listen to content rather than read it. This can significantly improve comprehension and engagement for learners who struggle with traditional reading methods. As Gambo et al. (2020) note, TTS systems have been instrumental in helping visually impaired individuals access information quickly and efficiently. Additionally, recent advancements in TTS technology have made it possible to produce human-like speech, further enhancing the user experience for students with disabilities. For example, AI-driven TTS programs can adjust the tone, speed, and inflection of speech to suit the needs of individual learners, making the content more engaging and easier to understand. These programs are particularly beneficial in educational settings where access to reading materials is crucial for academic success, as they enable students with disabilities to access written content independently and at their own pace. However, reliance on TTS should be carefully balanced with opportunities to develop independent reading skills where appropriate. Additionally, poorly designed systems may offer unnatural voice output or limited language support, which can affect comprehension and user engagement.

Predictive text tools leverage AI algorithms to assist students in generating written content more efficiently. These tools can suggest words or phrases based on the context of what the user is typing, which is especially helpful for students with writing difficulties or cognitive impairments. Predictive text technology can mitigate barriers associated with written expression, allowing students with disabilities to communicate their ideas more effectively (Goldman et al., 2023). By reducing the cognitive load associated with writing, predictive text tools enable students to focus on content creation rather than the mechanics of writing, thereby enhancing their overall learning experience. For students with SEN, predictive text tools can be transformative in helping them overcome challenges related to writing. For example, students with dysgraphia or other motor impairments may struggle with the physical act of writing, making it difficult for them to complete assignments or express their thoughts. Predictive text tools can alleviate this burden by suggesting relevant words and phrases, enabling students to compose written responses more efficiently and with less frustration. While predictive text reduces writing barriers, there is a risk that students may become overly dependent on suggestions, potentially limiting the development of independent spelling and composition skills. Educators should therefore integrate these tools alongside explicit instruction rather than as replacements for foundational writing support.

Personalized learning platforms utilize AI to tailor educational experiences to the individual needs of students. These platforms can analyze student performance data and adapt instructional materials accordingly, providing customized learning pathways that cater to each learner's strengths and weaknesses. For students with SEN, personalized learning platforms offer targeted support that addresses their specific challenges. A scoping review conducted by Fichten et al. (2022) found that personalized learning tools significantly enhance the educational experience for students with disabilities by providing tailored resources and feedback. Moreover, personalized learning platforms are particularly valuable in special education settings, where students often require individualized support to succeed. For example, AI-driven platforms can monitor a student's progress in real-time and adjust the content, pace, and difficulty level of tasks based on their performance. This ensures that students with disabilities are not overwhelmed by challenging material, while also providing opportunities for growth and skill development. Additionally, personalized learning platforms can offer alternative methods of engagement, such as interactive simulations, visual aids, or gamified learning activities, which can help keep students motivated and engaged in the learning process. Despite their adaptive capabilities, personalization systems depend on large volumes of learner data, raising concerns about privacy, algorithmic bias, and transparency in how recommendations are generated. Teachers must remain actively involved in interpreting AI outputs to ensure that instructional decisions remain context-sensitive and equitable.

Figure 1. AI-driven personalization process (source: author)

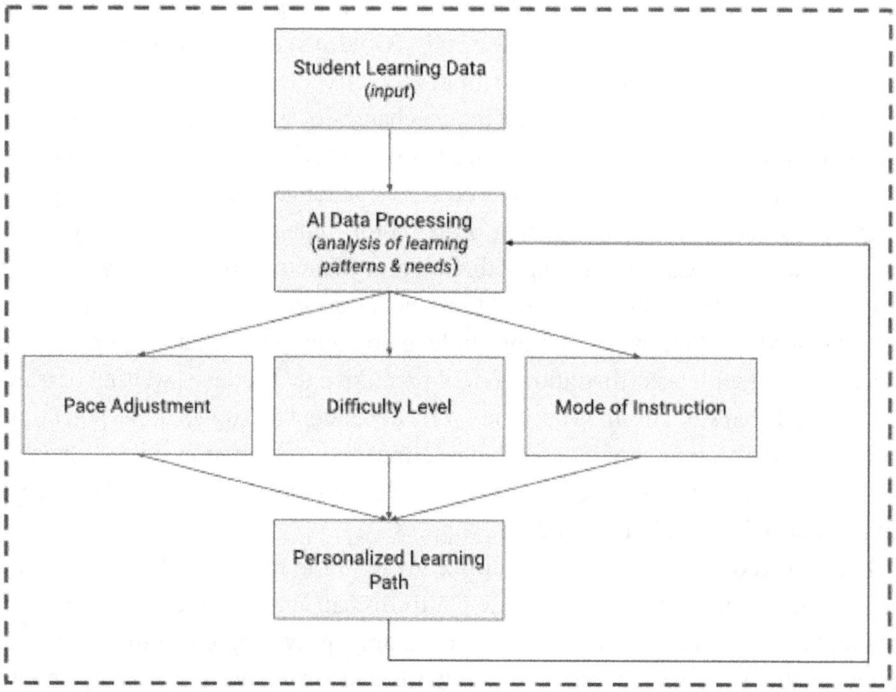

Figure 1 visualises the technical side of the AI-personalized learning process with the following components:

- Student Learning Data (Input)
  - Data Collected: Information about the student's learning progress, strengths, weaknesses, engagement levels, and performance on assessments or tasks.
  - Example: Test scores, time taken on tasks, error patterns, preferred learning modes (visual, auditory, etc.).
- AI Data Processing
  - AI Analysis: The AI system uses machine learning algorithms to process the data. It identifies trends, patterns, and learning gaps for each student.
  - Example: AI might identify that a student is struggling with comprehension of text-heavy content but performs better with video-based materials.
- Adaptation of Learning Materials (AI Output)

- Content Customization: Based on the AI analysis, the platform adapts the learning materials to better suit the student's needs. This could involve changing the medium, difficulty level, or mode of delivery.
- Example: For a student with ADHD, the platform might break down lessons into shorter, more interactive chunks, while a visually impaired student might receive text-to-speech or enlarged content.

- Personalized Learning Path Creation
  - Pace Adjustment: The AI system adjusts the pace of lessons, ensuring students are neither overwhelmed nor bored.
  - Example: Slowing down content delivery for students struggling with a concept or speeding up for those who grasp material quickly.
  - Difficulty Level: Based on progress, AI can adjust the complexity of tasks.
  - Example: A student who excels at basic math tasks might be given more challenging problems, while one who struggles may receive additional foundational tasks.
  - Mode of Instruction: AI can switch between visual, auditory, or kinesthetic learning modalities based on the student's learning preferences.
  - Example: A student with dyslexia might receive more visual or auditory content (e.g., videos, infographics, TTS tools).
- Ongoing Feedback Loop
  - Student Interaction and Feedback: As students interact with the personalized materials, new data is continuously gathered. AI refines its recommendations based on this ongoing feedback.
  - Example: A student's improved performance on visual content leads to more visual resources being incorporated, while areas of struggle are flagged for targeted intervention.
- Teacher/Parental Insights
  - Progress Reports and Interventions: AI generates reports for educators and parents, highlighting the student's strengths and areas needing attention, offering suggestions for further customization or human intervention.
  - Example: Reports on a student's improved reading comprehension might prompt the teacher to challenge the student with more advanced reading materials.

Augmentative and alternative communication (AAC) tools are designed to support communication for individuals with speech disabilities. These tools range from simple picture boards to sophisticated speech-generating devices that utilize AI to produce speech based on user input. AAC technologies have been shown to increase the participation and engagement of individuals with speech disabilities, improving their communication skills and fostering greater independence (Radici et al., 2023). AI-powered AAC tools can further enhance these capabilities by providing more responsive and personalized solutions that adapt to the user's needs. For example, AI-driven AAC devices can learn from a student's communication patterns over time, predicting commonly used words or phrases and suggesting them in real-time. This allows students with speech disabilities to communicate more efficiently and effectively, reducing the time and effort required to construct sentences or express their thoughts. Additionally, AI-powered AAC tools can integrate with other assistive technologies, such as speech recognition software or predictive text tools, to provide a seamless and comprehensive communication solution for students with disabilities. AI-powered AAC tools must also be carefully designed to reflect diverse communication styles and cultural contexts. Without inclusive datasets and ongoing personalization, these systems may fail to accurately predict or represent the user's intended expressions.

Across these tools, AI supports learning through several core mechanisms: reducing cognitive load (e.g., predictive text and TTS freeing working memory), increasing access to input and output channels (e.g., speech recognition and AAC), enabling adaptive scaffolding (e.g., personalization platforms adjusting difficulty and pacing), and enhancing engagement through multimodal and interactive formats. These mechanisms help explain why AI tools may produce improved participation and learning outcomes when aligned with learner profiles and instructional goals.

EVIDENCE AND EVALUATION CONSIDERATIONS

Although AI tools are increasingly present in inclusive classrooms, the strength of evidence supporting their effectiveness varies considerably. Communication-support technologies such as text-to-speech (TTS), speech recognition, and augmentative and alternative communication (AAC) tools are supported by a more established body of research demonstrating improved access and participation for students with disabilities. Writing-support tools such as predictive text systems also show moderate evidence of benefit, particularly in reducing cognitive load and improving written output for students with learning and motor challenges.

In contrast, AI-driven personalization platforms and adaptive learning systems remain an emerging area of research. Much of the current evidence is derived from short-term pilot implementations or small classroom studies, with limited longitudinal data on sustained academic, social, or independence outcomes. Similarly, innovative applications involving robotics and augmented reality are still largely experimental and require further validation across diverse learner populations and educational contexts.

These variations in evidentiary strength highlight the importance of cautious interpretation and ongoing evaluation. Schools and educators adopting AI technologies should monitor not only academic performance, but also participation, independence, engagement, and equity impacts to ensure that tools are producing meaningful and inclusive outcomes.

CASE STUDIES AND EXAMPLES

The implementation of AI technologies in educational settings has yielded numerous case studies and examples that demonstrate their effectiveness in supporting students with disabilities. These technologies, including speech recognition software, text-to-speech programs, predictive text tools, and personalized learning platforms, have been successfully integrated into various educational contexts to improve accessibility, communication, inclusivity, and learning outcomes. Table 2 presents specific examples and case studies illustrating the successful application of these AI technologies, enhancing written expression, reading comprehension, and instructional participation for students with disabilities.

Table 2. Case studies and examples of using AI to support students with SEN

Example	Case Study
Speech Recognition Technology in Writing	A study by Ok et al. (2022) explored the usage patterns and perceptions of speech recognition (SR) technology among students with high-incidence disabilities. The research found that when teachers introduced SR as part of writing instruction, students were able to engage more effectively in the writing process. The study highlighted that students who had the opportunity to use SR reported increased self-direction in their writing tasks, as they could choose when to utilize this assistive technology. This case illustrates how SR can empower students with disabilities to take control of their writing processes, ultimately enhancing their written expression.
SOLO Literacy Suite for Writing Instruction	An intervention study conducted by Park et al. (2017) combined teacher-directed writing instruction with the SOLO Literacy Suite, a digital tool designed to improve writing skills among students with disabilities. The results indicated that students who used the SOLO Literacy Suite showed significant improvements in their writing abilities compared to those who did not use the technology. This study underscores the potential of integrating writing technology into instructional practices to support students with disabilities in developing their writing skills.
Text-to-Speech Applications in Reading	A study by Bone and Bouck (2017) examined the effectiveness of TTS applications in supporting students who struggle with reading. The findings indicated that TTS technology significantly aided students with disabilities in completing reading assignments independently. By converting written text into spoken words, TTS applications helped students access information more easily, thereby enhancing their reading comprehension and engagement. This case exemplifies how TTS can serve as a critical tool for students with reading difficulties, allowing them to participate more fully in academic activities and reduce barriers to information access.
Predictive Text Tools for Writing Support	Goldman et al. (2023) highlighted the importance of predictive text tools in enhancing written expression for students with disabilities. Their research indicated that these tools, when integrated into writing instruction, provided students with valuable support in generating text. The predictive text technology allowed students to focus on content creation rather than the mechanics of writing, ultimately improving their writing outcomes. This example demonstrates how predictive text tools can effectively assist students with disabilities in overcoming barriers to written communication and improving the quality and fluency of written work.
Personalized Learning Platforms	The use of personalized learning platforms has also been shown to benefit students with disabilities. A scoping review conducted by Fichten et al. (2022) found that personalized learning tools significantly enhanced the educational experience for students with disabilities. These platforms adapt to individual learning needs, providing tailored resources and feedback that cater to each learner's strengths and challenges. This adaptability is crucial for fostering an inclusive learning environment where all students can thrive.

In addition to the examples in Table 2, at a more general level, Koch (2017) discussed the role of embedded assistive technology in supporting students with disabilities in school settings. The study highlighted how operating systems from Microsoft and Apple include built-in assistive technologies that are easy to access and use. These tools have been shown to enhance accessibility and support learning for students with sensory, physical, learning, and attention disabilities. This demonstrates the practical applications of embedded technology in fostering inclusivity. Overall, these examples highlight some of the benefits of using AI with SEN students, benefits which are more clearly explained in the following section. However, although these case studies confirm the instructional potential of AI, most research remains classroom-specific and small-scale. Future work must examine long-term outcomes, contextual barriers, and equitable implementation across diverse school systems.

EVIDENCE STRENGTH AND RESEARCH GAPS

Although the case examples summarized above illustrate promising applications of AI in inclusive education, the overall strength of the evidence base varies across tool categories. Communication and literacy support such as text-to-speech, speech recognition, and predictive writing tools show the most consistent positive findings related to improved access, participation, and learner independence. In contrast, AI-driven personalization systems and adaptive learning platforms remain supported largely by small-scale or short-term classroom studies, limiting the ability to generalize findings across diverse educational contexts. Emerging technologies such as robotics and augmented reality demonstrate innovative potential but are still in early exploratory phases with limited longitudinal validation. Consequently, while AI technologies offer meaningful opportunities to enhance inclusive education, current findings should be interpreted with caution, and further large-scale, cross-context research is needed to establish long-term impact and equitable implementation. Many existing studies rely on small participant samples, short intervention periods, or researcher-developed tools, which may limit external validity. As a result, claims about broad effectiveness should be interpreted as promising but provisional rather than conclusive.

IMPLEMENTATION REALITIES IN INCLUSIVE SETTINGS

Beyond questions of research strength, practical implementation conditions also shape the impact of AI in inclusive education. While AI technologies offer meaningful potential to enhance inclusion, their effectiveness depends heavily on the conditions under which they are implemented. Schools vary widely in infrastructure, staffing capacity, funding, and professional development opportunities, all of which influence how AI tools are selected, used, and sustained. Teachers may face increased workload when learning new systems, adapting materials, and interpreting AI-generated data, particularly in under-resourced contexts. In addition, procurement decisions are often shaped by cost constraints and vendor support structures rather than solely by pedagogical fit.

Successful implementation, therefore, requires more than access to technology; it demands ongoing training, technical support, leadership guidance, and alignment with individualized education planning processes such as IEP goals. Without these supports, AI tools risk becoming underused, misapplied, or inequitably distributed, potentially widening rather than reducing learning gaps. Recognizing these implementation realities helps situate AI as one component of a broader inclusive ecosystem rather than a standalone solution.

BENEFITS OF AI FOR STUDENTS WITH SEN

Building on the tool-specific evidence presented earlier, this section synthesizes broader outcome patterns across accessibility, engagement, personalization, and learner independence. It is evident from this chapter that AI offers transformative possibilities for students with SEN, enhancing their learning experiences in ways that were previously unimaginable. The integration of AI technologies in education supports personalized learning while improving accessibility, engagement, and overall academic success for students with various disabilities (James et al., 2018). As mentioned earlier in this chapter, one of the most significant benefits of AI in education is its capacity to deliver highly *personalized learning experiences* that accommodate each learner's unique learning needs and styles. AI-driven platforms can analyse student data in real time, identifying behavioural patterns, strengths, and adapting content, pace, and instructional methods accordingly. For example, AI can create tailored educational pathways for students with learning disabilities such as dyslexia or ADHD, ensuring that the content is presented in ways that align with their cognitive preferences. These platforms also adjust the task difficulty, suggest alternative engagement formats, and provide personalized feedback that is specific to the student's learning progress. This customization ensures that students with disabilities are not left behind and can engage with the curriculum at a pace suited to their abilities.

AI technologies have dramatically *improved accessibility* in educational environments, particularly for students with sensory, physical, or cognitive disabilities. AI-powered tools such as TTS (Buell et al., 2020) and speech recognition software break down barriers to learning by providing alternative ways to interact with academic content. For students with visual impairments, TTS converts written text to spoken words, providing independent access to instructional materials they would otherwise find challenging. Similarly, for students with motor disabilities, speech recognition software enables them to interact with digital platforms through voice commands, eliminating the need for traditional keyboard and mouse inputs. Moreover, AI-driven captioning tools can transcribe classroom discussions and provide real-time captions, which are invaluable for students with hearing impairments. Collectively, these tools promote equitable participation and ensure that students with disabilities can engage with the same instructional content as their peers, fostering a more inclusive and accessible learning environment.

Engagement is a critical factor of academic success for students with disabilities, many of whom may struggle to stay motivated in traditional learning environments. AI technologies, particularly those that utilize gamification, adaptive learning, and interactive content, have the potential to *increase student engagement* and make learning more enjoyable and responsive. Additionally, AI-powered learning platforms can tailor the delivery of content based on a student's interests, cognitive profiles, and engagement levels. For instance, students with autism spectrum disorder (ASD) can benefit from visually rich and interactive content that maintains focus and reduces distraction. Adaptive systems can also monitor fluctuations in engagement and automatically adjust the level of interactivity or task difficulty to sustain attention. By offering more engaging and interactive content, AI helps prevent the disengagement often seen in students with disabilities, who may feel frustrated or overwhelmed by traditional methods of instruction. This personalized engagement can lead to higher motivation and a more positive attitude toward learning.

A further significant benefit of AI for students with disabilities is the promotion of *independence* in their learning journey. Many AI tools are designed to be used independently, giving students the autonomy to control their learning pace and style (Evmenova et al., 2019). This independence is particularly important for students with SEN who might otherwise rely heavily on teacher assistance or adult support. For example, s AI-powered augmentative and alternative communication (AAC) tools enable students with communication challenges to express themselves in the classroom without the constant help of a teacher or aide. Similarly, students with physical disabilities can use AI-driven assistive technologies to navigate learning and digital environments, complete assignments, and communicate with greater efficiency. By fostering self-reliance, AI empowers students with disabilities to take control of their education and gain confidence in their abilities. This sense of empowerment is crucial for their academic success and overall well-being, as it enables them to feel more in control of their learning processes and outcomes.

AI benefits not only students with SEN directly but also *supports educators* in providing more effective instruction. Teachers often face challenges in meeting the diverse needs of students with disabilities, especially in inclusive classrooms. AI can assist teachers by providing real-time performance data, offering insights into areas where students need additional support, and suggesting targeted interventions (Garg & Sharma, 2020). AI-driven can also reduce the administrative burden on teachers by automating tasks such as grading, tracking student progress, and customizing lesson plans. This allows teachers to spend more time focusing on instruction and one-on-one interactions with students. Furthermore, AI technologies can offer professional development and training resources for educators, helping them develop the skills necessary to support students with disabilities more effectively. By enhancing teacher efficiency and instructional responsiveness, AI contributes to more inclusive learning environments and ensures that educators are better equipped to support students with diverse learning profiles.

CHALLENGES AND ETHICAL CONSIDERATIONS

Despite the substantial benefits demonstrated in this chapter, the successful application of AI in special education also requires a careful examination of its ethical, practical, and systemic implications. These considerations are essential to ensure that technological innovation does not compromise equity, privacy, or learner well-being. While the integration of AI in education holds great promise, particularly for students with disabilities, it is not without its challenges. Ethical concerns and practical limitations must be carefully considered to ensure that AI is applied in ways that protect the rights and dignity of all learners, particularly those from vulnerable groups (Nurjanah et al., 2024).

One of the most pressing ethical concerns regarding the use of AI in education is *data privacy*. AI technologies rely on vast amounts of data to function effectively. In special education, this data may include highly sensitive information about students' disabilities, learning needs, and performance. The collection, storage, and analysis of such personal data raise serious concerns about privacy and the potential for misuse. For students with disabilities, whose personal data may already make them more vulnerable to discrimination, robust data protection is essential. Educators, parents, and policymakers must therefore ensure that AI platforms comply with data protection regulations such as the General Data Protection Regulation (GDPR) in Europe, or similar laws in other regions. These regulations mandate that any collection or processing of student data should be transparent, consensual, and secure. Beyond regulatory compliance, there remains the ongoing challenge of data security, as AI systems are increasingly targeted for cyberattacks, which could lead to unauthorized access to sensitive student information. Developers and educators must prioritize security protocols to protect data from breaches, ensuring that student information is kept confidential and used solely for educational purposes.

Another critical ethical issue is the potential for *algorithmic bias* in AI systems. AI algorithms are only as unbiased as the data on which they are trained. If the datasets used to train AI models are not representative of the diversity of the student population, the resulting systems may perpetuate or even exacerbate existing biases. This is especially concerning for students with disabilities, who may already face systemic discrimination in educational settings (Popenici & Kerr, 2017). For example, AI-driven assessment tools could misinterpret the behaviors or learning patterns of students with disabilities, leading to unfair evaluations. Students with neurodevelopmental disorders, such as autism or ADHD, may display learning patterns that differ significantly from neurotypical students. If AI algorithms are not trained with these patterns in mind, they may unfairly categorize students with disabilities as underperforming, reinforcing harmful stereotypes and limiting opportunities for academic success. To mitigate this risk, developers must ensure that AI models are trained on diverse, representative datasets that include students with various disabilities. Furthermore, transparency in AI decision-making processes is crucial: educators and parents should be able to understand how AI systems arrive at their conclusions, allowing them to challenge or adjust decisions that may negatively impact students with disabilities. Ensuring fairness in AI applications requires continuous monitoring and updates to algorithms to reflect the diverse needs of the student population.

The increasing reliance on AI tools in education raises important concerns about maintaining an appropriate balance between human and technological support. Although AI has the potential to enhance learning outcomes for students with disabilities, *over-reliance on technology* may produce unintended consequences. Students may become overly dependent on AI tools, potentially diminishing their ability to develop essential cognitive, social, and problem-solving skills that are crucial for real-world success. For example, while AI-powered text-to-speech and speech recognition tools can significantly improve communication for students with disabilities; however, if used without appropriate moderation, these tools might limit opportunities for students to practice and refine their own communication skills. Similarly, while AI-driven personalized learning platforms can provide students with tailored educational experiences, they should not replace the vital role of human educators, who offer emotional support, pedagogical judgement, guidance, and adaptive thinking that technology cannot replicate. Needless to say, it is essential to strike a balance between using AI as a supportive tool and maintaining human oversight in the learning process. AI should complement, not replace, human interactions in education, particularly for students with disabilities who may require more nuanced and individualized support than AI alone can provide.

While AI has the potential to make education more accessible for students with SEN, concerns remain about the *accessibility* of AI technologies themselves. Many AI tools require expensive hardware, reliable internet access, and specialized training, which may not be available to all students or educational institutions, particularly those in low-income or rural areas. This digital divide can exacerbate existing inequalities, leaving students with disabilities in underserved communities at a further disadvantage. Additionally, while AI technologies are designed to enhance accessibility, poorly designed systems can inadvertently create new barriers. For example, an AI-based educational platform that is not compatible with screen readers or other assistive technologies may exclude students with visual or physical impairments. Similarly, AI systems that require complex navigation or extensive setup processes may be difficult for students with cognitive disabilities to use independently. To address these concerns, developers of AI tools must prioritize universal design principles, ensuring that these technologies are accessible to all students, regardless of their socioeconomic background or disability status. This includes designing AI systems that are compatible with a wide range of assistive devices, easy to use, and adaptable to different learning environments to prevent further marginalization of students with disabilities and to uphold the broader goal of inclusive education.

These concerns are particularly pronounced in low-resource and under-resourced educational settings. Schools in such contexts may face additional barriers, including limited funding for assistive and AI-enabled technologies, unreliable internet connectivity, insufficient technical support, and reduced access to teacher professional development. Without deliberate equity-focused planning, AI implementation risks reinforcing existing disparities rather than reducing them. Addressing these gaps requires not only technological solutions but also policy support, sustainable funding models, and capacity-building initiatives to ensure that inclusive AI practices are accessible across diverse educational environments. Without targeted funding models and policy safeguards, AI adoption risks becoming concentrated in already well-resourced schools, reinforcing rather than reducing educational inequities.

Another key ethical consideration is the role of *human oversight* in AI decision-making processes. Although AI systems can provide valuable insights and support, educators, parents, and administrators must retain ultimate responsibility for interpreting these outputs and making informed decisions about student outcomes. Blindly trusting AI-generated recommendations without critically evaluating their relevance or accuracy can lead to harmful consequences, particularly for students with disabilities who may have unique needs that AI systems cannot fully understand or accommodate. For instance, AI tools used for grading or assessment should complement rather than replace the nuanced judgment of a trained educator, who is better positioned to consider individual circumstances, developmental variability, and long-term progress. Similarly, decisions about interventions or accommodations for students with disabilities should always involve human stakeholders who understand the broader context of the student's educational journey. Ensuring meaningful human oversight in AI systems requires clear accountability structures and well-defined protocols for reviewing, interpreting, and validating AI-generated data. Schools and educational institutions must establish protocols and collaborative decision-making processes that engage both educators and parents, allowing them to scrutinize AI outputs and challenge decisions when necessary. This collaborative approach helps to mitigate the risks of AI errors or biases and ensures that AI tools are used ethically and effectively, responsibly, and in the best interests of students with disabilities.

Taken together, the benefits and limitations discussed in this chapter highlight the need for thoughtful innovation and strategic planning if AI is to meaningfully advance equitable and inclusive educational opportunities for students with disabilities.

FUTURE DIRECTIONS AND RECOMMENDATIONS

As the field of AI in education continues to evolve, its potential to further support students with disabilities becomes increasingly evident. Realizing these benefits, however, requires strategic planning, ongoing research, and a strong commitment to ethical and equitable implementation. In this section, we explore potential future trends in AI for special education and offer practical recommendations for educators, policymakers, and developers to ensure that these technologies are used effectively and equitably.

AI is a rapidly advancing field, and several emerging technologies hold the potential to significantly revolutionize special education. The development of more sophisticated AI tools that leverage advancements in robotics, natural language processing (NLP), and augmented reality (AR) could offer even more tailored and immersive learning experiences for students with disabilities. As these technologies mature, they will offer more nuanced instructional adaptations, greater assistive capabilities, and enhanced learning engagement- further expanding the possibilities for inclusive education.

Table 3. Emerging AI technologies

Technology	Description
AI-Driven Robotics	Robotics powered by AI can play a vital role in supporting students with physical and cognitive disabilities. These robots can serve as classroom assistants, helping students with mobility issues complete tasks and participate in group activities. For example, social robots have already shown promise in assisting students with autism spectrum disorder (ASD) by helping them develop communication and social skills in a non-judgmental, interactive way. As AI-driven robotics continues to evolve, we can expect more adaptive and responsive robots that provide personalized support to students with disabilities.
Advanced Natural Language (NLP) Processing	NLP technology is constantly improving, allowing AI systems to better understand and respond to human language. For students with communication disabilities, NLP could provide enhanced speech recognition and language generation tools, making it easier for them to express themselves in both written and verbal forms. The continued refinement of NLP models will lead to more accurate and contextually appropriate responses, improving communication aids for students with disabilities.
Augmented Reality (AR)	Augmented reality has the potential to create more immersive learning experiences by overlaying digital content onto the physical world. For students with disabilities, AR can provide interactive simulations that help them grasp complex concepts in a more tangible way. For instance, students with visual impairments could benefit from haptic feedback and auditory cues integrated into AR environments, allowing them to navigate and interact with content more effectively.

These emerging AI technologies illustrate the growing potential for more immersive, adaptive, and assistive learning environments in special education. However, realizing their full impact will require intentional design, equitable implementation, and ongoing collaboration between educators, policymakers, and developers.

Generative and Multimodal AI in Inclusive Education

Recent advances in generative and multimodal AI systems are beginning to influence inclusive educational practices. Generative AI tools can produce text, images, speech, and interactive content in response to user prompts, offering new possibilities for personalization and communication support. For students with SEN, these tools may assist with idea generation, language scaffolding, visual representation of concepts, and alternative modes of expression. For example, generative text tools can help students with writing difficulties organize their thoughts, while image-generation systems can support visual learners or students with communication challenges in expressing ideas.

However, the use of generative AI also introduces important considerations. These systems can produce inaccurate or misleading information, sometimes referred to as "hallucinations," which may confuse learners if not guided by educators. There is also a risk of over-dependence, where students rely on AI-generated responses rather than developing their own skills. Furthermore, concerns around data privacy, intellectual ownership, and safeguarding are particularly significant when these tools are used by vulnerable learners. As a result, generative AI should be integrated with clear human oversight, structured prompts, and instructional guidance to ensure it supports learning rather than replacing critical thinking or authentic expression.

Recommendations for Educators

Educators play a central role in the successful integration of AI technologies into the classroom. To ensure that AI is used effectively to support students with disabilities, teachers must be equipped with the knowledge and skills to implement these tools in pedagogically sound ways. Professional development should therefore extend beyond technical training to include instructional strategies that leverage AI for differentiation, accessibility, and individualized support. Schools and districts should prioritize sustained, practice-oriented professional learning that teaches educators how to leverage AI and integrate these tools into lesson design, assessment, and intervention planning to address the specific needs of students with disabilities.

Teachers should also critically assess the AI tools they adopt, ensuring that their features align with the learning needs, strengths, and contextual realities of their students. A balanced approach is essential, as over-reliance on AI may reduce opportunities for authentic human interaction, emotional support, and individualized judgment. Furthermore, teachers must stay informed about potential biases in AI systems and remain vigilant in questioning AI-generated recommendations that may not fully consider the complexities of individual learners. Also, teachers should work closely with special education specialists, data analysts, and technology developers to ensure that AI tools are being used appropriately and effectively. Through interdisciplinary collaboration and critical reflection, educators can ensure that AI is used as a complementary resource that enhances, not replaces, the relational and pedagogical dimensions of effective teaching.

A Stepwise Implementation Framework for Inclusive AI Integration

To translate these recommendations into practice, schools may benefit from a structured and phased approach to AI integration in inclusive settings:

1. **Needs Analysis** – Identify specific learning barriers, accessibility challenges, and instructional goals for students with SEN before selecting tools.
2. **Tool Selection Criteria** – Evaluate AI tools based on accessibility, data privacy safeguards, compatibility with assistive technologies, cultural and linguistic responsiveness, and alignment with IEP goals where applicable.

3. **Accessibility and Usability Checks** – Ensure tools are compatible with screen readers, alternative input devices, and diverse communication needs, and test usability with students and support staff.
4. **Professional Learning and Training** – Provide teachers and support staff with training not only on technical use but also on ethical, pedagogical, and inclusive integration strategies.
5. **Pilot Implementation** – Begin with small-scale trials to monitor how tools function in real classroom contexts and gather feedback from students, families, and educators.
6. **Monitoring and Evaluation** – Collect data on student engagement, learning progress, independence, and participation, while also reviewing any unintended consequences or accessibility barriers.
7. **Ongoing Review and Adjustment** – Use feedback and evidence to refine tool use, adjust instructional strategies, and ensure that AI continues to support inclusive goals rather than simply introducing new technologies.

This structured approach positions AI not as a standalone solution, but as part of a responsive and collaborative inclusive education ecosystem.

Recommendations for Policymakers

Policymakers have a responsibility to ensure that the implementation of AI technologies in education is equitable, ethical, and inclusive. Governments and educational authorities should develop clear regulatory frameworks and standards for the use of AI in schools, with explicit attention to the needs of students with disabilities. These standards should address issues such as data privacy, algorithmic fairness, and accessibility, ensuring that AI systems do not exacerbate existing inequalities or inadvertently marginalize vulnerable learners.

Policymakers must work to close the digital divide by ensuring that all schools, regardless of their location or socioeconomic status, have access to AI technologies. This includes investing in the necessary infrastructure, such as reliable internet access, hardware, and software, as well as providing funding for schools to adopt and implement AI-driven educational tools. Without such investments, students in underserved communities may be left behind, further widening the gap in educational outcomes. In addition to this, policymakers should incentivize research into new AI technologies that specifically target the needs of students with disabilities. By providing grants and other forms of support for research in this area, governments can foster innovation and ensure that the educational technology market continues to develop tools that benefit diverse learners. Moreover, collaboration between universities, research institutions, and technology companies should be encouraged to accelerate the development of AI solutions for special education.

Recommendations for Developers

AI developers are at the forefront of creating tools that can transform the educational landscape for students with disabilities. Developers must prioritize the principles of universal design, ensuring that AI tools are accessible to all students, regardless of their disabilities or learning needs. This includes creating interfaces that are intuitive, compatible with assistive technologies, and easy to navigate. AI tools should be flexible enough to accommodate the wide range of disabilities present in educational settings, from physical and sensory impairments to cognitive and learning challenges, supporting varied modalities of interaction and communication.

Collaboration with key stakeholders, including educators, families, students, and special education specialists, is essential throughout the design and development process. By involving these stakeholders in the design process, developers can gain insights into the practical challenges faced by students with disabilities and ensure that their products are responsive to real-world needs. Developers should also prioritize transparency and explainability in their systems, especially when AI is used to inform high-stakes educational decisions such as assessments, placement, or intervention. Educators and parents must be able to understand how AI models generate recommendations, outputs should be interpretable, reviewable, and open to challenge. Transparent design not only strengthens trust and ethical accountability but also mitigates risks related to bias, fairness, and inappropriate decision-making.

Evidence Strength and Research Limitations

Although the literature highlights promising applications of AI in special and inclusive education, the overall evidence base remains uneven. Some assistive applications, particularly in communication and access (such as text-to-speech, speech recognition, and AAC), are supported by a more established body of classroom research. However, many AI-driven personalization systems, adaptive platforms, and emerging technologies are still supported primarily by small-scale, short-term, or pilot studies. Longitudinal evidence examining sustained academic outcomes, social participation, independence, and equity impacts remains limited. Additionally, much of the existing research has been conducted in well-resourced educational contexts, raising questions about generalizability across diverse settings. These limitations underscore the need for cautious interpretation of current findings and for continued research that examines long-term, inclusive, and context-sensitive outcomes.

Future Research Directions

Future research is needed to strengthen the evidence base on AI in inclusive and special education. In particular, more longitudinal and large-scale studies are required to understand how AI tools influence not only academic outcomes but also communication, participation, independence, and social inclusion over time. Research should also explore how AI functions in diverse and under-resourced educational contexts, where infrastructure, training, and access may differ significantly from well-funded settings.

In addition, there is a need for interdisciplinary work that brings together educators, technologists, researchers, families, and students with disabilities to co-design and evaluate AI systems. Such collaboration can help ensure that emerging technologies are aligned with inclusive values, responsive to real-world classroom conditions, and sensitive to ethical and cultural considerations. Developing clearer evaluation frameworks and shared standards for measuring impact will be essential to guide responsible and equitable AI adoption in education.

CONCLUSION

The integration of AI into special education offers substantial potential to transform learning experiences for students with disabilities. As this chapter has demonstrated, AI technologies provide unprecedented opportunities for personalized learning, enhanced accessibility, increased engagement, and greater independence, helping to dismantle traditional barriers that have long hindered equitable participation in the educational environment. These innovations create new pathways for students with disabilities to access the curriculum, express themselves, and engage meaningfully with learning. However, the promise of AI must be balanced with a clear understanding of its challenges. Ethical concerns related to data privacy, algorithmic bias, and the over-reliance on technology underscore the importance of thoughtful, deliberate implementation. Ensuring that AI technologies are designed inclusively and deployed with careful consideration of students' diverse needs is essential for preventing further marginalization of vulnerable groups.

Looking ahead, the future of AI in special education is marked by rapid technological advancements and expanding possibilities. Emerging tools such as AI-driven robotics, advanced NLP, and AR will likely continue to reshape personalized and inclusive education in profound ways. These developments will demand ongoing collaboration between educators, policymakers, developers, and researchers to ensure that innovations are not only effective but ethical, transparent, and equitable. To maximize the benefits of AI while mitigating its risks, this chapter has proposed several key recommendations to guide this work: educators must be provided with professional development opportunities to effectively integrate AI into their teaching practice; policymakers must establish clear standards for equitable access and ethical use, and developers must prioritize universal design principles and transparency in AI tools.

Ultimately, the successful adoption of AI in special education depends on shared commitment to equity, inclusivity, and student-centred design. When guided by these principles, AI can serve as a tool for empowerment, providing students with disabilities the resources and support they need to thrive. By harnessing the transformative possibilities of AI while remaining attentive to its limitations, educational communities can create more responsive, supportive, and inclusive learning environments for all. The evidence reviewed suggests that AI's value in inclusive education is conditional rather than automatic, depending on pedagogical alignment, ethical governance, and sustained institutional support.

As this chapter concludes, it is important to remember that:

"The true power of AI in special education lies not in the technology itself, but in our collective commitment to using it ethically, inclusively, and in service of every learner's potential."

REFERENCES

Barua, P. D., Vicnesh, J., Gururajan, R., Oh, S. L., Palmer, E., Azizan, M. M., & Acharya, U. R. (2022). Artificial intelligence-enabled personalised assistive tools to enhance education of children with neurodevelopmental disorders—A review. *International Journal of Environmental Research and Public Health, 19*(3), 1192. DOI: 10.3390/ijerph19031192 PMID: 35162220

Bone, E. K., & Bouck, E. C. (2017). Accessible text-to-speech options for students who struggle with reading. *Preventing School Failure, 61*(1), 48–55. DOI: 10.1080/1045988x.2016.1188366

Buell, S., Langdon, P. E., Pounds, G., & Bunning, K. (2020). An open randomized controlled trial of the effects of linguistic simplification and mediation on the comprehension of "easy read" text by people with intellectual disabilities. *Journal of Applied Research in Intellectual Disabilities, 33*(2), 219–231. DOI: 10.1111/jar.12666 PMID: 31652030

CAST (2018). Universal Design for Learning Guidelines version 2.2.

D'Amico, F., Lancioni, G. E., De Marinis, F., Abbinante, F., Taurisano, P., Abbatantuono, C., & Alberti, G. (2023). A simple smartphone-aided program to support meaningful occupation in people with severe neuro-motor and speech disabilities. *International Journal of Rehabilitation Research. Internationale Zeitschrift fur Rehabilitationsforschung. Revue Internationale de Recherches de Readaptation, 46*(2), 205–208. DOI: 10.1097/mrr.0000000000000583 PMID: 37039592

Evmenova, A. S., & Regan, K. (2019). Supporting the writing process with technology for students with disabilities. *Intervention in School and Clinic, 55*(2), 78–85. DOI: 10.1177/1053451219837636

Fichten, C., Pickup, D., Asunsion, J., Jorgensen, M., Vo, C., Legault, A., & Libman, E. (2022). State of the research on artificial intelligence based apps for post-secondary students with disabilities. *Exceptionality Education International, 31*(1), 62–76. DOI: 10.5206/eei.v31i1.14089

Gambo, O., Adelokun, A., Gambo, I., & Afolayan, A. (2021). Planning Effective Learning for the Visually Impaired in Federal University in Osun State, Nigeria: Technology Perspective. *Malaysian Online Journal of Educational Technology, 9*(1), 80–96. DOI: 10.17220/mojet.2021.9.1.250

Garg, S., & Sharma, S. (2020). Impact of artificial intelligence in special need education to promote inclusive pedagogy. *International Journal of Information and Education Technology (IJIET), 10*(7), 523–527. DOI: 10.18178/ijiet.2020.10.7.1418

Goldman, S. R., Carreon, A., Smith, S. J., & Kurth, J. (2023). Exploring and implementing available writing educational technology for students with disabilities and their peers. *Journal of Special Education Technology, 38*(4), 563–572. DOI: 10.1177/01626434231155933

James, M., Besaw, J., & Jimenez, B. (2018). Using 3-D Printed Objects to Increase Comprehension for Students with Severe Disability. *Global Journal of Intellectual & Developmental Disabilities, 5*(2), 27–32. DOI: 10.19080/gjidd.2018.05.555658

Kamalov, F., Santandreu Calonge, D., & Gurrib, I. (2023). New era of artificial intelligence in education: Towards a sustainable multifaceted revolution. *Sustainability, 15*(16), 12451. DOI: 10.3390/su151612451

Koch, K. (2017). Stay in the box! Embedded assistive technology improves access for students with disabilities. *Education Sciences, 7*(4), 82. DOI: 10.3390/educsci7040082

Kuzdeuov, A., Mukayev, O., Nurgaliyev, S., Kunbolsyn, A., & Varol, H. A. (2024, February). ChatGPT for visually impaired and blind. In *2024 International Conference on Artificial Intelligence in Information and Communication (ICAIIC)* (pp. 722-727). IEEE. https://doi.org/DOI: 10.36227/techrxiv.22047080

Nurjanah, A., Salsabila, I. N., Azzahra, A., Rahayu, R., & Marlina, N. (2024). Artificial intelligence (ai) usage in today's teaching and learning process: A review. *Syntax Idea, 6*(3), 1517–1523. DOI: 10.46799/syntax-idea.v6i3.3126

Ok, M. W., Rao, K., Pennington, J., & Ulloa, P. R. (2022). Speech recognition technology for writing: Usage patterns and perceptions of students with high incidence disabilities. *Journal of Special Education Technology, 37*(2), 191–202. DOI: 10.1177/0162643420979929

Park, Y., Ambrose, G., Coleman, M. B., & Moore, T. C. (2017). The effects of teacher directed writing instruction combined with SOLO Literacy Suite. *Journal of Computer Assisted Learning, 33*(1), 20–34. DOI: 10.1111/jcal.12163

Popenici, S. A., & Kerr, S. (2017). Exploring the impact of artificial intelligence on teaching and learning in higher education. *Research and Practice in Technology Enhanced Learning, 12*(1), 22. DOI: 10.1186/s41039-017-0062-8 PMID: 30595727

Quinde, G. A. L., Muñoz, M. Y. T., Suárez, J. M. R., Villarreal, R. E. P., Vélez, W. A. Z., & Laínez, A. A. D. P. (2024). Perception of University Students on The Use of Artificial Intelligence (AI) Tools For The Development of Autonomous Learning. *Revista de Gestão Social e Ambiental, 18*(2), e06170–e06170. DOI: 10.24857/rgsa.v18n2-136

Radici, E., Heboyan, V., & De Leo, G. (2023). A speech-to-symbol app for supporting communication partner to model and improve vocabulary. *Child Language Teaching and Therapy*, *39*(3), 266–274. DOI: 10.1177/02656590231202857

Song, D. (2024). Artificial intelligence for human learning: A review of machine learning techniques used in education research and a suggestion of a learning design model. *American Journal of Education and Learning*, *9*(1), 1–21. DOI: 10.55284/ajel.v9i1.1024

Thomas, D. R., Gatz, E., Gupta, S., Aleven, V., & Koedinger, K. R. (2024, July). The Neglected 15%: Positive Effects of Hybrid Human-AI Tutoring Among Students with Disabilities. In *International Conference on Artificial Intelligence in Education* (pp. 409-423). Cham: Springer Nature Switzerland. https://doi.org/DOI: 10.35542/osf.io/y52ew

Tomlinson, C. A. (2014). The Differentiated Classroom: Responding to the Needs of All Learners.

Uluyol, Ç., & Aslan, C. (2022). Special Education Students' Attitudes towards Assistive Technologies. *Journal of Teacher Education and Lifelong Learning*, *4*(2), 124–132. DOI: 10.51535/tell.1177060

Zdravkova, K., Krasniqi, V., Dalipi, F., & Ferati, M. (2022). Cutting-edge communication and learning assistive technologies for disabled children: An artificial intelligence perspective. *Frontiers in Artificial Intelligence*, *5*, 970430. DOI: 10.3389/frai.2022.970430 PMID: 36388402

Chapter 7
Learning From Finland:
A Theoretical Approach to Implementing AI Curriculum in the UAE

Serena Aoun
http://orcid.org/0009-0001-7425-1246
Zayed University, UAE

ABSTRACT

The aim of the study is to examine how Finland implemented programming skills in its national curriculum to offer lessons for the implementation of the new National AI Curriculum introduced in the United Arab Emirates using Bernstein's curriculum model. This chapter adopts a conceptual and comparative approach, drawing on secondary literature and policy documents, and uses Bernstein's Curriculum Model as an analytical framework to interpret Finland's case and extract lessons for the UAE. The findings highlight strategies to ease the transition and make the implementation process smoother for different stakeholders. By synthesizing international best practices with the UAE's digital transformation goals, the chapter provides actionable recommendations for policymakers, curriculum designers, and educators seeking to bridge the gap between technological innovation and classroom practice. This chapter contributes to the global discourse on AI literacy in education by presenting the UAE as a case study of policy-driven innovation in a rapidly transforming educational landscape.

DOI: 10.4018/979-8-3373-6776-7.ch007

INTRODUCTION

Curricula are dynamic documents that constantly change and evolve in response to societies' needs. As societies advance and rely more on technology, curricula need to change to keep up with all the developments. This study is a theoretical, literature-based comparative analysis aimed at developing a conceptual framework for curriculum implementation. It examines how a specific curriculum innovation—the introduction of programming skills in Finland under transversal competencies—was implemented and uses these insights to inform the implementation of a newly introduced Artificial Intelligence (AI) curriculum in UAE schools.

The most recent wave of transformation stems from the increasing dependence on AI, which has implications across all levels of society. This is where the obsession about the usage of AI in education becomes the emergent behavior in these systems. For example, a recent study highlights that governments, such as the UK, are choosing AI in education due to its potential to enhance learning experiences and support educators in tasks such as lesson planning and assessment (Felix & Webb, 2024). AI is ultimately transforming societies and its integration into education is now a policy priority globally due to its numerous benefits. Another recent study conducted by Shoukat (2024), concludes that China and India found that adopting AI in educational systems enhanced the learning experience and outcomes for students. By integrating AI, governments aim to foster critical skills necessary for success in the 21st century, ultimately making the education system more effective and responsive to changing societal demands (Alkan, 2024). Alkan (2024) also highlights that AI in education improves student learning by providing personalized learning materials based on individual needs, monitoring performance, identifying weaknesses, and offering additional support in those areas. It doesn't come as a surprise why many governments around the world want to commit to AI integration in education and why funding is allocated towards this priority. These advantages align with governmental goals to improve academic results and prepare students for future challenges. However, we should not disregard that the integration of AI in education also presents challenges that require careful consideration and collaboration among stakeholders.

In 2017, the UAE government devised the UAE Strategy for AI 2031 with an eye on cutting costs in education and increasing the desire to learn. However, quite recently, the UAE also announced the rise of a new AI Curriculum which was introduced in May 2025 to be implemented in the 2025-2026 academic year in schools around the Emirates (AlKhaleej Times, 2025). Nonetheless, educators did not receive any practical implementation recommendations before they went on their summer break. The problem is that teachers will receive a new curriculum without localized research on proper implementation in the context of UAE despite the near start of the new academic year. While initiatives like the UAE AI Strategy 2031 aim to enhance AI curriculum integration, the practical implementation of these strategies remains a challenge (Calonge et al., 2025). Another study also found that while AI holds significant potential to enhance learning outcomes, bridge educational gaps, and support diverse student needs, challenges remain including ethical concerns, teacher preparedness, and the necessity for clear policy frameworks to regulate AI integration (Alhajji et al., 2025). These gaps between policy and classroom reality highlight an urgent need for evidence-informed implementation strategies that are tailored to the UAE's educational context—particularly as educators prepare to use the new AI curriculum with limited guidance.

Purpose of the Study

The purpose of this study is to look at a curriculum innovation that was introduced in another country, and extract lessons for UAE using a curriculum model. More precisely, this paper will look at how the programming curriculum addition was implemented in Finland's curriculum and try to develop a theory-based conceptual framework for implementing AI curricula in UAE schools. The author chose Finland's programming curriculum as a focal case due to its early and systemic implementation of digital skills education starting in 2016. According to Korhonen et al. (2023), the Finnish curriculum encourages an understanding of programming as a concept that is broader than merely coding or programming: it is a part of transversal competencies across disciplines, subject areas and grade levels. These characteristics make it a suitable reference point for analyzing how similar innovations, such as AI in education, might be implemented in other national contexts like the UAE. Finland's approach provides a strong example of how a national curriculum can meaningfully embed future-facing skills through structured, cross-disciplinary innovation.

This research relies on Bernstein's (1971) model of curriculum classification and framing because its synthesis integrates the structure of knowledge (classification) and pedagogy (framing). This framework can be used to analyze how the programming education was integrated within the Finnish national curriculum by assessing control over the knowledge boundaries and the communication rules in teaching for students in the framework. Through this lens the study investigates how curriculum innovation in Finland was done and what, to some extent, can be termed as parallel approaches and could adapt to strategize for teaching the AI curriculum in schools in the UAE with a focus on instructional freedom, interdisciplinary teaching, and supportive schooling frameworks. In brief, the focus of the study is to enrich knowledge on curriculum innovation by providing evidence-based strategies useful for UAE policymakers and educational leaders seeking to confront the task of implementing the AI curriculum in a contextually relevant and pedagogically appropriate manner. To achieve the aims of this study, the following research questions will be addressed.

Research Questions

- RQ1: What strategies and challenges influenced the implementation of programming as a curriculum innovation in Finland?
- RQ2: How can implementation strategies from Finland's curriculum innovation be adapted to support the implementation of AI education in the UAE?

These research questions address the growing global demand for effective AI integration in education by focusing on practical implementation strategies. By comparing Finland's advancements in implementing the programming curriculum innovation, this study aims to provide guidance to policymakers and educators in the UAE regarding the proper implementation of the new AI curriculum with a hope to overcome associating complexities. Furthermore, the study connects solid theoretical paradigms, such as Bernstein's model (1971), and practical curricular implementation to present a theory-informed framework that could facilitate pedagogically robust innovations in the UAE.

The literature reviewed in this chapter informs both research questions through exploring common strategies and challenges related to curriculum innovation in programming and AI education. Using Bernstein's five themes which are curriculum structure, pedagogic control, assessment strategies, teacher autonomy, and curriculum decision-making, provides the conceptual lens for reviewing Finland's implementation strategies (RQ1) and allows the interpretation of how strategies can be adapted to support the implementation of AI literacy in the UAE (RQ2).

Curriculum structure is used to compare the degree of classification between programming and AI skills in each context. Pedagogic control is analyzed through framing to explore how teachers structure and pace their lessons. Assessment strategies are explored to compare the learning outcomes are evaluated. Teacher autonomy is analyzed to understand teacher agency and flexibility in pedagogy. Finally, exploring curriculum decision-making to comprehend whether decisions come from government mandates or different bottom-up stakeholder participation. Together, these five themes provide an analytical lens to help us compare how different educational systems apply curriculum innovations into pedagogy. Figure 1 below demonstrates the conceptual framework for the comparative analysis using Bernstein's model.

Figure 1. Conceptual Framework: Comparative Analysis using Bernstein's Model

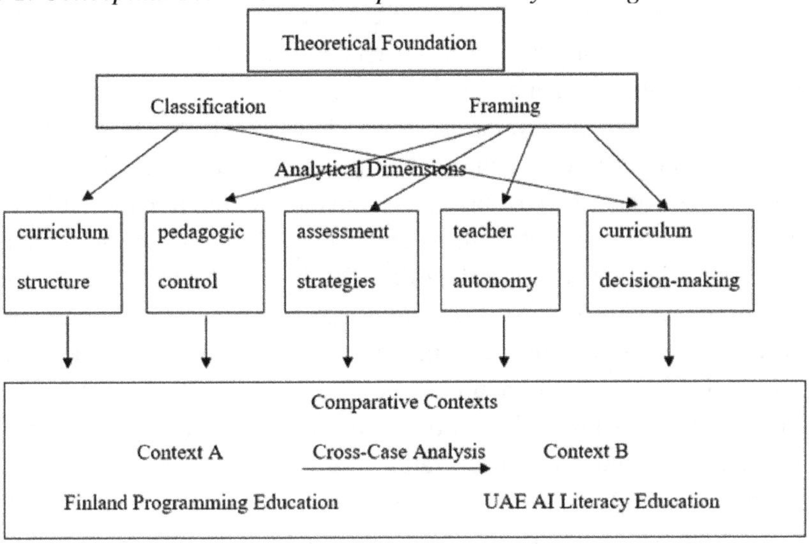

LITERATURE REVIEW

In order to understand the implementation strategies of the programming addition in the Finnish curriculum and try to derive lessons for the UAE, using Bernstein's model would be useful. Bernstein's work in "Class, Codes and Control" (1971) introduced classification and framing as key concepts to understand curricula and pedagogy. Classification refers to the boundaries between subjects and framing is the degree of control in the teaching and learning process (Bernstein, 1971). When subjects are clearly separated this means there is strong classification, and when knowledge is integrated across subjects this refers to weak classification. As for framing, strong framing means there is tight teacher control and a clear set of rules, while weak framing refers to student autonomy and open-ended inquiry (Bernstein, 1971).

With the recent wave of Arificial Intelligence taking over in educational settings, it is imperative for AI to be defined. A study conducted by Dai, Thomas, and Rawolle (2025) points that Artificial Intelligence is a big term which includes many techniques such as machine learning, expert systems, and more. However, in educational settings, teaching AI skills don't mean these technical systems, rather they are about fostering AI literacy in students. AI literacy is gaining the knowledge, skills, and ability to use and evaluate AI tools to create an impact (Choi et al.,

2025). In the context of this paper, teaching and integrating the AI curriculum will refer to AI literacy rather than the other techniques mentioned in other definitions.

With regards to this study, Finland's curriculum-which is characterised by interdisciplinary learning and a high level of student-centered approaches, has a weak classification and a weak framing. However, in the UAE the subjects are clearly separated with strong teacher control. This means the curriculum is strongly classified and framed according to Bernstein's model. Programming in Finland's case was integrated across subjects rather than a stand-alone subject, which confirms the weak classification mentioned earlier. Teachers in Finland can interpret the curriculum the way they see fit (weak framing), unlike the situation in the UAE. The difference in classification and framing shows how implementation strategies differ depending on curriculum models, governance, and cultural values.

Curriculum innovation refers to the systematic transformation of educational content, delivery methods, and organizational structures in response to societal needs or to improve student learning outcomes. Curriculum innovation involves deliberate changes to what is taught (content), how it is taught (pedagogy), when and where it is taught (structure), and how learning is assessed (evaluation) (Fullan, 2016). It is about moving away from traditional approaches and is often driven by technological advancements, new research, or societal demands. Curriculum innovation is more than just a series of isolated updates, as it involves systemic change that reshapes many aspects of education rather than making small disconnected tweaks (Fullan, 2016). The most tangible example of curriculum innovation is the shift from print to digital curricula. Digital innovations, such as e-learning platforms, enable the inclusion of interactive simulations, real-time updates, and adaptive learning pathways, offering opportunities for more personalized and flexible instruction (Sayed et al., 2022). Learning is no longer confined to the classroom, as digital tools support remote access and differentiated content. However, many innovative curricula combine traditional print materials with digital tools, using printed texts as core resources while integrating technology for interactive learning, assessments, and supplementary content (Voogt et al., 2013).

The integration of Information and Communication Technology (ICT) has become an imperative part of education, driving changes in curriculum design and delivery. ICT also influences how teachers design and assess learning, supporting formative data collection and individualized feedback (Anastasopoulou et al., 2024). While general ICT tools have long supported online learning and resource access, recent integration of programming and artificial intelligence represents a more profound shift in curriculum goals and instructional methods. A systemic review by Mills et al. (2024) highlights that programming education has evolved beyond teaching coding as a niche technical skill. It now emphasizes computational thinking, problem-solving, creativity, and critical thinking across various disciplines. The review underscores that integrating coding into curricula enhances students' abilities to reason and solve problems, preparing them for the digital knowledge economy (Mills et al., 2024). Another study by Sajja et al. (2023) discusses an AI assistant approach to demonstrate AI's potential in enhancing student engagement and learning outcomes through intelligent content delivery. These studies collectively affirm that programming education develops essential skills for the digital age, while AI technologies facilitate personalized and adaptive learning environments, transforming modern curriculum design and delivery. Understanding how technologies like programming and AI reshape curriculum structures raises critical questions about who controls knowledge, how learning is framed, and what forms of expertise are legitimized—issues central to Bernstein's theory.

Finland came a long way after the decision to reform their curriculum in 2016. They added transversal competencies with ICT and programming as keys areas. According to Pietarinen et al. (2016), the success of the implementation strategy of the Finnish curriculum was directly linked to the perceived educational impact for both the schools and the society. Furthermore, the transversal approach highlights programming as a key 21st-century skill that complements subject-specific learning, positioning it as a compulsory cross-curricular theme within the curriculum (Toikkanen & Leinonen, 2017). Programming was not introduced as an isolated subject, rather as a broader competence integrated across subjects, grade levels, and disciplinary boundaries, contributing to students' transversal skills development (Korhonen et al., 2022). This is a clear example of a weak classification according to Bernstein's model (1971).

As for implementation and teacher control, in Finland teachers are regarded as independent professionals with significant authority over classroom decisions and their own professional growth. Korhonen et al. (2022) mention that teachers design their lessons based on the national curriculum, tailoring them to meet the needs of their students and selecting the most appropriate teaching methods and resources. This reflects weak framing and a focus on student autonomy. It is also mentioned in the Finnish curriculum that the seven transversal competencies were devised to encourage students to recognize their uniqueness and strengths as their potential for development (Halinen, 2018), with a stong emphasis on formative assessment and feedback. These principles—cross-curricular integration, teacher autonomy, and formative practices—offer valuable insights for countries like the UAE, where curriculum innovation is emerging through AI-related reforms, often within more centralized, strongly classified frameworks.

However, despite curriculum reforms in 2016 many studies also show significant variation in how programming and computational thinking have been implemented across Finnish schools, largely influenced by teacher characteristics, motivation, and subject area (Leino et al., 2019; Kaarakainen et al., 2017; Hämäläinen et al.,

2021). Another study conducted by Pörn et al. (2021) found that participation in-service training courses significantly contributed to higher perceived preparedness, suggesting that such initiatives are crucial for enhancing teachers' confidence and effectiveness in teaching programming in primary education. Since this curriculum innovation was faced by some challenges, and because many teachers expressed concerns, the National Board of Education developed service training initiatives and a support network for teachers to help each other. Implementation often relied on individual teacher motivation and was particularly emphasized within STEAM-related subject areas, where teachers with higher affinity for programming were more likely to integrate programming into their instruction (Kaarakainen et al., 2017; Hämäläinen et al., 2021). These studies confirm that teachers in Finland can significantly impact reforms and how they are implemented.

Programming was not only integrated in different subjects in Finland, different countries followed the same trend as well. According to Mills et al. (2024), countries such as the United States, UK, Germany, Belgium and many others have embedded coding and computational thinking in their curriculum. These reforms were driven by governments that want to prepare their students to become digitally competent; which is a necessary skill for success in a rapidly evolving technological world. In the UK, computing was introduced as a compulsory subject in the national curriculum in 2014, emphasizing programming, algorithms, and digital literacy across all key stages (Department for Education, 2013). Likewise, in Singapore, the education system devised a "Code for Fun" initiative where computer science concepts were blended with problem-solving across subject areas (Gal, 2019). These examples highlight the global acknowledgement of the importance of digital fluency and the need to integrate programming not as a single subject, but as a transversal skill that supports 21st-century goals.

The UAE has positioned itself as a global leader in technological innovation, with AI at the center of its national development strategies. The National Strategy for AI 2031 was devised in 2017 with education as a key sector for AI integration. This strategy aims to boost government performance at all levels and use an integrated smart digital system that can overcome challenges (UAE Government, 2017). The main aim for education is to cut costs and enhance the desire for education. Recently in May 2025, the Ministry of Education in the UAE announced the integration of AI as an official subject in the school curriculum for kindergarten to grade 12 starting from 2025-2026 academic year (Khaleej Times, 2025). This initiative proves the shift in policy toward embedding AI literacy and computational thinking in the national curriculum to foster innovation, critical thinking, and digital fluency among Emirati students. This policy also demonstrates a transformation in curriculum design, where traditional subject boundaries may increasingly give way to interdisciplinary models that incorporate AI literacy within science, mathematics, and even humanities. Teacher training programs and curriculum development efforts are expected to evolve as well to support the successful implementation of this reform (Badoi-Hammami, 2023). The UAE's approach mirrors global trends, but also reflects a top-down implementation model with strong classification and framing, distinguishing it from more decentralized models like Finland's.

AI literacy has become an essential pedagogical practice highly dependent on teacher readiness, interdisciplinarity, and ethical governance rather than a technical competence. Nonetheless, key challenges such as teacher training, assessment, and AI ethics are still present and remain inconsistently addressed among different contexts. For example, a study conducted by Zhang and Zhang (2024) sheds light on the importance of incorporating AI in teacher training programs to enhance teaching practices. Prioritizing teacher competency in teaching AI literacy was also highlighted in a study conducted in China (Casal-Otero et al., 2023). Teachers' AI literacy is imperative for AI literacy education.

While teacher preparedness is a significant determinant of AI literacy implementation, other factors also play a role. Assessment is another dimension which is critical for the proper implementation of AI tools in the classroom. According to Williams (2023), assessment is vital for helping students and teachers set goals and measure their success. Furthermore, curriculum designers should be mindful of the type of assessments used since AI literacy focuses on skills and these skills need to have the proper assessment tools to measure them (Williams, 2023). However, assessning AI literacy can be challenging specifically if traditional assessments are being used. According to Swiecki et al. (2022), traditional assessments bring several issues such as difficulty for educators to assess AI tools, having these assessments only provide a snapshot of performance in addition to being uniform and unadaptable to different student backgrounds. A recent study by Chang and Choi (2025), highlighted the lack of standardized assessment tools to evaluate AI literacy competencies, which limits effective curriculum implementation and policy evaluation. Many issues are raised when it comes to adequately assessing AI literacy and the literature agrees on assessment as a main challenge in AI education.

Another factor that also impacts the implementation of AI in classroom practices is the ethical governance since it is essential for preparing students to engage with AI responsibly. A study conducted by Faisal (2025) in the UAE found that there are many educator concerns about data privacy and protection when it comes to AI adoption in schools. Another systematic review done by Huyen et al. (2025) highlights ethical challenges such as data security and privacy, discrimination and bias, excessive dependance on AI, and the complexity of AI algorithms. Therefore, it is imperative to use a comprehensive approach that balances technological advancement with human-centered principles to properly navigate AI adoption.

While many studies show the integration of programming in school curricula in different countries such as Finland, UK, and Singapore (Mills et al., 2024, Toikkanen & Leinonen, 2017), there remains a gap in research that explores how these experiences can inform the implementation of AI in education. This is particularly true in the UAE where the reform is happening rapidly without many guidelines for educators. Despite policy-level enthusiasm and investment, there is a lack of empirical and theory-informed frameworks guiding this transition. A study conducted by Khalil & Alsenaidi (2024) in Oman, found that professional development and targeted training for teachers are necessary for an AI-enhanced educational environment. This highlights the importance of conducting studies that focus specifically on the UAE context, using curriculum innovation theories like Bernstein's model of classification and framing (1971) to better understand and support how AI education is being introduced in schools in the presence of many challenges.

METHODOLOGY

This study adopts a qualitative, theoretical comparative analysis approach to explore curriculum innovation strategies in two national contexts: Finland and the UAE. Specifically, it compares the implementation of Finland's programming curriculum with the newly introduced AI curriculum in the UAE, using existing academic literature and policy documents. This method allows for an in-depth exploration of implementation processed through conceptual interpretation rather than empirical fieldwork. As Creswell (2013) emphasizes, qualitative research can be used to understand complex phenomena through rich, contextualized analysis grounded in theory. This study follows such a tradition by employing document analysis and theoretical interpretation to evaluate implementation strategies in Finland and extract lessons that may inform future AI curriculum implementation in the UAE. Document analysis is used to analyze publicly available sources such as the *Finnish National Core Curriculum* (Finnish National Agency for Education, 2016), the *UAE Artificial Intelligence Strategy 2031* (UAE Government, 2017), implementation reports from Finland, and peer-reviewed journal articles. According to Bowen (2009), document analysis is an efficient and effective method when the goal is to extract meaning and develop understanding from published materials such as curriculum frameworks, government policies, and peer-reviewed literature.

The research uses Bernstein's (1971) theory of classification and framing as the analytical framework. This lens is used to guide the thematic interpretation of how knowledge is structured and transmitted, and implemented in the two curriculum innovations. Bernstein's theoretical framework serves to investigate the processes by which curriculum knowledge is selected, organized, and recontextualized by various agents throughout the implementation phase. Classification relates to the delineation of boundaries among distinct forms of knowledge (e.g., disciplinary, vocational, interdisciplinary), whereas framing addresses the extent of control exerted by educators and learners over pedagogic discourse (i.e., instructional autonomy, sequencing, and pacing) (Bernstein, 1971). This analytical framework is particularly used for examining implementation, as it highlights the power dynamics inherent in the construction and dissemination of knowledge.

The analysis was based on Berstein's concepts which involve identifying themes related to curriculum structure, pedagogic control, assessment strategies, teacher autonnomy, and curriculum decision-making. These themes were traced across the Finnish case and the UAE's strategy documents to understand how curriculum reforms were framed and who the key recontextualizing agents are in each system. This is due to the fact that the UAE AI curriculum was not dissemenated in schools until the beginning of the new academic year. The documents were read multiple times to ensure contextual understanding. Then, selected parts of text were coded according to Bernstein's concepts. These coded segments were grouped into higher-order themes through comparison across the Finnish and UAE documents. The themes were retained only when they appeared consistently across multiple sources within each case and could be theoretically justified. The same coding framework and analytical criteria were applied in both cases to ensure consistency. Given that the UAE AI curriculum had not been fully disseminated yet in the schools during the time of the analysis, policy and strategy documents were treated as recontextualizing texts, allowing the examination of curriculum framing rather than enacted practice.

The rationale for choosing Finland lies in its internationally recognized approach to curriculum reform, particularly its early adoption of programming education as a transversal competence integrated across subject areas. Finland's reforms are known for being equity-oriented, systemically implemented, and supported by a coherent national strategy (Korhonen et al., 2023). In contrast, the UAE is at the early stages of implementing its AI curriculum. While the strategy has been launched, curriculum materials have not yet been distributed to schools, creating a unique opportunity to analyze its projected implementation in light of lessons from an established case. This theoretical and comparative approach is consistent with the tradition of conceptual analysis in curriculum studies, where the goal is to generate new insights and recommendations for implementation based on existing models and literature (Patton, 2002; Tisdell et al., 2025). This study did not involve human participants or primary data collection and therefore did not require ethical approval. This conceptual, implementation-focused comparative analysis aligns with traditions in curriculum studies that seek to generate theory-based insights and recommendations for practice through critical engagement with policy and reform literature (Patton, 2002; Tisdell et al., 2025). The use of Bernstein's theory provides a powerful framework for understanding how educational knowledge is shaped, controlled, and transmitted in policy implementation.

DISCUSSION

The following discussion is structured around five key themes derived from Bernstein's model and the research methodology: curriculum structure, teacher autonomy, pedagogic control, curriculum decision-making, and assessment strategies. When Finland decided to integrate programming across subjects, the plan and final goal were clear for everyone from the launch of the reform in 2016, which fostered engagement across stakeholders. This reflects a clearly articulated curriculum structure, where programming was clearly defined as a transversal skill integrated across subjects (Finnish National Agency for Education, 2016). The shared understanding across the system supported the implementation from the beginning.

In terms of teacher autonomy, some teachers in Finland faced this change with enthusiasm and high motivation. Teacher readiness varied in the application of ICT skills (Kaarakainen et al., 2017). Nonetheless, there were others who had concerns about their readiness and lacked the confidence to start designing lessons with this new integration (Hämäläinen et al., 2021). Consequently, the Finnish National Board of Education responded to these concerns and set up service training for teachers and created a collaborative network for support as well (Korhonen et al., 2022). Since teachers have the freedom in implementing the curriculum, this helped relieve some of the pressure exerted. The flexibility in the Finnish curriculum gave teachers the liberty of making pedagogical decisions that increased their confidence during the transition.

As for curriculum decision-making, Finland's reform treated teachers as key stakeholders with the ability to adapt this national policy framework. According to Korhonen et al. (2022), Finnish teachers can make decisions about their own teaching independently and they choose what to incorporate and what to disregard. This balance of top-down guidance with bottom-up input supported both coherence and responsiveness. Another study by Toikkanen and Leinonen (2017) highlights how teachers received in-service training to develop their digital competence skills. Teachers discussed the steps of implementation, and the brainstorming of ideas was interdisciplinary, since implementation happened across subjects. Nonetheless, there were challenges that arose during that time. Korhonen et al. (2022) highlight that many teachers didn't manage to gain digital competency skills and therefore data revealed that students didn't acquire the programming skills required.

When comparing the implementation of the curriculum innovation in Finland to the new AI curriculum currently being implemented in the UAE, we ought to consider the many differences that exist. First, there are fundamental variations in teachers' role between both countries, specifically teacher autonomy. In Finland, teachers are highly autonomous and can interpret the curriculum any way they see fit for their students. However, in the UAE, this is not possible as lessons are already handed in by the Ministry of Education for public schools. In contexts characterized by strong classification and framing such as the UAE, teachers' pedagogical discretion to modify lesson design is significantly constrained; it is more centralized. This impacts pedagogic control, as teachers in the UAE are limited in how they can frame and deliver the curriculum.

Furthermore, programming in Finland was integrated across different subjects, which aided in allowing teachers to rely on one another. Nonetheless, this is not the case in the UAE where the AI curriculum structure will be a standalone subject, divided and spread out in topics across different grade levels. The lack of interdisciplinary integration may limit opportunities for teachers to collaborate. The release of the curriculum only at the start of the academic year raises significant concerns regarding implementation readiness. Some ICT teachers might not be prepared to teach this subject and that would affect planning. There is already a high concern by teachers who might teach this curriculum because they don't have any material or lessons ready or prepared for the new academic year. It also remains unclear whether the AI curriculum will be mandatory in private schools, further adding ambiguity. However, the programming curriculum was clearly announced in Finland with a direct plan back in 2016.

As for assessment strategies, the emphasis in Finland is on formative assessment and feedback, while in the UAE it is traditionally summative. However there have been recent reforms that may introduce more formative elements (UAE Ministry of Education, 2023). Still, it remains unclear how assessment will be managed for the AI curriculum or what platform will be used in UAE. Overall, what is clear in this new curriculum innovation is that teachers in the UAE will have to teach AI literacy skills while they learn how to acquire these skills simultaneously. Without structured professional development and clear guidance on curriculum and assessment, this dual burden may pose a significant challenge in implementation.

CONCLUSION

The main purpose of this study was to derive best practices from Finland's implementation of its curriculum innovation and suggest ideas to facilitate the implementation if the AI curriculum in the UAE context while using Bernstein's Curriculum Model. It answers two main research questions revolving around the strategies and challenges that influenced the implementation of the programming curriculum in Finland, in addition to examining which implementation strategies can be adapted to support the implementation of the AI curriculum in the UAE. The novelty of this chapter lies in its comparative, theory-informed approach: instead of focusing solely on policy rhetoric, it critically analyzes how international practices can translate into actionable steps within the UAE context. This is an important topic which tries to close the gap of how stakeholders can implement and use AI in education as the wave of teaching AI literacy takes over the education scene. Moreover, despite policy-level enthusiasm and investment in the UAE, there is a lack of empirical and theory-informed frameworks guiding this transition.

These implications should not be interpreted as a simple policy transfer between contexts. Instead of encouraging direct policy borrowing, this comparison highlights the importance of contextual adaptation. Having teacher autonomy, curriculum flexibility and assessment strategies highly associated with strong classification and framing, requires structural redesign to align with centralized governance. Therefore, the Finnish case is best understood as providing analytical insights into enabling conditions rather than a model to be copied.

Considering the presented limitations, several recommendations are proposed to strengthen the implementation and evaluation of the AI curriculum in the UAE. The implementation of the AI curriculum in the UAE context should be rolled out in phases gradually. This will allow time for piloting, collecting feedback and improvements to instructional materials and assessment methods. Simultaneously, sustained efforts and solid funding allocated for professional development is essential to prepare teachers with the technical knowledge and pedagogical strategies needed to deliver the content effectively. This training however should be done during working hours and should cater to the linguistic and cultural needs in the UAE. Furthermore, before making AI a standalone subject, integrating AI in different subjects such as math, science, or ICT would ease the transition and would reduce the pressure on teachers and allow for interdisciplinary collaboration. Encouraging collaboration and giving teachers some flexibility will allow room for innovation. The content in this curriculum should be designed to suit UAE's culture and societal values while maintaining privacy. Finally, the UAE should move beyond high-stakes summative testing in this curriculum and focus more on formative assessments to allow for deeper student understanding, engagement, and reflective learning.

The main characteristics in Finland's education system rely on teacher autonomy and treating teachers as reflective academic experts. It is known for its equality and high quality of teaching and learning (Halinen, 2018). Furthermore, evaluation is done for improvement rather than ranking unlike in the UAE. Finland's experience offers concrete strategies in policy support, teacher training, and curriculum development. Using Berstein's model of classification and framing (1971) provided a lens to analyze key dimensions such as curriculum structure, pedagogic control, teacher autonomy, assessment strategies, and curriculum decision-making. This comparative analysis demonstrated that adopting a gradual, well-supported, and culturally responsive approach is essential for successful curriculum reform.

Limitations

This study highlights the need for future research on the implementation of the AI curriculum in the UAE. Future studies could explore how teacher autonomy, curriculum integration strategies, and assessment reforms influence the effectiveness of AI education in schools. Furthermore, future studies could investigate the impact of teacher training programs on teacher's pedagogical confidence and student progress in AI skills. There is a lack of research on AI ethics as well as how culturally responsive the stakeholders will be. As the UAE moves forward with its AI curriculum, research should track the rollout process and examine how theoretical frameworks like Bernstein's model can guide adaptation and policy refinement over time.

Recommendations

Future studies could adopt a longitudinal approach to track the roll out of the AI curriculum to allow different stakeholders such as policymakers and educational leaders understand how gradual implementation and professional development could impact the effectiveness of the curriculum. Furthermore, future research could focus on the impact of professional development on the students' AI literacy skills.

REFERENCES

Alhajji, R. A. Y., Almansoori, A. G., & Alyammahi, A. (2025). Harnessing AI for EFL educational advancement: A reflection on policy, practice, and pedagogy within the Ministry of Education in the UAE.

Alkan, A. (2024). *Use of artificial intelligence in education. Journal of the Human and Social Science Researches*. Itobiad., DOI: 10.15869/itobiad.1331201

Anastasopoulou, E., Konstantina, G., Tsagri, A., Schoina, I., Travlou, C., Mitroyanni, E., & Lyrintzi, T. (2024). The impact of digital technologies on formative assessment and the learning experience. *Technium Education and Humanities*, *10*, 115–126. DOI: 10.47577/teh.v10i.12113

Badoi-Hammami, M. (2023). The reality of practical training programs for teachers in light of technological development and continuous modern innovations: Challenges and opportunities. *Journal Plus Education*, *33*(Special Issue), 165–180. DOI: 10.24250/jpe/si/2023/mbh

Bernstein, B. (1971). Class, codes and control: Vol. 1. *Theoretical studies towards a sociology of language*. Routledge & Kegan Paul.

Bowen, G. A. (2009). Document analysis as a qualitative research method. *Qualitative Research Journal*, *9*(2), 27–40.

Calonge, D. S., Kamalov, F., Aguerrebere, P. M., Hassock, L., Smail, L., Yousef, D., Thadani, D. R., Kwong, T., & Abdulla, N. (2025). Upskilling and reskilling in the United Arab Emirates: Future-proofing careers with AI skills. *Journal of Adult and Continuing Education*. DOI: 10.1177/14779714251315288

Casal-Otero, L., Catala, A., Fernández-Morante, C., Taboada, M., & Cebreiro, B. (2023). AI literacy in K-12: A systematic literature review. *International Journal of STEM Education*, *10*(1). Advance online publication. DOI: 10.1186/s40594-023-00418-7

Chang, C. I., & Choi, W. C. (2025). Exploring Challenges and Opportunities in Artificial Intelligence (AI) Literacy and Educational AI Development: A Qualitative Study of Teachers and Researchers' Perspectives. *Perspectives*. DOI: 10.20944/preprints202508.1077.v1

Choi, W. C., Chang, C. I., Choi, I. C., Lam, L. C., Leong, K. I., & Ng, S. I. (2025). Artificial Intelligence (AI) Literacy in Education: Definition, Competencies, Opportunities and Challenges. *Preprints*. DOI: 10.20944/preprints202508.0497.v1

Creswell, J. W. (2013). *Qualitative inquiry and research design: Choosing among five approaches* (3rd ed.). SAGE Publications.

Dai, R., Thomas, M. K. E., & Rawolle, S. (2025). The roles of AI and educational leaders in AI-assisted administrative decision-making: A proposed framework for symbiotic collaboration. *Australian Educational Researcher*, *52*, 1471–1487. DOI: 10.1007/s13384-024-00771-8

Department for Education. (2013). *National curriculum in England: Computing programmes of study*.https://assets.publishing.service.gov.uk/government/uploads/system/uploads/attachment_data/file/239033/PRIMARY_national_curriculum_-_Computing.pdf

Faisal, R. (2025). Ethical AI integration in education: Policies, challenges, and strategies for bridging digital divides in emerging economies. *Crossroads of Social Inquiry*, *1*(2), 1–18. DOI: 10.64851/csi.v1i2.28

Felix, J. A., & Webb, L. (2024). Use of artificial intelligence in education delivery and assessment. DOI: 10.58248/pn712

Finnish National Agency for Education. (2016). National core curriculum for basic education 2014 [). Finnish National Board of Education.]. *Publications*, *2016*, 5.

Fullan, M. (2016). *The new meaning of educational change*. Teachers college press.

Gal, D. (2019). Coding for fun or for the future? RSIS Commentary. S. Rajaratnam School of International Studies.

Government, U. A. E. (2017). *UAE Strategy for Artificial Intelligence.*_https://u.ae/en/about-the-uae/strategies-initiatives-and-awards/strategies-plans-and-visions/government-services-and-digital-transformation/uae-strategy-for-artificial-intelligence

Halinen, I. (2018). The new educational curriculum in Finland. *Improving the quality of childhood in Europe, 7*, 75-89.

Hämäläinen, R., Nissinen, K., Mannonen, J., Lämsä, J., Leino, K., & Taajamo, M. (2021). Understanding teaching professionals' digital competence: What do PIAAC and TALIS reveal about technology-related skills, attitudes, and knowledge? *Computers in Human Behavior*, *117*, 106672. DOI: 10.1016/j.chb.2020.106672

Huyen, N. T., Lien, N. P., & Thuy, P. T. (2025). Challenges of AI In education: A systematic review. IOSR. *Journal of Research & Method in Education*, *15*(3), 37–46. https://www.iosrjournals.org/iosr-jrme/papers/Vol-15%20Issue-3/Ser-1/F1503013746.pdf

Kaarakainen, M.-T., Kaarakainen, S.-S., Tanhua-Piiroinen, E., Viteli, J., Syvänen, A., & Kivinen, A. (2017). *Digiajan peruskoulu 2017 – tilannearvio ja toimenpidesuositukset* [Comprehensive school digitalisation: Status review and recommendations for action for 2017]. Prime Minister's Office.

Khalil, H., & Alsenaidi, S. (2024). Teachers' digital competencies for effective AI integration in higher education in Oman. *Journal of Education and e-learning Research*, *11*(4), 698–707. DOI: 10.20448/jeelr.v11i4.6097

Korhonen, T., Salo, L., Laakso, N., Seitamaa, A., Sormunen, K., Kukkonen, M., & Forsström, H. (2023). Finnish teachers as adopters of educational innovation: Perceptions of programming as a new part of the curriculum. *Computer Science Education*, *33*(1), 94–116.

Leino, K., Rikala, J., Puhakka, E., Niilo-Rämä, M., Sirén, M., & Fagerlund, J. (2019). *Digiloikasta digitaitoihin. Kansainvälinen monilukutaidon ja ohjelmoinnillisen ajattelun tutkimus (ICILS 2018)* [From digital leap to ICT skills: International computer and information literacy study with computational thinking assessment (ICILS 2018)]. Finnish Institute for Educational Research: University of Jyväskylä.

Mills, K. A., Cope, J., Scholes, L., & Rowe, L. (2024). Coding and computational thinking across the curriculum: A review of educational outcomes. *Review of Educational Research*. Advance online publication. DOI: 10.3102/00346543241241327

Patton, M. Q. (2002). *Qualitative research and evaluation methods* (Vol. 3). Sage.

Pietarinen, J., Pyhältö, K., & Soini, T. (2016). Large-scale curriculum reform in Finland –exploring the interrelation between implementation strategy, the function of the reform, and curriculum coherence. *Curriculum Journal*, *28*(1), 22–40. DOI: 10.1080/09585176.2016.1179205

Pörn, R., Hemmi, K., & Kallio-Kujala, P. (2021). *Inspiring or confusing – a study of Finnish 1–6 teachers' relation to teaching programming*. *9*(1), 366–396. DOI: 10.31129/LUMAT.9.1.1355

Sajja, R., Sermet, Y., Cikmaz, M., Cwiertny, D., & Demir, I. (2023). Artificial intelligence-enabled intelligent assistant for personalized and adaptive learning in higher education. *arXiv preprint arXiv:2309.10892*. https://arxiv.org/abs/2309.10892

Sayed, W. S., Noeman, A. M., Abdellatif, A., Abdelrazek, M., Badawy, M. G., Hamed, A., & El-Tantawy, S. (2022). AI-based adaptive personalized content presentation and exercises navigation for an effective and engaging E-learning platform. *Multimedia Tools and Applications*, *82*(3), 3303–3333. DOI: 10.1007/s11042-022-13076-8

Shoukat, R. (2024). Harnessing AI for Educational Transformation: A Comparative Study of China, India and Pakistan. *Strategic Studies, 44*(1).

Swiecki, Z., Khosravi, H., Chen, G., Martinez-Maldonado, R., Lodge, J. M., Milligan, S., Selwyn, N., & Gašević, D. (2022). Assessment in the age of artificial intelligence. Computers & Education. *Artificial Intelligence*, *3*, 100075. DOI: 10.1016/j.caeai.2022.100075

Tisdell, E. J., Merriam, S. B., & Stuckey-Peyrot, H. L. (2025). *Qualitative research: A guide to design and implementation*. John Wiley & Sons.

Toikkanen, T., & Leinonen, T. (2017). The code ABC MOOC: Experiences from a coding and computational thinking MOOC for Finnish primary school teachers. In Rich, P., & Hodges, C. (Eds.), *Emerging Research, Practice, and Policy on Computational Thinking. Educational Communications and Technology: Issues and Innovations*. Springer., DOI: 10.1007/978-3-319-52691-1_15

Voogt, J., Erstad, O., Dede, C., & Mishra, P. (2013). Challenges to learning and schooling in the digital networked world of the 21st century. *Journal of Computer Assisted Learning*, *29*(5), 403–413. DOI: 10.1111/jcal.12029

Williams, R. (2023). A review of assessments in K-12 AI literacy curricula. *Retrieved*, (October), 25.

Zhang, J., & Zhang, Z. (2024). AI in teacher education: Unlocking new dimensions in teaching support, inclusive learning, and digital literacy. *Journal of Computer Assisted Learning*, *40*(4), 1871–1885. DOI: 10.1111/jcal.12988

Chapter 8
Regulating AI for Education:
Accountability, Accreditation, and QA in MENA

Mustafa Kayyali
http://orcid.org/0000-0003-3300-262X
Maaref University of Applied Sciences, Syria

ABSTRACT

This chapter examines how MENA education systems can regulate AI not as an afterthought but as a core dimension of academic quality and institutional legitimacy. It first traces the emerging uses of AI in schools and universities and shows how opaque algorithms unsettle traditional ideas of responsibility, authorship, and assessment. The chapter then explores how existing accreditation and quality assurance regimes—often designed for analogue institutions—can be reimagined to address issues such as data governance, algorithmic bias, learning analytics, and AI-assisted assessment. Drawing on regional policy documents and illustrative institutional practices, it proposes principles, indicators, and review processes that embed accountability into the design, procurement, and deployment of AI tools. Rather than importing ready-made global templates, the chapter argues for context-sensitive regulatory frameworks that align with MENA socio-political realities while safeguarding learners' rights and public trust.

INTRODUCTION

In many classrooms across the MENA region, the arrival of AI is not a grand announcement but a quiet shift in habits. A teacher copies a prompt into a generative

DOI: 10.4018/979-8-3373-6776-7.ch008

tool to draft exam questions. A student, anxious about grades and family expectations, feeds an essay outline into a chatbot late at night. A university administrator checks a dashboard that predicts dropout risk, colour-coding students' futures in shades of green, yellow, and red. None of these actions feels like "regulation" in the formal sense. Yet each one is already redistributing responsibility, reshaping what quality means, and silently redefining what counts as legitimate learning and teaching.

The speed of this transformation is especially striking in MENA education systems, where demographic pressure, chronic underfunding, and long-standing aspirations for global competitiveness converge (Bhattarai & Yousef, 2025). Governments are trying to respond to soaring youth populations, ambitious national visions, and the constant comparison with international benchmarks. AI appears, at first glance, to be a convenient ally: automate grading, personalise learning, predict failure, detect plagiarism, produce "smart" content in multiple languages. It promises efficiency and modernity, two words that sit very comfortably in policy documents.

But beneath the optimistic rhetoric, profound questions remain unresolved. When an algorithm flags a student as "high risk" and the student is treated differently because of that label, who is accountable if the prediction is wrong? When generative AI rewrites a weak assignment into polished academic English, whose work is actually being assessed, and what does integrity look like in such a world? When a private edtech vendor integrates AI into the digital platform used by a public university, how can accreditation bodies judge the quality of this hybrid, partly outsourced pedagogical experience? These are not peripheral technical details (Hands, 2025). They go to the heart of what it means to run an educational system that is fair, trustworthy, and worthy of public investment.

Regulation, in this context, cannot be reduced to a set of prohibitions or a list of "dos and don'ts" circulated to schools and universities. It is better understood as an evolving ecosystem of norms, incentives, standards, and feedback loops that coordinate the behaviour of teachers, institutions, ministries, and technology providers. In the MENA region, this ecosystem is already dense. Ministries of education, councils for higher education, national accreditation agencies, professional bodies, and quality assurance units inside universities all have their own histories, hierarchies, and routines (Myburgh, 2021). AI does not arrive in a vacuum; it enters a regulatory environment shaped by decades of centralisation, examination culture, political sensitivities, and uneven digital capacity.

At the same time, AI unsettles the assumptions on which many of those structures were built. Traditional accreditation standards, for example, presuppose that curricula, assessment tools, and teaching materials are relatively stable and authored by identifiable humans. Quality assurance procedures assume that data about students and courses are collected and interpreted by people whose judgement can be questioned, reviewed, or corrected. In contrast, AI systems make it possible to generate content on demand, to update learning pathways in real time, and to rely on complex statistical models that are opaque to most educators who are affected by them. The very idea of "evidence" for quality – once comfortably anchored in syllabi, exam scripts, and course portfolios – is beginning to blur.

There is a risk, especially in the face of global pressure, that MENA education systems try to respond by importing ready-made regulatory frameworks from elsewhere: guidelines on trustworthy AI, references to international principles, alignment with foreign standards (Kassir, 2022). These can be useful starting points, but they rarely speak directly to the lived realities of a crowded public classroom in Cairo, a private university in the Gulf competing for international students, or a fragile institution in a conflict-affected area trying to keep basic services running. Regulation that does not listen to context remains thin; it may satisfy donors, but it does not necessarily protect learners or guide institutions.

This chapter starts from a different premise: that regulating AI for education in MENA is not only a technical exercise but a deeply political, ethical, and institutional project. It requires clarity about what kind of accountability is desirable and feasible in environments where power is often unevenly distributed and criticism of official systems can carry risk. It calls for reimagining accreditation so that it does not simply tick boxes about "use of technology" but actually interrogates the design, deployment, and impact of AI tools. And it demands that quality assurance move beyond compliance audits toward a more reflective practice of questioning how AI is changing learning relationships, academic culture, and institutional priorities.

The first thread the chapter explores is accountability. AI systems blur lines of responsibility precisely at the moment when demands for accountability in education are intensifying (Ojha et al, 2025). When plagiarism detection tools mislabel a student's original work as AI-generated, or when automated grading systems reproduce biases embedded in their training data, who answers to the student, the parents, and society? Within MENA, where authority in education is often centralised and respect for hierarchy remains strong, mechanisms for contesting algorithmic decisions are not always obvious. The chapter examines how accountability can be distributed – among ministries, institutions, vendors, and individuals – without becoming so diluted that nobody is truly answerable.

The second thread concerns accreditation. Across the region, accreditation has been used as a lever for modernisation, quality control, and international recognition. Yet the criteria and indicators that agencies rely on were often designed before AI became a mainstream educational technology. How should accrediting bodies evaluate programs that rely heavily on AI tutors, automated feedback, and learning analytics? What counts as sufficient transparency from AI vendors? How can accreditation visits and reports move beyond superficial mentions of "innovative technologies" to a more rigorous appraisal of the risks and benefits of AI integration? The chapter engages with these questions by reflecting on how standards, review processes, and external evaluation traditions in MENA might be reconfigured.

The third thread is quality assurance within institutions. Most universities in the region now have units or committees dedicated to quality, but their focus is often on documentation, reporting, and periodic reviews. AI challenges these routines. It changes how courses are designed, how students interact with content, how assessments are conducted, and how data is used to monitor performance. Quality assurance offices cannot remain on the sidelines, merely collecting statistics generated by AI platforms; they need to develop the capacity to interrogate the assumptions behind those statistics, to ask uncomfortable questions about equity, privacy, and pedagogical value, and to engage academic staff in critical reflection rather than mechanical compliance.

Throughout the chapter, the MENA perspective is central. The discussion does not treat the region as a monolith; instead, it recognises that there are sharp contrasts between oil-rich states investing heavily in digital infrastructure and countries grappling with conflict, economic crisis, or sanctions. Yet there are also shared features: young populations, pressure to show alignment with global trends, tensions between public and private sectors, and the persistent challenge of transforming formal policies into lived practice. By grounding the debate in these realities, the chapter argues that AI regulation cannot be imported wholesale; it must be translated, negotiated, and sometimes resisted.

Ultimately, the chapter invites readers – policymakers, accreditation leaders, quality assurance practitioners, and educators – to view AI not only as a technological tool but as a mirror that reflects back the strengths and weaknesses of existing systems. The way the region chooses to regulate AI in education will reveal what it truly values: efficiency or equity, control or trust, short-term performance indicators or long-term human development. Regulation, in this sense, is not just about controlling machines; it is about deciding what kind of educational future is worth building together.

REGULATING AI IN MENA EDUCATION: BETWEEN URGENCY AND UNCERTAINTY

Regulating AI in MENA education sits in a strange, almost uncomfortable in-between space (Reimer-Burgrova, 2022). On one side, there is a strong sense that something has to be done quickly: ministries are under pressure, university leaders are fielding questions they cannot postpone, exam integrity is visibly shaken, and parents are starting to ask whether the tools on their children's phones are a blessing or a quiet threat. On the other side, the ground itself is moving. Nobody is fully sure what, precisely, needs to be regulated, or how long any rule will remain relevant before the next technical leap makes it look naïve or narrow. The result is a regulatory mood that oscillates between urgency and hesitation, as if the whole system is trying to run while learning how to walk again.

The urgency is not imaginary. MENA education systems are facing a compressed historical moment: a large youth population demanding credible skills and pathways, ambitious national visions tying education to competitiveness and digital transformation, and a lingering anxiety about "falling behind" in the global race for innovation (Bhattarai & Yousef, 2025). AI slips neatly into this narrative. It is sold as an accelerator, a shortcut, a way to compensate for crowded classrooms, overworked teachers, and limited resources. For policy actors used to thinking in terms of national projects and rapid reform cycles, the message is seductive: adopt AI, and the system can leapfrog stages that other regions took decades to navigate. In that atmosphere, calls for regulation are easily framed as a question of speed: how fast can guidelines be drafted, frameworks updated, agencies retooled?

Yet urgency alone is a poor architect. Beneath the surface of confident slogans lies a dense fog of uncertainty. It is not only technical uncertainty about how specific models function, or where data is stored, or what future versions might be capable of. There is also deep normative uncertainty: what kind of student agency is desirable when AI can draft, summarise, translate, and simulate? How much automation in assessment is acceptable before the meaning of grading itself changes? When learning analytics predict "risk," what exactly is being predicted—effort, prior disadvantage, language background, teacher bias? These questions do not have ready-made answers, and they are felt acutely in systems where high-stakes examinations and credentialism are woven into social expectations.

This double uncertainty becomes sharper because AI is not entering an empty institutional landscape. Most MENA countries already have elaborate regulatory architectures for education—laws, bylaws, accreditation criteria, ministerial decisions, circulars, unwritten norms enforced through hierarchy rather than text (Buckner, 2021). These frameworks were crafted for an analogue or, at best, early digital environment. They presume that textbooks have identifiable authors, that exams can be invigilated in a single room, that plagiarism is a matter of copying from visible sources, and that "ICT" means a computer lab and a learning management system with limited functionality. AI-enabled platforms upset these assumptions in subtle and not-so-subtle ways, and the old rules start to look both inadequate and strangely heavy at the same time.

The temporal mismatch is striking. AI tools evolve on the scale of weeks and months; ministries legislate on the scale of years. A generative model is updated overnight, while a change in accreditation standards may require multiple committee cycles, consultations, approvals, and sometimes parliamentary endorsement.

In MENA bureaucracies—often centralised, cautious, and layered—this latency is amplified (Lynch & Heydemann, 2024). Regulators find themselves chasing a moving target. By the time a committee has agreed on a definition of "AI-based plagiarism," students and teachers are already working with a new class of multimodal tools that do not fit the original description. The sense of running behind is very real, and it feeds a quiet frustration inside institutions that are accustomed to being told to "comply" with norms that arrive late and feel disconnected from daily practice.

Table 1. Regulatory Actors and AI Responsibilities

Regulatory Actor	Primary AI–Education Responsibilities	Key Risks if Role is Weak	Illustrative Accountability Questions
Ministries of education / higher education	Set overarching principles for AI in education, define high-risk uses, and align AI governance with national visions and equity goals.	Fragmented regulations, over-reliance on imported models, and neglect of vulnerable learners in national AI strategies.	Has the ministry set clear red lines for AI in high-stakes exams and student profiling, and are they publicly communicated?
National accreditation and QA agencies	Translate principles into standards, criteria, and evidence requirements that scrutinise how AI is governed in programs and institutions.	Superficial treatment of AI as a tick-box, accrediting the appearance of innovation rather than its governance and impact.	Do accreditation standards ask how AI is governed, not just whether it is present, and is evidence triangulated with student voices?
Institutional quality assurance units	Interrogate how AI tools reshape teaching, assessment, and analytics; coordinate local policies, monitoring, and staff development.	Uncritical adoption of vendor defaults; hidden inequities in AI-driven assessment and analytics; QA reduced to paperwork.	Can the QA unit explain where AI is used on campus, what risks were mapped, and how staff and students were involved?
University / school leadership	Decide which AI systems to adopt, negotiate contracts, allocate resources, and model responsible AI use in institutional culture.	Ad hoc AI deployments driven by marketing or crisis, without due consideration of pedagogy, ethics, or long-term costs.	Are procurement decisions for AI tools accompanied by impact assessments and sunset clauses for problematic deployments?
Edtech and AI vendors	Design, localise, and support AI tools; provide transparent documentation on data use, risks, and performance in Arabic and other languages.	Opaque systems, unaddressed bias, poor localisation, and vendor lock-in that restrict institutional autonomy.	Can the vendor demonstrate fairness, robustness, and data safeguards for MENA learners, including in Arabic interfaces?
Students and families	Use AI tools responsibly, question unfair or opaque uses, and provide feedback on how AI affects learning, privacy, and well-being.	Normalisation of undisclosed AI assistance, reliance on unvetted tools, and silence about harmful experiences with AI.	Do students know when AI is influencing decisions about them and how to challenge those decisions if they seem unfair?

In such circumstances, different regulatory reflexes emerge. One reflex is defensive: prohibit first, think later. Some institutions react to AI by issuing blanket bans, equating any use of generative tools with cheating, and framing regulation primarily as surveillance and punishment. This approach feels safe in the short term; it signals to the public, and to political authorities, that the institution is "taking the issue seriously." Yet it also pushes AI use underground, encourages students to become more secretive, and prevents teachers from experimenting with constructive, transparent, pedagogically grounded uses of intelligent tools (Afable, 2025). The system ends up regulating the visible surface while the deeper transformations continue unchecked.

Another reflex is deferential: wait for others to decide. University leaders in the region sometimes look upward—to the ministry, the council for higher education, the national accreditation body—and avoid taking strong positions until a formal directive arrives. This is understandable in governance cultures where institutional autonomy is constrained and misalignment with central policy can be politically risky. But it also prolongs the period in which AI is used extensively without any internal safeguards, local guidelines, or context-specific reflection. In this waiting mode, regulation is imagined as something imported, a finished document that will eventually drop from above rather than a living process generated from within (Park, 2023).

There is also a more fragmented pattern, visible in some systems, where AI regulation is treated as a technical matter for the IT department or an ethical dilemma for academic integrity committees, without much dialogue between them. Security officers worry about data breaches and server locations; pedagogy specialists talk about learning outcomes and critical thinking; quality assurance units think in terms of indicators and documentation (Azem Qashou et al, 2025). Each group has a partial view, and without a coherent bridge, the resulting policies can be internally inconsistent—strict about some marginal issues, silent about others that are far more consequential, such as vendor lock-in or algorithmic bias in admissions and scholarship allocation.

Figure 1. Illustrative Balance of Regulatory Attention Across AI–Education Domains

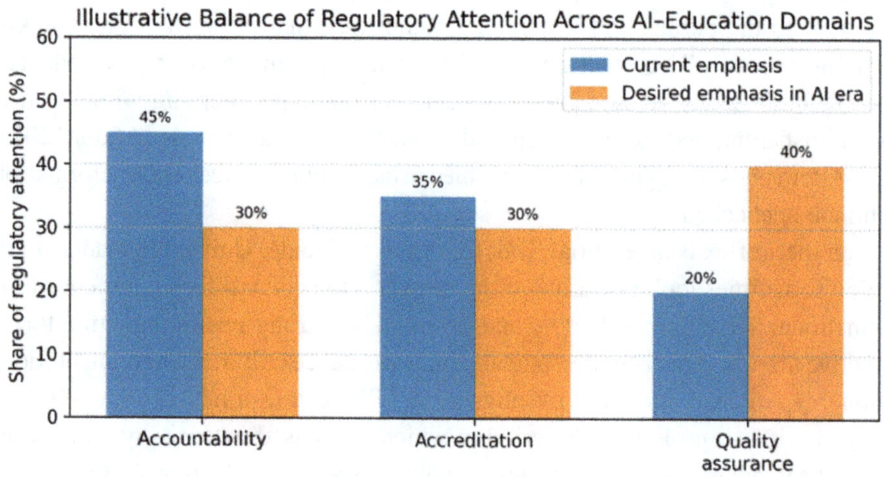

The uncertainty is compounded by asymmetries of knowledge and power between local regulators and global technology providers. Many AI tools arrive in the region as part of proprietary platforms whose inner workings are effectively opaque (Widder et al, 2024). Licensing contracts are dense; technical documentation is written for specialists and often in English only; claims about accuracy or fairness are presented as marketing rather than evidence. National regulators and accreditation teams, especially in smaller or resource-constrained countries, rarely have the capacity to audit these systems meaningfully. They must decide whether to trust vendors, rely on foreign regulatory decisions, or attempt some form of local evaluation with limited tools. None of these options is entirely comfortable.

Language adds another layer. Much of the frontier development in AI is optimised for English, with other languages—and dialects—added gradually and unevenly. For Arabic, and for the rich mix of languages used in MENA classrooms, performance can be patchy. A tool that behaves responsibly in one linguistic context may generate inaccuracies, biases, or cultural distortions in another. Regulators are left wondering: should an AI system be considered "fit for purpose" if its performance is significantly weaker in the language of instruction or the language of assessment? How does one codify that in regulation without inadvertently marginalising local languages even further?

Against this background, the call to regulate carries a certain tension. Act too fast, and the rules risk being shallow, reactive, or tied to specific tools that will soon be obsolete. Move too cautiously, and commercial pressures, institutional improvisation, and hidden practices will shape AI use in ways that are hard to reverse. The space between urgency and uncertainty is, in that sense, not just a problem but also a test of governance maturity: can systems learn to regulate iteratively, to acknowledge what they do not yet know, and to adjust without losing credibility? Some promising gestures are beginning to surface in regional debates (Sprongl, 2025). There is interest in principle-based approaches that articulate broad commitments—fairness, transparency, data protection, student well-being—without prescribing every technical detail. Such approaches can provide a compass rather than a detailed map, allowing institutions some room to adapt. There is also talk of regulatory sandboxes, where certain AI applications are piloted under close monitoring, with explicit conditions and evaluation mechanisms, before broader adoption. These ideas acknowledge uncertainty instead of denying it; they accept that learning about AI's impact is itself part of regulation.

Figure 2. Illustrative Regulatory Reflexes to AI in MENA Education

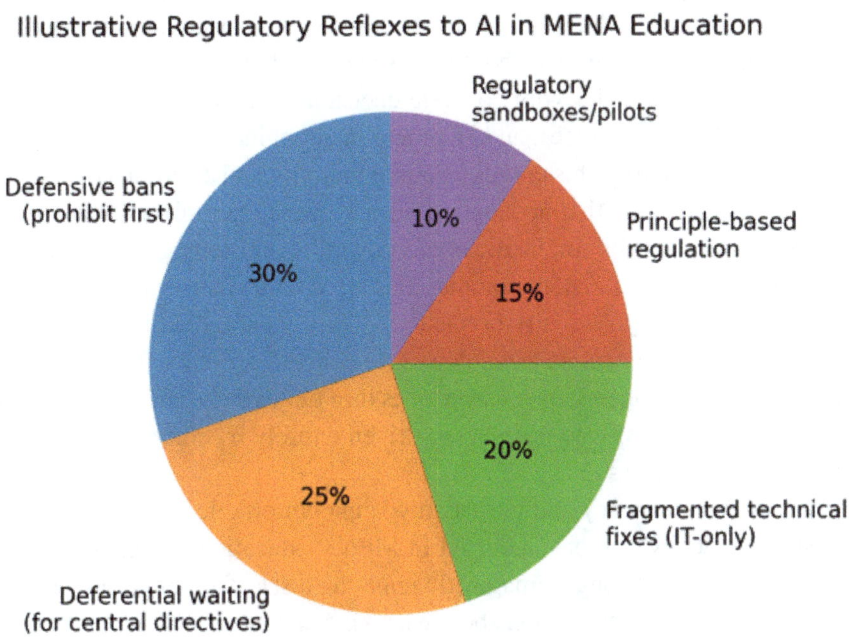

Still, translating these ideas into concrete policy is not straightforward. Principle-based regulation can easily slide into vagueness if it is not accompanied by clear expectations, enforcement mechanisms, and examples of what acceptable practice looks like in classrooms, examinations, and administrative processes. Sandboxes require institutional capacity, data governance arrangements, and a tolerance for experimentation that may clash with risk-averse political cultures (Fahy, 2022). In some MENA contexts, the fear of public scandal or reputational damage if a pilot goes wrong is strong enough to discourage visible experimentation altogether.

The urgency also has a geopolitical dimension. MENA countries are not only regulating AI for domestic use; they are positioning themselves vis-à-vis global discourses on "responsible AI," "trustworthy AI," and digital sovereignty. International partners, donors, and ranking agencies are watching. There is a temptation to produce regulations that look modern on paper—aligning with global language and fashionable frameworks—without fully grappling with local constraints. This performative layer can create a split reality: outwardly, the system appears aligned with international norms; inwardly, daily practices follow older logics or ad hoc improvisations in response to institutional pressures.

The most constructive responses seem to be those that accept the in-between state as inevitable rather than pathological. Urgency is not going away; the technological and political clock will keep ticking. Uncertainty is not a temporary glitch; it is built into AI's trajectory and into the complexity of education itself (Looi, 2024). The question, then, becomes how to inhabit this in-between space intentionally: how to craft regulations that are firm about values and flexible about mechanisms, how to link high-level principles with concrete decisions in admissions offices, exam boards, curriculum committees, and IT procurement units.

For MENA regulators, this entails a certain humility and a certain courage. Humility, in acknowledging that no single ministry, agency, or university can master the full spectrum of AI's implications alone, and that listening—to teachers, to students, to technical experts, to communities affected by data practices—is not a luxury but a regulatory necessity (Pederson, 2025). Courage, in being willing to say no to seductive but opaque technologies, to demand evidence from vendors, to revise previous decisions when consequences turn out to be harmful or unjust, and to protect educational spaces from being driven entirely by commercial logics or short-term political gains.

Sitting between urgency and uncertainty is uncomfortable, yet it is also where the most honest conversations about AI in MENA education can happen. In that space, regulation is no longer imagined simply as a set of prohibitions but as an ongoing, often messy conversation about what kind of educational future the region is willing to endorse, fund, and defend.

ACCREDITATION IN THE AGE OF AI: REDESIGNING STANDARDS, CRITERIA, AND EVIDENCE

Accreditation has always been slightly theatrical. Institutions stage their best version of themselves: polished self-study reports, curated evidence folders, orchestrated site visits where everyone knows roughly what they're supposed to say. Behind the performance, of course, there is real work, sometimes heroic, sometimes routine, occasionally just cosmetic. Now, AI walks onto this crowded stage, not as a quiet prop in the background, but as a force that can rewrite the script itself: how teaching happens, how students are assessed, how data circulates, how quality is narrated. Accreditation in the MENA region suddenly finds its old vocabulary straining (Boudihaj & Sahli, 2022). Standards, criteria, and "evidence" that once felt solid begin to wobble.

Many existing accreditation frameworks in the region were drafted for an era in which technology was an add-on. ICT appeared as a separate standard or a bullet point: availability of computer labs, use of learning management systems, basic digital literacy for staff and students. The underlying assumption was that the core of education—syllabi, assessments, contact hours, teaching methods—remained fundamentally human and stable, and that technology merely supported delivery. In such a world, accreditation reviewers could flip through a stack of syllabi, inspect exam papers, chat with faculty and students, and feel reasonably confident that they understood how learning was being organised.

AI quietly dissolves that comfort. When a learning management system incorporates generative tools that draft feedback, remix course readings, or auto-generate quiz questions, the boundary between content and platform becomes blurry. When students' trajectories are shaped by recommendation engines that nudge them toward certain resources, or when adaptive systems adjust difficulty levels on the fly, the curriculum is no longer just the written document submitted in the accreditation file; it is also whatever the AI system decides to show or hide at any given moment (Tariq, 2024). Classical accreditation standards—asking for "approved syllabi" and "aligned learning outcomes"—begin to feel slightly out of sync with what learners actually experience on their screens at midnight.

One of the most pressing questions, then, is deceptively simple: what counts as valid evidence in an AI-saturated environment? For decades, accreditation in MENA higher education has leaned heavily on artefacts that carry the aura of human authorship: course descriptions, final exams, samples of student work, external examiners' reports, minutes of committees (Naim et al, 2024). These artefacts are now increasingly entangled with AI. A course description might be drafted with extensive support from a language model. A set of exam questions may have been generated by an AI tool and then lightly edited. A student's essay could be a collage of human thought, machine-generated text, and paraphrasing tools, stitched together under pressure. If those documents are treated uncritically as transparent windows into quality, accreditation risks accrediting the eloquence of the machine rather than the integrity of the academic process.

Redesigning standards in this context requires a shift of emphasis. Instead of merely asking, "Is there a syllabus?" or "Is there a policy on academic integrity?", accreditation bodies need to probe how AI is integrated into the life of a program: what kinds of tools are used, under what conditions, with which safeguards, and with what reflective understanding from staff and students. Standards that once focused on the existence of policies now have to interrogate the depth of their implementation in a landscape where technology can easily outpace regulation. A generic statement that "AI is not allowed for assessments," for example, tells reviewers almost nothing in a context where enforcement is difficult and where the pressure to use AI—quietly—is strong.

Some MENA agencies have already introduced standards on "innovation," "digital learning," or "emerging technologies," but these often function as decorative add-ons, a way to signal modernity rather than to anchor serious scrutiny. In the age of AI, that cosmetic approach becomes dangerous. If "use of AI" is treated as an automatic plus—evidence of progress and sophistication—institutions may feel compelled to showcase AI deployments without fully grappling with their pedagogical or ethical implications. Accreditation would then unintentionally reward speed over reflection, adoption over governance (Bohlens, 2025). The standards themselves would become a kind of market signal: bring AI into the classroom, talk about it in the self-study report, and the agency will be pleased (Kayyali, 2025 B).

It is difficult, but necessary, to resist that drift. Redesigning criteria means asking less about whether AI is present and more about how it is governed (Alfrink et al, 2023). A program that uses AI tutors intensively but has a robust framework for oversight, clear rules on data use, documented staff training, and systematic feedback from students might deserve stronger recognition than a program that boasts of "cutting-edge AI integration" but offers little evidence of reflection or monitoring. This kind of distinction only emerges when criteria are reworded away from simple checklists—"the institution uses AI to support learning"—toward richer, more demanding formulations: "the institution demonstrates that the use of AI tools is aligned with learning outcomes, ethically justified, and subject to continuous evaluation."

For agencies in the MENA region, where accreditation is often both a quality mechanism and a political symbol, that shift will not come easily (Mansour et al, 2021). Many standards are embedded in law or regulation; any revision passes through slow bureaucratic channels. Yet the alternative—keeping criteria frozen while AI reshapes practice underneath—might be worse. A quiet gap opens between what accreditation documents describe and what classrooms actually feel like. Students and staff begin to treat accreditation language as ritual rather than reality, and the legitimacy of the system erodes. AI accelerates that erosion simply by making the gap harder to ignore.

The site visit, that ritual heart of accreditation, also needs rethinking. Traditionally, reviewers spend a few days on campus, conduct interviews, inspect facilities, and review documentation in person. With AI-driven systems, some of the most critical action happens in databases and logs and dashboards. A proctoring tool that disproportionately flags students with certain network conditions; a predictive model that systematically underestimates students from a particular region; an automated feedback system that generates formulaic, demotivating comments in Arabic but acceptable ones in English—none of this is visible from a campus tour or a conversation in the dean's office. Evidence lives in code, configuration files, vendor contracts, and data outputs. To engage with it, reviewers need new literacies.

That does not mean turning accreditation teams into software auditors. It does mean, however, that agencies need to broaden the profiles of their reviewers and rethink the kinds of questions they ask. A team visiting a university heavily reliant on AI-powered assessment tools should be able to ask, for instance, how error rates are monitored, whether false positives and false negatives are tracked, how often human review overrides automated decisions, and what patterns appear in those overrides. They should be able to examine, at least at a basic level, the documentation provided by vendors about fairness, bias mitigation, and localisation for Arabic or other regional languages, and to connect that information with the lived testimonies of students and instructors.

The notion of triangulation—comparing multiple sources of evidence—is not new in accreditation, but AI requires a more intensive version of it. A program might proudly show analytics dashboards suggesting high engagement and continuous improvement, yet student focus groups may describe a different reality: constant anxiety about being monitored, difficulty understanding how their data is used, or a sense that the platform's recommendations channel them into narrow paths. A redesigned evidence framework would treat these tensions not as noise to be smoothed over, but as critical signals about how AI is actually reshaping the educational experience. Numbers, narratives, screenshots, and policies all need to sit in the same room.

Regional particularities matter here. In some MENA contexts, agencies operate with limited financial and human resources; they already handle large numbers of institutions with small teams (Otman, 2021). Adding AI-related scrutiny can feel like yet another burden on overstretched systems. There is a risk that "AI standards" become a few extra lines in the manual, lightly touched during review and easily satisfied with generic statements. Breaking out of this pattern may require incremental moves: starting with a narrow set of core expectations around AI governance, piloting them with a subset of institutions, learning from the process, and gradually scaling up. Accreditation, to remain credible, will need to show that it can evolve iteratively rather than only through grand overhauls every decade.

Evidence itself will also need new forms. Self-study reports that merely list AI tools without critical reflection will not suffice. Agencies might begin to request AI impact statements at program or institutional level: concise analyses of where AI is used, what risks have been identified, what benefits are sought, and what mitigation strategies are in place (Kayyali, 2026). Long, wordy descriptions are not the point here; what matters is whether the institution has done the intellectual work of mapping its AI ecosystem and facing the uncomfortable questions that such mapping inevitably raises. Over time, these impact statements could become rich comparative material, helping agencies detect emerging patterns across institutions—shared vulnerabilities, good practices, or blind spots.

Another delicate area is the interplay between accreditation and commercial pressures. Edtech vendors have a strong incentive to present their AI products as accreditation-friendly, sometimes implying that their adoption will be viewed favourably by agencies or international quality networks. In a region keen to demonstrate modernity and innovation, such narratives can be persuasive. Accreditation bodies must be careful not to become unwitting marketing amplifiers (Labrecque et al, 2024). Redesigning standards means phrasing them in a technology-neutral way—focusing on outcomes, processes, and safeguards rather than on specific brands or solution types—and maintaining a clear distance from vendor endorsements. The credibility of the entire quality assurance ecosystem depends on that distance (Kayyali, 2024).

There is also the question of cross-border recognition. Many MENA institutions, especially private universities, seek international accreditation or alignment with foreign agencies. As AI reshapes pedagogy and assessment, divergent approaches to regulation may emerge: some agencies might ban certain tools outright, others allow them under conditions, others barely mention them. Institutions navigating multiple frameworks could face conflicting expectations. Regional agencies, by engaging in dialogue with peers abroad, can help ensure that their redesigned standards are not isolated but sit within a broader, evolving conversation about AI and quality in higher education. At the same time, they have an opportunity—if they choose to take it—to contribute perspectives grounded in multilingual, resource-constrained, and politically complex environments that global debates often overlook.

Underneath all these technicalities lies a more existential question for accreditation: what is being accredited, exactly, when AI saturates the educational environment? Is the agency certifying that minimum conditions still hold in spite of AI, that the traditional core remains untouched? Or is it consciously endorsing an evolving hybrid, where human and machine contributions to teaching, assessment, and academic decision-making are inextricably linked? Being honest about that question matters. When agencies pretend that nothing fundamental has changed, they push institutions to hide the extent of AI reliance, to treat it as a background tool not worth mentioning. When agencies lean the other way and romanticise AI as inherently transformative, they risk overlooking continuity, wisdom, and craft in established educational practices.

Redesigning standards, criteria, and evidence in the age of AI is, at heart, an exercise in intellectual honesty (Mann, 2024). It demands that accreditation systems admit the limits of their old instruments, that they resist both panic and hype, and that they cultivate a more nuanced gaze—one capable of seeing, at the same time, the promise of AI-powered personalisation and the dangers of datafied, surveilled learning. In the MENA region, where accreditation often carries the hopes of entire institutions for recognition, legitimacy, and survival, that gaze will need to be both critical and compassionate, attuned to constraints yet unwilling to rubber-stamp superficial digitalisation.

If accreditation can manage that balancing act—staying firm on values while nimble on methods—it may emerge from the AI upheaval not as a relic trying to catch up with technology, but as one of the few spaces where serious, evidence-based, ethically grounded conversations about AI in education are still possible. And that, given the noise and speed of the current moment, would already be a quiet but significant achievement.

QUALITY ASSURANCE FRAMEWORKS FOR AI-ENHANCED TEACHING, ASSESSMENT, AND ANALYTICS

Quality assurance units in many universities were never designed for this (Alzoubi, 2021). They were built for a world of syllabi in dusty folders, exam scripts stacked in cardboard boxes, and periodic reports that moved slowly through committees. Their natural habitat was the stable curriculum, the predictable semester, the familiar rhythm of lecturing, midterms, finals. Now they find themselves staring at dashboards, algorithmic risk scores, AI-generated feedback, and assessment systems that update overnight without warning. Quietly, almost without permission, the ground under "quality" has shifted.

AI-enhanced teaching promises a lot: personalised learning paths, rapid feedback, high-frequency formative assessment, multilingual support, and finely grained data about how students behave in digital spaces. The seduction is strong in MENA systems under strain—overcrowded classrooms, heavy teaching loads, pressure to modernise, chronic resource gaps (Boudihaj & Sahli, 2022). It is easy to nod along when a vendor or a visionary administrator says that AI can "support quality." Yet, the question that refuses to go away is less glamorous and far more mundane: who is actually making sure that these systems improve learning, rather than merely producing the appearance of sophistication?

Traditional quality assurance frameworks often sit several steps away from what truly happens between teacher and student (Shattuck, 2023). They revolve around inputs and formalities: staff qualifications, program specifications, documented learning outcomes, course evaluation forms, internal moderation reports. When AI enters teaching and assessment, this distance becomes hazardous. The most consequential decisions move into spaces that QA procedures seldom reach: the algorithm that decides which exercise a struggling student sees next; the classifier that labels a suspicious exam pattern; the automated marking system that allocates partial credit according to patterns found in historical data. Quality, in this new environment, is not just about the documented design of a course; it is also about the behaviour of systems that no single lecturer controls.

One way to think of quality assurance in AI-enhanced settings is as a shift from examining products to examining processes and infrastructures. Rather than asking only, "Is the course well designed on paper?" QA needs to ask, "How are AI tools chosen, configured, monitored, and revised over time, and who sits at the table when those choices are made?" Teaching is no longer only what the lecturer does in the classroom or on the LMS; it is what the combined ensemble of human educator and machine tutor delivers, sometimes in unpredictable ways (Kayyali, 2025 A).

Take AI-supported teaching assistants, for example. In theory, they can answer students' questions at any hour, provide examples, summarise readings, and explain difficult concepts in multiple languages. From a quality perspective, the question is not whether the bot exists but what epistemic authority it is given. Is it branded as an official institutional voice or as an experimental companion? Are students told how it works, what its limitations are, and what to do when it gives dubious answers? Are teachers trained to see the bot not as a threat but as an element they can orchestrate within their pedagogy? A serious QA framework will not treat the AI assistant as a neutral tool in the background; it will frame it as part of the teaching strategy that must align with learning outcomes, disciplinary expectations, and ethical commitments (Kasepalu et al, 2022).

Assessment raises even sharper tensions. AI-enhanced assessment spans a spectrum: from simple automated quizzes to complex essay scoring, code evaluation, oral exams with speech recognition, and remote proctoring. Each step along that spectrum increases the stakes. When marks are tied to algorithmic judgement, quality assurance cannot be satisfied with a few lines in a policy document saying that "systems are regularly updated" or "tools are aligned with outcomes." There needs to be evidence—real, sometimes uncomfortable evidence—about how well these systems work for different groups of learners, in different languages, under different conditions.

In many MENA countries, assessments carry heavy social and economic weight. One exam can determine access to scholarships, professional tracks, or migration opportunities. A misclassified script here is not a trivial glitch; it is a future diverted. QA frameworks, if they are to be honest, must insist on robustness checks: comparison between machine and human grading, analysis of discrepancies, awareness of where automated systems struggle (for example, writing that blends Arabic and English, or answers that are conceptually sound but linguistically imperfect). Such checks cannot remain technical curiosities locked in IT reports; they should become part of the QA conversation in program review committees, teaching and learning centres, and departmental meetings (Owen & Samson, 2025).

Learning analytics sits further in the background, yet its influence on quality is no less significant. Predictive dashboards can reshape how teachers perceive their students, how advisors allocate time, how institutions identify "problematic" courses or cohorts. On paper, analytics appears as a pure gift to QA: a constant flow of data showing engagement, progression, completion, bottlenecks. But data can tell very partial stories. Students who access the platform through unstable connections, those who rely on shared devices, or those who prefer to study offline may appear as disengaged ghosts in the system. A quality assurance framework that uncritically equates activity logs with learning risks reinforcing structural inequalities under a veneer of evidence-based decision-making.

The challenge, then, is not to reject AI-enhanced teaching, assessment, and analytics, but to cultivate a QA posture that treats them neither as magical solutions nor as invisible plumbing. That posture involves several quiet shifts.

First, QA needs to move closer to design. In the traditional model, quality units often evaluate after the fact: the course has run, the evaluation forms have been collected, external examiners have written their reports. With AI, many of the most consequential choices occur at the design and procurement stage: which platforms to adopt, what default settings to use, how to integrate tools into courses, what data to collect and store. QA frameworks in MENA institutions could introduce structured AI-readiness reviews before major deployments, bringing together IT, pedagogical experts, legal advisors, and student representatives to ask blunt questions about purpose, risk, and alignment with institutional values (Mohamed, 2025).

Second, the language of quality standards needs to acquire a new vocabulary. It is no longer enough to talk about "appropriateness of teaching methods" or "fairness of assessment procedures" in abstract terms. AI-enhanced environments require references to transparency, explainability, contestability, human oversight, and data minimisation. These are not fashionable buzzwords; they are conditions under which AI can be integrated without eroding trust. A framework that ignores them leaves QA practitioners speechless in front of systems they are supposed to judge.

Third, there is the matter of agency. In many MENA universities, quality assurance is perceived as something done to academics, not with them (Ehtiwesh & Maousa, 2023). AI-related QA will fail if it deepens that impression—if it arrives as new checklists from above, asking faculty to fill forms about "use of AI" without providing space for genuine reflection, doubt, and shared learning. A more generative model would treat teachers as co-investigators, inviting them to document how AI tools are actually playing out in their courses, what unanticipated effects they notice, where students flourish and where they flounder. Narratives, case vignettes, and pedagogical experiments become evidence alongside metrics.

There is also an emotional layer that QA frameworks typically ignore. AI-enhanced systems can trigger anxiety, resentment, fascination, and cynicism in both staff and students (Lin & Chen, 2024). A teacher who feels replaced by automated feedback; a student who feels constantly watched by proctoring software; an administrator tempted to use analytics as a blunt instrument to judge staff performance—these are quality issues, even if they do not fit neatly into standard indicators. If quality assurance is about the health of the educational ecosystem, then it must take seriously the affective climate created by AI tools: whether they foster a sense of possibility and support, or whether they generate a low-level, chronic feeling of being monitored and judged by inscrutable systems.

In the MENA context, where authority and respect are delicate currencies, ignoring this emotional dimension can backfire. Students who do not feel heard will develop informal strategies to evade or subvert systems they perceive as unfair. Staff who feel bypassed in AI decisions may quietly sabotage tools or comply in a minimal, performative way (Ivchyk, 2024). A QA framework attuned to AI would build in feedback channels that are not merely symbolic: anonymous student panels focused specifically on AI use, staff forums to share concerns, iterative revisions of guidelines based on lived experience rather than hypothetical scenarios.

None of this is simple, and it is easy to underestimate the resource implications. Many universities in the region struggle to maintain even basic QA routines; expecting them to suddenly develop high-level capacity to audit algorithms and interpret complex analytics is unrealistic. Yet the answer cannot be to abandon the field and leave AI governance entirely to vendors or a small circle of technical experts. A more modest but still meaningful step is to identify a small set of non-negotiables that every QA framework should include for AI-enhanced teaching and assessment: clarity about where and how AI is used; documented human oversight for high-stakes decisions; explicit channels for contesting outcomes influenced by algorithms; regular review of AI tools' performance with disaggregated data where possible.

Perhaps the most profound shift lies in how quality is narrated. For years, QA talk has been saturated with terms like "alignment," "efficiency," "continuous improvement." AI is perfectly suited to reinforce this language: it promises alignment at scale, efficiency through automation, improvement via near-real-time feedback loops. Yet educational quality, especially in fragile and rapidly changing MENA systems, is not only about smoothness and optimization (Abusamra et al., 2025).

It is also about resilience, critical thinking, ethical awareness, and the capacity of institutions to resist harmful uses of technology—even when those uses are profitable or politically convenient.

A QA framework that truly engages with AI-enhanced teaching, assessment, and analytics will eventually have to ask slightly awkward questions: Are we using this tool because it genuinely enriches learning or because it is impressive in marketing materials? Are we collecting this data because it helps students, or because we can? Are teachers becoming more reflective practitioners through their interactions with AI, or more passive supervisors of machine-driven processes? These questions cannot be reduced to tick-boxes, yet they belong at the heart of quality conversations.

In a sense, AI forces QA frameworks in MENA education to grow up. The era of equating quality with tidy documentation and compliant procedures was already fragile; AI simply exposes its limits with greater clarity. What is emerging, tentatively and unevenly, is an understanding that quality assurance in the age of AI is not a technical add-on but a new way of paying attention—a disciplined, ethically grounded attentiveness to how human and machine agents together shape what students come to know, to value, and to imagine as possible in their own futures.

TOWARDS A CONTEXT-SENSITIVE MENA REGULATORY MODEL: PATHWAYS, TENSIONS, AND FUTURE DIRECTIONS

Towards a context-sensitive regulatory model for AI in MENA education, it helps to start with something that often goes unsaid: the region is not a blank slate waiting for imported "best practices." It is a dense, layered field of laws, unwritten customs, political red lines, linguistic pluralism, fragile institutions, ambitious visions, private providers, and public distrust that coexist in uneasy proximity. Any regulatory framework that pretends this complexity does not exist will end up as one more elegant document in a drawer, quoted in conferences and quietly sidestepped in everyday practice.

There is, across many MENA systems, a recurring temptation to reach for ready-made models (Eriksson, 2024). A European AI act here, an OECD principle there, a UNESCO guideline translated quickly into Arabic and circulated as a sign of alignment with global norms. These instruments are not irrelevant, and they certainly should not be dismissed out of hand. Yet when they are cut and pasted into national strategies without serious localisation, they function a bit like borrowed clothes: impressive in the mirror, awkward in movement. A context-sensitive approach, by contrast, takes the messiness of the region as its starting point rather than an obstacle to be glossed over.

One possible pathway is to think in concentric circles of regulation rather than in a single monolithic law that promises to "solve" AI in education once and for all. At the outer circle sit broad national principles: commitments to equity, to the protection of learners' data, to transparency in high-stakes decisions, to safeguarding academic freedom, and to ensuring that AI deployments in education do not deepen existing social fractures. These principles need to be articulated in language that resonates locally, not just translated jargon. In some countries that might mean anchoring them in constitutional provisions around education and dignity; in others, referencing long-standing discourses about knowledge, justice, and public responsibility rooted in religious or cultural thought.

A second circle concerns sector-specific regulation. AI in education behaves differently from AI in finance or policing. The stakes are different, the power relations are different, and the temporal horizon is longer: the impact on a learner's trajectory may unfold across years. Ministries and higher education councils in MENA can carve out dedicated provisions for educational AI, specifying expectations around consent in the use of student data, thresholds for algorithmic involvement in grading and admissions, requirements for human review, and minimum standards for localisation in Arabic and other regional languages (Al-Zahrani & Alasmari, 2025). This is where the regulatory model begins to diverge deliberately from generic digital policy and starts to acknowledge the peculiar intimacy of education: its entanglement with identity, aspiration, and social mobility.

Closer to the centre lie institutional frameworks. No national regulation, however well crafted, can anticipate the countless decisions that universities and schools will have to make when they choose platforms, craft AI policies, and negotiate contracts with vendors. Context sensitivity here means recognising that MENA institutions sit on very different footing. An elite university in a Gulf capital, operating with considerable resources and a global faculty, does not face the same constraints as a teaching-oriented institution in a conflict-affected city where connectivity is fragile and staff are exhausted by daily survival. A regulatory model that ignores these differences will produce compliance theatre: glossy AI strategies in places that can afford them, and quiet improvisation in places that cannot.

To avoid that split, ministries can define minimum baselines while leaving room for varied paths above those baselines. For instance, every institution using AI in assessment could be required to have: (a) a public policy specifying where AI is permitted and where it is not; (b) a mechanism for students to appeal AI-influenced decisions; and (c) a designated body responsible for oversight of AI tools. Beyond that floor, institutions might be encouraged—through incentives, not only through sanctions—to experiment with more ambitious models: ethics committees that review new AI deployments, student advisory panels, or internal audit teams that periodically sample algorithmic decisions across courses.

The tensions begin to appear as soon as one tries to operationalise these ideas. Centralisation versus autonomy is perhaps the most persistent. Many MENA systems are habituated to highly centralised steering: curricula approved at ministerial level, textbook lists fixed nationally, exam formats standardised from the capital outward (Boudihaj & Sahli, 2022). AI regulation threatens to stretch that instinct to breaking point. Attempting to micro-regulate every tool, every use case, from the centre will slow innovation and drive usage into the shadows. Leaving everything to institutional discretion, on the other hand, risks creating a patchwork of standards, where some universities become contested testing grounds and others drift into uncritical dependence on vendors.

Table 2. Core Principles for a Context-Sensitive MENA AI Regulatory Model

Regulatory Principle	Operational Expectation in MENA Education	Example Mechanism	Possible Indicators
Context-sensitivity	AI regulation explicitly reflects demographic pressures, political constraints, linguistic diversity, and resource gaps in the region.	National AI-in-education guidelines that differentiate expectations for high-stakes exams, everyday teaching, and crisis contexts.	Evidence that AI policies reference MENA-specific challenges; stakeholder feedback on their relevance to local realities.
Transparency and explainability	Learners, staff, and regulators can understand, at an appropriate level, when and how AI systems influence educational decisions.	Institutional AI registers describing each tool's purpose, data flows, and limitations in language accessible to non-experts.	Proportion of AI tools documented in an accessible registry; survey data on staff and student awareness of AI use.
Contestability and redress	Students and staff have clear routes to question and appeal AI-influenced outcomes in admissions, assessment, or analytics.	Formal appeal procedures for AI-related decisions; requirement for human review before high-stakes automated outcomes are final.	Number and outcomes of AI-related appeals; time taken to resolve cases; qualitative feedback on perceived fairness.
Equity and inclusion	AI deployments are assessed for their impact on already marginalised groups and are used to narrow, not widen, opportunity gaps.	Equity impact assessments for major AI deployments; disaggregated monitoring of outcomes by gender, language, status, and location.	Trends in access, completion, and progression for vulnerable groups before and after AI deployment; qualitative student testimonies.
Data protection and digital sovereignty	Student data is collected minimally, stored securely, and processed under rules that respect local legal frameworks and sensitivities.	Data protection laws that cover educational AI; contractual clauses limiting cross-border transfers and secondary data use.	Audit reports on data handling; frequency of breaches; proportion of contracts with robust data protection clauses.

continued on following page

Table 2. Continued

Regulatory Principle	Operational Expectation in MENA Education	Example Mechanism	Possible Indicators
Human oversight and pedagogical fit	AI augments, rather than replaces, educators; tools are chosen because they genuinely support learning, not just efficiency.	Policy that bans fully automated grading in high-stakes exams; mandatory involvement of educators in AI configuration and review.	Share of high-stakes assessments that retain human markers; staff surveys on perceived pedagogical value of AI tools.
Iterative learning and adaptation	Regulation, standards, and local policies are updated regularly in light of new evidence, incidents, and technological change.	Time-limited approvals for certain AI tools; scheduled reviews of AI policies; regulatory sandboxes with built-in evaluation plans.	Frequency of AI policy updates; lessons-learned reports from sandboxes; adjustments made in response to documented incidents.

A context-sensitive model will not resolve this tension once and for all; it will have to live with it and tune it over time. One pragmatic route is to distinguish clearly between non-negotiable protections—child data, biometric information, cross-border data flows, high-stakes automated grading—and negotiable spaces where institutions can adapt more freely, such as the use of AI for low-stakes formative feedback or language support. Regulators would then focus their strictest enforcement on a small cluster of high-risk activities while encouraging openness and experimentation in lower-risk domains, provided certain transparency conditions are met.

Another tension runs between security-oriented thinking and rights-oriented thinking. In several MENA contexts, digital regulation has been shaped heavily by concerns around national security, public order, and control of information flows (Abdelmeguid, 2024). AI in education is easily pulled into that orbit. Learning analytics can be repurposed for surveillance; proctoring systems can morph into broader monitoring tools; content moderation, initially justified in the name of protecting students, can slide toward censorship of sensitive topics. A regulatory model that treats education only as an extension of security policy will eventually hollow out trust. Students and teachers will sense that AI tools are watching them more than helping them, and they will adjust their behaviour accordingly, often in ways that undermine the learning process.

Yet it would be naïve to suggest that MENA regulators should simply embrace a purely liberal, individual-rights framework detached from their political realities. The path forward is likely to be hybrid: recognising legitimate state concerns while insisting that educational AI be governed by a distinct set of guarantees—narrow purpose limitation, rigorous oversight of surveillance features, clear deletion timelines for sensitive data, and protections for academic inquiry even in contentious domains. These principles, if negotiated carefully, can create a narrow corridor in which educational AI can operate without becoming an all-purpose instrument of control.

Language and epistemic diversity introduce another layer of complexity (Pinho & Paz, 2024). A large share of the most capable AI models is developed and trained primarily in English and, to a lesser extent, other dominant languages. For Arabic, and for local dialects and minority languages in the region, performance can be fragile and uneven. There is a danger that educational AI will embody a subtle linguistic hierarchy: fluent, nuanced support in English; clumsy, error-prone behaviour in Arabic; near absence for Tamazight, Kurdish, or African languages spoken by migrant learners. A context-sensitive regulatory model cannot afford to be blind to this. It will need to ask, quite bluntly, whether tools used in public education meet minimum thresholds of quality in the languages where they are deployed—and, when they do not, whether their use should be curtailed or complemented by safeguards.

This is where regional collaboration becomes less of a slogan and more of a necessity. No single country in the region, even the wealthiest, will be able to fully shape the global trajectory of AI (Adams, 2024). Yet coalitions of agencies, ministries, and expert groups across MENA can pool capacity to evaluate tools, share benchmarks for Arabic and other regional languages, and articulate common expectations toward vendors. A shared repository of vetted tools, impact assessments, and case studies—kept honest by contributions from diverse systems, not only the usual flagships—could become part of the region's regulatory infrastructure, informal but influential.

Future directions will also be shaped by who gets invited into the regulatory conversation (Kayyali, 2025 C). Until now, much of the emerging policy talk around AI in education has taken place in closed rooms: senior officials, rectors, a handful of technical experts, sometimes international advisers. Students and frontline teachers appear mainly as objects of concern, not as actors with their own insights and fears. A context-sensitive model would deliberately puncture that pattern. Structured consultations with student unions, surveys that ask not just "Do you like AI?" but "Where did it help you?" and "Where did it harm you?", focus groups with teachers who have tried and abandoned certain tools—all of this can surface knowledge that would otherwise remain anecdotal and scattered.

Figure 3. Illustrative Iterative Maturity Pathway for AI Regulation in MENA Education

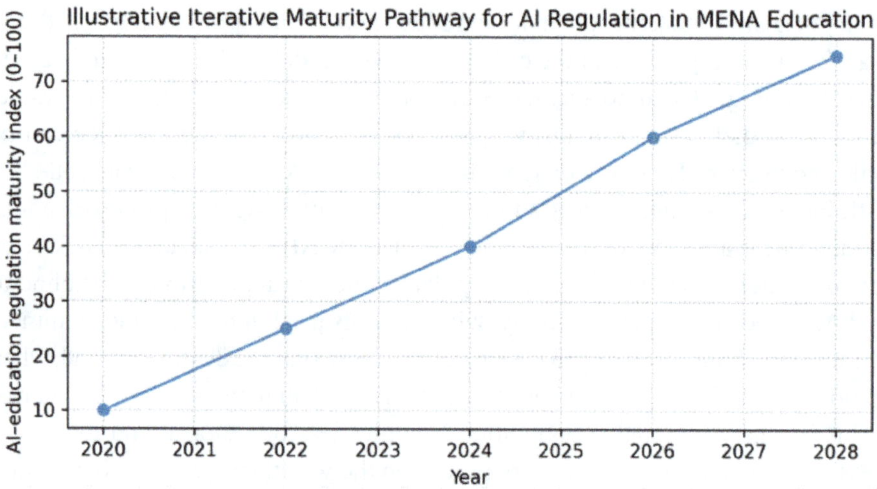

There's also the issue of temporal scale. Regulation is often imagined as something fixed: a law passed, a guideline issued, a circular signed. AI, by contrast, is shape-shifting; its capacities, business models, and social impacts mutate rapidly. MENA regulators who aim for a once-off, comprehensive framework will find themselves revising in a constant state of crisis (Eze, 2022). A more sustainable direction would be to treat AI regulation as an ongoing process, with built-in cycles of review, sunset clauses for certain permissions, and formal mechanisms to learn from incidents—failed deployments, scandals, or unexpected successes. This rhythm of deliberate revision is not natural in many bureaucracies in the region, which are often rewarded for stability and continuity, yet without it, AI will keep outgrowing whatever rules are put in place.

Another future horizon that deserves more explicit attention is capacity building. No model, however refined on paper, can function without people who understand both education and technology, and who can move between those worlds without getting lost. The region will need regulatory translators: individuals who can read a machine learning model card, interrogate a vendor about training data, and then switch registers to discuss the pedagogical implications with school leaders or faculty. These roles don't yet exist clearly in most MENA systems. They will have to be cultivated intentionally through joint programs across faculties of education, computer science, and law, through secondments between ministries and universities, and through regional networks that keep such people from feeling isolated or tokenistic.

Finally, a context-sensitive regulatory model will need to confront a subtle but powerful narrative that still lingers in parts of the region: the idea that technological modernity is something to be received, preferably whole and uncontested, from "advanced" countries. AI gives that story fresh fuel. Yet the same technology also creates an opening for a different storyline, one in which MENA actors do not simply comply with external standards but articulate their own terms of engagement, rooted in their histories and aspirations (Chelliah et al, 2023). When regulators in the region insist, for instance, that any AI tool used in public schooling must be auditable for bias against refugee children, or that university proctoring systems must be designed with low-bandwidth environments in mind, they are not simply protecting local users; they are contributing, however modestly, to a global conversation that has so far been dominated by other voices.

The pathways, tensions, and directions sketched here do not add up to a neat blueprint. They form, instead, a kind of regulatory cartography in progress—lines pencilled in, some to be erased, others to be deepened, all subject to revision as realities on the ground shift. What distinguishes a context-sensitive MENA model from an imported template is not that it is perfect, but that it is willing to be honest about its own constraints and to treat regulation less as a shield for appearances and more as a living practice of care for learners, educators, and institutions in a time when the boundaries between human judgement and machine output are increasingly tangled.

CONCLUSION

By the time one finishes tracing the threads of AI, accountability, accreditation, and quality assurance across MENA education systems, one realises that the core questions are less about technology and more about trust. Trust in institutions, in procedures, in the people who design and use AI tools, and in the idea that education remains, somehow, a fundamentally human endeavour even when mediated by complex algorithms. AI has not created the region's structural tensions, but it has made them more visible and, in many cases, more urgent.

The chapter has argued that regulating AI for education cannot be treated as a side project delegated to a technical committee or outsourced to an international consultant. It touches the deep architecture of education systems: who has the authority to decide what counts as valid knowledge, how success is defined and measured, and whose voices matter when policies are drafted and implemented. In a context where many decisions about curriculum, assessment, and institutional strategy are still highly centralised, the arrival of AI adds another layer of opacity. Without careful design, AI can become one more black box in a system already criticised for its lack of transparency.

Accountability, therefore, must be rethought in layered and relational terms. It is not enough to identify a legal "owner" of an AI system and declare that they are responsible. In practice, responsibility is shared and sometimes fragmented: ministries that mandate certain tools, universities that procure and integrate them, instructors who choose how to use them, students who may misuse them out of pressure or confusion, and vendors who design their models according to commercial logic. Good regulation acknowledges this complexity; poor regulation either pretends it does not exist or distributes blame so widely that no one feels compelled to act.

For MENA education systems, a promising path lies in building explicit accountability chains for AI use in education. That means defining, in policy and in practice, who is answerable for what. If a predictive model is used to allocate remedial support, there should be clear protocols on how decisions are made, documented, and reviewed – and routes for students to contest harmful or unjust outcomes. If generative AI is allowed in certain kinds of assignments, institutions need robust, public guidelines that articulate expectations, boundaries, and consequences in ways that are understandable to students and staff. When new AI tools are procured, procurement processes should require impact assessments that examine not only cost and functionality but also fairness, data protection, and pedagogical fit.

Accreditation can play a decisive role here, not as a distant inspector but as a translator between emerging AI practices and shared quality norms. Many agencies in the region are at a crossroads: they can either continue to treat technology as a marginal issue, ticking off boxes about "availability of e-learning platforms," or they can move toward a more substantive engagement with AI. The latter would mean updating standards to include criteria related to algorithmic transparency, ethical use of learning analytics, protection of student data, and institutional capacity to govern AI tools. It would also require training review teams who can actually read and interpret evidence about AI deployment, not merely accept polished narratives.

Yet accreditation agencies themselves need to be safeguarded from the temptation to treat AI regulation as a branding exercise. It is easy to insert elegant phrases about "responsible AI" into standards and reports while leaving the underlying practices unchanged. Genuine reform would involve rethinking site visit protocols, incorporating questions about how institutions involve stakeholders – including students – in decisions about AI, and insisting on concrete evidence that policies are not just on paper but alive in classrooms and digital spaces. In some cases, this may create friction with institutions that are wary of external scrutiny. That friction, if handled carefully, can be productive; it is often where real quality conversations begin.

Within institutions, quality assurance structures have the most intimate view of how AI is actually reshaping teaching, learning, and assessment. They see the small shifts that do not make headlines: lecturers quietly adjusting their assessment tasks because they suspect students are using AI; faculty meetings where colleagues disagree about whether using a chatbot is a form of cheating or a new literacy; administrators worrying about how to evaluate teaching when so much of the feedback to students is generated automatically. Quality assurance teams are positioned to turn these scattered experiences into shared reflection, but only if they are given both authority and freedom to ask difficult questions.

One of the key messages emerging from this chapter is that quality assurance in the age of AI must move beyond its bureaucratic reflexes. Instead of adding a few AI-related items to existing checklists, QA processes should invite departments and programs to analyse how AI is altering their assumptions about student work, assessment, and support. This could take the form of program-level AI impact reviews, teaching and learning workshops centred on AI ethics, or cross-unit committees that bring together IT, pedagogy, and quality professionals. These processes will be messy and sometimes uncomfortable. They will also be more honest than pretending that AI is just another tool to be slotted into existing frameworks without disturbance.

All of this unfolds against a backdrop of regional constraints that cannot be ignored. In many MENA countries, institutions operate under political and economic pressures that leave little room for experimentation. Data governance may be fragmented or weak. Imports of AI-based platforms may be driven by external funding conditions or vendor lobbying rather than careful pedagogical planning. Faculty may feel overwhelmed by constant waves of reform, and students may perceive AI primarily as a survival mechanism in an examination-driven culture. It would be naïve to suggest that regulation alone can resolve these structural issues.

Nevertheless, regulation – understood broadly as the constellation of rules, standards, and shared expectations – can either exacerbate or mitigate existing inequalities. If AI tools are adopted without scrutiny, they may deepen divides between well-resourced urban schools and under-resourced rural ones, between elite universities with strong digital infrastructures and fragile institutions struggling to stay afloat. If, on the other hand, AI governance is explicitly linked to equity, inclusion, and the protection of vulnerable learners, it can push institutions to ask who benefits from AI, who is left behind, and what trade-offs are being made in the name of efficiency.

The chapter has also hinted at an opportunity that is easy to overlook: the possibility for MENA to develop its own regulatory imagination rather than simply reacting to global models. There is no obligation to mirror every clause of European or North American policies. Instead, regional actors can draw selectively on international principles while grounding them in local legal traditions, cultural values, and educational priorities. This might mean, for example, foregrounding issues of linguistic diversity, recognising the political sensitivities of data storage and cross-border data flows, or giving particular attention to the use of AI in contexts of displacement and crisis where education systems are already fragile.

Regional collaboration will be critical. No single country, especially those with limited regulatory capacity, can tackle these questions alone. Networks of accreditation agencies, quality assurance bodies, and universities across the Arab world and wider MENA region could jointly develop guidelines, share case studies, and learn from both successes and failures. Such collaboration would not only spread good practice; it would also help resist the tendency to accept imported edtech and AI systems on vendor terms, without adequate negotiation or adaptation.

Looking ahead, the most constructive stance toward AI in MENA education is neither unquestioning enthusiasm nor fearful prohibition. It is a form of cautious, informed, and values-driven engagement. That means recognising AI's genuine potential to support differentiated instruction, to relieve teachers of some routine tasks, and to open new avenues for creativity and multilingual learning – while simultaneously insisting on clear lines of accountability, transparent accreditation criteria, and quality assurance mechanisms that see beyond the dashboards and analytics to the actual lives of learners and educators.

In the end, AI will not decide what MENA education becomes; people will, through the choices they make about regulation, investment, and everyday practice. The question is whether those choices will be made consciously, openly, and with a sense of responsibility to future generations, or whether they will be left to a mix of market pressures, technological momentum, and ad hoc reactions. Accountability, accreditation, and quality assurance may sound like technical terms, but in the context of AI they are really just different ways of asking the same thing: are we building an educational system in which we would trust our own children to learn?

If the answer to that question is to be yes, regulation cannot be an afterthought attached to AI once the systems are already entrenched. It must be woven into the design, procurement, deployment, and evaluation of AI from the outset. It must be revisited as technologies and contexts change. And it must be grounded in a simple, stubborn commitment: that every new tool adopted in the name of progress should, at the very least, strengthen rather than erode the human relationships and ethical responsibilities at the heart of education.

REFERENCES

Abdelmeguid, H. (2024). Digital Repression in the Middle East: The Strategic Weaponization of Cybercrime Laws in MENA. McGill Undergraduate Law Review, (9).

Abusamra, A., Muhtaseb, K., & Awawdeh, R. (2025). How should E-learning be conceptualized in the context of higher education in MENA region? *Social Sciences & Humanities Open*, *12*, 101808.

Adams, R. (2024). *The new empire of AI: the future of global inequality*. John Wiley & Sons.

Afable, L. (2025). Embracing or Resisting AI: Exploring the Teachers' Perspectives on Student Use of Artificial Intelligence. Available at *SSRN* 5314276.

Al-Zahrani, A. M., & Alasmari, T. M. (2025). A comprehensive analysis of AI adoption, implementation strategies, and challenges in higher education across the Middle East and North Africa (MENA) region. *Education and Information Technologies*, •••, 1–51.

Alfrink, K., Keller, I., Kortuem, G., & Doorn, N. (2023). Contestable AI by design: Towards a framework. *Minds and Machines*, *33*(4), 613–639.

Alzoubi, A. (2021). The impact of process quality and quality control on organizational competitiveness at 5-star hotels in Dubai. International Journal of Technology [IJTIM]. *Innovation and Management*, *1*(1), 54–68.

Azem Qashou, A. M., Bahar, N., & Mohamed, H. (2025). Qualitative Exploration of Data Security Risks in Mobile Cloud Computing for Higher Education. *Security and Privacy*, *8*(2), e70001.

Bhattarai, K., & Yousef, M. (2025). Education challenges and opportunities. The Middle East: Past, Present, and Future, 255-266.

Bohlens, C. (2025). Corruption in accreditation at HEIs: when corruption erodes trust in higher learning. In *Navigating Quality Assurance and Accreditation in Global Higher Education* (pp. 165–192). IGI Global Scientific Publishing.

Boudihaj, A., & Sahli, M. (2022). Education in the MENA Region. In World Education Patterns in the Global South: The Ebb of Global Forces and the Flow of Contextual Imperatives (pp. 19-41). Emerald Publishing Limited.

Buckner, E. (2021). *Degrees of dignity: Arab higher education in the global era*. University of Toronto Press.

Chelliah, P. R., Jayasankar, V., Agerstam, M., Sundaravadivazhagan, B., & Cyriac, R. (2023). *The power of artificial intelligence for the next-generation oil and gas industry: Envisaging AI-inspired intelligent energy systems and environments*. John Wiley & Sons.

Ehtiwesh, I., & Maousa, O. (2023). Examining Perceptions of Academic And Support Staff on Quality Assurance Accreditation in Higher Education in Developing Nations. *Education & Youth Research, 3*(2), 76–86.

Eriksson, A. K. (2024). Absent the silently invisible: Rethinking model victimhood under the "Comfort Women" system. *Hypatia*, •••, 1–15.

Eze, I. F. (2022). Framework for critical thinking among internal auditing students using technology-based educational intervention (Doctoral dissertation, Cape Peninsula University of Technology).

Fahy, L. A. (2022). Regulator reputation and the successful governance of innovation: Lessons from financial technology supervision (Doctoral dissertation, Utrecht University).

Hands, L. (2025). Just (ifying) algorithms: Data-driven automated predictions about unobservable targets and the General Data Protection Regulation (Doctoral dissertation).

Ivchyk, V. (2024). Breaking through obstacles to AI selection in management. Collection of scientific papers «SCIENTIA», (December 20, 2024; Chicago, USA), 39-48.

Kasepalu, R., Prieto, L. P., Ley, T., & Chejara, P. (2022). Teacher artificial intelligence-supported pedagogical actions in collaborative learning coregulation: A wizard-of-oz study. [). Frontiers Media SA.]. *Frontiers in Education, 7*, 736194.

Kassir, H. A. N. (2022). Neoliberal Globalization, Education Policies and Strategies Adopted in Science Curriculum Reform in the United Arab Emirates: A Case Study Based on the Views of Ministry of Educat ion Stakeholders (Doctoral dissertation, The University of Liverpool (United Kingdom)).

Kayyali, M. (2024). *Quality assurance and accreditation in higher education: issues, models, and best practices*. Springer Nature.

Kayyali, M. (2025 A). AI in Higher Education: Revolutionizing Curriculum and Administration. In AI Adoption and Diffusion in Education (pp. 31-62). IGI Global Scientific Publishing.

Kayyali, M. (2025 B). Ethical Implications of Generative AI in Education: Privacy, Bias, and Integrity. In Transformative AI Practices for Personalized Learning Strategies (pp. 185-218). IGI Global Scientific Publishing.

Kayyali, M. (2025 C). The Future of AI in Education: Predictions and Emerging Trends. Next-Generation AI Methodologies in Education, 367-406.

Kayyali, M. (2026). The Impact of AI on Classroom Dynamics in Higher Education: Shifting Roles for Professors and Students. In Responsible AI Integration in Education (pp. 151-180). IGI Global Scientific Publishing.

Labrecque, L. I., Peña, P. Y., Leonard, H., & Leger, R. (2024). Not all sunshine and rainbows: Exploring the dark side of AI in interactive marketing. *Journal of Research in Interactive Marketing*, *18*(5), 970–999.

Lin, H., & Chen, Q. (2024). Artificial intelligence (AI)-integrated educational applications and college students' creativity and academic emotions: Students and teachers' perceptions and attitudes. *BMC Psychology*, *12*(1), 487. PMID: 39285268

Looi, C. K. (2024). Charting the uncertain future of AI and education: Promises, challenges and opportunities. *Pedagogies*, *19*(3), 477–486.

Lynch, M., & Heydemann, S. (2024). *Two*. Understanding State Weakness in the Middle East and North Africa.

Mann, H. (2024). *Artificial Integrity: The paths to leading AI toward a human-centered future*. John Wiley & Sons.

Mansour, W., Boyd, A., & Walshe, K. (2021). National accreditation programmes for hospitals in the Eastern Mediterranean Region: Case studies from Egypt, Jordan, and Lebanon. *The International Journal of Health Planning and Management*, *36*(5), 1500–1520. PMID: 33949699

Mohamed, E. M. M. (2025). Degree of Government AI Readiness of Mena Countries and Its Impact on Banking Performance (Master's thesis, Hamad Bin Khalifa University (Qatar)).

Myburgh, Z. (2021). Quality management of reaccreditation processes in private higher education institutions in South Africa (Doctoral dissertation, University of Pretoria (South Africa)).

Naim, A., Saklani, A., Khan, S. A., & Malik, P. K. (Eds.). (2024). *Evaluating global accreditation standards for higher education*. IGI Global.

Ojha, M. kumar Mishra, A., Kandpal, V., & Singh, A. (2025). The Ethical Dimensions of AI Development in the Future of Higher Education: Balancing Innovation with Responsibility. In Ethical Dimensions of AI Development (pp. 401-436). IGI Global.

Otman, K. (2021). Small and medium enterprises in the Middle East and North Africa region. *International Journal of Business and Management, 16*(5), 12–21.

Owen, A., & Samson, E. (2025). *Validating AI/ML-Based Systems: Frameworks for Testing Model Accuracy*. Fairness, Robustness, and Generalization in QA.

Park, S. (2023). Bridging the global divide in AI regulation: A proposal for a contextual, coherent, and commensurable framework. *Wash. Int'l LJ, 33*, 216.

Pederson, J. D. (2025). AI Associate: Examining Artificial Intelligence and Its Potential Impact on the Pastoral Ministry (Doctoral dissertation).

Pinho, A. S., & Paz, A. L. (2024). Diversity and epistemological plurality: Thinking interculturality 'otherwise'. *Language and Intercultural Communication, 24*(4), 261–265.

Reimer-Burgrova, H. (2022). *Politics of Violence and Fear in MENA*. Palgrave Macmillan.

Shattuck, K. (Ed.). (2023). *Assuring quality in online education: Practices and processes at the teaching, resource, and program levels*. Taylor & Francis.

Sprongl, I. (2025). Agile Governance in the Real World: Balancing Autonomy, Regulation, and Learning in Complex Systems. Regulation, and Learning in Complex Systems (May 09, 2025).

Tariq, M. U. (2024). Navigating the personalization pathway: Implementing adaptive learning technologies in higher education. In *Adaptive Learning Technologies for Higher Education* (pp. 265–291). IGI Global.

Widder, D. G., Whittaker, M., & West, S. M. (2024). Why 'open'AI systems are actually closed, and why this matters. *Nature, 635*(8040), 827–833. PMID: 39604616

KEY TERMS AND DEFINITIONS

Accountability Chain: the distributed but traceable set of actors (ministries, institutions, vendors, educators, students) who share responsibility for AI decisions and their consequences in education.

Accreditation in the Age of AI: the reworked standards, evidence, and site-visit practices that must scrutinise how AI tools reshape curricula, assessment, and learning quality.

AI–Education Regulation in MENA: the evolving mix of laws, standards, and informal norms that govern how AI can be used in schools and universities across the region.

Context-Sensitive Regulation: an approach that refuses copy-paste global models and instead builds AI rules that reflect MENA's political, linguistic, demographic, and resource realities.

Iterative Governance: a regulatory stance that treats AI rules as living instruments, revised regularly through sandboxes, feedback loops, and learning from incidents rather than frozen once in law.

Quality Assurance for AI-Enhanced Systems: institutional processes that interrogate not just documents, but also how AI-driven teaching, assessment, and analytics actually behave in practice.

Regulatory Reflexes: typical initial reactions to AI in MENA education, such as blanket bans, waiting for central directives, fragmented IT fixes, or more reflective principle-based approaches.

Chapter 9
Teachers' Readiness for Generative AI in K-12 Education: An Exploratory Study in Sharjah

Mohammed Rizkallah
http://orcid.org/0009-0002-6201-9607
Sharjah Education Academy, UAE

Noha Osman
http://orcid.org/0009-0007-9658-2007
Independent Researcher, Egypt

ABSTRACT

This chapter examines how K–12 teachers in Sharjah experience and interpret the emergence of generative artificial intelligence (GenAI) within their professional practice. Using an exploratory qualitative design, data were collected through interviews and written responses from participating teachers. The literature situates GenAI within debates on AI literacy, teacher confidence, professional development, and institutional governance in centralized education systems. The conceptual framework understands teacher readiness as an institutionally mediated positioning shaped by confidence, ethical judgment, and perceived policy conditions. Findings indicate widespread awareness of GenAI alongside fragmented pedagogical understanding, variable confidence in supervising student use, and persistent uncertainty linked to assessment and institutional expectations. The discussion highlights the importance of institutional clarity and coordinated professional learning in shaping teachers' readiness toward GenAI.

DOI: 10.4018/979-8-3373-6776-7.ch009

INTRODUCTION

The rapid emergence of generative artificial intelligence (GenAI) has introduced new forms of uncertainty into K–12 educational practice. While GenAI tools have become increasingly visible within schools, policy discourse, and professional conversations, their presence raises questions that extend beyond technical adoption. Teachers are required to interpret how these technologies align with curriculum expectations, assessment practices, ethical responsibility, and institutional accountability, often in the absence of clear, shared guidance.

In centralized education systems, these interpretive demands are particularly pronounced. Teachers operate within tightly regulated environments shaped by standardized curricula, formal accountability mechanisms, and policy-driven reform agendas. Within such systems, engagement with emerging technologies is not merely a matter of individual readiness or innovation, but is mediated by institutional expectations, leadership interpretation, and perceived professional risk. As GenAI evolves, teachers are increasingly positioned at the intersection of innovation and regulation, required to make instructional decisions under conditions of ambiguity.

This chapter examines how K–12 teachers in Sharjah perceive, interpret, and navigate the emergence of GenAI within their professional practice, without seeking to establish causal relationships or evaluate the effectiveness of artificial intelligence (AI) integration. Specifically, the study explores how teachers understand the technology, how confident they feel engaging with it, how they interpret institutional signals, and how they negotiate perceived benefits alongside ethical and pedagogical concerns.

Adopting an exploratory qualitative approach, the study treats teachers' accounts as situated interpretations shaped by institutional context rather than as indicators of adoption success or resistance. In doing so, it shifts attention away from individual deficit explanations and toward the structural, professional, and governance conditions under which teachers encounter GenAI. By examining teachers' positioning within a centralized K–12 system, the study offers insight into how emerging educational technologies are navigated in practice when policy, professional development, and ethical guidance remain in flux.

The findings provide an interpretive account of teacher engagement with GenAI that is attentive to institutional context, professional agency, and the governance of educational change. The chapter contributes to existing scholarship by extending conceptual discussions of AI adoption to include affective, ethical, and governance-related dimensions within K–12 contexts. Practically, it offers analytically grounded insights to inform professional development design, leadership decision-making, and policy conversations related to responsible AI use in schools. While context-specific to Sharjah, the findings may offer transferable insights for other policy-driven or centralized education systems facing similar challenges.

Guided by a conceptual framework integrating AI literacy, Technological Pedagogical Content Knowledge (TPACK), teacher confidence, self-efficacy, and institutional conditions, the study employs thematic analysis of interview data to examine how these dimensions intersect within a centralized education system. The aim is not to evaluate the effectiveness of AI integration or to establish causal relationships, but to offer an interpretive account of how teachers position themselves in relation to GenAI under conditions of evolving policy, ethical uncertainty, and uneven professional support.

LITERATURE REVIEW

Generative AI in Contemporary Education

GenAI technologies, including systems such as ChatGPT, Copilot, Gemini, and other classroom-focused AI platforms, have begun to transform the educational landscape. These tools have introduced new possibilities for instructional support, feedback generation, and differentiated learning while simultaneously raising concerns related to assessment, academic integrity, and ethical use (Wang et al., 2024; Zhai, 2024; Echave et al., 2024). Unlike earlier educational technologies, GenAI tools can generate original content in response to natural-language prompts, positioning them as both pedagogical resources and sources of professional uncertainty for teachers (Al-Abdullatif, 2024; Cordero et al., 2024).

Educators now face the dual challenge of understanding these tools while integrating them meaningfully into their teaching practices (Minnillo et al., 2024; Zhai, 2024). Although the potential for GenAI to enhance instruction, personalize learning, and support creative resource development is widely recognized (Echave et al., 2024; Khalil & Alsenaidi, 2024), the literature consistently highlights a gap between technological capability and teacher readiness (Magat & Sangalang, 2024; Roshan et al., 2024). Research consistently highlights that teachers' attitudes, confidence, and professional preparedness play a central role in determining how AI is interpreted and enacted in classroom practice (Minnillo et al., 2024; Roshan et al., 2024).

Globally, education systems are exploring how AI can support the development of 21st-century competencies, including creativity, critical thinking, and digital literacy (Fundi et al., 2024; Khalil & Alsenaidi, 2024). At the same time, concerns related to misinformation, inequitable access, data privacy, and ethical responsibility continue to shape institutional responses to AI integration (Hojeij et al., 2024).

Within centralized education systems such as those of the United Arab Emirates (UAE), this gap is shaped not only by individual teacher preparedness but also by system-level governance, curricular regulation, and institutional expectations. K–12 education in Sharjah operates under the oversight of federal and emirate-level authorities, with strong emphasis on quality assurance, curriculum alignment, and accountability to national development priorities (Gaad et al., 2006; Kippels & Ridge, 2019). These structures have historically supported large-scale reform and standardization, but may constrain local flexibility in responding to rapidly emerging technologies.

Sharjah provides a particularly informative context for examining teachers' engagement with GenAI. Operating within a centralized and policy-driven education system, Sharjah schools span public, private, and international sectors while adhering to shared regulatory frameworks and accountability structures (Mozelius et al., 2024; Nyaaba & Zhai, 2024). Teachers in this context are required to navigate global AI discourses alongside local curriculum mandates, assessment regimes, and institutional norms. As a result, the introduction of GenAI has created conditions in which teachers must interpret emerging technologies in the absence of fully articulated policies or consistent professional guidance (Khlaif et al., 2024; Cordero et al., 2024).

Professional development emerges as a pivotal factor in bridging the gap between technological capability and teacher readiness. Studies suggest that structured, hands-on professional development can increase teachers' confidence in integrating GenAI, highlighting its relevance in the literature (Cordero et al., 2024; Yang et al., 2024). However, access to meaningful training remains uneven, with many educators reporting limited exposure, insufficient guidance, and uncertainty regarding ethical use (Aljemely, 2024; Hojeij et al., 2024).

In the Sharjah context, curriculum reform and technology integration have been framed as mechanisms for improving international competitiveness and student performance on global benchmarks such as Programme for International Student Assessment (PISA) and Trends in International Mathematics and Science Study (TIMSS) (Kippels & Ridge, 2019; Shemaili, 2022). While these priorities have accelerated digital infrastructure investment, the literature suggests that professional learning has not always evolved at the same pace as policy aspirations, particularly in relation to emerging and less clearly regulated technologies such as GenAI (Gaad et al., 2006).

This review synthesizes current research on teacher confidence, professional development, and AI literacy, not to establish consensus, but to surface recurring tensions, constraints, and unresolved questions, adopting an integrated conceptual lens that combines AI literacy, TPACK, and teacher self-efficacy (Al-Abdullatif, 2024; Wang et al., 2024). It identifies recurring themes, explores persistent barriers, and highlights opportunities for research and practice that inform effective, ethical, and sustainable AI integration. Positioning this synthesis within the Sharjah K–12 system allows for examination of how global discourses on AI readiness intersect with centralized governance structures, curriculum mandates, and institutional expectations that shape teachers' professional agency and confidence in practice (Kippels & Ridge, 2019; Shemaili, 2022).

Professional Development, Teacher Readiness, and Institutional Support

In this review, teacher readiness for GenAI is not treated as a singular or purely technical capacity. Readiness is understood as a context-dependent and institutionally mediated condition shaped by teachers' confidence, professional preparedness, access to professional development, ethical considerations, and the clarity of institutional expectations. This framing reflects the view that teachers' engagement with GenAI is influenced not only by individual knowledge or skill, but by the structural, professional, and governance conditions within which instructional decisions are made.

Professional development is consistently identified as a cornerstone of effective GenAI integration. Studies reveal that programs emphasizing experiential learning, iterative reflection, and authentic classroom application significantly improve teachers' proficiency and confidence (Anggrisia et al., 2024; Cordero et al., 2024; Zulianti et al., 2024). When professional development couples theoretical grounding with subject-specific, context-relevant practice, teachers are better able to translate AI concepts into meaningful instructional strategies (Al-Abdullatif, 2024; Ding et al., 2024).

Professional development is frequently cited as a central mechanism for supporting teacher readiness. Furthermore, professional development initiatives that integrate technical instruction with pedagogical application, ethical reflection, and collaborative learning have been associated with stronger AI literacy and self-efficacy (Ding et al., 2024; Zulianti et al., 2024). Frameworks such as TPACK provide conceptual guidance for aligning AI use with subject-specific instructional goals (Al-Abdullatif, 2024; Zakaria & Hashim, 2024). Nevertheless, the literature suggests that many professional development offerings remain tool-focused or short-term, offering limited support for teachers' affective, ethical, and contextual concerns (Hur, 2024; Minnillo et al., 2024).

Beyond technical competence, socio-emotional and motivational factors play a crucial role. Peer collaboration, mentorship, and supportive learning communities bolster teachers' willingness to experiment with AI and reduce anxiety associated with new technologies (MacDowell et al., 2024; Prilop et al., 2024; Hur, 2024). Trust in AI systems, perceived ease of use, and clear ethical frameworks further mediate teacher confidence, demonstrating the interdependence of technical, cognitive, and affective dimensions in professional development design (Al-Abdullatif, 2024; Khlaif et al., 2024). In this context, teacher confidence extends beyond technical proficiency to include comfort in supervising student use of GenAI, addressing ethical concerns, and aligning AI-supported practices with curricular and assessment expectations (Aljemely, 2024; Baule & O'Connell, 2024).

Moreover, teachers frequently encounter insufficient training, uneven access to infrastructure, and ongoing ethical concerns around academic integrity, bias, and student overreliance (Roshan et al., 2024). Cultural and emotional factors, including skepticism about AI's impact on creativity and critical thinking, further complicate adoption (Daskalaki et al., 2024; Zhai, 2024). These factors show the necessity of integrating ethical and reflective discussions into professional development content, enabling teachers to contextualize AI use rather than merely mastering technical operations (Cordero et al., 2024; Estaiteyeh & McQuirter, 2024). Furthermore, the literature suggests that professional development influences teachers' readiness for GenAI through its interaction with emotional, ethical, and institutional conditions.

Within the Sharjah K–12 education system, professional development is traditionally structured through centrally coordinated initiatives aligned with national curriculum reform and quality assurance agendas (Gaad et al., 2006; Kippels & Ridge, 2019). While this model enables system-wide dissemination of training, the literature suggests that it may constrain responsiveness to emerging pedagogical needs, particularly when technologies evolve more rapidly than formal professional development cycles.

Research on teacher development in the UAE further highlights persistent structural challenges, including uneven access to sustained professional learning opportunities and somewhat limited alignment between training, classroom realities, and evaluative expectations (Gaad et al., 2006; Shemaili, 2022). These conditions shape how teachers experience professional learning, influencing both their confidence and their willingness to integrate novel tools such as GenAI into instructional practice.

Institutional Support and Policy Clarity. Institutional support complements professional development by providing scaffolds that connect technological knowledge with pedagogical reasoning. Frameworks such as TPACK and cognitive apprenticeship facilitate deliberate AI integration, while organizational structures such as mentorship, shared reflection, and collaborative problem-solving enhance emotional resilience and foster a culture of innovation (Walter, 2024; Ding et al., 2024; Zakaria & Hashim, 2024).

In centralized systems such as Sharjah's, institutional support is closely tied to policy clarity, leadership interpretation of national directives, and the degree of autonomy afforded to schools and teachers (Kippels & Ridge, 2019). The literature indicates that when institutional expectations remain ambiguous, particularly regarding acceptable AI use, teachers may default to caution or avoidance, regardless of individual competence or motivation.

Clear policies, resource allocation, and sustained infrastructure investment remain critical to ensuring that teachers can adopt AI confidently and equitably across diverse classroom contexts (Cordero et al., 2024; Khlaif et al., 2024; Mozelius et al., 2024).

Teacher Attitudes, Confidence, and Self-Efficacy

Teacher Attitudes. Teacher attitudes have long been recognized as fundamental to educational quality and student success. These attitudes, comprising beliefs, feelings, and predispositions toward teaching, students, and academic practices, influence virtually every aspect of teachers' professional work, from lesson planning and instructional delivery to assessment and interactions with students, colleagues, and families (Leonard, 2025; Zhang & Han, 2008). Despite decades of research, understanding and shaping teacher attitudes remains a persistent challenge in education, as attitudes are complex, multifaceted constructs influenced by personal, professional, and contextual factors (Aung & Sakurai, 2023).

In research on technology adoption and innovation in education, teacher attitudes are frequently positioned as antecedent orientations that shape openness to change, perceptions of professional risk, and receptiveness to institutional guidance, particularly under conditions of uncertainty (Aung & Sakurai, 2023; Borja-Tomás et al., 2025; Zhai, 2024). Within the context of AI in education, attitudinal dispositions toward innovation, ethics, and change have been shown to influence how teachers initially interpret emerging technologies, even prior to considerations of technical competence or instructional confidence (Daskalaki et al., 2024; Roshan et al., 2024).

Teacher attitudes are typically conceptualized as multidimensional constructs encompassing cognitive, affective, and behavioral components (Borja-Tomás et al., 2025; Williams et al., 2021). The cognitive dimension includes teachers' beliefs about teaching, learning, and students' capabilities. The affective dimension encompasses emotional responses and feelings toward the profession, students, and educational practices. The behavioral dimension reflects teachers' predispositions to act in particular ways in educational settings (Amka, 2020).

Components, Influences on, and Impact of Teacher Attitude. Teachers' attitudes towards their profession often reflect their commitment to teaching and their willingness to engage with students. A positive attitude is associated with a strong commitment to professional development and a desire to improve teaching practices (Vats, 2019; Hardwick-Morris, 2022). Attitudes, which encompass emotional reactions to teaching, can be positive or negative. Teachers with positive attitudes are more likely to create supportive and engaging classroom environments, which enhance student learning (Gelişli et al., 2024; Ch, 2019). Furthermore, teachers' beliefs about their students' abilities and potential significantly impact their teaching methods and student outcomes, where high expectations and a belief in students' capabilities are linked to better student performance (Gelişli et al., 2024; Ch, 2019).

Teachers with more experience and those who engage in continuous professional development tend to have more positive attitudes towards teaching. This is often due to increased confidence and competence in their teaching abilities (Hardwick-Morris, 2022). School culture, administrative support, and available resources can also influence teachers' attitudes. Supportive environments that value creativity and innovation can foster positive attitudes and encourage creative teaching practices (Muskan et al., 2025). Teachers' personal beliefs and cultural backgrounds also shape their attitudes towards teaching and their interactions with students. These beliefs influence how teachers perceive their roles and responsibilities within the educational system (Vats, 2019; Kavitha, 2014).

Positive teacher attitudes are associated with higher levels of student engagement and achievement. Teachers who demonstrate enthusiasm and support can motivate students and create a conducive learning environment (Ch, 2019). In inclusive classrooms, teachers' attitudes toward students with disabilities play a crucial role in inclusive education outcomes. Positive attitudes contribute to more effective teaching strategies and improved student outcomes (Williams & Pelt, 2021). Moreover, teachers with favorable attitudes toward their profession are more likely to adopt innovative and student-centered teaching methods, leading to dynamic and engaging learning experiences (Muskan et al., 2025).

This suggests that teacher attitudes are shaped through an interaction of professional experience, institutional environment, and broader cultural expectations, rather than by individual disposition alone (Aung & Sakurai, 2023; Hardwick-Morris, 2022; Muskan et al., 2025).

While teacher attitudes shape general orientations toward innovation and pedagogical change, the literature consistently distinguishes these dispositions from confidence and self-efficacy, which refer more specifically to teachers' judgments about their capability to perform particular instructional tasks (Bandura, 1997; Borja-Tomás et al., 2025; Prilop et al., 2024). In studies of AI adoption in education, confidence and self-efficacy have therefore been used to capture teachers' perceived readiness to engage with AI tools in practice, particularly within institutional, ethical, and governance-related constraints (Al-Abdullatif, 2024; MacDowell et al., 2024).

Teacher Confidence. Teacher confidence refers to a general sense of assurance in one's teaching abilities and professional competence. While closely related to self-efficacy, confidence represents a broader belief in one's capacity to function effectively as a teacher across contexts (Julaihi et al., 2020).

In research on educational technology adoption, teacher confidence has been shown to be particularly salient under conditions of rapid technological change, where uncertainty regarding acceptable use, assessment implications, and professional risk complicates instructional decision-making (Prilop et al., 2024; Roshan et al., 2024). In studies of GenAI in education, confidence therefore functions less as a stable trait and more as a situational judgment shaped by institutional guidance, ethical clarity, and perceived support structures (Al-Abdullatif, 2024; MacDowell et al., 2024).

Existing research identifies teacher confidence as a key factor shaping engagement with GenAI in educational settings (Yang et al., 2024; Zakaria & Hashim, 2024). Confidence in this context extends beyond technical proficiency to include teachers' comfort in supervising student use, addressing ethical concerns, and aligning AI-supported practices with curricular and assessment expectations (Aljemely, 2024; Baule & O'Connell, 2024). However, confidence levels remain uneven, influenced by subject background, prior technological experience, and the degree of institutional clarity surrounding acceptable AI use (MacDowell et al., 2024; Prilop et al., 2024).

Components, Influences on, and Impact of Teacher Confidence. Continuous professional development is crucial in enhancing teacher confidence. Teachers who participate in ongoing training programs report increased confidence in teaching complex subjects and implementing curricular reforms (Sibomana et al., 2024; Batonghinog & Chavez, 2025).

Additionally, experience contributes significantly to confidence development. Educators with more years of teaching experience tend to have higher confidence levels, as they are more familiar with classroom challenges and effective instructional strategies (McDaniel, 1999). Teachers with deeper subject understanding also demonstrate greater instructional confidence, which translates into improved student engagement and teaching effectiveness (Holm, 2025).

Confident teachers are more effective in motivating students and fostering engaging learning environments, encouraging positive student attitudes toward learning (Sibomana et al., 2024). Furthermore, a positive correlation exists between teacher confidence and student outcomes, as confident teachers are more motivated and effective in instructional delivery (Law-Davis, 2023).

This suggests that teacher confidence influences instructional practice most strongly when supported by coherent institutional expectations and professional learning opportunities, rather than operating as an independent determinant of teaching effectiveness (Sibomana et al., 2024; Prilop et al., 2024).

Teacher Self-Efficacy. Teacher self-efficacy is defined as teachers' beliefs in their capacity to influence student learning and engagement positively (García-de-Olalla et al., 2025; Hoy, 2022). It is consistently associated with improved teaching quality, innovation, and effective classroom management (Na & Isa, 2024).

Within the context of AI adoption, teacher self-efficacy has been used to capture educators' perceived capability to engage with complex, ethically sensitive technologies that intersect with assessment, supervision, and accountability demands

(Al-Abdullatif, 2024; Wang et al., 2024). Unlike general confidence, self-efficacy in this domain reflects task-specific judgments about managing AI-supported learning activities under institutional and governance constraints.

Teacher self-efficacy develops through mastery experiences, vicarious experiences, verbal persuasion, and the regulation of affective states (Lazarides & Warner, 2020). Building on this theoretical foundation, numerous validated scales have been developed to measure teacher self-efficacy across educational contexts (Lingán-Huamán et al., 2023; Manman et al., 2025). Empirical research using these measures demonstrates that teacher self-efficacy varies across educational levels and cultural contexts, with studies conducted in China, Turkey, and Australia revealing context-dependent patterns (Wulandari et al., 2023; Manman et al., 2025). In addition, gender differences have been observed, particularly among early childhood educators (Winy & Wisudawati, 2023).

Components, Influences on, and Impact of Teacher Self-Efficacy. Bandura identified four primary sources of teacher self-efficacy: mastery experiences, vicarious experiences, verbal persuasion, and physiological and affective states (Gavora et al., 2024; Pfitzner-Eden, 2016). Among these, mastery experiences are the strongest predictors of self-efficacy, particularly among advanced preservice teachers (Pfitzner-Eden, 2016). Emotional states and vicarious experiences also contribute to the development of self-efficacy, while the influence of social persuasion varies by school context (Gavora et al., 2024). Building on these sources, interventions that emphasize mastery experiences significantly improve teacher self-efficacy, especially for preservice teachers (Täschner et al., 2024). Reflective elements further strengthen efficacy development by enabling teachers to learn from experience (Täschner et al., 2024). Moreover, professional development programs centered on self-efficacy have been shown to improve teaching quality and workforce preparedness (Na & Isa, 2024).

Teacher self-efficacy has been shown to shape instructional practice and learning outcomes. Teachers with high self-efficacy are more likely to adopt new teaching methods, set challenging goals, and manage classrooms effectively (Lazarides & Warner, 2020). In vocational education contexts, teacher self-efficacy predicts student academic performance, particularly in dimensions related to engagement (García-de-Olalla et al., 2025). Self-efficacy also enhances teaching efficiency by enabling teachers to maximize student learning under constrained conditions (Saharia & Begum, 2025).

Given its influence on teaching practice and student outcomes, enhancing teacher self-efficacy should be a core focus of professional development, as it directly shapes attitudes, confidence, and instructional practice (Tekin, 2023). Understanding factors such as teaching experience and educational background allows professional development programs to be tailored to diverse teacher needs (Akdemir, 2018).

Relationships Between Attitudes, Confidence, and Self-Efficacy. A significant positive relationship exists between teachers' attitudes toward their profession and their self-efficacy beliefs. Teachers with positive attitudes tend to demonstrate higher self-efficacy, resulting in improved instructional effectiveness and student outcomes (Paniamogan & Dioso, 2024; Akdemir, 2018). Pre-service teachers with positive professional attitudes similarly exhibit stronger self-efficacy beliefs (Şen, 2021).

Teacher confidence is closely linked to self-efficacy, with studies showing a strong positive correlation between the two constructs (Julaihi et al., 2020). Teachers with high self-efficacy are typically more confident in managing classrooms, implementing instructional strategies, and engaging students (Hurakadli, 2015; Eroglu & Ünlü, 2015). This interaction also influences student attitudes toward learning, contributing to improved educational outcomes (Lazo, 2024).

Conceptually, self-efficacy encompasses both personal teaching competence and general teaching efficacy, reflecting beliefs about overcoming external constraints to student learning (Phil, 2013). Teachers with strong self-efficacy are therefore more inclined to adopt innovative practices and foster positive learning environments (Kazempour, 2014; Kırkıç & Çetinkaya, 2020).

Challenges. Despite its importance, teacher self-efficacy research lacks longitudinal and experimental designs that isolate the effects of its four sources (Lazarides & Warner, 2020). Existing scales may not adequately capture environmental influences on efficacy beliefs, highlighting the need for improved measurement tools (Woodcock & Tournaki, 2022). Moreover, regional disparities and ongoing educational reforms further shape teacher self-efficacy, emphasizing the need for context-sensitive interventions (Hua et al., 2025).

The literature indicates that while teacher attitudes shape general orientations toward innovation, confidence and self-efficacy more directly mediate teachers' readiness to engage with generative AI in practice, particularly within centralized education systems where policy clarity, assessment norms, and institutional support structures condition professional action (Al-Abdullatif, 2024; MacDowell et al., 2024; Prilop et al., 2024). This distinction informs the present study's analytical focus on confidence and self-efficacy as institutionally mediated dimensions of teachers' positioning toward GenAI.

Theoretical Perspectives: AI Literacy and Teacher Self-Efficacy

AI Literacy as a Foundational Construct in the UAE K–12 Context. AI literacy has emerged as a foundational requirement for effective human–machine cooperation in education. For teachers, AI literacy encompasses not only familiarity with AI tools but also an understanding of their pedagogical affordances, limitations, and ethical implications (Al-Abdullatif, 2025). In K–12 contexts, this literacy is particularly significant due to safeguarding responsibilities, developmental considerations, and the need to mediate students' engagement with AI technologies.

Within the Gulf Cooperation Council (GCC) region, the UAE has articulated ambitious national strategies to position education as a driver of innovation and knowledge-based economic development. Initiatives such as the UAE AI Strategy and We the UAE 2031 Vision emphasize the integration of digital and AI-related competencies across educational systems (Magat & Sangalang, 2024; UNESCO, 2024). These policy directions signal strong institutional expectations regarding technological engagement, even as classroom-level guidance for emerging tools such as GenAI continues to evolve.

Within the UAE, AI literacy is positioned as part of broader national strategies aimed at digital transformation and innovation in education. The Sharjah K–12 education system operates under centralized regulatory oversight, with an explicit emphasis on technological integration, smart learning initiatives, and preparation for global competitiveness (Kippels & Ridge, 2019; Shemaili, 2022). As a result, teachers are increasingly expected to engage with emerging technologies, including AI, even as formal guidance on classroom-level implementation continues to evolve.

AI-integrated teacher preparation programs are designed to support personalized learning, collaborative pedagogies, and sociocultural engagement in classrooms (Massouti, 2025). These initiatives signal institutional expectations and policy direction rather than evidence of uniform classroom-level enactment.

In parallel, AI tools have been incorporated into teacher licensing and certification processes through adaptive assessment systems and blockchain-based credentialing, reflecting a national effort to align educator competencies with emerging technological standards (Abdallah et al., 2024). These developments situate AI literacy not only as an individual teacher capacity but also as an institutional expectation shaped by national policy and governance structures.

Professional development initiatives in the UAE reflect this emphasis, with programs increasingly designed to introduce foundational AI concepts alongside ethical considerations and practical applications. These initiatives aim to foster collaborative professional learning communities and align teacher practice with national modernization goals (Massouti, 2025; Abdallah & Awad, 2024). However, the literature suggests that AI literacy development remains uneven, particularly when policy aspirations outpace classroom-level pedagogical support.

Ethical AI Literacy and Governance in Sharjah Schools. Ethical considerations are central to AI literacy in K–12 education and are particularly pronounced in highly regulated systems such as the UAE. Ethical frameworks adapted for school contexts emphasize principles of transparency, fairness, responsibility, privacy, and beneficence, while also foregrounding pedagogical appropriateness, children's rights, and teacher well-being (Adams et al., 2023). These principles align with the UAE's broader focus on responsible AI practices, including equity, inclusivity, and data protection in educational settings (Alqodsi et al., 2024; Abdallah & Awad, 2025). Together, these policy-oriented approaches reinforce the importance of embedding ethical reasoning within both professional development and everyday instructional decision-making.

Despite this policy-level emphasis, institutional governance at the school level often lags behind technological adoption. Many schools continue to rely on acceptable use policies that do not explicitly address GenAI, creating ambiguity for teachers regarding permissible classroom practices (Marcus-Quinn & McCoy, 2025). In Sharjah, this lack of AI-specific guidance can result in inconsistent interpretations of ethical responsibility and academic integrity.

The literature, therefore, highlights the need for adaptive governance frameworks that translate national AI strategies into actionable school-level policies. Such frameworks are particularly important in centralized systems, where alignment between ministry-level direction, school leadership, and classroom practice shapes teachers' perceptions of risk, accountability, and professional autonomy (Salha et al., 2024; Gouseti et al., 2024).

Teacher Self-Efficacy as a Mediating Lens in AI Adoption. Within the centralized, policy-driven, and ethically regulated institutional contexts described above, teacher self-efficacy functions as a critical mediating construct linking AI literacy, professional development, and classroom enactment. Self-efficacy theory conceptualizes teachers' beliefs in their ability to organize and execute instructional actions under specific conditions, including the integration of unfamiliar or rapidly evolving technologies (Berg, 2022).

In the UAE context, teacher self-efficacy is shaped not only by individual competence but also by the clarity of institutional expectations and the availability of structured support. Professional development initiatives, collaborative learning opportunities, and leadership alignment play a significant role in reinforcing teachers' beliefs that they can responsibly supervise student AI use, redesign assessments, and address ethical concerns (Bauml & Kyzar, 2025; Novariza, 2023). Where guidance is fragmented or policy signals are unclear, teachers may experience reduced self-efficacy despite high levels of technical exposure.

Ongoing training initiatives and extensive instructional documentation aim to ensure that teachers are equipped to implement curriculum reforms and technology-enhanced practices effectively (Gaad et al., 2006; Kippels & Ridge, 2019). However, uneven access to AI-specific training and lingering concerns around ethical responsibility and workload continue to influence teachers' confidence in adopting AI at scale (Mohebi, 2025).

This dynamic is particularly relevant in Sharjah, where teachers are expected to balance innovation with accountability to national standards and assessment regimes.

In such contexts, self-efficacy becomes closely tied to perceptions of institutional trust and support rather than individual skill alone.

Technology Adoption Frameworks, TPACK, and Teacher Agency. Technology adoption frameworks such as the Technology Acceptance Model (TAM) and the Unified Theory of Acceptance and Use of Technology (UTAUT) provide additional insight into teachers' engagement with AI technologies. These models emphasize perceived usefulness, perceived ease of use, and social influence as predictors of adoption (Salele & Khan, 2022; Naseri & Abdullah, 2024). However, in centralized education systems such as the UAE, these adoption factors interact strongly with governance structures and professional norms, shaping how adoption decisions are interpreted and enacted.

The TPACK framework is particularly relevant in centralized and policy-driven education systems such as Sharjah's, as it emphasizes pedagogical coherence and alignment between technology use, curriculum expectations, and subject knowledge (Alshamsi, 2025). In Sharjah schools, where curriculum reform and digital integration are ongoing priorities, TPACK provides a lens for understanding how teachers negotiate AI use within existing instructional and assessment constraints.

Within these centrally governed and policy-driven conditions, self-efficacy operates as a mediator, influencing whether teachers perceive themselves as capable of applying AI in ways that are pedagogically sound and institutionally acceptable (Li & Hidayat, 2025). This mediating role of self-efficacy highlights the role of teacher agency in shaping how AI policies and professional development initiatives are translated into classroom practice.

Implications for Conceptual Framing. These aforementioned theoretical perspectives synthesize AI literacy, teacher self-efficacy, and institutional governance as interdependent constructs within the Sharjah and UAE education context. Teachers' engagement with GenAI is shaped not only by access to tools or training, but by their beliefs about instructional agency, ethical responsibility, and the clarity of institutional expectations.

This synthesis informs the conceptual framework adopted in the present study, which conceptualizes teacher confidence in students' use of GenAI as emerging at the intersection of AI literacy, professional development, self-efficacy, and institutional support within a centralized, policy-driven education system. Consistent with the exploratory qualitative orientation of the study, this conceptual framing does not posit predictive or causal relationships among constructs, but instead delineates analytically relevant dimensions that inform the interpretation of teachers' experiences with GenAI.

Unresolved Tensions and Gaps in the Literature

Despite growing scholarly attention to AI in education, several gaps remain. Empirical research examining K–12 teachers' experiences with GenAI, particularly within GCC contexts, remains limited (Cordero et al., 2024; Magat & Sangalang, 2024). Much of the existing literature focuses on higher education or presents conceptual discussions that do not fully account for classroom-level constraints in primary and secondary schooling (Al-Abdullatif, 2024; Roshan et al., 2024).

Moreover, while AI literacy and TPACK frameworks offer valuable theoretical perspectives, fewer studies examine how these constructs interact with teacher self-efficacy, ethical concerns, and institutional support to shape teachers' positioning toward AI use (Wang et al., 2024; Zakaria & Hashim, 2024). Emotional readiness, professional risk perception, and collaborative support structures remain underexplored, despite evidence that these factors mediate teachers' confidence and willingness to engage with emerging technologies (MacDowell et al., 2024; Prilop et al., 2024).

Ethical considerations related to academic integrity, data privacy, and equity similarly remain insufficiently integrated into professional development and policy discussions, particularly in K–12 contexts where safeguarding responsibilities and accountability structures are pronounced (Estaiteyeh & McQuirter, 2024).

These gaps point not to a lack of consensus, but to unresolved tensions regarding how professional, ethical, and institutional conditions shape teachers' readiness to engage with generative AI in K–12 education systems.

Explicit Mapping to the Conceptual Framework

The reviewed literature directly informs the conceptual framework guiding this study by identifying interrelated constructs that shape teachers' engagement with GenAI in K–12 education. Teacher AI literacy emerges as a foundational capacity enabling teachers to understand AI systems, evaluate pedagogical appropriateness, and navigate ethical considerations within classroom practice (Al-Abdullatif, 2025; Adams et al., 2023). Prior research on teacher self-efficacy and confidence contributes to this framework by clarifying how beliefs about competence, instructional control, and risk management underpin teachers' confidence in engaging with AI and guiding students' use responsibly (Hoy, 2022; Julaihi et al., 2020; Lazarides & Warner, 2020).

Professional development and institutional support are positioned as interconnected conditions that shape teacher AI literacy and confidence through experiential learning, collaboration, and reflective practice (Cordero et al., 2024). These conditions also influence teachers' confidence in students' use of GenAI by providing, or withholding, clear expectations, safeguards, and pedagogical models for responsible integration. Institutional governance, expressed through leadership practices, policy frameworks, infrastructure, and ethical guidelines, operates as a cross-cutting contextual influence that enables or constrains teacher agency (Khlaif et al., 2024; Marcus-Quinn & McCoy, 2025).

Within the UAE and Sharjah context, centralized regulation, national AI strategies, and teacher licensing reforms further condition these relationships, highlighting the interaction between individual capacities, professional confidence, and systemic structures rather than isolated skill acquisition. Ethical concerns and institutional clarity function as cross-cutting considerations across all constructs, shaping how teachers interpret their responsibilities, assess acceptable practice, and position themselves in relation to GenAI. This mapping is intended to clarify analytically relevant relationships identified in the literature, rather than to propose predictive or causal pathways among constructs.

CONCEPTUAL FRAMEWORK

This study is guided by a conceptual framework (Figure 1 below) that synthesizes insights from existing literature to inform the interpretation of teachers' experiences with GenAI in K–12 education. The framework functions as a heuristic and interpretive lens, rather than a predictive or causal model. It does not propose linear relationships or outcomes; instead, it highlights key dimensions that shape how teachers understand, experience, and navigate the use of GenAI within their professional and institutional contexts.

Throughout this chapter, 'teacher confidence' refers to teachers' comfort and perceived readiness to engage with GenAI in professional practice, while 'confidence in students' use of GenAI' refers specifically to teachers' comfort in supervising, permitting, and guiding student engagement.

Figure 1. Conceptual Framework Guiding Interpretation of Teachers' Readiness Toward GenAI

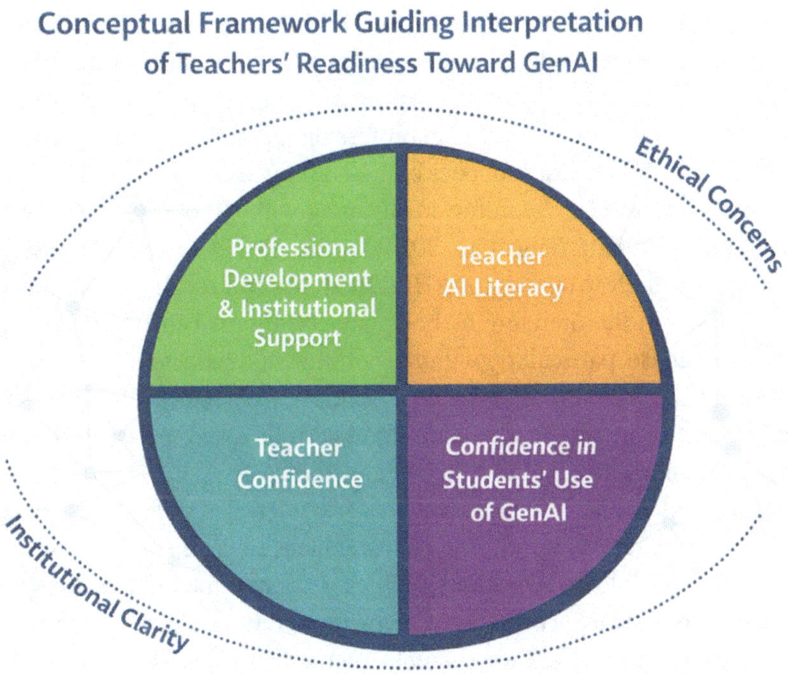

The framework comprises four interrelated constructs: professional development and institutional support, teacher AI literacy, teacher confidence, and teachers' confidence in students' use of GenAI, alongside two cross-cutting considerations: ethical concerns and institutional clarity. These constructs are treated as overlapping and context-dependent dimensions rather than sequential stages, reflecting the complex and situated nature of teachers' engagement with emerging educational technologies.

Professional development and institutional support are conceptualized as contextual conditions through which teachers encounter GenAI in educational settings. Prior research emphasizes that structured, practice-oriented professional development can shape how teachers interpret the instructional possibilities of GenAI (Anggrisia et al., 2024; Cordero et al., 2024; Zulianti et al., 2024). Frameworks such as TPACK and cognitive apprenticeship are frequently cited as approaches that integrate theoretical grounding with hands-on application (Al-Abdullatif, 2024; Ding et al., 2024). Within this framework, professional development is not positioned as a determining factor, but as one element of the broader institutional environment that informs teachers' opportunities to engage with AI pedagogically and ethically.

Teacher AI literacy refers to teachers' understandings of how GenAI functions, including its capabilities, limitations, and potential applications in educational contexts (Zakaria & Hashim, 2024; Zulianti et al., 2024). In this framework, AI literacy is understood as variable and evolving, shaped by prior experience, disciplinary norms, and institutional contexts, rather than as a fixed or uniform competency.

Teacher confidence is conceptualized as a situational and context-dependent orientation toward the use of GenAI in professional practice. Existing research indicates that hands-on experience, peer collaboration, and socio-emotional support are associated with teachers' comfort in engaging with AI tools (MacDowell et al., 2024; Prilop et al., 2024; Yang et al., 2024), while limited exposure or insufficient support may contribute to uncertainty (Hur, 2024; Minnillo et al., 2024). Confidence is also discussed in the literature as being shaped by trust in AI systems and by perceived ease of use, particularly within environments characterized by supportive institutional policies (Al-Abdullatif, 2024; Khlaif et al., 2024). Within this framework, confidence is treated not as an individual trait alone, but as an orientation negotiated within institutional and ethical constraints.

The framework further attends to teachers' confidence in students' use of GenAI, encompassing teachers' comfort in allowing student engagement, supervising use, and navigating ethical considerations such as academic integrity and responsible application. This dimension reflects teachers' interpretations of risk, responsibility, and pedagogical legitimacy when students interact with GenAI tools.

Two cross-cutting considerations, ethical concerns and institutional clarity, are understood as moderating influences across all dimensions of the framework. Ethical concerns, including issues related to academic integrity, fairness, and responsible use, are widely identified in the literature as shaping educators' engagement with AI (Cordero et al., 2024; Estaiteyeh & McQuirter, 2024; Hojeij et al., 2024). Institutional clarity, including the presence or absence of explicit policies and leadership guidance, is similarly recognized as shaping teachers' interpretations of acceptable practice and professional risk (Cordero et al., 2024; Khlaif et al., 2024; Mozelius et al., 2024).

Overall, this conceptual framework provides a structured lens for examining how teachers position themselves in relation to GenAI under conditions of evolving technology and institutional uncertainty. It informs analytic sensitization during data analysis while remaining open to variation, contradiction, and emergent insights from teachers' accounts. Accordingly, the framework does not prescribe analytic categories in advance, but supports interpretive engagement with teachers' accounts as situated and contextually produced.

METHODOLOGY

Research Design and Epistemological Positioning

This study adopted an exploratory qualitative research design to examine K–12 teachers' perceptions and experiences related to the use of GenAI in educational settings in Sharjah. The study is grounded in an interpretivist orientation, which assumes that teachers' understandings of GenAI are socially constructed and shaped by professional, institutional, and contextual conditions. Accordingly, the study sought to explore how teachers interpret and navigate the emergence of GenAI rather than to test hypotheses, measure outcomes, or evaluate the effectiveness of AI integration.

The qualitative approach was selected to capture the complexity and nuance of teachers' perspectives in relation to an emerging and rapidly evolving educational phenomenon (Creswell, 2013; Merriam & Tisdell, 2016). This design enabled in-depth examination of how teachers make sense of GenAI within their professional practice and institutional contexts.

Participants and Context

The study involved 15 K–12 teachers currently teaching in Sharjah. As outlined in Table 1, participants represented a range of teaching phases and subject areas, providing diverse perspectives on GenAI use across school contexts. Teaching phases included Early Years, Primary, Lower Secondary, and Upper Secondary. Subject areas represented were English, Mathematics, Science, ICT, Social Studies, and Early Years. Information regarding school type (e.g., public, private, international) was not collected to avoid overinterpreting institutional variation beyond the study's exploratory scope. All participants reported between 1 and 10 years of teaching experience, with a minimum of one year of experience within the UAE education system, ensuring familiarity with local curricular structures and institutional expectations.

Table 1. Participant Characteristics

Characteristic	Description
Number of participants	15
Teaching phases	Early Years, Primary, Lower Secondary, Upper Secondary
Subject areas	English, Mathematics, Science, ICT, Social Studies, Early Years
School type	Not collected / not reported
Teaching experience	1–10 years (minimum ≥ 1 year)

Recruitment and Sampling

Participants were recruited using purposive sampling through professional networks, school contacts, and referrals. Purposive sampling was selected to ensure inclusion of teachers with varied subject backgrounds, teaching phases, and levels of exposure to GenAI, which is appropriate for exploratory qualitative research and supports the generation of rich, contextually grounded data (Palinkas et al., 2015). Inclusion criteria required participants to be currently teaching at the K–12 level in Sharjah and to have a minimum of one year of teaching experience.

Participation was voluntary, and teachers self-selected into the study after receiving an invitation and information about the research aims and procedures. The sample was not intended to be representative; rather, it was designed to support in-depth exploration of teachers' experiences within a specific institutional context.

Data Collection Procedures

Data were collected in May 2025 through semi-structured interviews designed to explore teachers' conceptual understandings of GenAI, confidence and comfort levels, perceived risks and benefits, prior experiences, and professional development needs. The semi-structured protocol was informed by the conceptual framework, with prompts designed to elicit accounts related to AI literacy, professional development and institutional support, teacher confidence, ethical concerns, and perceived institutional clarity.

To accommodate participants' schedules and preferences, a mixed-format approach was employed, including:

- In-person interviews, audio-recorded with consent
- Online/video-call interviews, audio-recorded with consent
- Written responses for participants preferring asynchronous engagement

All data collection formats followed the same semi-structured interview protocol to ensure consistency across modes. Synchronous interviews lasted approximately 45–60 minutes, while written responses were comparable in depth and detail. Audio-recorded interviews were transcribed verbatim, and written responses were integrated into the dataset for analysis.

Saturation and Sample Adequacy

Sample adequacy was assessed through thematic sufficiency rather than numerical thresholds. As data collection and analysis progressed, recurring patterns and concepts became increasingly stable across participants, teaching phases, and subject areas. Data collection concluded when additional interviews were no longer yielding substantively new analytic insights, indicating that the dataset was sufficient to support the exploratory aims of the study, consistent with reflexive approaches to qualitative analysis (Braun & Clarke, 2006).

Data Analysis

Data were analyzed using reflexive thematic analysis, following Braun and Clarke's six-phase approach: familiarization, initial coding, theme development, theme review, theme definition, and reporting (Braun & Clarke, 2006). Analysis was iterative, with codes and themes refined through multiple review cycles. Both inductive and deductive coding strategies were employed, allowing themes to emerge from the data while remaining informed by sensitizing concepts related to AI literacy, teacher confidence, professional development, and institutional structures.

Patterns were examined across interview modes, subject areas, and teaching phases to identify variation and convergence. Analytic decisions were documented throughout the process, supporting transparency and consistency in theme development. Reflexive practices were applied throughout the analysis to support thoughtful interpretation and minimize the undue influence of researcher assumptions (Braun & Clarke, 2019).

The conceptual framework informed analytic sensitization by guiding attention to relevant dimensions of teachers' experiences, but did not determine coding decisions or theme development.

Researcher Reflexivity and Positioning

The researcher brings professional experience in education within policy-regulated and institutionally structured contexts, which informed sensitivity to issues of governance, accountability, and professional risk in teachers' accounts. Reflexive awareness was maintained throughout data collection and analysis through analytic memoing and ongoing consideration of how prior assumptions could shape interpretation. Attention to contradictory and marginal cases further supported reflexive engagement and mitigated the privileging of dominant narratives.

Trustworthiness and Rigor

Trustworthiness was supported through multiple strategies addressing credibility, dependability, confirmability, and transparency. Credibility was enhanced through the collection of rich, in-depth data across multiple formats and participant backgrounds. Dependability was supported by a clearly articulated and iterative analytic process, while confirmability was strengthened through reflexive engagement with assumptions and deliberate attention to contradictory cases. Transparency was ensured by explicitly documenting analytic steps and decision-making processes throughout the analysis, consistent with established qualitative research standards (Creswell, 2013; Merriam & Tisdell, 2016).

Treatment of Deviant and Contradictory Cases

Variation and contradiction were treated as analytically informative rather than problematic. Participants whose views diverged from dominant patterns were examined closely to refine theme boundaries and prevent overgeneralization. These cases contributed to a more nuanced understanding of how teachers position themselves in relation to GenAI under differing institutional and professional conditions, consistent with reflexive thematic analysis principles (Braun & Clarke, 2006).

Ethical Considerations

Ethical approval was obtained prior to data collection. Participants provided informed consent and were assured of confidentiality, voluntary participation, and the right to withdraw at any time. Pseudonyms were used to protect identities, and all identifying information was removed from transcripts. Data were securely stored on password-protected devices accessible only to the research team.

FINDINGS

Findings Overview

The analysis of interviews with K–12 teachers in Sharjah identified four interrelated themes describing how teachers experience, interpret, and navigate the emergence of GenAI within their institutional contexts. These themes capture variation in teachers' awareness and conceptual understanding of AI, their confidence and comfort in using it, their experiences of professional development and institutional guidance, and their perceptions of potential benefits alongside ethical concerns. The findings reflect differences in how teachers position themselves in relation to GenAI within their professional practice, under conditions of uneven training and unclear institutional expectations. These themes represent teachers' reported experiences and interpretations within this sample and are not intended to indicate prevalence or generalizability across the wider Sharjah or UAE teaching population.

Summary of Findings

The themes in Table 2 are presented in relation to the study's conceptual framework, reflecting analytically distinct but interrelated dimensions of teachers' positioning toward GenAI.

Table 2. Summary of Key Themes and Illustrative Evidence from Teacher Interviews

Theme	Analytical Definition	Illustrative Evidence (from interview data)
Awareness and Conceptual Understanding of AI in Education	Captures how teachers recognize GenAI as an emerging presence in education while holding uneven and sometimes fragmented understandings of its functions and pedagogical relevance. Reflects variation in conceptual depth rather than simple awareness or exposure.	References to AI as a tool for "coding education, creative thinking, and research skills"; framings of AI as supporting "enhancing literacy and writing" or "brainstorming ideas"; descriptions of AI as "vague" or "misunderstood"; associations of AI primarily with cheating, plagiarism, or automated content generation
Confidence and Comfort Levels with Generative AI	Describes teachers' self-reported confidence in engaging with GenAI in classroom contexts, shaped by subject background, prior experience with technology, and perceived clarity of institutional expectations. Reflects differences in willingness to guide or permit student use rather than adoption levels alone.	Accounts from ICT and Computer Science teachers describing comfort due to prior experience with coding and digital tools; reports of feeling "unprepared" or "unsure" among early years, language, and humanities teachers; concerns about allowing independent student use due to misinformation and overreliance
Professional Development Gaps and Institutional Ambiguity	Represents teachers' accounts of limited pedagogically grounded professional development and unclear institutional policies regarding AI use. Captures structural conditions contributing to individualized decision-making and uneven practices across departments.	Descriptions of training focused on a single AI tool rather than pedagogy; characterizations of professional development as "too technical and not pedagogical"; statements reflecting uncertainty about what is permitted due to lack of school-level policy; references to informal departmental practices versus avoidance
Perceived Benefits and Ethical Concerns	Encompasses teachers' recognition of GenAI's instructional and efficiency-related benefits alongside persistent ethical, pedagogical, and equity-related concerns. Reflects coexistence of perceived value and caution rather than evaluative judgment.	References to personalization, differentiation, creativity, and workload reduction; descriptions of AI supporting independent learning and idea generation; concerns about academic integrity, overreliance, bias, equity, data privacy, and safety for younger learners

Awareness and Conceptual Understanding of AI in Education

Theme Definition (Analytical). This theme captures how teachers recognize GenAI as an emerging presence in educational contexts while holding uneven and, at times, fragmented understandings of its functions and pedagogical relevance. Awareness in this theme does not imply depth of understanding or instructional integration; rather, it reflects how teachers conceptualize what GenAI is, what it can do, and how it is framed within their school environments.

Evidence Display. Participants commonly demonstrated a baseline awareness of GenAI, frequently referencing widely known tools such as ChatGPT, Copilot, Gemini, and other classroom-oriented AI platforms. These references suggest that GenAI has entered teachers' professional discourse and everyday vocabulary. However, the presence of AI in professional discourse did not necessarily correspond with shared pedagogical frameworks or institutional guidance on its instructional use. Accounts varied in how AI was understood and positioned in relation to teaching and learning.

Some teachers articulated relatively expansive conceptualizations, describing AI as a tool that could support "coding education, creative thinking, and research skills." Others framed AI more narrowly, emphasizing its potential for "enhancing literacy and writing" or providing new ways for students to "brainstorm ideas." These accounts reflected differing perceptions of AI's instructional scope rather than uniform understandings of its role.

At the same time, several participants characterized AI as a "vague" or "misunderstood" concept within their school contexts. Some teachers reported that colleagues primarily associated AI with cheating, plagiarism, or automated content generation, framing it as a potential threat rather than a pedagogical resource. In these accounts, conversations about AI at the school level were described as largely reactive, focused on preventing misuse instead of exploring instructional possibilities. As one teacher noted, "We know it's important, but we don't yet know how it fits into each subject."

Teachers also described a sense that the rapid evolution of GenAI outpaced their schools' collective understanding of the technology. Although awareness was widespread, participants indicated that uncertainty about AI's capabilities and limitations shaped how it was discussed and understood within professional communities.

Explicit Variation. While most participants were aware of GenAI tools, the depth and clarity of conceptual understanding varied across teachers, with some articulating pedagogical possibilities and others describing AI primarily in terms of risk, misuse, or uncertainty within their school contexts. Within the conceptual framework, this variation in awareness highlights AI literacy as an uneven and evolving dimension shaped by institutional discourse rather than uniform exposure or training.

Confidence and Comfort Levels with Generative AI

Theme Definition (Analytical). This theme describes teachers' self-reported confidence and comfort in engaging with GenAI in classroom contexts. It captures how teachers position themselves in relation to AI use, shaped by subject background, prior experience with technology, and perceived clarity of institutional expectations. These accounts reflect teachers' perceived readiness and comfort in engaging with GenAI under existing institutional conditions.

Evidence Display. Participants reported wide variation in confidence levels when engaging with GenAI. Teachers with backgrounds in ICT, Computer Science, and STEM subjects generally described moderate to high confidence, often drawing on prior experience with coding, robotics, or other digital tools. These teachers indicated that their familiarity with technological systems enabled them to explain AI processes to students and reduced feelings of intimidation. One Computer Science teacher remarked, "Because I already teach coding, I can explain how the AI arrives at an answer, so I'm not intimidated by it." Such teachers were more likely to allow students to experiment with AI under structured conditions.

In contrast, teachers working in early childhood education, languages, humanities, and the arts more frequently described lower levels of confidence. Several reported feeling "unprepared" or "unsure" about how to guide students in using AI responsibly. These accounts often referenced uncertainty rather than resistance, with teachers expressing concern about making inappropriate instructional decisions in the absence of clear guidance.

Across subject areas, uncertainty was frequently linked to the lack of explicit institutional policies regarding acceptable AI use. Teachers described hesitancy about permitting student use without knowing "what's allowed and what's not," expressing concern about inadvertently crossing unclear boundaries. These concerns reflect teachers' perceptions of professional risk in the absence of clearly articulated institutional expectations. As one participant stated, "We want to use it, but we don't want to cross a line we didn't know existed."

A majority of participants reported discomfort with unrestricted student use of GenAI. Concerns focused on misinformation, overreliance on AI-generated responses, and challenges in distinguishing between student-generated and AI-assisted work. One teacher noted, "I'm not confident that students can use it independently without replacing their thinking." As a result, teachers described a range of classroom approaches, including structured integration, cautious experimentation, and avoidance of AI use altogether.

Explicit Variation. Confidence and comfort levels varied notably by subject background and prior technological experience, with teachers in ICT- and STEM-related disciplines reporting greater confidence than those teaching early years, languages, and humanities, particularly in contexts where institutional guidance was perceived as unclear. Within the conceptual framework, confidence is understood as a situational orientation shaped by institutional clarity, subject norms, and prior technological experience rather than as a stable individual attribute.

Professional Development Gaps and Institutional Ambiguity

Theme Definition (Analytical). This theme captures teachers' accounts of limited access to pedagogically grounded professional development related to GenAI, alongside unclear institutional policies governing its use. Rather than reflecting individual motivation or resistance, this theme represents the structural conditions within which teachers are required to make instructional decisions, often in the absence of formal guidance.

Evidence Display. Across interviews, teachers consistently described professional development related to GenAI as insufficient or misaligned with classroom needs. Participants emphasized that available training opportunities were often limited in scope and focused primarily on demonstrating specific AI tools rather than addressing pedagogical integration. Several teachers noted that such sessions did not provide guidance on how AI could be meaningfully incorporated into teaching practices, assessment, or student learning. One participant explained, "We had a workshop on using one AI tool, but it didn't explain how to use it in teaching, or how to guide students."

Others characterized existing professional development as "too technical and not pedagogical," reporting that training did not address practical classroom concerns such as curriculum alignment, assessment design, or student autonomy. As a result, teachers described uncertainty about how to translate technical knowledge into instructional practice, despite expressing interest in learning more about AI.

Institutional ambiguity further shaped teachers' experiences. Participants frequently reported the absence of clear, school-level policies specifying acceptable or appropriate uses of GenAI. In the absence of formal guidance, teachers described being left to interpret boundaries individually, often erring on the side of caution. This caution reflects teachers' perceptions of professional and ethical risk in the absence of clear institutional authorization. As one teacher stated, "I don't know what's allowed and what's not. Until the school tells us, it's hard to be confident."

This lack of institutional clarity contributed to uneven practices across departments. Some teachers described informal collaboration within teams to develop shared understandings or tentative guidelines, while others reported avoiding AI use altogether due to uncertainty. Participants suggested that such inconsistencies could result in students encountering differing expectations across classrooms, depending on teacher discretion rather than coordinated policy.

Teachers also expressed a desire for professional development that extended beyond technical demonstrations to include practical, subject-specific applications and opportunities for collaborative reflection. Participants described themselves as "willing but unsupported," emphasizing that interest in GenAI was not matched by institutional structures to support informed implementation.

Explicit Variation. Teachers' experiences of professional development and institutional guidance varied across schools and departments, with some teams developing informal approaches to AI use while others avoided engagement altogether in the absence of clear policy direction. Within the conceptual framework, professional development and institutional support are understood as contextual conditions that shape teachers' confidence and AI literacy rather than as direct drivers of instructional change.

Perceived Benefits and Ethical Concerns

Theme Definition (Analytical). This theme encompasses teachers' accounts of the potential instructional and practical benefits of GenAI alongside their expressed ethical, pedagogical, and equity-related concerns. It captures the coexistence of perceived value and caution in teachers' perspectives, without positioning either as dominant or evaluative.

Evidence Display. Across interviews, teachers described a range of potential benefits associated with the use of GenAI in educational settings. Participants frequently cited enhanced personalization and differentiation, noting that AI could support students with varying learning needs. Teachers also referenced improved access to instructional materials and support for multilingual learners, as well as increased opportunities for creativity and idea generation. Several participants described AI as a tool that could reduce teacher workload by assisting with the creation of worksheets, rubrics, feedback, and enrichment materials.

Some teachers highlighted AI's capacity to support independent learning. Participants noted that students could use AI to ask questions they might hesitate to raise in class, or to receive scaffolding when struggling with writing or generating ideas. These accounts positioned AI as a supplementary resource that could extend learning beyond direct teacher instruction.

At the same time, teachers consistently articulated ethical and pedagogical concerns that constrained their enthusiasm. Participants across subject areas expressed apprehension regarding academic integrity, particularly the potential for students to rely on AI-generated content in ways that replace essential cognitive processes. These concerns were frequently articulated in relation to the absence of clear institutional guidance on assessment design and acceptable AI use. Concerns about misinformation and the difficulty of distinguishing between student-generated and AI-assisted work were also commonly reported. As one teacher stated, "AI could replace effort," reflecting unease about students bypassing meaningful learning.

Equity and safety concerns were particularly salient for younger learners. Teachers raised questions about age-appropriate use, access disparities, and the potential risks associated with students' exposure to AI-generated content. Broader concerns about bias in AI outputs and data privacy were also mentioned, with some participants noting uncertainty about how student information might be used or stored by AI systems. One teacher reflected, "We don't fully understand what the AI is doing with the information."

Explicit Variation. While many participants identified potential instructional benefits of GenAI, the emphasis placed on ethical, equity, and safety concerns varied across teachers, with some focusing primarily on academic integrity and cognitive impact and others highlighting issues of data privacy, bias, and age-appropriateness. Within the conceptual framework, ethical concerns are understood as cross-cutting influences that shape teachers' confidence and willingness to engage with GenAI under conditions of institutional uncertainty.

Findings Synthesis

These four themes illustrate how teachers navigate the emergence of GenAI through interrelated but distinct dimensions of awareness, confidence, institutional context, and ethical positioning. These themes reflect patterns of experience across the sample rather than indicators of prevalence or generalizability. While awareness of GenAI tools was widespread, conceptual understanding varied in depth and clarity, shaping how teachers framed AI within their professional practice. Confidence and comfort levels differed across subject backgrounds and prior technological experience, particularly in contexts where institutional expectations were perceived as unclear. Teachers' accounts of professional development and policy ambiguity highlighted the structural conditions under which instructional decisions were made, rather than differences in individual motivation, contributing to uneven practices across departments and schools. At the same time, teachers articulated both perceived benefits and ethical concerns, reflecting a coexistence of optimism and caution rather than a singular stance toward AI use. These findings depict variation in how teachers position themselves in relation to GenAI, consistent with the study's conceptual framework emphasizing institutionally mediated engagement.

DISCUSSION

Interpreting Teachers' Positioning Toward Generative AI in Sharjah K–12 Contexts

This study adopts an exploratory qualitative design to examine how K–12 teachers in Sharjah experience and interpret the emergence of GenAI within their professional practice. The discussion does not seek to establish causal relationships or evaluate the effectiveness of AI integration. Rather, it offers an interpretive analysis of how teachers' positioning toward GenAI takes shape under specific institutional, ethical, and governance conditions within a centralized education system. In this study, teacher readiness is understood not as a measure of technical preparedness or adoption, but as an institutionally mediated positioning toward GenAI, shaped by confidence, ethical judgement, and perceived governance conditions. These interpretations are grounded in the Sharjah context and are intended to inform understanding of similar centralized education systems, rather than to support generalizable claims.

Across the findings, three cross-cutting analytical insights emerge. First, awareness of GenAI does not translate into pedagogical coherence, as teachers' understandings remain fragmented and uneven. Second, teacher confidence functions less as an individual attribute and more as an institutionally mediated position shaped by policy clarity, leadership interpretation, and assessment expectations. Third, ethical concerns surrounding GenAI are closely tied to governance and assessment regimes instead of solely to individual teacher dispositions. These insights are discussed below in relation to existing literature on AI literacy, self-efficacy, professional development, and institutional support.

Awareness Without Pedagogical Coherence. The findings indicate that while GenAI has entered teachers' professional vocabulary, awareness alone does not ensure a coherent pedagogical understanding of its role in teaching and learning. This finding directly reflects tensions identified in the literature, where increased exposure to AI tools is often assumed to signal readiness, despite cautions that familiarity does not necessarily translate into pedagogical, ethical, or curricular coherence (Al-Abdullatif, 2025; Zhai, 2024). In the present study, teachers' accounts reflected varied conceptual framings of GenAI, ranging from expansive instructional possibilities to narrow associations with academic misconduct.

This fragmentation complicates assumptions in the literature that increasing exposure or technical familiarity will naturally lead to pedagogically meaningful integration (Echave et al., 2024; Magat & Sangalang, 2024). Instead, the findings suggest that awareness operates as a necessary but insufficient condition for pedagogical engagement. Within Sharjah's centralized system, where curricular alignment and accountability are emphasized (Kippels & Ridge, 2019), the absence of shared pedagogical framing may intensify uncertainty rather than resolve it. Teachers' cautious positioning can therefore be understood not as resistance, but as a response to incomplete interpretive guidance regarding how GenAI fits within existing instructional norms.

Confidence as an Institutionally Mediated Position. Rather than functioning solely as an individual psychological trait, teacher confidence in this study appears closely linked to institutional conditions. This finding reflects and extends existing literature that associates confidence and self-efficacy with technical competence or experience, while also emphasizing the role of contextual and organizational influences (Julaihi et al., 2020; Holm, 2025). While subject background and prior exposure to technology shaped teachers' comfort levels, confidence was also contingent on perceived policy clarity, leadership expectations, and assessment norms.

Self-efficacy theory conceptualizes teachers' beliefs in their capacity to act effectively under specific conditions (Hoy, 2022; Lazarides & Warner, 2020). In Sharjah, those conditions are defined by centralized governance, evolving AI-related directives, and strong accountability structures. When institutional expectations regarding acceptable GenAI use remained ambiguous, teachers' confidence was constrained regardless of individual competence. This finding specifies how institutional trust and governance clarity mediate confidence, particularly when emerging technologies introduce ethical and evaluative uncertainty.

The observed variation in confidence across subject areas further supports this interpretation. Teachers working in disciplines with clearer technical traditions or assessment practices reported greater comfort, whereas others expressed hesitation linked to uncertainty about supervision, boundaries, and evaluation. These patterns suggest that confidence is not merely developed through skill acquisition, but negotiated within institutional frameworks that define acceptable pedagogical risk. This interpretation aligns with the study's conceptual framework, which conceptualizes teacher confidence as an institutionally mediated orientation rather than a stable individual attribute.

Professional Development as a Mediating, Not Determining, Condition. Consistent with prior research, professional development emerged as an important mediating factor in teachers' engagement with GenAI (Cordero et al., 2024; Zulianti et al., 2024). However, the findings caution against positioning professional development as a singular or determining solution for teacher readiness. While teachers expressed strong interest in pedagogically grounded and collaborative professional learning, professional development alone did not resolve uncertainty when institutional guidance and assessment expectations remained unclear.

This finding refines literature that positions professional development as the primary lever for AI integration (Anggrisia et al., 2024; Yang et al., 2024). Within centralized systems such as Sharjah's, professional development operates alongside governance structures, leadership interpretation, and policy signals that collectively shape teacher agency (Gaad et al., 2006; Kippels & Ridge, 2019). When these elements are misaligned, professional development may increase awareness and technical familiarity without enabling confident pedagogical enactment.

Framing professional development as a mediating condition aligns with conceptual models that situate professional learning within broader institutional ecosystems rather than as an isolated intervention. The findings therefore suggest that professional development is most effective when embedded within coherent policy frameworks, ethical guidance, and leadership support that collectively legitimize pedagogical experimentation. This interpretation is consistent with the study's conceptual framework, which positions professional development as a contextual condition interacting with institutional clarity and ethical governance rather than as a determining driver of instructional change.

Ethics, Assessment, and the Governance of Risk. Teachers' ethical concerns regarding GenAI were closely intertwined with assessment practices and institutional governance. Concerns about plagiarism, overreliance, originality, and data privacy reflect tensions widely identified in responsible AI literature (Adams et al., 2023; Marcus-Quinn & McCoy, 2025). Importantly, in the present study these concerns were not framed as abstract ethical dilemmas, but as practical uncertainties tied to classroom assessment and professional accountability.

Assessment regimes play a central role in shaping how teachers interpret ethical risk. In systems where academic integrity is closely monitored and evaluative standards are tightly regulated, uncertainty around acceptable GenAI use heightens perceived professional vulnerability. In this sense, teachers' ethical caution reflects institutional risk management rather than individual reluctance or resistance to innovation. This finding reflects existing scholarship on responsible AI in education by demonstrating how ethical positioning is mediated through governance and assessment structures in practice (Adams et al., 2023; Marcus-Quinn & McCoy, 2025).

In Sharjah's policy-driven context, teachers' ethical positioning can thus be understood as a governance issue rather than an individual moral stance. When AI-specific assessment guidance is absent or inconsistent, teachers may default to caution to protect both students and themselves. This highlights the importance of governance frameworks that translate national AI strategies into actionable, classroom-level expectations, particularly within centralized education systems.

The discussion reinforces that teachers' positioning toward GenAI in Sharjah is best understood as a negotiated, institutionally situated orientation rather than a function of individual readiness, attitudes, or technical competence alone. Teachers' awareness, confidence, ethical reasoning, and professional judgement are shaped through ongoing interpretation of policy signals, assessment expectations, leadership practices, and governance structures within a centralized system. Rather than framing hesitation or caution as resistance, the findings suggest that teachers' responses to GenAI reflect rational engagement with institutional uncertainty and professional accountability. This interpretive perspective reinforces the study's conceptual framing of readiness as context-dependent and relational, and highlights the need to examine GenAI adoption not only through individual capacities, but through the institutional conditions that enable or constrain pedagogical agency. These insights provide a foundation for considering how policy, professional development, and governance frameworks might more coherently support teachers' engagement with GenAI, a focus taken up in the concluding section.

PRACTICAL IMPLICATIONS AND RECOMMENDATIONS

Conceptual Implications: Distributing Responsibility Beyond Teachers

The findings suggest that responsibility for GenAI integration extends beyond individual teachers. Teacher hesitancy should not be interpreted as a deficit or resistance, but as a rational response to institutional ambiguity. Within centralized education systems, leadership mediation, policy clarity, and assessment alignment play critical roles in shaping teachers' professional agency.

This interpretation reflects the study's conceptual framework, which positions teachers' engagement with GenAI as emerging at the intersection of individual capacities and institutional conditions rather than as an individual responsibility alone.

Rather than positioning teachers as primary agents of change, these findings suggest the need for coordinated institutional responses that align professional development, governance structures, and ethical frameworks. Such alignment supports conditions under which teachers can engage with GenAI in ways that are pedagogically meaningful, ethically responsible, and professionally legitimate.

The findings further highlight that institutional conditions shape teachers' confidence, ethical positioning, and willingness to engage with AI. Professional development, leadership interpretation, assessment regimes, and policy clarity function collectively as structural influences that enable or constrain pedagogical agency. These influences emphasize the role of governance coherence in shaping the conditions under which responsible AI use becomes pedagogically viable, particularly within education systems such as Sharjah's.

At the classroom level, the findings suggest that teachers' cautious engagement with GenAI reflects rational responses to ethical and evaluative uncertainty rather than resistance to innovation. Institutional guidance that clarifies acceptable use, assessment boundaries, and supervisory expectations may reduce perceived professional risk and support more consistent practice across subjects and school contexts. In this sense, the implications of the study extend beyond technical training toward the broader coordination of policy, leadership, and professional learning that legitimizes thoughtful experimentation while safeguarding ethical and pedagogical standards.

Professional Development Design

The literature indicates that professional development for GenAI integration should extend beyond tool-focused training toward sustained, context-sensitive models that integrate AI literacy, pedagogical reasoning, and ethical reflection. Experiential learning, discipline-specific applications, and collaborative inquiry are consistently associated with stronger teacher confidence and self-efficacy. Embedding mastery experiences and reflective components is particularly important for strengthening self-efficacy and reducing anxiety associated with AI use.

Institutional Support and Governance

Institutional support is critical to translating professional learning into sustained classroom practice. Updated acceptable use policies, AI-specific ethical guidelines, and leadership alignment are necessary to reduce uncertainty and support consistent implementation. Governance frameworks emphasizing transparency, equity, accountability, and adaptive policy development provide the structural conditions that enable teachers to act confidently and responsibly.

Academic Integrity and Assessment Practices

Concerns related to plagiarism, overreliance, and misuse of GenAI highlight the importance of aligning assessment practices with ethical and pedagogical expectations. Within centralized systems, uncertainty surrounding acceptable assessment practices can heighten perceived professional risk and contribute to cautious or inconsistent classroom use. Addressing academic integrity as part of institutional guidance and assessment design, rather than solely as an individual enforcement issue, may support more coherent and ethically grounded engagement with GenAI across classrooms.

Leadership, Culture, and Equity

Leadership plays a central role in shaping the institutional conditions under which teachers engage with GenAI. Clear expectations, consistent messaging, and attention to equity and access are essential to ensuring that AI integration does not exacerbate existing disparities within and across school systems. Attention to teacher well-being remains particularly important in contexts where innovation is introduced alongside strong accountability pressures.

LIMITATIONS AND ANALYTICAL BOUNDARIES

This study is context-specific, drawing on qualitative data from a purposive sample of K–12 teachers in Sharjah. The findings reflect self-reported perceptions at a particular moment in time and do not claim representativeness across the UAE or broader regional contexts. As an interpretive qualitative study, the analysis does not establish causal relationships or measure instructional outcomes. These boundaries frame the study's contribution as analytic rather than predictive, offering insight into how teachers' positioning toward GenAI is shaped within specific institutional conditions. The value of the study lies in its capacity to illuminate patterns of positioning rather than to forecast outcomes.

As a qualitative, context-specific study, the intent is not statistical generalization but analytic transferability. Readers may assess the relevance of these insights to comparable centralized or policy-driven schooling contexts by considering the study's contextual details, participant characteristics, and institutional conditions described in this chapter. The findings are therefore offered as interpretive propositions that may inform understanding in similar settings, rather than as claims about prevalence or population-level effects.

FUTURE RESEARCH DIRECTIONS

This study points to several avenues for future research. Longitudinal qualitative or mixed-methods studies could examine how teachers' confidence, AI literacy, and ethical positioning evolve as institutional policies and professional development mature. Comparative research across emirates, school sectors, or governance models may further illuminate how centralized and decentralized systems differently shape teachers' engagement with GenAI. Future work incorporating student perspectives, classroom artifacts, or assessment practices could also deepen understanding of how GenAI is enacted in practice and how ethical, pedagogical, and institutional considerations interact over time.

CONCLUSION

This chapter examined how K–12 teachers in Sharjah experience and interpret the emergence of GenAI within their professional and institutional practice. Adopting an exploratory qualitative design, the study focused on teachers' perceptions, confidence, professional learning experiences, and ethical positioning rather than on evaluating effectiveness or impact. The findings shed light on how teachers' engagement with GenAI is shaped by uneven conceptual understanding, variable confidence, professional learning conditions, and persistent institutional ambiguity.

Across the analysis, awareness of GenAI emerged as widespread but insufficient for coherent pedagogical integration. Teachers' confidence in engaging with AI, particularly in supervising student use, was not solely a function of technical skill or individual disposition, but was closely mediated by subject background, prior experience, and, critically, by the clarity of institutional expectations. Professional development functioned as an important but non-determining condition: while teachers expressed strong interest in structured and collaborative learning opportunities, professional learning alone did not resolve uncertainty in the absence of clear policy guidance and assessment alignment.

Ethical concerns related to academic integrity, overreliance, equity, and data privacy featured prominently in teachers' accounts and were closely intertwined with governance and accountability structures. Rather than reflecting resistance to innovation, teachers' cautious positioning toward GenAI can be understood as a rational response to professional risk within a centralized and policy-driven education system. These findings stress the importance of viewing teacher confidence and agency as institutionally situated rather than individually deficient.

The chapter contributes conceptually by advancing an integrative framework that situates AI literacy, teacher confidence, professional development, and institutional support as interdependent dimensions shaping teachers' positioning toward GenAI, informed by research on teacher self-efficacy. By emphasizing ethical concerns and institutional clarity as cross-cutting influences, the study extends existing discussions of technology adoption to account for governance, assessment regimes, and professional accountability in highly regulated schooling contexts.

While the findings are specific to Sharjah, they offer analytically transferable insights for comparable centralized or policy-driven education systems grappling with the introduction of GenAI. Rather than prescribing technical solutions, the study highlights the importance of coordinated institutional responses that align professional learning, leadership interpretation, policy guidance, and ethical frameworks. Such alignment creates conditions under which teachers can engage with GenAI in ways that are pedagogically meaningful, ethically responsible, and professionally legitimate.

REFERENCES

Abdallah, A. K., Khanbooli, B. A., Kaabi, N. A. M. A., & Awadhi, M. A. A. (2024). Bridging innovative technologies with progressive educational governance. In *Advances in educational technologies and instructional design* (pp. 84–99). IGI Global. https://doi.org/DOI: 10.4018/979-8-3693-0880-6.ch007

Abdallah, R., & Awad, M. J. (2025). Integrating Artificial Intelligence and Technology Into UAE Teacher Licensing Systems for Global Education Reforms. 211–250. https://doi.org/DOI: 10.4018/979-8-3373-0837-1.ch008

Adams, C., Pente, P., Lemermeyer, G., & Rockwell, G. (2023). Ethical principles for artificial intelligence in K–12 education. *Computers & Education: Artificial Intelligence*, *4*, 100131. Advance online publication. DOI: 10.1016/j.caeai.2023.100131

Akdemir, Ö. A. (2018). An investigation of the relationship between prospective teachers' self-efficacy beliefs and their attitudes towards the teaching profession. *[Journal title not provided]*, *5*(3), 157–164. https://doi.org/DOI: 10.20448/JOURNAL.509.2018.53.157.164

Al-Abdullatif, A. M. (2024). Modeling teachers' acceptance of generative artificial intelligence use in higher education: The role of AI literacy, intelligent tpack, and perceived trust. *Education Sciences*, *14*(11), 1209–1209. DOI: 10.3390/educsci14111209

Al-Abdullatif, A. M. (2025). Auditing AI literacy competency in K–12 education: The role of awareness, ethics, evaluation, and use in human–machine cooperation. *Systems*, *13*(6), 490. Advance online publication. DOI: 10.3390/systems13060490

Aljemely, Y. (2024). Challenges and best practices in training teachers to utilize artificial intelligence: A systematic review. *Frontiers in Education*. Advance online publication. DOI: 10.3389/feduc.2024.1470853

Alqodsi, E. M., Jadalhaq, I. M., Maknouzi, M. E. H. E., & Abdulhay, I. E. (2024). Promoting responsible AI practices. In *Advances in educational technologies and instructional design* (pp. 195–211). IGI Global. https://doi.org/DOI: 10.4018/979-8-3693-0880-6.ch014

Alshamsi, A. M. O. (2025). Integration of transformative leadership, artificial intelligence, and the TPACK framework for efficient pedagogy: A documentary analysis. *International Journal of Learning. Teaching and Educational Research*, *24*(9), 47–63. DOI: 10.26803/ijlter.24.9.47

Amka, A. (2020). Teacher attitude for better education: The relationship between affection, support and religiosity in the success of inclusive education. *Talent Development & Excellence, 12*(1), 1894–1909. https://doi.org/DOI: 10.35542/osf.io/qxeby

Anggrisia, N. F., Basori, B., Mubarok, H., & Degaf, A. (2024). Empowering madrasah teachers in Mojokerto through AI-based applications: Enhancing teaching competence and classroom engagement. *Journal of Social Outreach, 3*(2), 130–141. DOI: 10.15548/jso.v3i2.9895

Aung, P. S., & Sakurai, R. (2023). Factors influencing teachers' attitudes towards inclusive education in Myanmar. *World Journal of Educational Research (Los Angeles, Calif.), 10*(3), 24–39. DOI: 10.22158/wjer.v10n3p24

Bandura, A. (1997). *Self-efficacy: The exercise of control.* W. H. Freeman.

Batonghinog, P. J., & Chavez, J. C. (2025). Professional development training and academic support: Predictors of teachers' confidence in curriculum change. *Journal of Interdisciplinary Perspectives, 3*(7). Advance online publication. DOI: 10.69569/jip.2025.327

Baule, S. M., & O'Connell, J. S. (2024). Harnessing generative AI for educator professional development. *Advances in educational technologies and instructional design book series*, 77-114. https://doi.org/DOI: 10.4018/979-8-3373-1017-6.ch003

Bauml, M., & Kyzar, K. (2025). "I can do this!" How early childhood teacher education influences preservice teachers' confidence for teaching. *Journal of Early Childhood Teacher Education.* Advance online publication. DOI: 10.1080/10901027.2024.2439869

Berg, D. D. (2022). Over 40 years of teacher self-efficacy research. In *Oxford handbook of self-efficacy.* Oxford University Press., DOI: 10.1093/oxfordhb/9780199841332.013.30

Borja-Tomás, C., Ríos-Jiménez, M. A., & García-Jiménez, M. (2025). *Actitudes del profesorado universitario que predicen el desarrollo de una buena práctica educativa: Una revisión sistemática.* European Public & Social Innovation Review., DOI: 10.31637/epsir-2025-1799

Braun, V., & Clarke, V. (2006). Using thematic analysis in psychology. *Qualitative Research in Psychology, 3*(2), 77–101.

Braun, V., & Clarke, V. (2019). Reflecting on reflexive thematic analysis. *Qualitative Research in Sport, Exercise and Health, 11*(4), 589–597.

Ch, A. H. (2019). Relationship between teachers' attitude and college students' learning. *Research on Humanities and Social Sciences*, *9*(3), 23–30.

Cordero, J., Torres-Zambrano, J., & Cordero-Castillo, A. (2024). Integration of generative artificial intelligence in higher education: Best practices. *Education Sciences*, *15*(1), 32–32. DOI: 10.3390/educsci15010032

Creswell, J. W. (2013). *Qualitative inquiry and research design: Choosing among five approaches* (3rd ed.). SAGE.

Daskalaki, E., Psaroudaki, K., & Fragopoulou, P. (2024). Navigating the future of education: Educators' insights on AI integration and challenges in Greece, Hungary, Latvia, Ireland, and Armenia. https://doi.org//arxiv.2408.15686DOI: 10.48550

Ding, A. E., Shi, L., Yang, H., & Choi, I. (2024). Enhancing teacher AI literacy and integration through different types of cases in teacher professional development. *Computers and Education Open*. Advance online publication. DOI: 10.1016/j.caeo.2024.100178

Echave, J. A., Donato, V. J. P., & Acosta, O. D. (2024). Embracing generative AI in education: Exploring teachers' perceptions, practices, and potential impact. *Jurnal Pendidikan Indonesia Gemilang*, *4*(2), 211–232. DOI: 10.53889/jpig.v4i2.458

Eroglu, C., & Ünlü, H. (2015). Self-efficacy: Its effects on physical education teacher candidates' attitudes toward the teaching profession. *Kuram ve Uygulamada Eğitim Bilimleri*, *15*(1), 201–212. DOI: 10.12738/ESTP.2015.1.2282

Estaiteyeh, M., & McQuirter, R. (2024). Generative or degenerative?! Implications of AI tools in pre-service teacher education and reflections on instructors' professional development. *Brock Education Journal*, *33*(3). Advance online publication. DOI: 10.26522/brocked.v33i3.1176

Fundi, M., Sanusi, I. T., Oyelere, S. S., & Ayere, M. (2024). Advancing AI education: Assessing Kenyan in-service teachers' preparedness for integrating artificial intelligence in competence-based curriculum. *Computers in Human Behavior Reports*. Advance online publication. DOI: 10.1016/j.chbr.2024.100412

Gaad, E., Arif, M., & Scott, F. (2006). Systems analysis of the UAE education system. *International Journal of Educational Management*, *20*(4), 291–303. DOI: 10.1108/09513540610665405

Gavora, P., Pacholík, V., Navrátilová, H., & Puhrová, B. P. (2024). Self-efficacy učitelů 1. stupně základní školy: Zdroje jeho zlepšení. *Orbis Scholae*. Advance online publication. https://doi.org/DOI: 10.14712/23363177.2024.13

Gelişli, Y., Kazykhankyzy, L., & Göksu, D. Y. (2024). Development of "Teachers' Attitude Scale Towards Students": Validity and reliability analysis. *Gazi Eğitim Fakültesi Dergisi*, *44*(3), 2009–2027. DOI: 10.17152/gefad.1534467

Gouseti, A., James, F., Fallin, L., & Burden, K. (2024). The ethics of using AI in K–12 education: A systematic literature review. *Technology, Pedagogy and Education*, •••, 1–22. Advance online publication. DOI: 10.1080/1475939X.2024.2428601

Hardwick-Morris, M. (2022). Secondary school teachers' attitudes towards the teaching profession. *The Research Probe*, *2*(1). Advance online publication. DOI: 10.53378/352893

Hojeij, Z., Kuhail, M. A., & ElSayary, A. (2024). Investigating in-service teachers' views on ChatGPT integration. *Interactive Technology and Smart Education*. Advance online publication. DOI: 10.1108/itse-04-2024-0094

Holm, J. L. (2025). Developing mathematics teacher confidence through increasing understanding of mathematics. *Open Access Government*, *45*(1), 290–291. DOI: 10.56367/oag-045-11870

Holzmann, P., Schwarz, E. J., & Audretsch, D. B. (2020). Understanding the determinants of novel technology adoption among teachers: The case of 3D printing. *The Journal of Technology Transfer*, *45*(1), 259–275. DOI: 10.1007/S10961-018-9693-1

Hoy, A. W. (2022). Gaining efficacy with experience: From teacher education to classroom practice. In *Oxford research encyclopedia of education*. Routledge., DOI: 10.4324/9781138609877-ree19-1

Hua, S., Mansor, A. N., & Jamaludin, K. A. (2025). Teachers' self-efficacy beliefs in China: A literature review (2015–2025). *Deleted Journal*, *4*, 456. Advance online publication. DOI: 10.56294/mw2025456

Hur, J. W. (2024). Fostering AI literacy: Overcoming concerns and nurturing confidence among preservice teachers. *Information and Learning Science*. Advance online publication. DOI: 10.1108/ils-11-2023-0170

Hurakadli, B. M. (2015). *Relationship between attitude towards the teaching profession and teachers' self-efficacy beliefs* [Unpublished manuscript].

Julaihi, N. H., Ying, L. C., Li, V. L., & Bakri, S. R. A. (2020). Confidence level and self-efficacy beliefs of mathematics teachers: Evidence from Sarawak. *International Journal of Social and Management Studies*, *4*(2), 1–23. DOI: 10.24191/IJSMS.V4I2.8145

Kavitha, K. (2014). *Attitude of secondary school teachers*. [Unpublished manuscript].

Kazempour, M. (2014). The interrelationship of science experiences, beliefs, attitudes, and self-efficacy: A case study of a pre-service teacher with positive science attitude and high science teaching self-efficacy. *Journal of Education and Learning, 8*(1), 51–64. DOI: 10.11591/EDULEARN.V8I1.205

Khalil, H., & Alsenaidi, S. (2024). Teachers' digital competencies for effective AI integration in higher education in Oman. *Journal of Education and e-learning Research, 11*(4), 698–707. DOI: 10.20448/jeelr.v11i4.6097

Khlaif, Z. N., Ayyoub, A. A., Hamamra, B., Bensalem, E., Mitwally, M. A. A., Ayyoub, A., Hattab, M., & Shadid, F. (2024). University teachers' views on the adoption and integration of generative AI tools for student assessment in higher education. *Education Sciences, 14*(10), 1090–1090. DOI: 10.3390/educsci14101090

Kippels, S., & Ridge, N. (2019). The growth and transformation of K–12 education in the UAE. In *Education in the United Arab Emirates* (pp. 37–55). Springer., DOI: 10.1007/978-981-13-7736-5_3

Kırkıç, K. A., & Çetinkaya, F. (2020). The relationship between preschool teachers' self-efficacy beliefs and their teaching attitudes. *International Journal of Evaluation and Research in Education, 9*(4), 807–815. DOI: 10.11591/ijere.v9i4.20670

Kurniahtunnisa, K., Manuel, M. Y., Aini, M. S., & Agustina, T. P. (2025). Persepsi dan sikap siswa terhadap penggunaan artificial intelligence. *Scholaria: Jurnal Pendidikan dan Kebudayaan, 15*(1), 47–59. https://doi.org/DOI: 10.24246/j.js.2025.v15.i1.p47-59

Law-Davis, S. (2023). Early childhood teachers' confidence to teach religious education and the influences impacting their teaching in Catholic primary schools. *Religions, 14*(2), 198. Advance online publication. DOI: 10.3390/rel14020198

Lazarides, R., & Warner, L. M. (2020). Teacher self-efficacy. In *Oxford research encyclopedia of education.* Oxford University Press., DOI: 10.1093/acrefore/9780190264093.013.890

Lazo, K. P. M. (2024). The interaction between teachers' efficacy and students' attitudes toward effective learning in state universities and colleges of the Philippines. *International Journal of Advanced and Applied Sciences, 11*(7), 75–86. DOI: 10.21833/ijaas.2024.07.010

Li, Q., & Hidayat, R. (2025). The mediating role of self-efficacy and belief between technological pedagogical content knowledge and modes of technology use among elementary school teachers in China. *International Journal of Educational Reform.* Advance online publication. DOI: 10.1177/10567879251345810

Lingán-Huamán, S. K., Mamani-Benito, O., Castillo-Blanco, R., Cabrera-Orosco, I., Rodríguez-Sosa, J., & Carranza-Esteban, R. F. (2023). Teacher self-efficacy: Development, validity, and factorial invariance of a brief measure in Peruvian university professors. *Frontiers in Education*, *8*, 1211487. Advance online publication. DOI: 10.3389/feduc.2023.1211487

MacDowell, P., Moskalyk, K., Korchinski, K., & Morrison, D. (2024). Preparing educators to teach and create with generative artificial intelligence. *Canadian Journal of Learning and Technology*, *50*(4), 1–23. DOI: 10.21432/cjlt28606

Magat, R. J. B., & Sangalang, E. M. (2024). Teachers' familiarity, perceptions, and training needs on the use of ChatGPT in mathematics instruction. *International Journal of Education in Mathematics, Science and Technology*, 1471-1487. https://doi.org/DOI: 10.46328/ijemst.4332

Manman, D., Chularut, P., & Ayudhaya, P. K. N. (2025). A study on defining and evaluating teacher self-efficacy for pre-service English teachers in China. *International Journal of Sociologies and Anthropologies Science Reviews*, *5*(6), 611–622. DOI: 10.60027/ijsasr.2025.7619

Marcus-Quinn, A., & McCoy, S. (2025). *Future proofing schools: Bringing school policies into the AI era* (Version 2). OSF Preprints. https://doi.org/DOI: 10.35542/osf.io/mujkh_v2

Massouti, A. (2025). *Promoting artificial intelligence in UAE's teacher education*. IGI Global. [Book title not provided], DOI: 10.4018/979-8-3373-0837-1.ch009

McDaniel, J. E. (1999). *Teacher confidence and attitude regarding performance assessment* (Master's thesis, Fort Hays State University). Fort Hays State University. https://doi.org/DOI: 10.58809/MXEB4276

Merriam, S. B., & Tisdell, E. J. (2016). *Qualitative research: A guide to design and implementation* (4th ed.). Jossey-Bass.

Minnillo, S., Jones, L., & Barrio-García, S. D. (2024). AI in the L2 classroom: Serving language educators through professional development. *Journal of Linguistics and Language Teaching*, *16*(1). Advance online publication. DOI: 10.5070/l2.21198

Mohebi, L. (2025). Exploring the integration of AI in education. In *Advances in computational intelligence and robotics* (pp. 371–386). IGI Global. https://doi.org/DOI: 10.4018/979-8-3693-7332-3.ch022

Mozelius, P., Håkansson Lindqvist, M., Cleveland-Innes, M., Jaldemark, J., & Sundgren, M. (2024). *Educating the educators on generative artificial intelligence in higher education*. In *Proceedings of the International Conference on AI Research* (Vol. 4, pp. 296–302). https://doi.org/DOI: 10.34190/icair.4.1.3026

Na, C., & Isa, Z. (2024). Exploring the influence of teacher self-efficacy on teaching quality in higher vocational education. *DREAM*, *3*(7). Advance online publication. DOI: 10.56982/dream.v3i07.246

Naseri, R. N. N., & Abdullah, M. S. (2024). Understanding AI technology adoption in educational settings: A review of theoretical frameworks and their applications. *Information Management and Business Review*, *16*(3), 174–181. DOI: 10.22610/imbr.v16i3(i).3963

Novariza, B. (2023). *Enhancing teacher self-efficacy: A framework for structured continuous professional development*. Managere. *Indonesian Journal of Educational Management*, *5*(3), 330–341. DOI: 10.52627/managere.v5i3.414

Nyaaba, M., & Zhai, X. (2024). Generative AI professional development needs for teacher educators. https://doi.org/DOI: 10.61969/jai.1385915

Palinkas, L. A., Horwitz, S. M., Green, C. A., Wisdom, J. P., Duan, N., & Hoagwood, K. (2015). Purposeful sampling for qualitative data collection and analysis in mixed method implementation research. *Administration and Policy in Mental Health*, *42*, 533–544. DOI: 10.1007/s10488-013-0528-y

Paniamogan, J. D., & Dioso, E. D. (2024). *Relationship between teachers' attitude and self-efficacy: A descriptive correlational study*. EPRA International Journal of Environmental, Economics, Commerce and Educational Management., DOI: 10.36713/epra17840

Pfitzner-Eden, F. (2016). Why do I feel more confident? Bandura's sources predict preservice teachers' latent changes in teacher self-efficacy. *Frontiers in Psychology*, *7*, 1486. Advance online publication. DOI: 10.3389/fpsyg.2016.01486

Phil, M. (2013). *Relationship between attitude towards teaching profession and teachers' self-efficacy beliefs* [Unpublished manuscript].

Prilop, C. N., Mah, D., Jacobsen, L. J., Hansen, R. R., Weber, K. E., & Hoya, F. (2024). Generative AI in teacher education: Using AI-enhanced methods to explore teacher educators' perceptions. https://doi.org/DOI: 10.31219/osf.io/szcwb

Roshan, S., Iqbal, S. Z., & Qing, Z. (2024). Teacher training and professional development for implementing AI-based educational tools. *Journal of Asian Development Studies*. https://doi.org/DOI: 10.62345/jads.2024.13.2.154

Saharia, B., & Begum, J. (2025). Self-efficacy: A determining factor of teaching efficiency. *International Journal of Research and Scientific Innovation, 12*(7), 81–88. DOI: 10.51244/ijrsi.2025.120700009

Salele, N., & Khan, M. S. H. (2022). Engineering trainee-teachers' attitudes toward technology use in pedagogical practices: Extending the computer attitude scale (CAS). *SAGE Open, 12*(2), 21582440221102436. Advance online publication. DOI: 10.1177/21582440221102436

Salha, S., Mousa, A., & Khayat, S. (2024). Artificial intelligence in education (AIED) policies in school contexts: A mixed-methods study. *Leadership and Policy in Schools*. Advance online publication. DOI: 10.1080/15700763.2024.2443675

Şen, Ş. (2021). The study of relationship between pre-service teachers' self-efficacy beliefs and attitudes towards the teaching profession. *MIER Journal of Educational Studies, Trends and Practices*, 23–32. https://doi.org/DOI: 10.52634/mier/2019/v9/i1/1380

Shemaili, M. A. (2022). Science education in the United Arab Emirates. In *Science education in the Arab Gulf states* (pp. 225–241). Springer., DOI: 10.1007/978-981-16-6955-2_14

Sibomana, A., Mukagihana, J., & Ndiritu, J. (2024). *Teacher training programs and secondary mathematics and science teachers' attitudes and confidence in teaching*. BonView International Journal of Curriculum and Education., DOI: 10.47852/bonviewijce42022797

Täschner, J., Dicke, T., Reinhold, S., & Holzberger, D. (2024). "Yes, I can!" A systematic review and meta-analysis of intervention studies promoting teacher self-efficacy. *Review of Educational Research*. Advance online publication. DOI: 10.3102/00346543231221499

Tekin, O. (2023). The mediating role of teacher self-efficacy in predicting teachers' research attitudes. *Teacher Development, 27*(3), 314–332. DOI: 10.1080/13664530.2023.2201579

UNESCO. (2024). *We the UAE 2031 Vision*. Policy Monitoring Platform. UNESCO. https://www.unesco.org/creativity/en/policy-monitoring-platform/we-uae-2031-vision

Vats, R. (2019). A study of teachers' attitude towards the teaching profession. *International Education and Research Journal, 5*(4).

Walter, A. L. (2024). Utilizing language-generating artificial intelligence (LGAI) in educational planning: A case study. *Journal of Interdisciplinary Teacher Leadership*. https://doi.org/DOI: 10.46767/kfp.2016-0052

Wang, K., Ruan, Q., Zhang, X., Fu, C., & Duan, B. (2024). Pre-service teachers' GenAI anxiety, technology self-efficacy, and tPACK: Their structural relations with behavioral intention to design GenAI-assisted teaching. *Behavioral Science, 14*. Advance online publication. DOI: 10.3390/bs14050373

Williams, S. H., & Pelt, R. M. (2021). How teachers' attitudes impact the inclusive classroom. *International Journal of Education and Social Science Research, 4*(1), 13–21. DOI: 10.37500/IJESSR.2021.4103

Woodcock, S., & Tournaki, N. (2022). Bandura's triadic reciprocal determinism model and teacher self-efficacy scales: A revisit. *Teacher Development, 27*(1), 75–91. DOI: 10.1080/13664530.2022.2150285

Wulandari, A., Sukarno, S., & Matsuri, M. (2023). Bibliometric analysis of teacher self-efficacy in primary education. *Al-Ishlah, 15*(2), 1664–1676. DOI: 10.35445/alishlah.v15i2.3063

Yang, Y., Tseng, C. C., & Lai, S. (2024). Enhancing teachers' self-efficacy beliefs in AI-based technology integration into English-speaking teaching through a professional development program. *Teaching and Teacher Education*. Advance online publication. DOI: 10.1016/j.tate.2024.104582

Zakaria, N. Y. K., & Hashim, H. (2024). Shaping the future of education: Conceptualising pre-service teachers' perspectives on artificial intelligence (AI) integration. *International Journal of Academic Research in Business & Social Sciences*. Advance online publication. DOI: 10.6007/ijarbss/v14-i5/21584

Zhai, X. (2024). Transforming teachers' roles and agencies in the era of generative AI: Perceptions, acceptance, knowledge, and practices. *arXiv.org, abs/2410.03018*. https://doi.org//arxiv.2410.03018DOI: 10.48550

Zhang, L., & Han, Z. (2008). A teaching attitude adjusting model for college teachers based on attitude theories. *International Education Studies, 1*(1). Advance online publication. DOI: 10.5539/ies.v1n1p64

Zulianti, H., Hastuti, H., Nurchurifiani, E., Hastomo, T., Maximilian, A., & Ajeng, G. D. (2024). Enhancing novice EFL teachers' competency in AI-powered tools through a tpack-based professional development program. *World Journal of English Language, 15*(3), 117–117. DOI: 10.5430/wjel.v15n3p117

Compilation of References

Abdaljaleel, M., Barakat, M., Alsanafi, M., Salim, N. A., Abazid, H., Malaeb, D., Mohammed, A. H., Hassan, B. R., Wayyes, A. M., Farhan, S. S., Khatib, S. E., Rahal, M., Sahban, A., Abdelaziz, D. H., Mansour, N. O., AlZayer, R., Khalil, R., Fekih-Romdhane, F., Hallit, R., & Sallam, M. (2024). A multinational study on the factors influencing university students' attitudes and usage of ChatGPT. *Scientific Reports*, *14*(1), 1983. DOI: 10.1038/s41598-024-52549-8 PMID: 38263214

Abdallah, A. K., Khanbooli, B. A., Kaabi, N. A. M. A., & Awadhi, M. A. A. (2024). Bridging innovative technologies with progressive educational governance. In *Advances in educational technologies and instructional design* (pp. 84–99). IGI Global. https://doi.org/DOI: 10.4018/979-8-3693-0880-6.ch007

Abdallah, R., & Awad, M. J. (2025). Integrating Artificial Intelligence and Technology Into UAE Teacher Licensing Systems for Global Education Reforms. 211–250. https://doi.org/DOI: 10.4018/979-8-3373-0837-1.ch008

Abdelmeguid, H. (2024). Digital Repression in the Middle East: The Strategic Weaponization of Cybercrime Laws in MENA. McGill Undergraduate Law Review, (9).

Abdelnour-Nocera, J., Nobarany, S., & Parmiggiani, E. (2021). Contextual and cultural perspectives in human-centred computing. *Interacting with Computers*, *33*(2), 117–123. DOI: 10.1093/iwc/iwab006

Abukhalaf, S., Charles, T., & Hill, C. (2024). The Metaverse as a Virtual Learning Space: Perceptions from the UAE. *Journal of Ecohumanism*, *3*(5), 1037–1052. DOI: 10.62754/joe.v3i5.3954

Abusamra, A., Muhtaseb, K., & Awawdeh, R. (2025). How should E-learning be conceptualized in the context of higher education in MENA region? *Social Sciences & Humanities Open*, *12*, 101808.

Acton, R., & Glasgow, P. (2015). Teacher wellbeing in Neoliberal contexts: A review of the literature. *The Australian Journal of Teacher Education, 40*(8). Advance online publication. DOI: 10.14221/ajte.2015v40n8.6

Adams, C., Pente, P., Lemermeyer, G., & Rockwell, G. (2023). Ethical principles for artificial intelligence in K–12 education. *Computers & Education: Artificial Intelligence, 4*, 100131. Advance online publication. DOI: 10.1016/j.caeai.2023.100131

Adams, R. (2024). *The new empire of AI: the future of global inequality*. John Wiley & Sons.

Adly, A. A. (2020). On the quest for economic prosperity: A higher education strategic perspective for the MENA region. *arXiv preprint arXiv:2009.14408.*

Afable, L. (2025). Embracing or Resisting AI: Exploring the Teachers' Perspectives on Student Use of Artificial Intelligence. Available at *SSRN* 5314276.

AI Assessment Scale Project. (2026). Custom AIAS GPT [Generative AI tool; response generated using prompt about examples of AI-resistant assessments]. AI Assessment Scale. https://aiassessmentscale.com/

Akdemir, Ö. A. (2018). An investigation of the relationship between prospective teachers' self-efficacy beliefs and their attitudes towards the teaching profession. *[Journal title not provided], 5*(3), 157–164. https://doi.org/DOI: 10.20448/JOURNAL.509.2018.53.157.164

Al-Abdullatif, A. M. (2024). Modeling teachers' acceptance of generative artificial intelligence use in higher education: The role of AI literacy, intelligent tpack, and perceived trust. *Education Sciences, 14*(11), 1209–1209. DOI: 10.3390/educsci14111209

Al-Abdullatif, A. M. (2025). Auditing AI literacy competency in K–12 education: The role of awareness, ethics, evaluation, and use in human–machine cooperation. *Systems, 13*(6), 490. Advance online publication. DOI: 10.3390/systems13060490

Al-Azzam, S. H., & Al-Oudat, M. (2025). Artificial Intelligence-Based Classification and Prediction of Academic and Psychological Challenges in Higher Education. *Educational Process: International Journal, 15*, e2025150. DOI: 10.22521/edupij.2025.15.150

Aldossary, A. S., Aljindi, A. A., & Alamri, J. M. (2024). The role of generative AI in education: Perceptions of Saudi students. *Contemporary Educational Technology, 16*(4), ep536. DOI: 10.30935/cedtech/15496

Aldreabi, H., Dahdoul, N. K. S., Alhur, M., Alzboun, N., & Alsalhi, N. R. (2025). Determinants of student adoption of Generative AI in Higher Education. *Electronic Journal of e-Learning, 23*(1), 15–33. DOI: 10.34190/ejel.23.1.3599

Alfrink, K., Keller, I., Kortuem, G., & Doorn, N. (2023). Contestable AI by design: Towards a framework. *Minds and Machines, 33*(4), 613–639.

Alhajji, R. A. Y., Almansoori, A. G., & Alyammahi, A. (2025). Harnessing AI for EFL educational advancement: A reflection on policy, practice, and pedagogy within the Ministry of Education in the UAE.

Aljemely, Y. (2024). Challenges and best practices in training teachers to utilize artificial intelligence: A systematic review. *Frontiers in Education*. Advance online publication. DOI: 10.3389/feduc.2024.1470853

Alkan, A. (2024). *Use of artificial intelligence in education. Journal of the Human and Social Science Researches*. Itobiad., DOI: 10.15869/itobiad.1331201

Alkaramneh, M. S., Al-Taj, H., Ghanem, B. O., Sheirah, K. A., Ghedhaifi, H., & Shatat, N. (2025). The Degree to Which Faculty Members at Jordanian Universities Employ Artificial Intelligence Applications in Education and Scientific Research. *The Journal of Educators Online, 22*(3), n3.

Allen, K., Kern, M. L., Vella-Brodrick, D., Hattie, J., & Waters, L. (2018). What schools need to know about fostering school belonging: A meta-analysis. *Educational Psychology Review, 30*(1), 1–34. DOI: 10.1007/s10648-016-9389-8

Alnaqbi, A. M. A., & Yassin, A. M. (2021). Current status, challenges, and strategies of artificial intelligence and e-learning in the UAE military education system. *International journal of sustainable construction engineering and technology, 12*(3), 352-361.

Alotaibi, N. S., & Alshehri, A. H. (2023). Prospers and obstacles in using artificial intelligence in Saudi Arabia higher education institutions—The potential of AI-based learning outcomes. *Sustainability, 15*(13), 10723.

Alqodsi, E. M., Jadalhaq, I. M., Maknouzi, M. E. H. E., & Abdulhay, I. E. (2024). Promoting responsible AI practices. In *Advances in educational technologies and instructional design* (pp. 195–211). IGI Global. https://doi.org/DOI: 10.4018/979-8-3693-0880-6.ch014

Alrayes, A., Henari, T. F., & Ahmed, D. A. (2024). ChatGPT in education–Understanding the Bahraini academics perspective. *Electronic Journal of e-Learning, 22*(2), 112–134. DOI: 10.34190/ejel.22.2.3250

Alshamsi, A. M. O. (2025). Integration of transformative leadership, artificial intelligence, and the TPACK framework for efficient pedagogy: A documentary analysis. *International Journal of Learning. Teaching and Educational Research, 24*(9), 47–63. DOI: 10.26803/ijlter.24.9.47

Alshamy, A., Al-Harthi, A. S. A., & Abdullah, S. (2025). Perceptions of Generative AI Tools in Higher Education: Insights from Students and Academics at Sultan Qaboos University. *Education Sciences, 15*(4), 501. DOI: 10.3390/educsci15040501

Alsharefeen, R., & Sayari, N. A. (2025). Examining academic integrity policy and practice in the era of AI: A case study of faculty perspectives. *Frontiers in Education, 10*. Advance online publication. DOI: 10.3389/feduc.2025.1621743

Alshehhi, N., Alzouebi, K., & Charles, T. (2024). Perspectives On Game-Based Learning Within The Higher Education Sector. *Educational Administration: Theory and Practice, 30*(5), 3229–3233. DOI: 10.53555/kuey.v30i5.2153

Alwakid, W. N., Dahri, N. A., Humayun, M., & Alwakid, G. N. (2025). Exploring the role of AI and teacher competencies on instructional planning and student performance in an Outcome-Based Education System. *Systems, 13*(7), 517. DOI: 10.3390/systems13070517

Al-Zahrani, A. M., & Alasmari, T. M. (2025). A comprehensive analysis of AI adoption, implementation strategies, and challenges in higher education across the Middle East and North Africa (MENA) region. *Education and Information Technologies*, •••, 1–51.

Alzoubi, A. (2021). The impact of process quality and quality control on organizational competitiveness at 5-star hotels in Dubai. International Journal of Technology [IJTIM]. *Innovation and Management, 1*(1), 54–68.

Amka, A. (2020). Teacher attitude for better education: The relationship between affection, support and religiosity in the success of inclusive education. *Talent Development & Excellence, 12*(1), 1894–1909. https://doi.org/DOI: 10.35542/osf.io/qxeby

Anastasopoulou, E., Konstantina, G., Tsagri, A., Schoina, I., Travlou, C., Mitroyanni, E., & Lyrintzi, T. (2024). The impact of digital technologies on formative assessment and the learning experience. *Technium Education and Humanities, 10*, 115–126. DOI: 10.47577/teh.v10i.12113

Anggrisia, N. F., Basori, B., Mubarok, H., & Degaf, A. (2024). Empowering madrasah teachers in Mojokerto through AI-based applications: Enhancing teaching competence and classroom engagement. *Journal of Social Outreach, 3*(2), 130–141. DOI: 10.15548/jso.v3i2.9895

Ateeq, A., Alzoraiki, M., Milhem, M., Beshr, B. A. H., & Al Meer, S. (2024). Does Information Communication Technology Has Influence on Quality University Education on Gulf University: Literature Review. *The AI Revolution: Driving Business Innovation and Research, 1*, 565–574.

Aung, P. S., & Sakurai, R. (2023). Factors influencing teachers' attitudes towards inclusive education in Myanmar. *World Journal of Educational Research (Los Angeles, Calif.), 10*(3), 24–39. DOI: 10.22158/wjer.v10n3p24

Ayed, I. A. H. (2022). *Oman higher education institutions dealing with artificial intelligence* (Doctoral dissertation, Universidade do Minho (Portugal)).

Azem Qashou, A. M., Bahar, N., & Mohamed, H. (2025). Qualitative Exploration of Data Security Risks in Mobile Cloud Computing for Higher Education. *Security and Privacy, 8*(2), e70001.

Azmi, S., Iahad, N. A., & Ahmad, N. (2015). Gamification in online collaborative learning for programming courses: A literature review. *Journal of Engineering and Applied Sciences (Asian Research Publishing Network), 10*(23), 1–3.

Azzam, A., & Charles, T. (2024). A Review of Artificial Intelligence in K-12 Education. *Open Journal of Applied Sciences, 14*, 2088–2100. DOI: 10.4236/ojapps.2024.148137

Azzam, A., & Charles, T. (2025). K-12 STEM Teachers' Experiences with Artificial Intelligence. *TEM Journal, 14*(1), 463-468. https://doi.org/DOI: 10.18421/TEM141-41

Badoi-Hammami, M. (2023). The reality of practical training programs for teachers in light of technological development and continuous modern innovations: Challenges and opportunities. *Journal Plus Education, 33*(Special Issue), 165–180. DOI: 10.24250/jpe/si/2023/mbh

Bai, L. Y., Li, Z. Y., Wu, W. X., Liu, L. Y., Chen, S. P., Zhang, J., & Zhu, J. N. Y. (2022). Student-Teacher Relationship: Its Measurement and Effect on Students' Trait, Performance, and Wellbeing in Private College. *Frontiers in Psychology, 13*, 793483. DOI: 10.3389/fpsyg.2022.793483 PMID: 35360560

Bakker, A. B., & Demerouti, E. (2017). Job demands-resources theory: Taking stock and looking forward. *Journal of Occupational Health Psychology, 22*(3), 273–285. DOI: 10.1037/ocp0000056 PMID: 27732008

Bálint-Svella, É. (2021). Prospective Preschool and Primary School Teachers' Knowledge and Opinion about Gamification. *Acta Didactica Napocensia, 14*(1), 104–114.

Bandura, A. (1997). *Self-efficacy: The exercise of control*. W. H. Freeman.

Barahona Mora, A. (2020). Gamification for classroom management: An implementation using classdojo. *Sustainability*, *12*(22), 9371. DOI: 10.3390/su12229371

Barua, P. D., Vicnesh, J., Gururajan, R., Oh, S. L., Palmer, E., Azizan, M. M., & Acharya, U. R. (2022). Artificial intelligence-enabled personalised assistive tools to enhance education of children with neurodevelopmental disorders—A review. *International Journal of Environmental Research and Public Health*, *19*(3), 1192. DOI: 10.3390/ijerph19031192 PMID: 35162220

Bashir, A., Nomaan, S., & Hysaj, A. (2025). Generative AI in education: Exploring EAP faculty perspectives at a multicultural UAE university. In Coman, A., & Vasilache, S. (Eds.), Lecture Notes in Computer Science: Vol. 15786. *HCII 2025* (pp. 125–140). Springer., DOI: 10.1007/978-3-031-93539-8_9

Batonghinog, P. J., & Chavez, J. C. (2025). Professional development training and academic support: Predictors of teachers' confidence in curriculum change. *Journal of Interdisciplinary Perspectives*, *3*(7). Advance online publication. DOI: 10.69569/jip.2025.327

Baule, S. M., & O'Connell, J. S. (2024). Harnessing generative AI for educator professional development. *Advances in educational technologies and instructional design book series*, 77-114. https://doi.org/DOI: 10.4018/979-8-3373-1017-6.ch003

Bauml, M., & Kyzar, K. (2025). "I can do this!" How early childhood teacher education influences preservice teachers' confidence for teaching. *Journal of Early Childhood Teacher Education*. Advance online publication. DOI: 10.1080/10901027.2024.2439869

Baxter, G., & Sommerville, I. (2011). Socio-technical systems: From design methods to systems engineering. *Interacting with Computers*, *23*(1), 4–17. DOI: 10.1016/j.intcom.2010.07.003

Baytiyeh, H. (2022). Artificial intelligence and the future of higher education in the Arab world. *International Journal of Educational Development*, *89*, 102550. DOI: 10.1016/j.ijedudev.2021.102550

Benjamin, R. (2019). *Race after technology: Abolitionist tools for the new Jim Code*. Polity Press.

Berente, N., Gu, B., Recker, J., & Santhanam, R. (2021). Managing artificial intelligence. *Management Information Systems Quarterly*, *45*(3), 1433–1450. DOI: 10.25300/MISQ/2021/16274

Berg, D. D. (2022). Over 40 years of teacher self-efficacy research. In *Oxford handbook of self-efficacy*. Oxford University Press., DOI: 10.1093/oxfordhb/9780199841332.013.30

Bernstein, B. (1971). Class, codes and control: Vol. 1. *Theoretical studies towards a sociology of language*. Routledge & Kegan Paul.

Bhattarai, K., & Yousef, M. (2025). Education challenges and opportunities. The Middle East: Past, Present, and Future, 255-266.

Bicen, H., & Kocakoyun, S. (2018). Perceptions of students for gamification approach: Kahoot as a case study. *International Journal of Emerging Technologies in Learning, 13*(2).

Bilgin, C. U., & Gul, A. (2020). Investigating the effectiveness of gamification on group cohesion, attitude, and academic achievement in collaborative learning environments. *TechTrends, 64*(1), 124–136.

Blodgett, S. L., Barocas, S., Daumé, H., & Wallach, H. (2020). Language (Technology) is Power: A Critical Survey of "Bias" in NLP. *arXiv*. DOI: 10.48550/arXiv.2005.14050

Bohlens, C. (2025). Corruption in accreditation at HEIs: when corruption erodes trust in higher learning. In *Navigating Quality Assurance and Accreditation in Global Higher Education* (pp. 165–192). IGI Global Scientific Publishing.

Bone, E. K., & Bouck, E. C. (2017). Accessible text-to-speech options for students who struggle with reading. *Preventing School Failure, 61*(1), 48–55. DOI: 10.1080/1045988x.2016.1188366

Borja-Tomás, C., Ríos-Jiménez, M. A., & García-Jiménez, M. (2025). *Actitudes del profesorado universitario que predicen el desarrollo de una buena práctica educativa: Una revisión sistemática*. European Public & Social Innovation Review., DOI: 10.31637/epsir-2025-1799

Borji, A. (2023). A categorical archive of ChatGPT failures. *arXiv*. DOI: 10.48550/arxiv.2302.03494

Boubker, O. (2024). From chatting to self-educating: Can AI tools boost student learning outcomes? *Expert Systems with Applications, 238*, 121820. DOI: 10.1016/j.eswa.2023.121820

Boudihaj, A., & Sahli, M. (2022). Education in the MENA Region. In World Education Patterns in the Global South: The Ebb of Global Forces and the Flow of Contextual Imperatives (pp. 19-41). Emerald Publishing Limited.

Bowen, G. A. (2009). Document analysis as a qualitative research method. *Qualitative Research Journal*, *9*(2), 27–40.

Braun, V., & Clarke, V. (2006). Using thematic analysis in psychology. *Qualitative Research in Psychology*, *3*(2), 77–101. DOI: 10.1191/1478088706qp063oa

Braun, V., & Clarke, V. (2019). Reflecting on reflexive thematic analysis. *Qualitative Research in Sport, Exercise and Health*, *11*(4), 589–597.

Braun, V., & Clarke, V. (2023). Toward good practice in thematic analysis: Avoiding common problems and be(com)ing a knowing researcher. *International Journal of Transgender Health*, *24*(1), 1–6. DOI: 10.1080/26895269.2022.2129597 PMID: 36713144

Broadbent, J., Panadero, E., Lodge, J. M., & Fuller-Tyszkiewicz, M. (2023). The self-regulation for learning online (SRL-O) questionnaire. *Metacognition and Learning*, *18*(1), 135–163. DOI: 10.1007/s11409-022-09319-6 PMID: 36065225

Bronfenbrenner, U. (1979). *The ecology of human development: Experiments by nature and design*. Harvard University Press.

Buckner, E. (2021). *Degrees of dignity: Arab higher education in the global era*. University of Toronto Press.

Buell, S., Langdon, P. E., Pounds, G., & Bunning, K. (2020). An open randomized controlled trial of the effects of linguistic simplification and mediation on the comprehension of "easy read" text by people with intellectual disabilities. *Journal of Applied Research in Intellectual Disabilities*, *33*(2), 219–231. DOI: 10.1111/jar.12666 PMID: 31652030

Calonge, D. S., Kamalov, F., Aguerrebere, P. M., Hassock, L., Smail, L., Yousef, D., Thadani, D. R., Kwong, T., & Abdulla, N. (2025). Upskilling and reskilling in the United Arab Emirates: Future-proofing careers with AI skills. *Journal of Adult and Continuing Education*. DOI: 10.1177/14779714251315288

Casal-Otero, L., Catala, A., Fernández-Morante, C., Taboada, M., & Cebreiro, B. (2023). AI literacy in K-12: A systematic literature review. *International Journal of STEM Education*, *10*(1). Advance online publication. DOI: 10.1186/s40594-023-00418-7

CAST (2018). Universal Design for Learning Guidelines version 2.2.

CAST. (2018). *Universal Design for Learning Guidelines version 2.2*. https://udlguidelines.cast.org/

Ch, A. H. (2019). Relationship between teachers' attitude and college students' learning. *Research on Humanities and Social Sciences*, *9*(3), 23–30.

Chaaban, Y., Qadhi, S., Chen, J., & Du, X. (2024). Understanding researchers' AI readiness in a higher education context: Q methodology research. *Education Sciences*, *14*(7), 709. DOI: 10.3390/educsci14070709

Chang, C. I., & Choi, W. C. (2025). Exploring Challenges and Opportunities in Artificial Intelligence (AI) Literacy and Educational AI Development: A Qualitative Study of Teachers and Researchers' Perspectives. *Perspectives*. DOI: 10.20944/preprints202508.1077.v1

Charles, R., & Charles, T. (2024). High school students' perceptions of using AI for learning. *Voice of the Publisher*, *10*, 284–297. DOI: 10.4236/vp.2024.103024

Charles, T. (2022). The past, present, and future of assessments in the higher education sector. In Hill, C., Lamie, J., & Gore, T. (Eds.), *The evolution of transnational education* (pp. 126–136). Routledge., DOI: 10.4324/9781003225386

Charles, T. (2025). AI in Professional Development for English Language Teachers. In Ali, M., Anwar, M., Fazal, S., & Ayyaz, S. (Eds.), *AI Applications for English Language Learning* (pp. 73–92). IGI Global Scientific Publishing., DOI: 10.4018/979-8-3693-9077-1.ch004

Charles, T., & Hill, C. (2025). Micro-credentials and AI in higher education: Transforming professional development. In ElSayary, A. (Ed.), *Prompt engineering and generative AI applications for teaching and learning* (pp. 1–14). IGI Global Scientific Publishing., DOI: 10.4018/979-8-3693-7332-3.ch001

Charles, T., & Papadaki, M. (2025). Ethical Leadership in Technology Integration and Digital Education. In Soles, B., & Meyerott, T. (Eds.), *Diverse Leadership Perspectives in Education: From K-12 to Higher Education* (pp. 437–454). IGI Global Scientific Publishing., DOI: 10.4018/979-8-3693-6115-3.ch016

Charles, T., Zoelfakar, S., & Sebastian, S. (2025). Micro-Credentials in Vocational and Professional Training. In *Integrating Micro-Credentials With AI in Open Education* (pp. 217–250). IGI Global Scientific Publishing., DOI: 10.4018/979-8-3693-5488-9.ch010

Chelliah, P. R., Jayasankar, V., Agerstam, M., Sundaravadivazhagan, B., & Cyriac, R. (2023). *The power of artificial intelligence for the next-generation oil and gas industry: Envisaging AI-inspired intelligent energy systems and environments*. John Wiley & Sons.

Chen, L., Chen, P., & Lin, Z. (2020). Artificial intelligence in education: A review. *IEEE Access : Practical Innovations, Open Solutions*, *8*, 75264–75278.

Chen, X., Xie, H., Zou, D., & Hwang, G. J. (2020). Application and theory gaps during the rise of artificial intelligence in education. *Computers and Education: Artificial Intelligence*, *1*, 100002.

Chen, X., Zou, D., Xie, H., Cheng, G., & Liu, C. (2022). Two decades of artificial intelligence in education. *Journal of Educational Technology & Society*, *25*(1), 28–47.

Chiang, C., & Lee, H. (2023). Can large language models be an alternative to human evaluations? *arXiv*. DOI: 10.48550/arxiv.2305.01937

Choi-Lundberg, D. L., Butler-Henderson, K., Harman, K., & Crawford, J. (2023). A systematic review of digital innovations in technology-enhanced learning designs in higher education. *Australasian Journal of Educational Technology*, *39*(3), 133–162. DOI: 10.14742/ajet.7615

Choi, W. C., Chang, C. I., Choi, I. C., Lam, L. C., Leong, K. I., & Ng, S. I. (2025). Artificial Intelligence (AI) Literacy in Education: Definition, Competencies, Opportunities and Challenges. *Preprints*. DOI: 10.20944/preprints202508.0497.v1

Collie, R. J. (2023). The Tripartite Occupational Well-Being Scale: Evidence of Validity Among Teachers. *Journal of Psychoeducational Assessment*, *42*(1), 46–59. DOI: 10.1177/07342829231202313

Contractor, R., & Reyes, D. (2025). Generative AI in higher education: Evidence from an elite college. *arXiv*. https://arxiv.org/abs/2508.00717

Corbin, T., Bearman, M., Boud, D., & Dawson, P. (2025). The wicked problem of AI and assessment. *Assessment & Evaluation in Higher Education*, •••, 1–17. DOI: 10.1080/02602938.2025.2553340

Corbin, T., Dawson, P., Nicola-Richmond, K., & Partridge, H. (2025). 'Where's the line? It's an absurd line': Towards a framework for acceptable uses of AI in assessment. *Assessment & Evaluation in Higher Education*, •••, 1–13. DOI: 10.1080/02602938.2025.2456207

Cordero, J., Torres-Zambrano, J., & Cordero-Castillo, A. (2024). Integration of generative artificial intelligence in higher education: Best practices. *Education Sciences*, *15*(1), 32–32. DOI: 10.3390/educsci15010032

Crawford, K. (2021). *Atlas of AI: Power, politics, and the planetary costs of artificial intelligence*. Yale University Press.

Creswell, J. W. (2013). *Qualitative inquiry and research design: Choosing among five approaches* (3rd ed.). SAGE Publications.

Curren, R., Boniwell, I., Ryan, R. M., Oades, L., Brighouse, H., Unterhalter, E., Kristjánsson, K., de Ruyter, D., Macleod, C., Morris, I., & White, M. (2024). Finding consensus on well-being in education. *Theory and Research in Education*, *22*(2), 117–157. DOI: 10.1177/14778785241259852

D'Amico, F., Lancioni, G. E., De Marinis, F., Abbinante, F., Taurisano, P., Abbatantuono, C., & Alberti, G. (2023). A simple smartphone-aided program to support meaningful occupation in people with severe neuro-motor and speech disabilities. *International Journal of Rehabilitation Research. Internationale Zeitschrift fur Rehabilitationsforschung. Revue Internationale de Recherches de Readaptation*, *46*(2), 205–208. DOI: 10.1097/mrr.0000000000000583 PMID: 37039592

D'Mello, S., & Kory, J. (2015). A review and meta-analysis of multimodal affect detection systems. *ACM Computing Surveys*, *47*(3), 1–36. DOI: 10.1145/2682899

Dabis, A., & Csáki, C. (2024). AI and ethics: Investigating the first policy responses of higher education institutions to the challenge of generative AI. *Humanities & Social Sciences Communications*, *11*(1), 1–13. DOI: 10.1057/s41599-024-03526-z

Dai, R., Thomas, M. K. E., & Rawolle, S. (2025). The roles of AI and educational leaders in AI-assisted administrative decision-making: A proposed framework for symbiotic collaboration. *Australian Educational Researcher*, *52*, 1471–1487. DOI: 10.1007/s13384-024-00771-8

Daskalaki, E., Psaroudaki, K., & Fragopoulou, P. (2024). Navigating the future of education: Educators' insights on AI integration and challenges in Greece, Hungary, Latvia, Ireland, and Armenia. https://doi.org//arxiv.2408.15686DOI: 10.48550

Davis, F. D. (1989). Perceived usefulness, perceived ease of use, and user acceptance of information technology. *Management Information Systems Quarterly*, *13*(3), 319–340. DOI: 10.2307/249008

Dawson, P., Bearman, M., Dollinger, M., & Boud, D. (2024). Validity matters more than cheating. *Assessment & Evaluation in Higher Education*, *49*(7), 1005–1016. DOI: 10.1080/02602938.2024.2386662

Deci, E. L., & Ryan, R. M. (2000). The "what" and "why" of goal pursuits: Human needs and the self-determination of behavior. *Psychological Inquiry*, *11*(4), 227–268.

Demaidi, M. N. (2025). Artificial intelligence national strategy in a developing country. *AI & Society*, *40*(2), 423–435.

Department for Education. (2013). *National curriculum in England: Computing programmes of study*.https://assets.publishing.service.gov.uk/government/uploads/system/uploads/attachment_data/file/239033/PRIMARY_national_curriculum_-_Computing.pdf

Dichev, C., & Dicheva, D. (2017). Gamifying education: what is known, what is believed and what remains uncertain: a critical review. *International Journal of Educational Technology in Higher Education, 14*, 1–36. DOI: 10.1186/s41239-017-0042-5

Ding, A. E., Shi, L., Yang, H., & Choi, I. (2024). Enhancing teacher AI literacy and integration through different types of cases in teacher professional development. *Computers and Education Open*. Advance online publication. DOI: 10.1016/j.caeo.2024.100178

Dreer, B. (2023). On the outcomes of teacher wellbeing: A systematic review of research. *Frontiers in Education, 14*, 1205179. Advance online publication. DOI: 10.3389/fpsyg.2023.1205179 PMID: 37575417

Dweck, C. S. (2006). *Mindset: The new psychology of success*. Random House.

Dwork, C., & Roth, A. (2014). The algorithmic foundations of Differential Privacy. *Foundations and Trends in Theoretical Computer Science*, *9*(3–4), 211–407. DOI: 10.1561/0400000042

Echave, J. A., Donato, V. J. P., & Acosta, O. D. (2024). Embracing generative AI in education: Exploring teachers' perceptions, practices, and potential impact. *Jurnal Pendidikan Indonesia Gemilang*, *4*(2), 211–232. DOI: 10.53889/jpig.v4i2.458

Ehtiwesh, I., & Maousa, O. (2023). Examining Perceptions of Academic And Support Staff on Quality Assurance Accreditation in Higher Education in Developing Nations. *Education & Youth Research*, *3*(2), 76–86.

El-Kassas, M., Khalifa, R., Medhat, M. A., Yilmaz, Y., Tumi, A., Labidi, A., & AlNaamani, K. M. (2025). Mapping artificial intelligence adoption in hepatology practice and research: Challenges and opportunities in MENA region. *Frontiers in Medicine*, *12*, 1630831. PMID: 41020250

Elsawah, W., & Charles, T. (2023). Investigating Emirati Students' Practices of Learning Block-Based Programming in an Online Learning Context: Evidence from a UAE National Program. In *BUiD Doctoral Research Conference 2022: Multidisciplinary Studies* (pp. 131-142). Cham: Springer Nature Switzerland. DOI: 10.1007/978-3-031-27462-6_12

Eriksson, A. K. (2024). Absent the silently invisible: Rethinking model victimhood under the “Comfort Women” system. *Hypatia*, •••, 1–15.

Eroglu, C., & Ünlü, H. (2015). Self-efficacy: Its effects on physical education teacher candidates’ attitudes toward the teaching profession. *Kuram ve Uygulamada Eğitim Bilimleri, 15*(1), 201–212. DOI: 10.12738/ESTP.2015.1.2282

Escalante, J., Pack, A., & Barrett, A. (2023). AI-generated feedback on writing: Insights into efficacy and ENL student preference. *International Journal of Educational Technology in Higher Education, 20*(1). Advance online publication. DOI: 10.1186/s41239-023-00425-2

Estaiteyeh, M., & McQuirter, R. (2024). Generative or degenerative?! Implications of AI tools in pre-service teacher education and reflections on instructors’ professional development. *Brock Education Journal, 33*(3). Advance online publication. DOI: 10.26522/brocked.v33i3.1176

Evangelista, E. D. L. (2025). Ensuring academic integrity in the age of ChatGPT: Rethinking exam design, assessment strategies, and ethical AI policies in higher education. *Contemporary Educational Technology, 17*(1), ep559. DOI: 10.30935/cedtech/15775

Evmenova, A. S., & Regan, K. (2019). Supporting the writing process with technology for students with disabilities. *Intervention in School and Clinic, 55*(2), 78–85. DOI: 10.1177/1053451219837636

Eze, I. F. (2022). Framework for critical thinking among internal auditing students using technology-based educational intervention (Doctoral dissertation, Cape Peninsula University of Technology).

Fadlelmula, F. K., & Qadhi, S. M. (2024). A systematic review of research on artificial intelligence in higher education: Practice, gaps, and future directions in the GCC. *Journal of University Teaching & Learning Practice, 21*(6), 146–173.

Fahy, L. A. (2022). Regulator reputation and the successful governance of innovation: Lessons from financial technology supervision (Doctoral dissertation, Utrecht University).

Faisal, R. (2025). Ethical AI integration in education: Policies, challenges, and strategies for bridging digital divides in emerging economies. *Crossroads of Social Inquiry, 1*(2), 1–18. DOI: 10.64851/csi.v1i2.28

Federiakin, D., Molerov, D., Zlatkin-Troitschanskaia, O., & Maur, A. (2024). Prompt engineering as a new 21st century skill. *Frontiers in Education, 9*. Advance online publication. DOI: 10.3389/feduc.2024.1366434

Felix, J. A., & Webb, L. (2024). Use of artificial intelligence in education delivery and assessment. DOI: 10.58248/pn712

Fichten, C., Pickup, D., Asunsion, J., Jorgensen, M., Vo, C., Legault, A., & Libman, E. (2022). State of the research on artificial intelligence based apps for post-secondary students with disabilities. *Exceptionality Education International, 31*(1), 62–76. DOI: 10.5206/eei.v31i1.14089

Finnish National Agency for Education. (2016). National core curriculum for basic education 2014 [). Finnish National Board of Education.]. *Publications, 2016*, 5.

Floridi, L., Cowls, J., Beltrametti, M., Chatila, R., Chazerand, P., Dignum, V., Luetge, C., Madelin, R., Pagallo, U., Rossi, F., Schafer, B., Valcke, P., & Vayena, E. (2018). AI4People, an ethical framework for a good AI Society: Opportunities, Risks, principles, and recommendations. *Minds and Machines, 28*(4), 689–707. DOI: 10.1007/s11023-018-9482-5 PMID: 30930541

Fredricks, J. A., Blumenfeld, P. C., & Paris, A. H. (2004). School Engagement: Potential of the Concept, State of the Evidence. *Review of Educational Research, 74*(1), 59–109. DOI: 10.3102/00346543074001059

Fullan, M. (2016). *The new meaning of educational change*. Teachers college press.

Fundi, M., Sanusi, I. T., Oyelere, S. S., & Ayere, M. (2024). Advancing AI education: Assessing Kenyan in-service teachers' preparedness for integrating artificial intelligence in competence-based curriculum. *Computers in Human Behavior Reports*. Advance online publication. DOI: 10.1016/j.chbr.2024.100412

Gaad, E., Arif, M., & Scott, F. (2006). Systems analysis of the UAE education system. *International Journal of Educational Management, 20*(4), 291–303. DOI: 10.1108/09513540610665405

Gal, D. (2019). Coding for fun or for the future? RSIS Commentary. S. Rajaratnam School of International Studies.

Gambo, O., Adelokun, A., Gambo, I., & Afolayan, A. (2021). Planning Effective Learning for the Visually Impaired in Federal University in Osun State, Nigeria: Technology Perspective. *Malaysian Online Journal of Educational Technology, 9*(1), 80–96. DOI: 10.17220/mojet.2021.9.1.250

Garg, S., & Sharma, S. (2020). Impact of artificial intelligence in special need education to promote inclusive pedagogy. *International Journal of Information and Education Technology (IJIET), 10*(7), 523–527. DOI: 10.18178/ijiet.2020.10.7.1418

Gavora, P., Pacholík, V., Navrátilová, H., & Puhrová, B. P. (2024). Self-efficacy učitelů 1. stupně základní školy: Zdroje jeho zlepšení. *Orbis Scholae*. Advance online publication. https://doi.org/DOI: 10.14712/23363177.2024.13

Gelişli, Y., Kazykhankyzy, L., & Göksu, D. Y. (2024). Development of "Teachers' Attitude Scale Towards Students": Validity and reliability analysis. *Gazi Eğitim Fakültesi Dergisi*, *44*(3), 2009–2027. DOI: 10.17152/gefad.1534467

Giannakos, M., Azevedo, R., Brusilovsky, P., Cukurova, M., Dimitriadis, Y., Hernandez-Leo, D., & Rienties, B. (2024). The promise and challenges of generative AI in education. *Behaviour & Information Technology*, *44*(11), 2518–2544. DOI: 10.1080/0144929X.2024.2394886

Gocen, A., & Aydemir, F. (2020). Artificial intelligence in education and schools. *Research on Education and Media*, *12*(1), 13–21.

Godwin-Jones, R., O'Neill, E., & Ranalli, J. (2024). Integrating AI tools into instructed second language acquisition. In Chapelle, C. A., Beckett, G. H., & Ranalli, J. (Eds.), *Exploring artificial intelligence in applied linguistics* (pp. 9–23). Iowa State University Digital Press., DOI: 10.31274/isudp.2024.154.02

Goldman, S. R., Carreon, A., Smith, S. J., & Kurth, J. (2023). Exploring and implementing available writing educational technology for students with disabilities and their peers. *Journal of Special Education Technology*, *38*(4), 563–572. DOI: 10.1177/01626434231155933

Gouseti, A., James, F., Fallin, L., & Burden, K. (2024). The ethics of using AI in K–12 education: A systematic literature review. *Technology, Pedagogy and Education*, •••, 1–22. Advance online publication. DOI: 10.1080/1475939X.2024.2428601

Government, U. A. E. (2017). *UAE Strategy for Artificial Intelligence.* https://u.ae/en/about-the-uae/strategies-initiatives-and-awards/strategies-plans-and-visions/government-services-and-digital-transformation/uae-strategy-for-artificial-intelligence

Government, U. A. E. (2024) '*UAE National Strategy for Artificial Intelligence 2031*'. Retrieved November 08, 2025, from https://ai.gov.ae/strategy

Grove, M. (2025). *It's time we moved the generative AI conversation on - HEPI*. HEPI. Retrieved November 29, 2025, from https://www.hepi.ac.uk/2025/07/16/its-time-we-moved-the-generative-ai-conversation-on/

Guest, G., Namey, E., Taylor, J., Eley, N., & McKenna, K. (2017). Comparing focus groups and individual interviews: Findings from a randomized study. *International Journal of Social Research Methodology, 20*(6), 693–708. DOI: 10.1080/13645579.2017.1281601

Gutierrez Jr, R. (2024). Ethical Horizons in AI: Navigating Opportunities and Upholding Values in the MENA Landscape. *Volume (2). Maǧalla al-Nūr li-l-dirāsāt al-insāniyya .. doi: . v2*, (4).DOI: <ALIGNMENT.qj></ALIGNMENT>10.69513/jnfh

Halinen, I. (2018). The new educational curriculum in Finland. *Improving the quality of childhood in Europe, 7*, 75-89.

Hämäläinen, R., Nissinen, K., Mannonen, J., Lämsä, J., Leino, K., & Taajamo, M. (2021). Understanding teaching professionals' digital competence: What do PIAAC and TALIS reveal about technology-related skills, attitudes, and knowledge? *Computers in Human Behavior, 117*, 106672. DOI: 10.1016/j.chb.2020.106672

Hamed, A. E., & Ismael, B. B. (2024). AI-Driven Opportunistic Learning: Enhancing Personalized Educational Experiences for Arab Learners in the MENA Region. *Journal of Scientific Development for Studies and Research (JSD), 5*(20), 206_225-206_225.

Hands, L. (2025). Just (ifying) algorithms: Data-driven automated predictions about unobservable targets and the General Data Protection Regulation (Doctoral dissertation).

Hardwick-Morris, M. (2022). Secondary school teachers' attitudes towards the teaching profession. *The Research Probe, 2*(1). Advance online publication. DOI: 10.53378/352893

Hill, C., Abu-Ayyash, E., & Charles, T. (2023). By nature, a social animal: An exploration of perceptions of online group work. *Cambridge Journal of Education, 53*(5), 665–681. DOI: 10.1080/0305764X.2023.2206795

Hojeij, Z., Kuhail, M. A., & ElSayary, A. (2024). Investigating in-service teachers' views on ChatGPT integration. *Interactive Technology and Smart Education*. Advance online publication. DOI: 10.1108/itse-04-2024-0094

Holmes, W. (2020). Artificial intelligence in education. In *Encyclopedia of education and information technologies* (pp. 88–103). Springer International Publishing.

Holmes, W., Porayska-Pomsta, K., Holstein, K., Sutherland, E., Baker, T., Shum, S. B., & Koedinger, K. R. (2022). Ethics of AI in education: Towards a community-wide framework. *International Journal of Artificial Intelligence in Education, 32*(3), 504–526.

Holm, J. L. (2025). Developing mathematics teacher confidence through increasing understanding of mathematics. *Open Access Government, 45*(1), 290–291. DOI: 10.56367/oag-045-11870

Holzmann, P., Schwarz, E. J., & Audretsch, D. B. (2020). Understanding the determinants of novel technology adoption among teachers: The case of 3D printing. *The Journal ofTechnology Transfer, 45*(1), 259–275. DOI: 10.1007/S10961-018-9693-1

Hossain, Z., Alwreikat, A., Khan, G. A., Alotaibi, F. A., Biswas, M. S., & Sbeity, F. (2025). AI Literacy and Perception Among Library and Information Science Students in South Asia and the Middle East. *Science & Technology Libraries*, •••, 1–21. DOI: 10.1080/0194262X.2025.2484280

Howard, J. L., Bureau, J., Guay, F., Chong, J. X., & Ryan, R. M. (2021). Student motivation and associated outcomes: A meta-analysis from self-determination theory. *Perspectives on Psychological Science, 16*(6), 1300–1323. DOI: 10.1177/1745691620966789 PMID: 33593153

Hoy, A. W. (2022). Gaining efficacy with experience: From teacher education to classroom practice. In *Oxford research encyclopedia of education*. Routledge., DOI: 10.4324/9781138609877-ree19-1

Hua, S., Mansor, A. N., & Jamaludin, K. A. (2025). Teachers' self-efficacy beliefs in China: A literature review (2015–2025). *Deleted Journal, 4*, 456. Advance online publication. DOI: 10.56294/mw2025456

Huma, T., Ahmed, S., Mahmood, W., Khan, A., Afridi, A. K., Huma, T., Ahmed, S., Mahmood, W., Khan, A., & Afridi, A. K. (2025). AI adoption in Higher Education: A Comparative study of Institutional readiness and challenges. *Social Science Review Archives., 3*(4), 304–312. DOI: 10.70670/sra.v3i4.1117

Hurakadli, B. M. (2015). *Relationship between attitude towards the teaching profession and teachers' self-efficacy beliefs* [Unpublished manuscript].

Hur, J. W. (2024). Fostering AI literacy: Overcoming concerns and nurturing confidence among preservice teachers. *Information and Learning Science*. Advance online publication. DOI: 10.1108/ils-11-2023-0170

Huyen, N. T., Lien, N. P., & Thuy, P. T. (2025). Challenges of AI In education: A systematic review. IOSR. *Journal of Research & Method in Education, 15*(3), 37–46. https://www.iosrjournals.org/iosr-jrme/papers/Vol-15%20Issue-3/Ser-1/F1503013746.pdf

Hwang, G. J., Xie, H., Wah, B. W., & Gašević, D. (2020). Vision, challenges, roles and research issues of Artificial Intelligence in Education. *Computers and Education: Artificial Intelligence, 1*, 100001.

Ivchyk, V. (2024). Breaking through obstacles to AI selection in management. Collection of scientific papers «SCIENTIA», (December 20, 2024; Chicago, USA), 39-48.

Jaleel, B., & Saber, H. (2025). The United Arab Emirates as an International Education Hub: Assessing Progress Toward a Knowledge-Based Economy. *Journal of Studies in International Education*. Advance online publication. DOI: 10.1177/10283153251364511

James, M., Besaw, J., & Jimenez, B. (2018). Using 3-D Printed Objects to Increase Comprehension for Students with Severe Disability. *Global Journal of Intellectual & Developmental Disabilities, 5*(2), 27–32. DOI: 10.19080/gjidd.2018.05.555658

Jennings, P. A., & Greenberg, M. T. (2009). The prosocial classroom: Teacher social and emotional competence in relation to student and classroom outcomes. *Review of Educational Research, 79*, 491–525. DOI: 10.3102/0034654308325693

Jeno, L. M., Vandvik, V., Eliassen, S., & Grytnes, J. A. (2019). Testing the novelty effect of an m-learning tool on internalization and achievement: A Self-Determination Theory approach. *Computers & Education, 128*, 398–413. DOI: 10.1016/j.compedu.2018.10.008

Ji, Y., Zhong, M., Lyu, S., Li, T., Niu, S., & Zhan, Z. (2025). How does AI literacy affect individual innovative behavior: The mediating role of psychological need satisfaction, creative self-efficacy, and self-regulated learning. *Education and Information Technologies, 30*(11), 16133–16162. DOI: 10.1007/s10639-025-13437-4

Jobin, A., Ienca, M., & Vayena, E. (2019). The global landscape of AI ethics guidelines. *Nature Machine Intelligence, 1*(9), 389–399. DOI: 10.1038/s42256-019-0088-2

Julaihi, N. H., Ying, L. C., Li, V. L., & Bakri, S. R. A. (2020). Confidence level and self-efficacy beliefs of mathematics teachers: Evidence from Sarawak. *International Journal of Social and Management Studies, 4*(2), 1–23. DOI: 10.24191/IJSMS.V4I2.8145

Kaarakainen, M.-T., Kaarakainen, S.-S., Tanhua-Piiroinen, E., Viteli, J., Syvänen, A., & Kivinen, A. (2017). *Digiajan peruskoulu 2017 – tilannearvio ja toimenpidesuositukset* [Comprehensive school digitalisation: Status review and recommendations for action for 2017]. Prime Minister's Office.

Kamalov, F., Santandreu Calonge, D., & Gurrib, I. (2023). New era of artificial intelligence in education: Towards a sustainable multifaceted revolution. *Sustainability, 15*(16), 12451.

Kapp, K. M. (2012). *The gamification of learning and instruction: Game-based methods and strategies for training and education*. Pfeiffer.

Kasepalu, R., Prieto, L. P., Ley, T., & Chejara, P. (2022). Teacher artificial intelligence-supported pedagogical actions in collaborative learning coregulation: A wizard-of-oz study. [). Frontiers Media SA.]. *Frontiers in Education, 7*, 736194.

Kassir, H. A. N. (2022). Neoliberal Globalization, Education Policies and Strategies Adopted in Science Curriculum Reform in the United Arab Emirates: A Case Study Based on the Views of Ministry of Educat ion Stakeholders (Doctoral dissertation, The University of Liverpool (United Kingdom)).

Kavitha, K. (2014). *Attitude of secondary school teachers*. [Unpublished manuscript].

Kayyali, M. (2025 A). AI in Higher Education: Revolutionizing Curriculum and Administration. In AI Adoption and Diffusion in Education (pp. 31-62). IGI Global Scientific Publishing.

Kayyali, M. (2025 B). Ethical Implications of Generative AI in Education: Privacy, Bias, and Integrity. In Transformative AI Practices for Personalized Learning Strategies (pp. 185-218). IGI Global Scientific Publishing.

Kayyali, M. (2025 C). The Future of AI in Education: Predictions and Emerging Trends. Next-Generation AI Methodologies in Education, 367-406.

Kayyali, M. (2026). The Impact of AI on Classroom Dynamics in Higher Education: Shifting Roles for Professors and Students. In Responsible AI Integration in Education (pp. 151-180). IGI Global Scientific Publishing.

Kayyali, M. (2024). *Quality assurance and accreditation in higher education: issues, models, and best practices*. Springer Nature.

Kazempour, M. (2014). The interrelationship of science experiences, beliefs, attitudes, and self-efficacy: A case study of a pre-service teacher with positive science attitude and high science teaching self-efficacy. *Journal of Education and Learning, 8*(1), 51–64. DOI: 10.11591/EDULEARN.V8I1.205

Kern, M., Waters, L. E., Adler, A., & White, M. A. (2015). A multidimensional approach to measuring well-being in students: Application of the PERMA Framework. *The Journal of Positive Psychology*, *10*, 262–271. DOI: 10.1080/17439760.2014.936962 PMID: 25745508

Khadragy, S., Selim, N., Hassan, D., Hegazy, A., & Ali, S. (2024). Exploring the effects of using AI technologies in higher education institutions in UAE. *Journal of Curriculum and Teaching*, *13*(5), 10. DOI: 10.5430/jct.v13n5p10

Khalil, H., & Alsenaidi, S. (2024). Teachers' digital competencies for effective AI integration in higher education in Oman. *Journal of Education and e-learning Research*, *11*(4), 698–707. DOI: 10.20448/jeelr.v11i4.6097

Khlaif, Z. N., Ayyoub, A. A., Hamamra, B., Bensalem, E., Mitwally, M. A. A., Ayyoub, A., Hattab, M., & Shadid, F. (2024). University teachers' views on the adoption and integration of generative AI tools for student assessment in higher education. *Education Sciences*, *14*(10), 1090–1090. DOI: 10.3390/educsci14101090

Khosravi, H., Shum, S. B., Chen, G., Conati, C., Tsai, Y. S., Kay, J., ... & Gašević, D. (2022). Explainable artificial intelligence in education. *Computers and education: artificial intelligence, 3*, 100074.

Killingback, C., Tomlinson, A., & Stern, J. (2024). Compassionate pedagogy in higher education: A scoping review. *Journal of University Teaching & Learning Practice*, *21*(10). Advance online publication. DOI: 10.53761/7yvrw787

Kippels, S., & Ridge, N. (2019). The growth and transformation of K–12 education in the UAE. In *Education in the United Arab Emirates* (pp. 37–55). Springer., DOI: 10.1007/978-981-13-7736-5_3

Kırkıç, K. A., & Çetinkaya, F. (2020). The relationship between preschool teachers' self-efficacy beliefs and their teaching attitudes. *International Journal of Evaluation and Research in Education*, *9*(4), 807–815. DOI: 10.11591/ijere.v9i4.20670

Kitzinger, J. (1995). Qualitative Research: Introducing focus groups. *BMJ (Clinical Research Ed.)*, *311*(7000), 299–302. DOI: 10.1136/bmj.311.7000.299 PMID: 7633241

Klimova, B., & Pikhart, M. (2025). Exploring the effects of artificial intelligence on student and academic well-being in Higher Education: A mini-review. *Frontiers in Psychology*, *16*. Advance online publication. DOI: 10.3389/fpsyg.2025.1498132 PMID: 39963679

Knox, J. (2020). Artificial intelligence and education in China. *Learning, Media and Technology*, *45*(3), 298–311.

Koch, K. (2017). Stay in the box! Embedded assistive technology improves access for students with disabilities. *Education Sciences*, *7*(4), 82. DOI: 10.3390/educsci7040082

Korhonen, T., Salo, L., Laakso, N., Seitamaa, A., Sormunen, K., Kukkonen, M., & Forsström, H. (2023). Finnish teachers as adopters of educational innovation: Perceptions of programming as a new part of the curriculum. *Computer Science Education*, *33*(1), 94–116.

Korpershoek, H., Canrinus, E. T., Fokkens-Bruinsma, M., & de Boer, H. (2019). The relationships between school belonging and students' motivational, social-emotional, behavioural, and academic outcomes in secondary education: A meta-analytic review. *Research Papers in Education*, *35*(6), 641–680. DOI: 10.1080/02671522.2019.1615116

Kotamjani, S. S., Shirinova, S., Muratova, K., & Sharma, M. (2024). Exploring Students' Perspectives on Generative AI for Academic Purposes in Uzbekistan's Higher Education. *Association for Computing Machinery*, 986–994. https://doi.org/DOI: 10.1145/3726122.3726266

Krueger, R. A., & Casey, M. A. (2014). *Focus groups: A Practical Guide for Applied Research*. SAGE Publications.

Kurniahtunnisa, K., Manuel, M. Y., Aini, M. S., & Agustina, T. P. (2025). Persepsi dan sikap siswa terhadap penggunaan artificial intelligence. *Scholaria: Jurnal Pendidikan dan Kebudayaan, 15*(1), 47–59. https://doi.org/DOI: 10.24246/j.js.2025.v15.i1.p47-59

Kurtz, G., Amzalag, M., Shaked, N., Zaguri, Y., Kohen-Vacs, D., Gal, E., Zailer, G., & Barak-Medina, E. (2024). Strategies for Integrating Generative AI into Higher Education: Navigating Challenges and Leveraging Opportunities. *Education Sciences*, *14*(5), 503. DOI: 10.3390/educsci14050503

Kuzdeuov, A., Mukayev, O., Nurgaliyev, S., Kunbolsyn, A., & Varol, H. A. (2024, February). ChatGPT for visually impaired and blind. In *2024 International Conference on Artificial Intelligence in Information and Communication (ICAIIC)* (pp. 722-727). IEEE. https://doi.org/DOI: 10.36227/techrxiv.22047080

Kwet, M. (2019). Digital colonialism: US Empire and the new imperialism in the Global South. *Race & Class*, *60*(4). Advance online publication. DOI: 10.1177/0306396818823172

Laal, M., & Ghodsi, S. M. (2012). Benefits of collaborative learning. *Procedia: Social and Behavioral Sciences*, *31*, 486–490. DOI: 10.1016/j.sbspro.2011.12.091

Labrecque, L. I., Peña, P. Y., Leonard, H., & Leger, R. (2024). Not all sunshine and rainbows: Exploring the dark side of AI in interactive marketing. *Journal of Research in Interactive Marketing*, *18*(5), 970–999.

Lampou, R. (2023). The integration of artificial intelligence in education: Opportunities and challenges. *Review of Artificial Intelligence in Education*, *4*, e15–e15.

Larcombe, W., Baik, C., & Finch, S. (2021). Exploring course experiences that predict psychological distress and mental wellbeing in Australian undergraduate and graduate coursework students. *Higher Education Research & Development*, •••, 1–16. DOI: 10.1080/07294360.2020.1865284

Law-Davis, S. (2023). Early childhood teachers' confidence to teach religious education and the influences impacting their teaching in Catholic primary schools. *Religions*, *14*(2), 198. Advance online publication. DOI: 10.3390/rel14020198

Lazo, K. P. M. (2024). The interaction between teachers' efficacy and students' attitudes toward effective learning in state universities and colleges of the Philippines. *International Journal of Advanced and Applied Sciences*, *11*(7), 75–86. DOI: 10.21833/ijaas.2024.07.010

Lee, D., & Palmer, E. (2025). Prompt engineering in higher education: A systematic review to help inform curricula. *International Journal of Educational Technology in Higher Education*, *22*(1). Advance online publication. DOI: 10.1186/s41239-025-00503-7

Leijen, Ä., Pedaste, M., & Baucal, A. (2024). A new psychometrically validated questionnaire for assessing teacher agency in eight dimensions across pre-service and in-service teachers. *Frontiers in Education*, *9*. Advance online publication. DOI: 10.3389/feduc.2024.1336401

Leino, K., Rikala, J., Puhakka, E., Niilo-Rämä, M., Sirén, M., & Fagerlund, J. (2019). *Digiloikasta digitaitoihin. Kansainvälinen monilukutaidon ja ohjelmoinnillisen ajattelun tutkimus (ICILS 2018)* [From digital leap to ICT skills: International computer and information literacy study with computational thinking assessment (ICILS 2018)]. Finnish Institute for Educational Research: University of Jyväskylä.

Liang, W., Yuksekgonul, M., Mao, Y., Wu, E., & Zou, J. (2023). GPT detectors are biased against non-native English writers. *Patterns (New York, N.Y.)*, *4*(7), 100779. DOI: 10.1016/j.patter.2023.100779 PMID: 37521038

Liberati, A., Altman, D. G., Tetzlaff, J., Mulrow, C., Gøtzsche, P. C., Ioannidis, J. P., Clarke, M., Devereaux, P. J., Kleijnen, J., & Moher, D. (2009). The PRISMA statement for reporting systematic reviews and meta-analyses of studies that evaluate healthcare interventions: Explanation and elaboration. *BMJ (Clinical Research Ed.), 339*. Advance online publication. DOI: 10.1136/bmj.b2700 PMID: 19622552

Li, H. (2025). Students' wellbeing in positive higher education: Conceptual frameworks and influencing factors. *Frontiers in Education, 10*. Advance online publication. DOI: 10.3389/feduc.2025.1607364

Li, K. C., Chong, G. H. L., Wong, B. T. M., & Wu, M. M. F. (2025). A TAM-Based analysis of Hong Kong undergraduate students' attitudes toward generative AI in higher education and employment. *Education Sciences, 15*(7), 798. DOI: 10.3390/educsci15070798

Lingán-Huamán, S. K., Mamani-Benito, O., Castillo-Blanco, R., Cabrera-Orosco, I., Rodríguez-Sosa, J., & Carranza-Esteban, R. F. (2023). Teacher self-efficacy: Development, validity, and factorial invariance of a brief measure in Peruvian university professors. *Frontiers in Education, 8*, 1211487. Advance online publication. DOI: 10.3389/feduc.2023.1211487

Lin, H., & Chen, Q. (2024). Artificial intelligence (AI)-integrated educational applications and college students' creativity and academic emotions: Students and teachers' perceptions and attitudes. *BMC Psychology, 12*(1), 487. PMID: 39285268

Li, Q., & Hidayat, R. (2025). The mediating role of self-efficacy and belief between technological pedagogical content knowledge and modes of technology use among elementary school teachers in China. *International Journal of Educational Reform*. Advance online publication. DOI: 10.1177/10567879251345810

Liu, G. L., Darvin, R., & Ma, C. (2024). Exploring AI-mediated informal digital learning of English (AI-IDLE): A mixed-method investigation of Chinese EFL learners' AI adoption and experiences. *Computer Assisted Language Learning, 38*(7), 1632–1660. DOI: 10.1080/09588221.2024.2310288

Lochmiller, C. (2021). Conducting Thematic Analysis with Qualitative Data. *The Qualitative Report*. Advance online publication. DOI: 10.46743/2160-3715/2021.5008

Looi, C. K. (2024). Charting the uncertain future of AI and education: Promises, challenges and opportunities. *Pedagogies, 19*(3), 477–486.

Luckin, R., Holmes, W., Griffiths, M., & Forcier, L. B. (2016). *Intelligence unleashed: An argument for AI in education*. Pearson.

Luo, J., & Dawson, P. (2025). Exploring value judgements in grading: Will teachers mark down student work assisted by GenAI, and should they? *Studies in Higher Education*, •••, 1–15. DOI: 10.1080/03075079.2025.2552825

Luo, J., Zheng, C., Yin, J., & Teo, H. H. (2025b). Design and assessment of AI-based learning tools in higher education: A systematic review. *International Journal of Educational Technology in Higher Education*, *22*(1), 42. DOI: 10.1186/s41239-025-00540-2

Lutfi, A., & Hidayah, R. (2021). Applying gamification to improve the quality of teaching and learning of Chemistry in high schools: A case study of Indonesia. *Asia-Pacific Forum on Science Learning & Teaching*, *20*(2), 1–17.

Lynch, M., & Heydemann, S. (2024). *Two*. Understanding State Weakness in the Middle East and North Africa.

MacDowell, P., Moskalyk, K., Korchinski, K., & Morrison, D. (2024). Preparing educators to teach and create with generative artificial intelligence. *Canadian Journal of Learning and Technology*, *50*(4), 1–23. DOI: 10.21432/cjlt28606

Magat, R. J. B., & Sangalang, E. M. (2024). Teachers' familiarity, perceptions, and training needs on the use of ChatGPT in mathematics instruction. *International Journal of Education in Mathematics, Science and Technology*, 1471-1487. https://doi.org/DOI: 10.46328/ijemst.4332

Manman, D., Chularut, P., & Ayudhaya, P. K. N. (2025). A study on defining and evaluating teacher self-efficacy for pre-service English teachers in China. *International Journal of Sociologies and Anthropologies Science Reviews*, *5*(6), 611–622. DOI: 10.60027/ijsasr.2025.7619

Mann, H. (2024). *Artificial Integrity: The paths to leading AI toward a human-centered future*. John Wiley & Sons.

Mansour, W., Boyd, A., & Walshe, K. (2021). National accreditation programmes for hospitals in the Eastern Mediterranean Region: Case studies from Egypt, Jordan, and Lebanon. *The International Journal of Health Planning and Management*, *36*(5), 1500–1520. PMID: 33949699

Marcus-Quinn, A., & McCoy, S. (2025). *Future proofing schools: Bringing school policies into the AI era* (Version 2). OSF Preprints. https://doi.org/DOI: 10.35542/osf.io/mujkh_v2

Massouti, A. (2025). *Promoting artificial intelligence in UAE's teacher education*. IGI Global. [Book title not provided], DOI: 10.4018/979-8-3373-0837-1.ch009

Maxwell, D., Oyarzun, B., Kim, S., & Bong, J. Y. (2025). Generative AI in Higher Education: Demographic differences in student perceived readiness, benefits, and challenges. *TechTrends*. Advance online publication. DOI: 10.1007/s11528-025-01109-6

McCarthy, J., Minsky, M. L., Rochester, N., & Shannon, C. E. (2006). A proposal for the dartmouth summer research project on artificial intelligence, august 31, 1955. *AI Magazine*, *27*(4), 12–12. DOI: 10.1609/aimag.v27i4.1904

McDaniel, J. E. (1999). *Teacher confidence and attitude regarding performance assessment* (Master's thesis, Fort Hays State University). Fort Hays State University. https://doi.org/DOI: 10.58809/MXEB4276

Mehrabi, N., Morstatter, F., Saxena, N., Lerman, K., & Galstyan, A. (2022). A survey on bias and fairness in machine learning. *ACM Computing Surveys*, *54*(6), 1–35. DOI: 10.1145/3457607

Merino-Campos, C. (2025). The impact of artificial intelligence on personalized learning in higher education: A systematic review. *Trends in Higher Education*, *4*(2), 17. DOI: 10.3390/higheredu4020017

Mills, K. A., Cope, J., Scholes, L., & Rowe, L. (2024). Coding and computational thinking across the curriculum: A review of educational outcomes. *Review of Educational Research*. Advance online publication. DOI: 10.3102/00346543241241327

Minnillo, S., Jones, L., & Barrio-García, S. D. (2024). AI in the L2 classroom: Serving language educators through professional development. *Journal of Linguistics and Language Teaching*, *16*(1). Advance online publication. DOI: 10.5070/l2.21198

Mohamed, E. M. M. (2025). Degree of Government AI Readiness of Mena Countries and Its Impact on Banking Performance (Master's thesis, Hamad Bin Khalifa University (Qatar)).

Mohebi, L. (2025). Exploring the integration of AI in education. In *Advances in computational intelligence and robotics* (pp. 371–386). IGI Global. https://doi.org/ DOI: 10.4018/979-8-3693-7332-3.ch022

Mohebi, L. (2025). A qualitative study on the integration of AI in Education: Perceptions, challenges, and opportunities among selective In-Service and Pre-service teachers in the UAE. In *Lecture notes in educational technology* (pp. 113–126). Springer., DOI: 10.1007/978-981-96-4952-5_8

Moher, D., Shamseer, L., Clarke, M., Ghersi, D., Liberati, A., Petticrew, M., Shekelle, P., & Stewart, L. A.Prisma-P Group. (2015). Preferred reporting items for systematic review and meta-analysis protocols (PRISMA-P) 2015 statement. *Systematic Reviews*, *4*(1), 1. DOI: 10.1186/2046-4053-4-1 PMID: 25554246

Mollick, E., & Mollick, L. (2024). Instructors as Innovators: A future-focused approach to new AI learning opportunities, with prompts. *arXiv*. DOI: 10.48550/arxiv.2407.05181

Morgan, D. L. (1997). *Focus groups as qualitative research*. SAGE Publications.

Moukhliss, G., Lahyani, K., & Diab, G. (2024). The Impact of Artificial Intelligence on Research and Higher Education in Morocco. [EduLearn]. *Journal of Education and Learning*, *18*(4), 1292–1300. DOI: 10.11591/edulearn.v18i4.21511

Mozelius, P., Håkansson Lindqvist, M., Cleveland-Innes, M., Jaldemark, J., & Sundgren, M. (2024). *Educating the educators on generative artificial intelligence in higher education*. In *Proceedings of the International Conference on AI Research* (Vol. 4, pp. 296–302). https://doi.org/DOI: 10.34190/icair.4.1.3026

Mustafa, M. Y., Tlili, A., Lampropoulos, G., Huang, R., Jandrić, P., Zhao, J., Salha, S., Xu, L., & Panda, S., Kinshuk, López-Pernas, S., & Saqr, M. (2024). A systematic review of literature reviews on artificial intelligence in education (AIED): A roadmap to a future research agenda. *Smart Learning Environments*, *11*, 59. DOI: 10.1186/s40561-024-00350-5

Myburgh, Z. (2021). Quality management of reaccreditation processes in private higher education institutions in South Africa (Doctoral dissertation, University of Pretoria (South Africa)).

Myin-Germeys, I., Kasanova, Z., Vaessen, T., Vachon, H., Kirtley, O., Viechtbauer, W., & Reininghaus, U. (2018). Experience sampling methodology in mental health research: New insights and technical developments. *World Psychiatry; Official Journal of the World Psychiatric Association (WPA)*, *17*(2), 123–132. DOI: 10.1002/wps.20513 PMID: 29856567

Mzwri, K., & Turcsányi-Szabo, M. (2025). The impact of prompt engineering and a generative AI-Driven tool on autonomous learning: A case study. *Education Sciences*, *15*(2), 199. DOI: 10.3390/educsci15020199

Na, C., & Isa, Z. (2024). Exploring the influence of teacher self-efficacy on teaching quality in higher vocational education. *DREAM*, *3*(7). Advance online publication. DOI: 10.56982/dream.v3i07.246

Naim, A., Saklani, A., Khan, S. A., & Malik, P. K. (Eds.). (2024). *Evaluating global accreditation standards for higher education*. IGI Global.

Naseri, R. N. N., & Abdullah, M. S. (2024). Understanding AI technology adoption in educational settings: A review of theoretical frameworks and their applications. *Information Management and Business Review*, *16*(3), 174–181. DOI: 10.22610/imbr.v16i3(i).3963

Nazim, M., & Alzubi, A. A. F. (2025). Empowering EFL teachers' perceptions of generative AI-mediated self-professionalism. *PLoS One*, *20*(6), e0326735. DOI: 10.1371/journal.pone.0326735 PMID: 40549814

Nimmo, R., Constantinides, M., Zhou, K., Quercia, D., & Stumpf, S. (2024). User Characteristics in Explainable AI: The Rabbit Hole of Personalization? *Association for Computing Machinery*, 1–13. https://doi.org/DOI: 10.1145/3613904.3642352

Novariza, B. (2023). *Enhancing teacher self-efficacy: A framework for structured continuous professional development*. Managere. *Indonesian Journal of Educational Management*, *5*(3), 330–341. DOI: 10.52627/managere.v5i3.414

Nurjanah, A., Salsabila, I. N., Azzahra, A., Rahayu, R., & Marlina, N. (2024). Artificial intelligence (ai) usage in today's teaching and learning process: A review. *Syntax Idea*, *6*(3), 1517–1523. DOI: 10.46799/syntax-idea.v6i3.3126

Nurunnabi, M., Mitchell, C., Koubaa, A., & Hoke, T. (2023). *Sustainable Development Goals and AI integration into Curricula in the MENA Region. Report*. Prince Sultan University.

Nyaaba, M., & Zhai, X. (2024). Generative AI professional development needs for teacher educators. https://doi.org/DOI: 10.61969/jai.1385915

Oades, L. G., Robinson, P., Green, S., & Spence, G. B. (2011). Towards a positive university. *The Journal of Positive Psychology*, *6*(6), 432–439. DOI: 10.1080/17439760.2011.634828

OECD. (n.d.). *Teachers' occupational well-being framework*. OECD.

Ojha, M. kumar Mishra, A., Kandpal, V., & Singh, A. (2025). The Ethical Dimensions of AI Development in the Future of Higher Education: Balancing Innovation with Responsibility. In Ethical Dimensions of AI Development (pp. 401-436). IGI Global.

Ok, M. W., Rao, K., Pennington, J., & Ulloa, P. R. (2022). Speech recognition technology for writing: Usage patterns and perceptions of students with high incidence disabilities. *Journal of Special Education Technology*, *37*(2), 191–202. DOI: 10.1177/0162643420979929

Otman, K. (2021). Small and medium enterprises in the Middle East and North Africa region. *International Journal of Business and Management, 16*(5), 12–21.

Ouyang, F., & Jiao, P. (2021). Artificial intelligence in education: The three paradigms. *Computers and Education: Artificial Intelligence, 2*, 100020.

Owen, A., & Samson, E. (2025). *Validating AI/ML-Based Systems: Frameworks for Testing Model Accuracy*. Fairness, Robustness, and Generalization in QA.

Page, M. J., McKenzie, J. E., Bossuyt, P. M., Boutron, I., Hoffmann, T. C., Mulrow, C. D., ... & Moher, D. (2021). The PRISMA 2020 statement: an updated guideline for reporting systematic reviews. *bmj, 372*. https://doi.org/DOI: 10.1136/bmj.n71

Palinkas, L. A., Horwitz, S. M., Green, C. A., Wisdom, J. P., Duan, N., & Hoagwood, K. (2015). Purposeful sampling for qualitative data collection and analysis in mixed method implementation research. *Administration and Policy in Mental Health, 42*, 533–544. DOI: 10.1007/s10488-013-0528-y

Paniamogan, J. D., & Dioso, E. D. (2024). *Relationship between teachers' attitude and self-efficacy: A descriptive correlational study*. EPRA International Journal of Environmental, Economics, Commerce and Educational Management., DOI: 10.36713/epra17840

Park, S. (2023). Bridging the global divide in AI regulation: A proposal for a contextual, coherent, and commensurable framework. *Wash. Int'l LJ, 33*, 216.

Park, Y., Ambrose, G., Coleman, M. B., & Moore, T. C. (2017). The effects of teacher directed writing instruction combined with SOLO Literacy Suite. *Journal of Computer Assisted Learning, 33*(1), 20–34. DOI: 10.1111/jcal.12163

Patton, M. Q. (2002). *Qualitative research and evaluation methods* (Vol. 3). Sage.

Patton, M. Q. (2025). *Qualitative research & evaluation methods* (4th ed.). Sage Publications.

Pederson, J. D. (2025). AI Associate: Examining Artificial Intelligence and Its Potential Impact on the Pastoral Ministry (Doctoral dissertation).

Pedro, F., Subosa, M., Rivas, A., & Valverde, P. (2019). Artificial intelligence in education: Challenges and opportunities for sustainable development.

Perkins, M., Furze, L., Roe, J., & MacVaugh, J. (2024). The Artificial Intelligence Assessment Scale (AIAS): A framework for ethical integration of generative AI in educational assessment. *Journal of University Teaching & Learning Practice, 21*(6), 49–66. DOI: 10.53761/q3azde36

Pfitzner-Eden, F. (2016). Why do I feel more confident? Bandura's sources predict preservice teachers' latent changes in teacher self-efficacy. *Frontiers in Psychology*, *7*, 1486. Advance online publication. DOI: 10.3389/fpsyg.2016.01486

Phil, M. (2013). *Relationship between attitude towards teaching profession and teachers' self-efficacy beliefs* [Unpublished manuscript].

Pietarinen, J., Pyhältö, K., & Soini, T. (2016). Large-scale curriculum reform in Finland –exploring the interrelation between implementation strategy, the function of the reform, and curriculum coherence. *Curriculum Journal*, *28*(1), 22–40. DOI: 10.1080/09585176.2016.1179205

Pinho, A. S., & Paz, A. L. (2024). Diversity and epistemological plurality: Thinking interculturality 'otherwise'. *Language and Intercultural Communication*, *24*(4), 261–265.

Popenici, S. A., & Kerr, S. (2017). Exploring the impact of artificial intelligence on teaching and learning in higher education. *Research and Practice in Technology Enhanced Learning*, *12*(1), 22. DOI: 10.1186/s41039-017-0062-8 PMID: 30595727

Porayska-Pomsta, K., Holmes, W., & Nemorin, S. (2023). The ethics of AI in education. In Du Boulay, B., Mitrovic, A., & Yacef, K. (Eds.), *Handbook of Artificial Intelligence in Education* (pp. 571–604). Edward Elgar Publishing., DOI: 10.4337/9781800375413.00038

Pörn, R., Hemmi, K., & Kallio-Kujala, P. (2021). *Inspiring or confusing – a study of Finnish 1–6 teachers' relation to teaching programming*. *9*(1), 366–396. DOI: 10.31129/LUMAT.9.1.1355

Prilop, C. N., Mah, D., Jacobsen, L. J., Hansen, R. R., Weber, K. E., & Hoya, F. (2024). Generative AI in teacher education: Using AI-enhanced methods to explore teacher educators' perceptions. https://doi.org/DOI: 10.31219/osf.io/szcwb

Quinde, G. A. L., Muñoz, M. Y. T., Suárez, J. M. R., Villarreal, R. E. P., Vélez, W. A. Z., & Laínez, A. A. D. P. (2024). Perception of University Students on The Use of Artificial Intelligence (AI) Tools For The Development of Autonomous Learning. *Revista de Gestão Social e Ambiental*, *18*(2), e06170–e06170. DOI: 10.24857/rgsa.v18n2-136

Radici, E., Heboyan, V., & De Leo, G. (2023). A speech-to-symbol app for supporting communication partner to model and improve vocabulary. *Child Language Teaching and Therapy*, *39*(3), 266–274. DOI: 10.1177/02656590231202857

Raji, I. D., Kumar, I. E., Horowitz, A., & Selbst, A. (2022). The fallacy of AI functionality. *2022 ACM Conference on Fairness Accountability and Transparency,* 959–972. https://doi.org/DOI: 10.1145/3531146.3533158

Reimer-Burgrova, H. (2022). *Politics of Violence and Fear in MENA*. Palgrave Macmillan.

Rittel, H. W., & Webber, M. M. (1973). Dilemmas in a general theory of planning. *Policy Sciences, 4*(2), 155–169. DOI: 10.1007/BF01405730

Roll, I., & Wylie, R. (2016). Evolution and revolution in artificial intelligence in education. *International Journal of Artificial Intelligence in Education, 26*(2), 582–599.

Rose, D., & Dalton, B. (2009). Learning to read in the digital age. *Mind, Brain and Education : the Official Journal of the International Mind, Brain, and Education Society, 3*(2), 74–83. DOI: 10.1111/j.1751-228X.2009.01057.x

Roshan, S., Iqbal, S. Z., & Qing, Z. (2024). Teacher training and professional development for implementing AI-based educational tools. *Journal of Asian Development Studies*. https://doi.org/DOI: 10.62345/jads.2024.13.2.154

Rudolph, J., Tan, S., & Tan, S. (2023). ChatGPT: Bullshit spewer or the end of traditional assessments in higher education? *Journal of Applied Learning & Teaching, 6*(1), 342–363. https://search.informit.org/doi/10.3316/informit.T2025102700003092061569891

Saharia, B., & Begum, J. (2025). Self-efficacy: A determining factor of teaching efficiency. *International Journal of Research and Scientific Innovation, 12*(7), 81–88. DOI: 10.51244/ijrsi.2025.120700009

Sailer, M., & Homner, L. (2020). The gamification of learning: A meta-analysis. *Educational Psychology Review, 32*(1), 77–112. DOI: 10.1007/s10648-019-09498-w

Sajja, R., Sermet, Y., Cikmaz, M., Cwiertny, D., & Demir, I. (2023). Artificial intelligence-enabled intelligent assistant for personalized and adaptive learning in higher education. *arXiv preprint arXiv:2309.10892*. https://arxiv.org/abs/2309.10892

Salah, R. M., Alves, G. R., & Guerreiro, P. (2014, February). Reshaping higher education systems in the MENA region: The contribution of remote and virtual labs. In *2014 11th International Conference on Remote Engineering and Virtual Instrumentation (REV)* (pp. 240-245). IEEE.

Salele, N., & Khan, M. S. H. (2022). Engineering trainee-teachers' attitudes toward technology use in pedagogical practices: Extending the computer attitude scale (CAS). *SAGE Open, 12*(2), 21582440221102436. Advance online publication. DOI: 10.1177/21582440221102436

Salem, M. A., Zakaria, O. M., Aldoughan, E. A., Khalil, Z. A., & Zakaria, H. M. (2025). Bridging the AI Gap in Medical Education: A Study of Competency, Readiness, and Ethical Perspectives in Developing Nations. *Computers, 14*(6), 238. DOI: 10.3390/computers14060238

Salha, S., Mousa, A., & Khayat, S. (2024). Artificial intelligence in education (AIED) policies in school contexts: A mixed-methods study. *Leadership and Policy in Schools*. Advance online publication. DOI: 10.1080/15700763.2024.2443675

Saqr, M., Fors, U., & Tedre, M. (2023). Digital transformation in MENA higher education: A review and framework. *Education and Information Technologies, 28*(1), 43–64. DOI: 10.1007/s10639-022-11098-7

Sayed, W. S., Noeman, A. M., Abdellatif, A., Abdelrazek, M., Badawy, M. G., Hamed, A., & El-Tantawy, S. (2022). AI-based adaptive personalized content presentation and exercises navigation for an effective and engaging E-learning platform. *Multimedia Tools and Applications, 82*(3), 3303–3333. DOI: 10.1007/s11042-022-13076-8

Seligman, M. E. P. (2011). *Flourish: A visionary new understanding of happiness and well-being*. Free Press.

Selwyn, N. (2022). The future of AI and education: Some cautionary notes. *European Journal of Education, 57*, 620–631. DOI: 10.1111/ejed.12532

Selwyn, N., Ljungqvist, M., & Sonesson, A. (2025). When the prompting stops: Exploring teachers' work around the educational frailties of generative AI tools. *Learning, Media and Technology, 50*(3), 310–323. DOI: 10.1080/17439884.2025.2537959

Şen, Ş. (2021). The study of relationship between pre-service teachers' self-efficacy beliefs and attitudes towards the teaching profession. *MIER Journal of Educational Studies, Trends and Practices*, 23–32. https://doi.org/DOI: 10.52634/mier/2019/v9/i1/1380

Sengar, S. S., Hasan, A. B., Kumar, S., & Carroll, F. (2024). Generative artificial intelligence: A systematic review and applications. *Multimedia Tools and Applications, 84*(21), 23661–23700. DOI: 10.1007/s11042-024-20016-1

Sergeeva, O. V., Zheltukhina, M. R., Shoustikova, T., Tukhvatullina, L. R., Dobrokhotov, D. A., & Kondrashev, S. V. (2025). Understanding higher education students' adoption of generative AI technologies: An empirical investigation using UTAUT2. *Contemporary Educational Technology, 17*(2), ep571. DOI: 10.30935/cedtech/16039

Shabara, R., ElEbyary, K., & Boraie, D. (2024). Teachers or ChatGPT: The issue of accuracy and consistency in l2 assessment. *Teaching English with Technology, 24*(2), 71–92. DOI: 10.56297/vaca6841/LRDX3699/XSEZ5215

Shattuck, K. (Ed.). (2023). *Assuring quality in online education: Practices and processes at the teaching, resource, and program levels.* Taylor & Francis.

Shemaili, M. A. (2022). Science education in the United Arab Emirates. In *Science education in the Arab Gulf states* (pp. 225–241). Springer., DOI: 10.1007/978-981-16-6955-2_14

Shneiderman, B. (2020). Human-Centered Artificial Intelligence: Reliable, Safe & Trustworthy. *International Journal of Human-Computer Interaction, 36*(6), 495–504. DOI: 10.1080/10447318.2020.1741118

Shoukat, R. (2024). Harnessing AI for Educational Transformation: A Comparative Study of China, India and Pakistan. *Strategic Studies, 44*(1).

Shwedeh, F., Salloum, S. A., Aburayya, A., Fatin, B., Elbadawi, M. A., Ghurabli, Z. A., & Dabbagh, T. A. (2024). AI adoption and educational sustainability in higher education in the UAE. In Al-Marzouqi, A., Salloum, S. A., Al-Saidat, M., Aburayya, A., & Gupta, B. (Eds.), *Artificial Intelligence in Education: The Power and Dangers of ChatGPT in the Classroom* (pp. 201–229). Springer., DOI: 10.1007/978-3-031-52280-2_14

Sibomana, A., Mukagihana, J., & Ndiritu, J. (2024). *Teacher training programs and secondary mathematics and science teachers' attitudes and confidence in teaching.* BonView International Journal of Curriculum and Education., DOI: 10.47852/bonviewijce42022797

Smith, B. L., & MacGregor, J. T. (1992) "What is collaborative learning?" In Goodsell, A., Maher, M., Tinto, V., Smith, B.L., MacGregor J. T. (Eds.), *Collaborative Learning: A Sourcebook for Higher Education.* National Center on postsecondary teaching, learning, and assessment publishing, Pennsylvania State University, USA.

Smith, B. W., Dalen, J., Wiggins, K., Tooley, E., Christopher, P., & Bernard, J. (2008). The brief resilience scale: Assessing the ability to bounce back. *International Journal of Behavioral Medicine, 15*(3), 194–200. DOI: 10.1080/10705500802222972 PMID: 18696313

Sokal, L., Trudel, L. E., & Babb, J. (2020). Canadian teachers' attitudes toward change, efficacy, and burnout during the COVID-19 Pandemic. *International Journal of Educational Research Open, 1*, 100016. Advance online publication. DOI: 10.1016/j.ijedro.2020.100016

Solis-Grant, M. J., Espinoza-Parçet, C., Sepúlveda-Carrasco, C., Pérez-Villalobos, C., Rodríguez-Núñez, I., Pincheira-Martínez, C., Gómez-Varela, J. P., & Aránguiz-Ibarra, D. (2022). Inclusion at universities: Psychometric properties of an inclusive management scale as perceived by students. *PLoS One*, *17*(1), e0262011. DOI: 10.1371/journal.pone.0262011 PMID: 34995314

Song, D. (2024). Artificial intelligence for human learning: A review of machine learning techniques used in education research and a suggestion of a learning design model. *American Journal of Education and Learning*, *9*(1), 1–21. DOI: 10.55284/ajel.v9i1.1024

Sousa, A. E., & Cardoso, P. (2025). Use of generative AI by higher education students. *Electronics (Basel)*, *14*(7), 1258. DOI: 10.3390/electronics14071258

Sprongl, I. (2025). Agile Governance in the Real World: Balancing Autonomy, Regulation, and Learning in Complex Systems. Regulation, and Learning in Complex Systems (May 09, 2025).

Suárez, P. J. O., Romary, L., & Sagot, B. (2020). A Monolingual Approach to Contextualized Word Embeddings for Mid-Resource Languages. *arXiv,* 1703–1714. https://aclanthology.org/2020.acl-main.156/

Swidan, A., Lee, S. Y., & Romdhane, S. B. (2025). College students' use and perceptions of AI tools in the UAE: Motivations, ethical concerns and institutional guidelines. *Education Sciences*, *15*(4), 461. DOI: 10.3390/educsci15040461

Swiecki, Z., Khosravi, H., Chen, G., Martinez-Maldonado, R., Lodge, J. M., Milligan, S., Selwyn, N., & Gašević, D. (2022). Assessment in the age of artificial intelligence. Computers & Education. *Artificial Intelligence*, *3*, 100075. DOI: 10.1016/j.caeai.2022.100075

Tarafdar, M., Cooper, C. L., & Stich, J. (2019). The Technostress Trifecta - techno eustress, techno distress and design: Theoretical directions and an agenda for research. *Information Systems Journal*, *29*(1), 6–42. DOI: 10.1111/isj.12169

Tariq, M. U. (2024). Navigating the personalization pathway: Implementing adaptive learning technologies in higher education. In *Adaptive Learning Technologies for Higher Education* (pp. 265–291). IGI Global.

Täschner, J., Dicke, T., Reinhold, S., & Holzberger, D. (2024). "Yes, I can!" A systematic review and meta-analysis of intervention studies promoting teacher self-efficacy. *Review of Educational Research*. Advance online publication. DOI: 10.3102/00346543231221499

Tausch, A. P., & Menold, N. (2016). Methodological aspects of focus groups in health research. *Global Qualitative Nursing Research, 3*. Advance online publication. DOI: 10.1177/2333393616630466 PMID: 28462326

Tekin, O. (2023). The mediating role of teacher self-efficacy in predicting teachers' research attitudes. *Teacher Development*, *27*(3), 314–332. DOI: 10.1080/13664530.2023.2201579

Thomas, D. R., Gatz, E., Gupta, S., Aleven, V., & Koedinger, K. R. (2024, July). The Neglected 15%: Positive Effects of Hybrid Human-AI Tutoring Among Students with Disabilities. In *International Conference on Artificial Intelligence in Education* (pp. 409-423). Cham: Springer Nature Switzerland. https://doi.org/DOI: 10.35542/osf.io/y52ew

Tisdell, E. J., Merriam, S. B., & Stuckey-Peyrot, H. L. (2025). *Qualitative research: A guide to design and implementation*. John Wiley & Sons.

Toikkanen, T., & Leinonen, T. (2017). The code ABC MOOC: Experiences from a coding and computational thinking MOOC for Finnish primary school teachers. In Rich, P., & Hodges, C. (Eds.), *Emerging Research, Practice, and Policy on Computational Thinking. Educational Communications and Technology: Issues and Innovations*. Springer., DOI: 10.1007/978-3-319-52691-1_15

Tomlinson, C. A. (2014). The Differentiated Classroom: Responding to the Needs of All Learners.

Tondeur, J., Howard, S. K., & Yang, J. (2021). One-size does not fit all: Towards an adaptive model to develop preservice teachers' digital competencies. *Computers in Human Behavior, 116*, 106659. DOI: 10.1016/j.chb.2020.106659

Trigui, H., Guerfali, F., Harigua-Souiai, E., Qasrawi, R., Atri, C., Sokhn, E. S., & Znaidi, S. (2024). Exploring AI governance in the Middle East and North Africa (MENA) region: Gaps, efforts, and initiatives. *Data & Policy*, *6*, e83.

Uluyol, Ç., & Aslan, C. (2022). Special Education Students' Attitudes towards Assistive Technologies. *Journal of Teacher Education and Lifelong Learning*, *4*(2), 124–132. DOI: 10.51535/tell.1177060

UNESCO. (2021). *Recommendation on the ethics of artificial intelligence*. Paris: UNESCO. https://unesdoc.unesco.org/ark:/48223/pf0000381137

UNESCO. (2023). *Global Education Monitoring Report Summary 2023: Technology in education, A tool on whose terms?* Paris: UNESCO. https://www.unesco.org/gem-report/en/publication/technology-education

UNESCO. (2024). *We the UAE 2031 Vision*. Policy Monitoring Platform. UNESCO. https://www.unesco.org/creativity/en/policy-monitoring-platform/we-uae-2031-vision

United Nations. (2015) *'Sustainable Development Goal 4: Ensure inclusive and equitable quality education and promote lifelong learning opportunities for all'*. Retrieved November 08, 2025, from https://sdgs.un.org/goals/goal4

Uygun, E. (2026). Clashing AIs: Artificial intelligence literacy and academic integrity in an EFL context. *Journal of Academic Ethics*, *24*, 7. DOI: 10.1007/s10805-025-09676-2

Vashishth, T. K., Sharma, V., Sharma, K. K., Kumar, B., Panwar, R., & Chaudhary, S. (2024). AI-Driven Learning Analytics for Personalized Feedback and Assessment in Higher Education. In Nguyen, T., & Vo, N. (Eds.), *Using Traditional Design Methods to Enhance AI-Driven Decision Making* (pp. 206–230). IGI Global Scientific Publishing., DOI: 10.4018/979-8-3693-0639-0.ch009

Vats, R. (2019). A study of teachers' attitude towards the teaching profession. *International Education and Research Journal*, *5*(4).

Vaughn, S., Schumm, J., & Sinagub, J. (1996). *Focus group interviews in education and psychology*. SAGE Publications., DOI: 10.4135/9781452243641

Von Winckelmann, S., Henry, M., & Mackenzie, A. (2024). Empowering Educators: A Case Study on Establishing AI Competency and Confidence. In Crompton, H., & Burke, D. (Eds.), *Artificial Intelligence Applications in K-12 - Theories, Ethics, and Case Studies for Schools*. Routledge., DOI: 10.4324/9781003440192

Voogt, J., Erstad, O., Dede, C., & Mishra, P. (2013). Challenges to learning and schooling in the digital networked world of the 21st century. *Journal of Computer Assisted Learning*, *29*(5), 403–413. DOI: 10.1111/jcal.12029

Waked, A. N., Abdelsalam, H., Ashraf, M. W., Pilotti, M., & El Alaoui, K. (2024). The impact of falsely detecting AI-generated text on academic assessment. In Shelley, M., & Ozturk, O. T. (Eds.), *Proceedings of ICRES 2024 International Conference on Research in Education and Science* (pp. 573-586), Antalya, Turkiye. ISTES.

Walter, A. L. (2024). Utilizing language-generating artificial intelligence (LGAI) in educational planning: A case study. *Journal of Interdisciplinary Teacher Leadership*. https://doi.org/DOI: 10.46767/kfp.2016-0052

Walters, W. H., & Wilder, E. I. (2023). Fabrication and errors in the bibliographic citations generated by ChatGPT. *Scientific Reports, 13*(1), 14045. DOI: 10.1038/s41598-023-41032-5 PMID: 37679503

Walton, G. M., & Cohen, G. L. (2011). A brief social-belonging intervention improves academic and health outcomes of minority students. *Science, 331*(6023), 1447–1451. DOI: 10.1126/science.1198364 PMID: 21415354

Wang, F., Li, N., Cheung, A. C. K., & Wong, G. K. W. (2025). In GenAI we trust: An investigation of university students' reliance on and resistance to generative AI in language learning. *International Journal of Educational Technology in Higher Education, 22*(1). Advance online publication. DOI: 10.1186/s41239-025-00547-9

Wang, K., Ruan, Q., Zhang, X., Fu, C., & Duan, B. (2024). Pre-service teachers' GenAI anxiety, technology self-efficacy, and tPACK: Their structural relations with behavioral intention to design GenAI-assisted teaching. *Behavioral Science, 14*. Advance online publication. DOI: 10.3390/bs14050373

Wang, Z., Chai, C.-S., Li, J., & Lee, V. W. (2025). Assessment of AI ethical reflection: The development and validation of the AI Ethical Reflection Scale (AIERS) for university students. *International Journal of Educational Technology in Higher Education, 22*(1). Advance online publication. DOI: 10.1186/s41239-025-00519-z

Weng, X., XIA, Q., Gu, M., Rajaram, K., & Chiu, T. K. (2024). Assessment and learning outcomes for generative AI in higher education: A scoping review on current research status and trends. *Australasian Journal of Educational Technology, 40*(6), 37–55. DOI: 10.14742/ajet.9540

Widder, D. G., Whittaker, M., & West, S. M. (2024). Why 'open'AI systems are actually closed, and why this matters. *Nature, 635*(8040), 827–833. PMID: 39604616

Wiethof, C., Tavanapour, N., & Bittner, E. (2021). Designing and evaluating a collaborative writing process with gamification elements: Toward a framework for gamifying collaboration processes. *AIS Transactions on Human-Computer Interaction, 13*(1), 38–61. DOI: 10.17705/1thci.00141

Williamson, B., & Hogan, A. (2020). *Commercialisation and privatisation in/of education in the context of Covid-19*. Education International. https://eprints.qut.edu.au/216577/

Williamson, B., & Eynon, R. (2020). Historical threads, missing links, and future directions in AI in education. *Learning, Media and Technology, 45*(3), 223–235. DOI: 10.1080/17439884.2020.1798995

Williams, R. (2023). A review of assessments in K-12 AI literacy curricula. *Retrieved*, (October), 25.

Williams, S. H., & Pelt, R. M. (2021). How teachers' attitudes impact the inclusive classroom. *International Journal of Education and Social Science Research, 4*(1), 13–21. DOI: 10.37500/IJESSR.2021.4103

Woodcock, S., & Tournaki, N. (2022). Bandura's triadic reciprocal determinism model and teacher self-efficacy scales: A revisit. *Teacher Development, 27*(1), 75–91. DOI: 10.1080/13664530.2022.2150285

World Economic Forum. (2025). *AI in Action: Beyond Experimentation to Transform Industry*. Retrieved from https://reports.weforum.org/docs/WEF_AI_in_Action_Beyond_Experimentation_to_Transform_Industry_2025.pdf

Wulandari, A., Sukarno, S., & Matsuri, M. (2023). Bibliometric analysis of teacher self-efficacy in primary education. *Al-Ishlah, 15*(2), 1664–1676. DOI: 10.35445/alishlah.v15i2.3063

Xanthopoulou, D., Bakker, A. B., Demerouti, E., & Schaufeli, W. B. (2007). The role of personal resources in the job demands-resources model. *International Journal of Stress Management, 14*(2), 121–141. DOI: 10.1037/1072-5245.14.2.121

Xia, Q., Weng, X., Ouyang, F., Lin, T. J., & Chiu, T. K. (2024). A scoping review on how generative artificial intelligence transforms assessment in higher education. *International Journal of Educational Technology in Higher Education, 21*(1), 40. DOI: 10.1186/s41239-024-00468-z

Yang, Y., Tseng, C. C., & Lai, S. (2024). Enhancing teachers' self-efficacy beliefs in AI-based technology integration into English-speaking teaching through a professional development program. *Teaching and Teacher Education*. Advance online publication. DOI: 10.1016/j.tate.2024.104582

Yan, Y., Liu, H., & Chau, T. (2025). A systematic review of AI ethics in education: Challenges, policy gaps, and future directions. *Journal of Global Information Management, 33*(1), 1–50. DOI: 10.4018/JGIM.386381

Yaşar, H., Kıyıcı, M., & Karatas, A. (2020). The views and adoption levels of primary school teachers on gamification, problems and possible solutions. *Participatory Educational Research, 7*(3), 265–279. DOI: 10.17275/per.20.46.7.3

Yeager, D. S., & Dweck, C. S. (2012). Mindsets that promote resilience: When students believe that personal characteristics can be developed. *Educational Psychologist, 47*(4), 302–314. DOI: 10.1080/00461520.2012.722805

Yeo, M. A. (2023). Academic integrity in the age of Artificial Intelligence (AI) authoring apps. *TESOL Journal, 14*(3). Advance online publication. DOI: 10.1002/tesj.716

Yusuf, A., Pervin, N., & Román-González, M. (2024). Generative AI and the future of higher education: A threat to academic integrity or reformation? Evidence from multicultural perspectives. *International Journal of Educational Technology in Higher Education, 21*(1). Advance online publication. DOI: 10.1186/s41239-024-00453-6

Zakaria, N. Y. K., & Hashim, H. (2024). Shaping the future of education: Conceptualising pre-service teachers' perspectives on artificial intelligence (AI) integration. *International Journal of Academic Research in Business & Social Sciences*. Advance online publication. DOI: 10.6007/ijarbss/v14-i5/21584

Zdravkova, K., Krasniqi, V., Dalipi, F., & Ferati, M. (2022). Cutting-edge communication and learning assistive technologies for disabled children: An artificial intelligence perspective. *Frontiers in Artificial Intelligence, 5*, 970430. DOI: 10.3389/frai.2022.970430 PMID: 36388402

Zhai, X. (2024). Transforming teachers' roles and agencies in the era of generative AI: Perceptions, acceptance, knowledge, and practices. *Journal of Science Education and Technology*. Advance online publication. DOI: 10.1007/s10956-024-10174-0

Zhang, J., & Zhang, Z. (2024). AI in teacher education: Unlocking new dimensions in teaching support, inclusive learning, and digital literacy. *Journal of Computer Assisted Learning, 40*(4), 1871–1885. DOI: 10.1111/jcal.12988

Zhang, L., & Han, Z. (2008). A teaching attitude adjusting model for college teachers based on attitude theories. *International Education Studies, 1*(1). Advance online publication. DOI: 10.5539/ies.v1n1p64

Zhan, Y., Boud, D., Dawson, P., & Yan, Z. (2025). Generative artificial intelligence as an enabler of student feedback engagement: A framework. *Higher Education Research & Development, 44*(5), 1289–1304. DOI: 10.1080/07294360.2025.2476513

Zhao, C. (2025). AI-assisted assessment in higher education: A systematic review. *Journal of Educational Technology and Innovation, 6*(4). Advance online publication. DOI: 10.61414/jeti.v6i4.209

Zheng, L., Long, M., Zhong, L., & Gyasi, J. F. (2022). The effectiveness of technology-facilitated personalized learning on learning achievements and learning perceptions: A meta-analysis. *Education and Information Technologies, 27*(8), 11807–11830. DOI: 10.1007/s10639-022-11092-7

Zulianti, H., Hastuti, H., Nurchurifiani, E., Hastomo, T., Maximilian, A., & Ajeng, G. D. (2024). Enhancing novice EFL teachers' competency in AI-powered tools through a tpack-based professional development program. *World Journal of English Language*, *15*(3), 117–117. DOI: 10.5430/wjel.v15n3p117

About the Contributors

Tendai Charles, Educated in Russell Group universities, Dr. Charles has a PhD in Education from the University of York, awarded in 2018. He joined the Faculty of Education at the British University in Dubai in 2019 as an Assistant Professor, was the inaugural Director of the Centre for Research in Digital Education, and is presently Programme Coordinator for their Masters in Education. He is a post-positivist researcher with over 40 publications, who specialises in evidence-based education, technology-enhanced learning and second language acquisition. Dr. Charles is an Accredited Researcher with the UK Government's Office for National Statistics, and is a Fellow of the UK's Royal Statistical Society. To-date, he has supervised over 60 postgraduate theses/dissertations, and as a Fellow of the Higher Education Academy (FHEA), his excellence in teaching is internationally recognised.

Christopher Hill has worked in international higher education since 2008 and is an OBHE Associate, HEA Fellow, Specialist for the Hong Kong Council for Accreditation of Academic and Vocational Qualifications, an Adjunct Researcher for the Higher Evaluation and Accreditation Council of Taiwan and External Examiner for the University of Birmingham. Prof. Hill is currently Vice President of Research and Innovation at the Canadian University in Dubai. Prof. Hill's research interests include TNE and its impact on national systems; the role of online learning; and the development of international education and the student experience in the global arena. Prof. Hill is widely published, is a regular keynote speaker on the subject of international education, cultural teaching, TNE and institutional development, and a member of eight international journal editorial boards and a peer reviewer for a further ten journals. Prof. Hill hosts the Think Education podcast that provides a platform for reflection and discussion on research practice and teaching and learning within higher education.

***

Siham Abukhalaf is a PhD in Education student at Deakin University in Australia.

Rania Al-Tanna holds a Master's in Education from the British University in Dubai.

Khadeegha Alzouebi is an associate professor of Educational Leadership. She has worked extensively on school reform and school effectiveness both in the UK and in the United Arab United. She has worked in the Education field in many capacities from classroom teaching at both undergraduate and postgraduate level, to project directorship, to leading school reform, and postgraduate research supervision. Khadeegha has developed a research interest that is particularly concerned with enhancing the effectiveness of leaders and managers through the use of innovative technological practices while looking at factors that influence organisational learning and the different leadership styles reflected in schools with a strongly international perspective.

Kingsley Asante, dedicated and innovative educator with expertise in TESOL, Business, ICT integration, and academic leadership. Committed to advancing education through research, technology, and professional development. Recognised for excellence in student engagement, building positive relationships, giving outstanding feedback to students and fostering a culture of learning

Asim Bashir is a Lecturer and Assessment Coordinator at the University of Birmingham Dubai. He holds a Doctorate in Education and has over twenty years of experience in higher education, specialising in academic literacy, assessment design, and faculty development. His research focuses on Generative AI adoption in higher education, HE pedagogy, and digital literacy. Dr. Bashir is an Advance HE Senior Fellow and assessor, actively contributing to mentoring and professional recognition initiatives across the Gulf region. He has presented and published on AI in education, academic integrity, and inclusive assessment design.

Dina Darwish, is the Vice Dean of Faculty of Computer Science and IT at the Ahram Canadian University, Egypt. She obtained her Ph.D. from Cairo University in Engineering. She is a professor now, with special focuses on artificial intelligence and with many publications in topics such as Artificial Intelligence, Internet of Things, Big Data Analytics, Quantum Computing, Blockchain Applications, Cloud Computing Applications, Wireless Ad Hoc Networks, Web 3 Technologies, Chatbots Development, and more. She has edited more than 20 specialized books in this field.

Pamela Johnson is a curriculum coordinator at the University of Birmingham Dubai, and she provides teacher professional development and curriculum support as a Specialist with the U.S. State Department's English Language Programs. Before joining the university, she consulted with higher education faculty across various disciplines on technology, pedagogy, and course content. Her professional interests include technology, assessment, artificial intelligence, and information and media literacy.

Sanjeev Kumar Is a Professor in Lovely Professional University Punjab India. He received Undergraduate in Hotel Management from Osmania University, Postgraduate in Tourism Management from Madurai Kamaraj University. He completed Doctor of Philosophy in Hospitality Management in 2019 from Amity University Jaipur India. His research areas lies in food Service Industry, his research focuses on Alcoholic beverages, Event management and Sustainable Management Practices, Metaverse, AI Machine Learning and Artificial Intelligence. He published more than 80 research papers, articles and chapters in Scopus Indexed, UGC Approved and peer reviewed Journals and books. Dr. Sanjeev Kumar participated and acted as resource person in various National and International conferences, seminars, session chair, research workshops and industry talks and his work has been widely cited. Dr. Sanjeev also edited more than 20 books with various International Publishers such as IGI Global, Cambridge Scholars, Emerald, CABI, Bentham Science, Taylor & Francis. Dr Sanjeev is an active researcher and has published numerous research articles in prestigious National and International journals and books.

Noha Osman is an aspiring Ph.D. student and accomplished Senior Educational Officer with a dynamic career dedicated to shaping the future of education. Her journey, from her current role to her earlier experiences as a Kindergarten teacher, has inspired her commitment to student-centered learning. Noha is dedicated to nurturing individual student needs, promoting engagement, and leading curriculum development to fuel educational excellence.

Karim Ragab is a UAE-based school leader and STEM educator with 22 years' experience spanning teaching, curriculum development, and K–12 leadership. He is Vice Principal at Ittihad Private School–Mamzar, where he has led literacy/numeracy initiatives, strengthened instructional quality, and driven measurable gains. Previously, Karim served as Principal for the Applied Technology High Schools (Dubai and Umm Al Quwain). An active IEEE member, he previously developed national Applied Technology curricula and mentored students for Emirates/WorldSkills competitions. He represented the UAE as the CNC turning expert in the WorldSkills competitions (Leipzig 2013 and São Paulo 2015). Karim holds an MSc in Mechanical Engineering (American University of Sharjah) and a BSc from Alexandria University, and he is completing a PhD in Educational Technology (Universidad de Córdoba, expected Mar 2026). His recent publications focus on interactive technology in STEM education and energy efficiency in schools.

Mohammed Rizkallah has over a decade of experience in education, serving recently as a postgraduate instructor in the American University in Cairo's Professional Educators Diploma. He has developed, taught, and trained instructors of the STEAM (Science, Technology, Engineering, Arts, Mathematics) track in that program. Dr. Rizkallah has also worked as the Project Director of the Bachelor's in Business Administration in the Arabic language at University of the People. Alongside working with universities, he also has worked as a consultant with more than 20 schools in Cairo, Egypt, where he developed curricula, developed policies, trained and coached teachers and leaders, as well as oversaw the development of new programs and departments in different schools. Recently, he served as a consultant with UNICEF to conduct research to investigate girls' attitudes towards STEM field, and in another project to train refugee teachers in different communities.

Emre Uygun is a lecturer at the School of Foreign Languages, Bursa Uludağ University, and a PhD candidate in English Language Teaching. His main areas of interest include artificial intelligence–supported language learning, distance education, educational technology, teacher training, and English for Specific Purposes. He has contributed to national and international journals and book chapters, focusing on the integration of emerging technologies in language education, the design and evaluation of online and distance learning environments, and the professional development of language teachers, and continues to advance his research in the field of ELT.

Ghofran Yazbeck is a PhD in Education student at the British University in Dubai.

Index

A

C

D

E

F

G

H

I

K

M

P

Q

S

T

W

www.ingramcontent.com/pod-product-compliance
Lightning Source LLC
LaVergne TN
LVHW060004031026
849161LV00025B/1416